OXFORD
UNIVERSITY PRESS

PROGRESS

PSYCHOLOGY
for Cambridge International AS & A Level
2nd edition

Craig Roberts

Oxford excellence for Cambridge AS & A Level

OXFORD

OXFORD
UNIVERSITY PRESS

Great Clarendon Street, Oxford, OX2 6DP, United Kingdom

Oxford University Press is a department of the University of Oxford. It furthers the University's objective of excellence in research, scholarship, and education by publishing worldwide. Oxford is a registered trade mark of Oxford University Press in the UK and in certain other countries

British Library Cataloguing in Publication Data

Data available

978-0-19-839968-1

10 9 8 7 6 5 4 3 2 1

Paper used in the production of this book is a natural, recyclable product made from wood grown in sustainable forests. The manufacturing process conforms to the environmental regulations of the country of origin.

Printed in Great Britain by Bell and Bain Ltd., Glasgow

FSC MIX Paper from responsible sources FSC® C007785

Acknowledgements

The questions, example answers, marks awarded and/or comments that appear in this book and website were written by the authors. In examination, the way marks would be awarded to answers like these may be different.

The publishers would like to thank the following for permissions to use their photographs:

Cover image: Shutterstock; p31: Reprinted with permission of The Journal of Neuroscience,24:9903-9913; p40: Hank Morgan/Getty Images; p54: Lekcej/Shutterstock; p60(TL): Valentyn Volkov/Shutterstock; p60(C): Aprilphoto/Shutterstock; p60(B): Svariophoto/Shutterstock; p60(TR): Kuttelvaserova Stuchelova/Shutterstock; p70: Transmission of Aggression through Imitation of Aggressive Models/Albert Bandura, Dorothea Ross, and Sheila A. Ross ©1961; p74: Reprinted from Journal of the American Academy of Child & Adolescent Psychiatry, Case Study: Disgust and a Specific Phobia of Buttons/Lissette M. Saavedra,Wendy K. Silverman ©2002 with permission from Elsevier; p97: Photographee.eu/Shutterstock; p100: Photo is provided by the Primate Research Institute, Kyoto University; p101: Photo is provided by the Primate Research Institute, Kyoto University; p152(T): Karen Finlay, Vinay Kanetkar, Jane Londerville, Harvey H. C. Marmurek/The Physical and Psychological Measurement of Gambling Environments ©2006 Sage Publications; p152(B): Karen Finlay, Vinay Kanetkar, Jane Londerville, Harvey H. C. Marmurek/The Physical and Psychological Measurement of Gambling Environments ©2006 Sage Publications; p165: © Country Pride Truck Stops; p166: © Country Pride Truck Stops; p169: ©Stephani K. A. Robson; p177: Reprinted from Neural Predictors of Purchases/Brian Knutson, Scott Rick, G. Elliott Wimmer, Drazen Prelec, George Loewenstein/©2007 Elsevier Inc.; p179: Lars Hall/Petter Johansson; p182: Elizabeth Porublev, et al: "To wrap or not wrap? What is expected? Some initial findings from a study on gift wrapping", ANZMAC: Sustainable management and marketing conference. Melbourne, Australia. Dec. 2009. Reprinted by permission.; p202: Brian McKinstry/JI'Xiang Wang/©British Journal of General Practice 1991, 41,'275-279.; p219: Image reproduced with permission from Professor Paul M Watt and from Avita Medical Ltd.; p255: The Three Levels of Leadership/James Scouller/©Management Books 2000; p257: In Praise of Followers/Harvard Business Review, November 1988, Volume 66, issue 6/Robert Kelley.

Artwork by Greengate Publishing Services Ltd. and Q2A Media Services Pvt. Ltd.

The author and publisher are grateful to the following for permission to reprint copyright material:

Andrade, J: "What does doodling do?" *Applied Cognitive Psychology*, 2010, John Wiley & Sons, Copyright © 2009 John Wiley & Sons, Ltd. Reprinted by permission.

Auty, S and Lewis, C: Table from "Exploring children's choice: the reminder effect of product placement". *Psychology & Marketing*. Vol. 21, No. 9. John Wiley and Sons Reproduced by permission.

Baron-Cohen, S., Wheelwright, S., Hill, J., Raste, Y. and Plumb, I: The "Reading the Mind in the Eyes" Test Revised Version: A Study with Normal Adults, and Adults with Asperger Syndrome or High-functioning Autism. *Journal of Child Psychology and Psychiatry*, 2001, John Wiley & Sons. Copyright © 2001 John Wiley & Sons, Ltd. Reprinted by permission.

Blau, G.T. & Boal, K. T: "Conceptualizing how job involvement and organizational commitment affect turnover and absenteeism", *Academy of Management Review*. Vol. 12 No. 2, April 1987.

Blaszczynski, A and Nower, L: *Journal of Clinical Activities Assignments and Handouts in Psychotherapy Practice* Vol 2 (4) 2002.

Borda Mas, M., López Jiménez, A.M. and Pérez San Gregorio, M.A: "Blood-injection Phobia Inventory (BIPI): Development, reliability and validity". *Anales de Psicologia*. 2010, Vol. 26, No. 1. Reprinted by permission.

Budzynski, T. H. and Stoyva, J.M: "An instrument for producing deep muscle relaxation by means of analog information feedback". *Journal of Applied Behavior Analysis*. Vol. 2, No. 4, 1969. Reproduced by permission of John Wiley & Sons.

Burton et al: Table from "Firesetting, Arson, Pyromania, and the Forensic Mental Health Expert". *Journal of American Academy Psychiatric Law*. Vol. 40. © American Academy of Psychiatry and the Law. Reprinted with permission.

Chandola T., Britton, A., Brunner, E., Hemingway, H., Malik, M., Kumari, M., Badrick, E., Kivimaki, M. and Marmot, M: "Work stress and coronary heart disease: what are the mechanisms?" *European Heart Journal* (2008) 29. Reprinted by permission of Oxford University Press and Professor Tarani Chandola.

Da Silva Timossi, L, et al: "Valuation of Quality of Work Life: An Adaptation from The Walton's Owl Model". Xiv International Conference on Industrial Engineering and Operations Management Rio de Janeiro, Brazil, 13 to 16 October – 2008. Reprinted with permission of the authors.

Dayan, E. and Bar-Hillel, M: Table from p. 334 "Nudge to nobesity II: menu positions influence food orders". *Judgment and Decision Making*. Vol. 6, number 4. Reprinted by permission of E. Dayan and M. Bar-Hillel.

DiNardo et al: "Etiology and maintenance of dog fears". *Behaviour Research and Therapy*. Vol. 26, number 3, p.242, 1988.

Fischer, P. M. et al: "Brand Logo Recognition by Children aged 3 to 6 years: Mickey Mouse and Old Joe the Camel". JAMA. Vol. 266, Issue No. 22, 11 December 1991. Copyright © 1991 American Medical Association. Reproduced with permission. All rights reserved.

Gansberg, M: "37 who saw murder didn't call the police: Apathy at stabbing of Queen's woman shocks Inspector", The New York Times, 27 March 1964, copyright © The New York Times 1964. All Rights reserved. Used by permission of PARS International Corp and protected by the Copyright Laws of the United States. The printing, copying, redistribution, or retransmission of this content without express permission is prohibited.

Gil, J. et al: "The differentiating behaviour of shoppers: clustering of individual movement traces in a supermarket". Proceedings of the 7th International Space Syntax Symposium, 2009. Reprinted by permission.

Gold, et al: "Rotating shift work, sleep, and accidents related to sleepiness in hospital nurses". *American Journal of Public Health*. Vol. 82 No. 7 1992.

Gottesman, I: "A Critical Review of Recent Adoption, Twin and Family Studies of Schizophrenia", *Schizophrenia Bulletin*: February 2976. Reproduced by permission of Professor Gottesman.

Grant, J: "Kleptomania Symptom Assessment Scale"© Jon Grant. Reprinted by permission.

Hayes, N: *Doing Psychological Research*. Copyright © Nicky Hayes, 2000, Open University Press. Reproduced with the kind permission of Open University Press. All rights reserved.

Hodgson, R.J. and Rachman, S: 1977. "Obsessional-compulsive complaints". Behav. Res. & Therapy. Vol. 15.

Holmes, T. H. and Rahe, R. H: 1967. "The Social Readjustment rating Scale". *Journal of Psychological Research*. Volume 11.

Kardes, F. R. et al: "The Role of the Need for Cognitive Closure in the Effectiveness of the Disrupt-Then-Reframe Influence Technique" from Journal of Consumer Research, October 2007, Oxford University Press. Reprinted by permission of Oxford University Press and the authors.

Knutson, B. et al: "Neural predictors of purchases". *Neuron*. Vol. 53 147–156, doi: 10.1016/j.neuron.2006.11.010 January 4, 2007 © 2007 Elsevier Inc.

Knutsson, A: "Health disorders of shift workers" *Occupational Medicine*, 2003, Vol. 53. Reprinted by permission of Professor Knutsson and Oxford University Press.

Kohli et al: Seven-point plan from 'Got slogan? Guidelines for creating effective slogans', *Business Horizons* Feb 2007. Reprinted by permission of Elsevier.

Kouzes, J. M. and Posner, B. Z: *Leadership practices inventory: LPI®*. Jossey-Bass. © Copyright 2013 by James M. Kouzes and Barry Z. Posner, www.leadershipchallenge.com. All rights reserved. Reprinted by permission of John Wiley & Sons Inc.

Continues on last page

INTRODUCTION

This book has been written as a companion to support you throughout your Cambridge International Examinations Psychology AS and A Level (9990 syllabus).

The book is divided into two parts: one for the AS Level and one for the A Level. The part for the AS Level will guide you through all of the 12 core studies and all of the research methods, issues, debates and evaluations. The part for the A Level will guide you through the two options you have chosen to study (from the four available). There are a range of activities throughout the book to get you thinking psychologically, which are ideal preparation for the examinations.

There is an accompanying Revision Guide, which is a separate book summarising all the key content of this book, that will help you when you are revising. As part of your revision, you can practise answering exam-style questions to the best of your ability using the accompanying website.

Author

Craig is a freelance tutor and author of psychology textbooks. He has been teaching for over 21 years and is a very experienced examiner with a number of national and international examination boards.

Acknowledgements

I have to thank everyone who has made an impact on my life and who support me through every venture I take on (which numbers many!). My family and close circle of friends have given eternal support and you all know who you are. A special thanks has to go out to Javi for being my pillar and to Brett "The Baron" Crowhurst for keeping me sane with my love of horses. I have to mention my cat Gingerella who helped a lot by sitting on various materials I needed to use when writing this book! Finally, thank you to all of the teachers I met in Boynton Beach, Florida; Mumbai and Bangalore, India; and Nairobi, Kenya for being truly inspirational and making every minute of writing this book worthwhile. I will be back!

Dedication

To Javi, Ness, Hannah & Josh. Always love you.

Support website

The accompanying support website has a range of material that can be used for revision purposes:

- Interactive activities for AS and A Level
- Example exam-style questions for Papers 1,2, 3 and 4.

Access it at:
www.oxfordsecondary.com/9780198399681

CONTENTS

RESEARCH METHODS

EXPERIMENTS

Laboratory

These take place in a situation or environment that is artificial to the participants in the study. There are two main types of variable that need to be considered when running any experiment.

Independent variable

The independent variable (IV) is the variable that the psychologist chooses to manipulate or change. This represents the different conditions that are being compared in any study. These usually form the *experimental condition* and the *control condition*. To make sure that only one factor is being changed in an experiment, the IV is divided into two groups. One group, called the control, is exposed to all of the experiment but does not get whatever is being tested or changed in the experiment. Essentially, it is used as a comparison group. At the same time, the experimental condition gets all of the experiment *plus* the one variable being tested by the experiment.

Dependent variable

The dependent variable (DV) is the variable that the psychologist chooses to measure. It is always hoped that the IV is directly affecting the DV in an experiment. The psychologist will attempt to *control* as many other variables as possible to try to ensure that it is the IV directly affecting the DV. There are different types of variable that can affect the DV as well that have to be controlled if possible. One type is called *participant variables*. These are the traits and behaviours (e.g. level of intelligence, prejudices or any previous experiences) that participants bring to the study that may affect the DV. There is usually an attempt at a *standardised procedure*.

For more on these two main types of variable, and other examples, see pages 2 and 11–12.

Strengths of laboratory experiments	Weaknesses of laboratory experiments
Laboratory experiments have high levels of standardisation and so can be replicated to test for reliability. As laboratory experiments have high levels of control, researchers can be more confident it is the IV directly affecting the DV.	As laboratory experiments take place in an artificial setting, it is said that they can lack ecological validity. Many laboratory experiments make participants take part in tasks that are nothing like real-life ones, so the tasks lack mundane realism. Participants usually know they are taking part in an experiment and they may respond to demand characteristics as something about the set-up indicates the aim of the experiment.

Field

These are experiments that take place in the participants' own natural environment rather than in an artificial laboratory. The researcher still tries to manipulate or change an IV while measuring the DV in an attempt to see how the IV affects the DV. There is an attempt to control other variables that could affect the DV. One type of these is called *situational variables*. These are variables from the setting that might affect the DV (e.g. the weather or time of day).

Strengths of field experiments	Weaknesses of field experiments
As field experiments take place in a realistic setting, it is said that they have ecological validity. As participants will not know they are taking part in a study, there will be little or no demand characteristics so behaviour is more likely to be natural and valid. (See more on demand characteristics on page 19.)	Situational variables can be difficult to control, so sometimes it is difficult to know whether it is IV affecting the DV. It could be an uncontrolled variable causing the DV to change. As participants will not know they are taking part in a study, there are issues with breaking ethical guidelines. These include the issues of informed consent and deception.

Natural

This is when researchers use a pre-existing or naturally occurring IV. There are certain instances where the experimenter cannot directly manipulate the IV under investigation. These usually take place in a real-life situation (e.g. the workplace or a hospital). Examples of the naturally occurring IVs that can be used in natural experiments include things such as caffeine consumption, a new care plan on a ward in a hospital or family size.

Strengths of natural experiments	Weaknesses of natural experiments
As the experiment is located in a natural setting exploiting a naturally occurring IV, the study should be high in ecological validity. As participants are usually unaware that a study is taking place, their behaviour is more likely to be natural and a valid representation of each person's behavioural repertoire.	It can be difficult to know whether the IV has caused an effect on the DV due to the lack of controls. Therefore, it is difficult to establish a cause-effect relationship. As the event is naturally occurring, it can be very difficult to replicate the experiment to test for reliability.

Evaluations of all experiments on validity, reliability and ethics

	Laboratory experiments	Field experiments	Natural experiments
Validity (see page 18)	These experiments have high internal validity because controls mean the researcher can be confident it is the IV directly affecting the DV. They have low external validity as it may be difficult to apply the findings to a real-life situation.	These experiments have lower internal validity as the researcher can control some variables but not all of them. There is stronger external validity than in laboratory experiments due to the "field" setting of the study.	These experiments have low internal validity as there is no control over any extraneous variables. Natural experiments have high external validity as they take place in participants' natural environment.
Reliability (see pages 19–20)	These have high levels of reliability because controls and standardised procedures allow for full replication.	These have medium levels of reliability as some elements of the study are controlled with some standardised procedures but full replication may be difficult.	These have low levels of reliability as there are hardly any controls or standardisation and this makes replication very difficult.
Ethics (see pages 13–17)	It is usually easy to gain informed consent. Deception can be dealt with through a full debrief. Participants know they are in a study so can withdraw at any time.	Researchers can gain informed consent from participants, but it is not always possible. Participants may not know they are part of a study which can make debriefing difficult and sometimes impossible. (Also, if participants do not know they are in a study their right to withdraw is invalidated.)	There are several issues. Informed consent can be very difficult to obtain, depending on the study. People may not know they are part of a study which can make debriefing difficult and sometimes impossible. (Also, if participants do not know they are in a study their right to withdraw is invalidated.)

Notes: Internal validity refers to whether it is the IV directly affecting the DV (and not some other variable or variables). External validity refers to the extent to which the findings of the study can be applied to real-life settings and to other people outside the sample.

SELF-REPORTS

Questionnaires

When a study uses a questionnaire, it is asking participants to answer a series of questions in the written form. A psychologist can use a variety of question types in a questionnaire-based study:

▶ **Likert scales** are statements (e.g. "Owning a pet is good for your psychological health") that participants read and then state whether they "Strongly agree", "Disagree", etc. with the statement.

▶ **Rating scales** are questions or statements where the participant gives an answer in the form of a number (e.g. "On scale of 0–10, how happy are you today?" Answer based on the scale 0 = not at all happy and 10 = very happy).

▶ **Open-ended** questions or statements allow participants to develop an answer and write it in their own words, as an answer, for example to "Tell me about a happy childhood memory".

▶ **Closed questions** are questions that can be answered "yes" or "no" or instructions with a set amount of options, for example "Pick the emotion that best describes how you feel today: happy, sad, cheerful, moody." Participants choose which answer best fits how they feel.

Strengths of questionnaires	Weaknesses of questionnaires
Participants may be more likely to reveal truthful answers in a questionnaire as it does not involve talking face to face with someone. A large sample of participants can answer the questionnaire in a short time span, which should increase the representativeness and generalisability of the findings.	Rather than giving truthful answers, participants may give socially desirable answers because they want to look good. This lowers the validity of the findings. If the questionnaire has a lot of closed questions participants might be forced into choosing an answer that does not reflect their true opinion.

Interviews

These are similar to questionnaires but answers are given in the spoken not written form. Interviewers ask a series of questions using the types highlighted above. They may record the interview so they can go back and transcribe exactly what participants said. Depending on what the psychologist is studying, there are three main types of interview.

Structured

Structured interviews use set questions. Each participant will be asked the same questions in the same order.

Unstructured

Unstructured interviews involve the interviewer having a theme or topic that needs to be discussed. The interviewer may have an initial question to begin the interview but each subsequent question is based on the response given by the participant.

Semi-structured

Semi-structured interviews involve certain questions that must be asked of participants. However, the interviewer can ask them in a different order and/or ask other questions to help clarify a participant's response.

Strength of interviews	Weakness of interviews
If the interview has a lot of open questions participants will reveal more of the reasons why they behave in a certain way or have a certain opinion.	Participants might be less likely to give truthful answers in interviews (maybe due to social desirability) as they are actually face to face with the interviewer and might not want to be judged.

Case studies

According to Shaughnessy and Zechmeister, a case study is "… an intensive description and analysis of a single individual" (1997: 308). As with correlations (see page 8), case studies are not a unique research method, they simply use other research methods in a quest for drawing a conclusion (e.g. naturalistic observation, interviews or questionnaires). Variables are not systematically controlled or altered as in single-case experimental designs. Case studies are simply in-depth detailed analyses of individuals or close-knit groups of people as in a family unit.

Sometimes case studies form longitudinal studies. This type of study extends over a period of time. The researcher studies the same individual or unit of individuals for a fixed amount of time (e.g. five years). This allows for an analysis of the development of behaviour over a time period. Of course, longitudinal studies do not have to be exclusively about one person or unit of individuals. They can involve following a cohort (group) of people for the purposes of analysing the development of behaviour.

Strengths of case studies	Weaknesses of case studies
As reserachers are focusing on one individual (or unit of individuals) they can collect rich, in-depth data that has details – this makes the findings more valid. Participants are usually studied as part of their everyday life, which means that the whole process tends to have ecological validity.	As researchers are focusing on one individual (or unit of individuals), the case may be unique. This makes generalisations quite difficult. As participants are studied in depth, an attachment could form between them and the researcher which could reduce the objectivity of the data collection and analysis of data. This could reduce the validity of the findings.

OBSERVATION

This research method involves observing people or animals and their behaviours. There are many different types of observation, as described below. However, there are some elements that are core to observations in general. Prior to observing, the psychologist must create a *behavioural checklist* (called an *ethogram* if observing non-humans). This checklist must name each behaviour that the psychologist is expecting see. In addition, a picture of the behaviour happening and a brief description of that behaviour is useful. This makes sure that if there is more than one observer, they are looking for the same behaviours. The checklist must be "tested" before the main observation to ensure that all potential behaviours are covered and the observers can use the checklist successfully. This is called a pilot observation. Additional behaviours may be added to the checklist after this process. An example of one of these can be found under structured observations.

In observations there are two ways in which an observer can "sample" behaviours:

1. Time sampling: behaviours are recorded in specified time intervals. Three types can be used:

   ▶ Instantaneous scan: the behaviour that is being shown by the person being observed is recorded at the start of each set time interval. For example, every 10 seconds whatever behaviour being shown by a child in the playground is recorded.

   ▶ Predominant activity scan: the observer records the most frequent behaviour shown by the person being observed in a set time period (e.g. in a 10-second period).

   ▶ One-zero scan: the observer records whether each behaviour happened (a 1) or did not happen (a 0) within the time period set. Frequency of that behaviour is *not* recorded, just whether it happened or not.

2. Event sampling: every time a behaviour is seen in the person being observed it is tallied. A set time period is decided upon before recording begins.

Strengths of observations in general	Weaknesses of observations in general
If participants are unaware that they are being observed then they should behave "naturally". This increases the ecological validity of the observation. As behaviours are "counted" and are hence quantitative, the process is objective and the data can be analysed statistically with minimal bias.	If participants are aware that they are being observed then they may not act "naturally" but show more socially desirable behaviours. This reduces the validity of findings. It may be difficult to replicate the study if it is naturalistic as many variables cannot be controlled. This reduces the reliability of the study.

Overt or covert

Observation can be overt or covert. The difference is:

▶ overt observation is when participants know who the researcher is and that they are being observed

▶ covert observation is when participants do not know that a researcher is in the group observing them.

Participant or non-participant

Participant observations are when the researcher becomes a part of the group the researcher wishes to observe. The researcher can be overt or covert about this. The researcher interacts with participants and takes notes on behaviours, participants' comments and any other relevant information.

Strengths of participant observations	Weaknesses of participant observations
Usually, the participants being observed are in a real-life setting so there is increased ecological validity. As observers become involved with the group they are more likely to understand the motives and reasons for behaviours. This increases the validity of findings.	There are ethical problems as the informed consent of those being placed into the group has not been sought or given. The presence of an outsider (the observer) can initially change the behaviours of the group members. This lowers the validity of findings.

Non-participant observations are when the researcher is "away" from the people or animals being observed. This can also be an overt or covert process. The researcher does not interact with any of the participants.

Strengths of non-participant observations	Weakness of non-participant observations
Participants' behaviour will not be affected by knowing they are being observed because the observers are out of sight. Researchers' observations are more likely to be objective as they are detached from the people they are observing.	It can be difficult to make detailed observations and to produce qualitative data that allows understanding as to *why* the behaviours are occurring.

Structured or unstructured

Structured observations are those where the observers have created a behavioural checklist in order to code the behaviour they are observing. For example, if researchers were interested in aggressive and affiliative play in children they would construct a behavioural checklist similar to the one on the next page.

Name of behaviour	Diagram	Description
Hitting		When one person purposively makes physical contact with another (e.g. hand to arm) – not accidental.
Hugging		When two people place their arms around each other in a non-aggressive way.

The observers can then tally how many times a behaviour occurs during the time period set aside to observe. They can use time or event sampling as outlined above.

Strength of structured observations	Weakness of structured observations
The coding system (via the behavioural checklist) allows objective quantitative data to be collected. This can then be analysed statistically.	The sampling of observed behaviour tends to be restrictive (e.g. time sampling) and does not give an idea of the reasons *why* the behaviours are occurring.

Unstructured observations are when observers note all the behaviours they can see in qualitative form over a period of time. No behavioural checklist is used as the observers simply record what is happening in real time.

Strength of unstructured observations	Weakness of unstructured observations
These types of observations can generate in-depth, rich qualitative data that can help explain *why* behaviours are occurring.	Observers may easily be drawn to noticeable or eye-catching behaviours that may not fully represent all the behaviours occurring during the observation period.

Naturalistic or controlled

Naturalistic observations take place in a person's or animal's own natural environment.

Strengths of naturalistic observations	Weaknesses of naturalistic observations
As participants are unaware that they are being watched, they should behave more naturally, removing the chances of demand characteristics affecting their behaviour. As the observation takes place in a natural setting for participants, there are increased levels of ecological validity.	There is very little control over extraneous variables, which makes it difficult to draw cause and effect conclusions about the observed behaviours. Replication may be difficult as there cannot be a totally standardised procedure due to possible extraneous variables. This makes it difficult to test for reliability.

Some observations take place in a controlled setting. For example, during an experiment in a laboratory room the observers could be behind a one-way mirror so they cannot be seen observing.

Strengths of controlled observations	Weaknesses of controlled observations
As the set-up is controlled, the observers can be more confident about what is causing any of the behaviours shown by participants. There is less risk of extraneous variables affecting participants' behaviour.	Carrying out the observations in an artificial setting can easily influence participants' behaviour. For example, children may be anxious in an environment that is different from their usual environment. As the setting is artificial, the findings may lack ecological validity.

Correlations

Correlations do not constitute a separate research method as such because other research methods are used to gain the data. Correlational designs look for relationships between the measures collected from other research methods (e.g. questionnaires or observations). Correlations can be defined as the relationship between two measured variables.

There are three broad categories that results of correlational studies can fall into: *positive*, *negative* or *no* correlation:

▶ A *positive correlation* takes the form that if one variable increases, the second variable is also likely to increase. For example, there may be a positive correlation between people's height and their shoe size in that we expect a taller person to have larger feet. As one variable increases, so does the other.

▶ A *negative correlation* takes the form that if one measured variable increases, the other measured variable decreases. For example, there may be a negative correlation between the number of therapy sessions a person has and the number of depressive symptoms the person exhibits – we expect that as the number of therapy sessions increase, the number of exhibited depressive symptoms decreases. As one variable increases, the other decreases.

▶ *No correlation* refers to the situation where no definite trend occurs and the two measured variables do not appear to be related to each other. For example, if we attempted to correlate the circumference of people's heads and then rated them on a "big-headedness scale", such as how much they liked to talk about their achievements and boost their ego, we would probably find no correlation.

Strengths of correlations	Weaknesses of correlations
Correlations are good for showing the relationship between two variables. Further research, such as experiments, can then be conducted to establish cause and effect between the variables. Correlations do not require any manipulation (researchers simply look at the relationship between two measures) so correlations can be used where experiments are either unethical or impractical.	There are issues of causality. If a correlation is reported in a study, researchers do not know if variable A is causing a change in variable B or if variable B is causing a change in variable A. There could also be a third variable causing changes in both A and B that has not been measured. Correlations are restricted to research where measurements are quantitative so cannot be used to investigate *why* behaviours are occurring.

AIMS AND HYPOTHESES

Aim

The aim is written before a study is run. It is a statement that tells people what the purpose of a study is. It does *not* predict the outcome of the study (a hypothesis does this) but merely states what the study is about. It can be written as a question. There are examples of aims for the 12 core studies you need to learn for your AS Level.

HYPOTHESIS

A hypothesis predicts the findings of a study. It is also written before the study is run. An experimental hypothesis always contains the IV and DV (fully operationalised). A correlational hypothesis will always have both measured variables operationalised. There are two main types of experimental or alternative hypotheses, as highlighted below.

Directional (one-tailed)

A directional, or one-tailed, hypothesis predicts a significant difference or correlation and also the *direction* of results. Here are two examples:

▶ Females will be able to spell more words correctly (out of 25 words) compared to males.

▶ There will be a positive correlation between the amount of hours spent revising for an AS Level Cambridge International Psychology examination and the final score a student achieves.

Non-directional (two-tailed)

A non-directional, or two-tailed, hypothesis still predicts a difference or correlation but *not* the expected direction of results. Here are two examples:

▶ There will be a difference in the number of words spelt correctly (out of 25 words) by females compared to males.

▶ There will be a correlation between the amount of hours spent revising for an AS Level Cambridge International Psychology examination and the final score a student achieves.

Null

A null hypothesis is necessary if we are going to use *inferential statistical tests* to examine whether we have found a significant difference or a significant correlation. These tests calculate how far the actual findings have deviated from chance. Here are some examples:

▶ Any difference in the number of words spelt correctly (out of 25 words) of females compared to males will be due to chance.

▶ Any correlation between the amount of hours spent revising for an AS Level Cambridge International Examinations Psychology exam and the final score a student achieves will be due to chance.

VARIABLES

Independent variable

This is the variable that researchers choose to manipulate or change. This represents the different conditions that are being compared in any study. For example, if a researcher wants to investigate memory in school children, then the variable that requires changing is age. Therefore, age is the IV. However, the IV requires some form of operationalisation. To do this, the researcher must clearly define what the different conditions are. For the memory in school children example above, the operationalised IV could be: level 1 = 5–6 years old; level 2 = 7–8 years old.

Dependent variable

The DV is the variable that researchers choose to measure. It is always hoped that the IV is directly affecting the DV in an experiment. Also, the DV needs some form of operationalisation. To achieve this, researchers must clearly define how they will measure.

Taking the example above of investigating memory in school children, the operationalised DV could be the amount of items that a child remembers after being shown a tray of objects containing a maximum of 25 objects.

EXPERIMENTAL DESIGN

Researchers who choose to use an experiment have to decide on an experimental (participant) design. This refers to how they allocate participants to the varying conditions of their experiment.

Independent measures

This is when a participant only takes part in one level of the IV. If the IV is naturally occurring (e.g. gender, age) then a researcher *must* use this type of design. In a true independent measures design, participants are *randomly allocated* to one level of the IV (so they get an equal chance of being placed in *any* level of the IV).

Strengths of independent measures	Weaknesses of independent measures
As participants only take part in one condition they are less likely to guess the aim of the study, therefore reducing the potential effects of demand characteristics. As participants only take part in one condition there are no order effects that can reduce the validity of findings. (See below for examples of order effects.)	There may be a problem with participant variables affecting the DV rather than the IV – even by chance, all people of a certain personality might form one condition and all people with a different personality might form the other condition – so it could be personality affecting the DV rather than the IV. More participants are required for this type of design compared to repeated measures.

Repeated measures

This is when a participant takes part in *all* of the levels of the IV. This *cannot* be used if the IV is naturally occurring (e.g. a participant cannot be a male and a female at the same time). Researchers must use

counterbalancing, which is sometimes called an ABBA design. For example, 50 per cent of participants do level A then level B of the IV and the other 50 per cent do level B then A.

Strengths of repeated measures	Weaknesses of repeated measures
Using repeated measures eliminates any effect of participant variables as all participants take part in all conditions, therefore they are controlled. Fewer participants are needed for this type of design than the number needed for independent measures design.	As all participants take part in all conditions, there is a chance of demand characteristics affecting the study – participants might work out the aim of the study and behave in a way to fulfil that rather than showing their true behaviour. Order effects can affect the findings of the study and reduce its validity. These are some examples: • Practice effect – participants get better at a task when they complete a similar one or the same one more than once. • Fatigue effect – the more tasks participants do the more tired they might become. • Boredom effect – repeating similar tasks can bore participants.

CONTROLLING OF VARIABLES

Controlling variables and standardisation of procedure

Obviously, any researcher would not want any variable to affect the DV except the IV. Therefore, researchers will find ways to control variables that could potentially do this. These are discussed below.

A standardised procedure is one where *all* participants follow the same *order of events* within a study. The only subtle difference would be which level of the IV a participant is exposed to. Aspects such as standardised instructions, standardised materials and a standardised location all form part of a standardised procedure. The more a procedure is standardised, the more likely it is that another researcher could replicate the study and test for reliability.

In contrast, when a researcher attempts to *control variables*, it is to strengthen the cause–effect relationship between the IV and the DV. Of course, standardising a procedure adds to this strengthening as it eliminates other variables that could have a direct or indirect effect on the DV.

Extraneous variables

These are variables that can influence the relationship between the IV and DV. They can affect the outcome of an experiment but they are not the variables of interest. Therefore, they add *error* to the experiment.

Uncontrolled variables

These are variables that cannot be controlled by a researcher. Examples are forces of nature, the weather or other aspects of the environment. Uncontrolled variables can have an impact on a study, for example by affecting the DV in an experiment or changing people's behaviours during an observation. These variables can lower the validity of findings.

Participant variables

Variables that the participant brings to the study can affect the DV rather than the IV. Examples of participant variables include prejudices, previous experiences with a similar study or task, level of intelligence, gender and personality.

These are some ways of helping to control participant variables:

▶ Participants can be randomised to each level of the IV. It is hoped that, by chance, these types of variables will "balance" themselves out across the levels.

▶ Repeated measures can be used where possible. If all participants take part in all levels of the IV then their participant variables are effectively controlled for.

Situational variables

Variables that the situation brings to the study can affect the DV rather than the IV. Examples of situational variables are noise, temperature, lighting and the weather.

Ways of helping to control situational variables include the following:

▶ The situation where the study takes place can be standardised. For example, the temperature and noise levels can be controlled.

▶ If using repeated measures, researchers can ensure that counterbalancing is used.

▶ A double-blind technique can be used. This is when the researcher does not know the full aim of the study and simply follows a standardised procedure (so the researcher does not know which condition participants are in). Also, participants are not told anything about which condition they are in.

TYPES OF DATA

Quantitative

Quantitative data is in the numerical form and researchers can perform statistical analyses on it. Anything in the form of a number is quantitative data.

Strengths of quantitative data	Problems with quantitative data
As the data are numerical, it allows easier comparison and statistical analysis to take place (e.g. the average score of two different groups of participants can easily be compared). As the data are numerical, analysis is objective and scientific – there is only minimal chance of researchers miscalculating the data and drawing invalid conclusions.	As the data are numerical, they miss out on valuable information. If the answer is simply yes/no or on a rating scale we do not know *why* participants chose the answers that they did. This approach can be seen as reductionist as researchers are reducing complex ideas and behaviours to a number or percentage.

Qualitative

Qualitative data take the form of descriptions via words, sentences and paragraphs. These data are rich in detail and are data where participants can explain their answers to questions asked.

Strengths of qualitative data	Problems with qualitative data
The data collected are in-depth responses in the words of participants so they are rich and in detail and represent what participants believe. Therefore, it can be argued that this approach is not reductionist. As the data come directly from participants we can understand *why* each participant thinks, feels or acts in a certain way.	The interpretation of the data could be subjective as we are dealing with words rather than numbers – a researcher could misinterpret what the participant was meaning to say or be biased against some of the participant's views. There may be researcher bias: the researcher might only select data that fits into the hypothesis or aim of the study. This cannot be done with quantitative data.

SAMPLING OF PARTICIPANTS

Sample and population

Participants are the people who choose to take part in a study. They form the sample of participants whom the study will be conducted on. It is hoped that these people represent a wider, target population (TP). The researcher must have a TP. This is the group of people a researcher studies in the same way in the hope that the findings can *generalise to* and be *representative of* that TP. For example, if a psychologist wants to investigate memory in school children then the researcher's TP might be children 5–8 years old. There are different *sampling techniques* that psychologists can use to help recruit their participants from the TP.

Opportunity

This technique involves the researcher recruiting participants who happen to be around at the time the researcher needs participants. Once the correct number has been chosen and those participants have completed the study, no more participants are asked.

Strength of opportunity sampling	Weakness of opportunity sampling
Large numbers of participants can be obtained relatively quickly and easily, because this method involves using people who are around at the time of the study.	A researcher is unlikely to gain a wide variety of participants to allow for generalisation because this technique draws in one type of person in the main.

Random

Random sampling involves every participant in the TP having an *equal chance of being chosen*. If the TP is small then potential participants can be numbered and, for example, chosen from a hat. If the TP is large, all potential participants can be numbered then a random number generator can be used to select the sample.

Strength of random sampling	Weakness of random sampling
The researcher can generalise to the TP with more confidence. This is because the sample is more likely to be representative of the TP.	Obtaining details of the TP from which draw the sample (e.g. lists of people in the TP) may be difficult. You cannot *guarantee* a representative sample as with random sampling, e.g. all chosen participants could be of one gender. With both techniques a researcher may find a "perfect" sample but may still have the problem that the participants will not take part in the study.

Volunteer (self-selecting)

This technique involves the researcher *advertising* for participants. It is frequently used in universities to recruit participants for a range of studies. Therefore, for this technique *participants* choose whether they want to participate or not.

Strength of volunteer sampling	Weakness of volunteer sampling
People are more likely to participate if they have already volunteered so the drop-out rate should be lower, making generalisations potentially stronger.	Using this technique a researcher is unlikely to gain a wide variety of participants to allow for generalisation. Instead, the group will consist only of the type of people who will volunteer to take part in research or in a particular study.

ETHICS

Guidelines for the use of humans

The British Psychology Society (BPS) updated some of its guidelines in 2014. Formerly the Code of Ethics and Conduct, the BPS guidelines are now called the Code of Human Research Ethics. Both sets of guidelines can be found at http://www.bps.org.uk/what-we-do/ethics-standards/ethics-standards.

The 2014 the Code of Human Research Ethics are a supplement to the 2009 guidelines rather than replacing them. As part of the 2014 update the BPS note:

> Researchers should respect the rights and dignity of participants in their research and the legitimate interests of stakeholders such as funders, institutions, sponsors and society at large. There are numerous reasons for behaving ethically. Participants in psychological research should have confidence in the investigators. Good psychological research is only possible if there is a mutual respect and trust between investigators and participants.
>
> Source: BPS, 2014: 4.

There are various ethical guidelines that a researcher has to consider when designing and running *any* study. The main aspects are highlighted below and the guidance is that given by the BPS in both of their documents.

Informed consent

The BPS Code of Human Research Ethics section on "Informing participants" states the following:

> Giving potential participants sufficient information about the research in an understandable form requires careful drafting of the information sheet. It is recommended that at least one pilot test of the processes for informing and debriefing participants be carried out with a naïve person having a literacy level at the lower end of the range expected in the planned research sample. In certain circumstances the aims of the research may be compromised by giving full information prior to data collection. In such cases, it should be made clear that this is the case in the information sheet and the means by which the withheld information will be given at the conclusion of data collection should be specified. The amount of information withheld and the delay in disclosing the withheld information should be kept to the absolute minimum necessary. The information sheet given to potential participants for them to keep should normally offer a clear statement of all those aspects of the research that are relevant for their decision about whether or not to agree to participation. The following list offers a series of headings for consideration. Not all of these will be relevant in specific cases.
>
> - The aim(s) of the project
> - The type(s) of data to be collected
> - The method(s) of collecting data
> - Confidentiality and anonymity conditions associated with the data including any exceptions to confidentiality, for example, with respect to potential disclosures
> - Compliance with the Data Protection Act and Freedom of Information Act
> - The time commitment expected from participants
> - The right to decline to offer any particular information requested by the researcher
> - The opportunity to withdraw from the study at any time with no adverse consequences
> - The opportunity to have any supplied data destroyed on request (up to a specified date)
> - Details of any risks associated with participation
> - If appropriate, a statement that recompense for time and inconvenience associated with participation will be given, without specifying the amount or nature of such recompense beyond the reimbursement of incurred expenses such as travel costs
> - The name and contact details of the Principal Investigator
> - The name and contact details of another person who can receive enquiries about any matters which cannot be satisfactorily resolved with the Principal Investigator
> - Details of any insurance indemnity for the research
> - Any debriefing that is planned
> - How the data will be used and planned outcomes
> - Potential benefits of the research
> - How the results of the research will be made available to participants.
>
> Which of these headings are appropriate, and the extent of information given under each, will depend on the nature of the research. The language should be clear and accessible to people with limited literacy, using short words and sentences, written in the active voice, and avoiding the use of technical terms. Sufficient time should be given for potential participants to absorb and consider the information given about the research and what is expected of their participation before they are asked to make a decision regarding participation.
>
> BPS Code of Human Research Ethics (2014: 18–19)

The following extracts are from the Code's "Documenting consent" and "Who can give consent?" sections.

Consent, whether in a verbal recording, electronic or hard copy form, should include an explicit statement confirming that information about the research has been given to the participant and has been understood. It is important that participants do not misunderstand any collection of health-related data from them as constituting any form of medical screening. Such misapprehensions might lead them to be less vigilant in relation to seeking medical attention for risks or symptoms of illness.

Source: BPS Code of Human Research Ethics (2014: 20)

The consent of participants in research, whatever their age or competence, should always be sought, by means appropriate to their age and competence level. For children under 16 years of age and for other persons where capacity to consent may be impaired the additional consent of parents or those with legal responsibility for the individual should normally also be sought. In special circumstances such as where it may be important that views of such participants or findings about them should not be suppressed, the rationale for not seeking parental consent should be clearly stated and approved by a REC.

Source: BPS Code of Human Research Ethics (2014: 20)

In relation to the gaining of consent from children and young people in school or other institutional settings, where the research procedures are judged by a senior member of staff or other appropriate professional within the institution to fall within the range of usual curriculum or other institutional activities, and where a risk assessment has identified no significant risks, consent from the participants and the granting of approval and access from a senior member of school staff legally responsible for such approval can be considered sufficient. Where these criteria are not met, it will be a matter of judgement as to the extent to which the difference between these criteria and the data gathering activities of the specific project warrants the seeking of parental consent from children under 16 years of age and young people of limited competence.

Source: BPS Code of Human Research Ethics (2014: 17)

Protection (physical and psychological)

The 2009 BPS guidelines state the requirement that participants leave any study in the same physical and psychological state as they entered. If a study requires negative imagery or makes participants think about negative things then a "positive mood" task must be used at the end of the study. For example, if a study is asking people to talk about or write about past relationships this may be upsetting so a researcher could show participants pictures of kittens and puppies at the end to invalidate any negative mood instilled by the study.

Psychologists should always:

▶ consider research from the viewpoint of participants to help eliminate potential risks to their psychological and physical wellbeing

▶ assess the risk of "harming" participants based on aspects such as sexual orientation, race, religion and family status

▶ refrain from financial incentives that may make participants risk harm beyond what they would do in their everyday lives.

Deception

The following extract is from the Code's "Deception" section.

To many outside the psychology profession, and to some within it, the idea of deceiving the participants in research is seen as quite inappropriate. The experience of deception in psychological research may have the potential to cause distress and harm, and can make the recipients cynical about the activities and attitudes of psychologists. However, since there are very many psychological processes that are modifiable by individuals if they are aware that they are being studied, the statement of the research focus in advance of the collection of data would make much psychological research impossible. There is a difference between withholding some of the details of the hypothesis under test and deliberately falsely informing the participants of the purpose of the research, especially if the information given implies a more benign topic of study than is in fact the case. This Code expects all psychologists to seek to supply as full information as possible to those taking part in their research, recognising that if providing all of that information at the start of a person's participation may not be possible for methodological reasons. If the reaction of participants when deception is revealed later in their participation is likely to lead to discomfort, anger or objections from the participants then the deception is inappropriate. If a proposed research study involves deception, it should be designed in such a way that it protects the dignity and autonomy of the participants. Where an essential element of the research design would be compromised by full disclosure to participants, the withholding of information should be specified in the project protocol that is subjected to ethics review and explicit procedures should be stated to obviate any potential harm arising from such withholding. Deception or covert collection of data should only take place where it is essential to achieve the research results required, where the research objective has strong scientific merit and where there is an appropriate risk management and harm alleviation strategy. Studies based on observation in natural settings must respect the privacy and psychological wellbeing of the individuals studied. Unless those observed give their consent to being observed, observational research is only acceptable in public situations where those observed would expect to be observed by strangers. Additionally, particular account should be taken of local cultural values and of the possibility of intruding upon the privacy of individuals who, even while in a normally public space, may believe they are unobserved.

Source: BPS Code of Human Research Ethics (2014: 24–25)

Confidentiality

The BPS guidelines are as follows.

> Subject to the requirements of legislation, including the Data Protection Act, information obtained from and about a participant during an investigation is confidential unless otherwise agreed in advance. Investigators who are put under pressure to disclose confidential information should draw this point to the attention of those exerting such pressure. Participants in psychological research have a right to expect that information they provide will be treated confidentially and, if published, will not be identifiable as theirs. In the event that confidentiality and/or anonymity cannot be guaranteed, the participant must be warned of this in advance of agreeing to participate. The duty of confidentiality is not absolute in law and may in exceptional circumstances be overridden by more compelling duties such as the duty to protect individuals from harm. Where a significant risk of such issues arising is identified in the risk

assessment, specific procedures to be followed should be specified in the protocol.

Source: BPS Code of Human Research Ethics (2014: 22)

Privacy

A researcher should make it clear that participants have the right to ignore any questions or aspect of a study that they do not want to answer or engage in. This protects individuals' privacy. Also, studies should try to refrain from making people reveal personal details that they would not reveal in their everyday lives.

Debriefing

The BPS Code of Human Research Ethics states the following.

> As outlined in the Code of Ethics and Conduct…, when the research data gathering is completed, especially where any deception or withholding of information has taken place, it is important to provide an appropriate debriefing for participants. In some circumstances, the verbal description of the nature of the investigation will not be sufficient to eliminate all possibility of harmful after-effects. For example, following an experiment in which negative mood was induced, it would be ethical to induce a happy mood state before the participant leaves the experimental setting.

Source: BPS Code of Human Research Ethics (2014: 26)

The BPS Code of Ethics and Conduct (2009) included the following guidance.

> 3.4 Standard of debriefing of research participants
>
> *Psychologists should:*
>
> (i) Debrief research participants at the conclusion of their participation, in order to inform them of the outcomes and nature of the research, to identify any unforeseen harm, discomfort, or misconceptions, and in order to arrange for assistance as needed.
>
> (ii) Take particular care when discussing outcomes with research participants, as seemingly evaluative statements may carry unintended weight.

Source: BPS Code of Ethics and Conduct (2009: 20)

Guidelines for the use of animals

The following comments are taken from the BPS Guidelines for Psychologists Working With Animals published in 2012.

Replacement: Psychologists should at least consider using video footage of animal behaviour or computer simulations where possible.

Species and strain: Psychologists should choose a species that is scientifically and ethically suitable for the intended use. Choosing an appropriate subject species usually requires knowledge of that species' natural history and some judgement of its level of sentience. Knowledge of an individual animal's previous experience, such as whether or not it was bred in captivity, is also important. When the use involves regulated procedures, and when a variety of species can be used, the psychologist should employ the species which, in the opinion of the psychologist and other qualified colleagues, is likely to suffer least while still attaining the scientific objective, and must justify their choice in any project licence application (BPS: 2012: 5).

Numbers: Under the Animal (Scientific Procedures) Act 1986, psychologists should always use the smallest number of animals that still accomplishes the research aims and goals. This could be calculated via pilot study work and statistical programs.

Procedures: A range of well-documented procedures are contained in the Animal (Scientific Procedures) Act of 1986. They cover any procedure that involves a protected species that may cause pain, suffering or lasting harm or distress. Psychologists should always consider research that enriches rather than deprives, for example. Procedures that may cause discomfort, injury, stress, etc. need a *project licence* which will specify the species, number of animals and procedures that are allowed. To gain the licence there has to be a careful cost-benefit analysis. Psychologists must also hold a *personal licence* that shows they are competent in following regulated procedures set out by the Act. The rest of the section on animal ethics covers aspects of the following regulated procedures.

Pain and distress: Part of this is covered in the Procedures section above, but the BPS guidelines also note that holders of a *personal licence* should minimise any pain, suffering or distress that might arise from their research. Also, "whatever procedure is in use, any adverse effects on animals must be recognised and assessed, and immediate action taken wherever necessary" (BPS, 2014: 7).

Housing: Caging conditions should take into account the social behaviour of the species. Caging in isolation may be stressful to social animals; overcrowding may also cause distress, and possible harm through aggression. Because the degree of stress experienced by an animal can vary with species, age, sex, reproductive condition, developmental history, depression of the immune system and social status, the natural social behaviour of the animals concerned and their previous social experience must be considered in order to minimise such stress (BPS 2012: 8).

Reward, deprivation and aversive stimuli: It is not always necessary to provide all species of animals with *ad libitum* food intake, and, in some cases, this may even be considered harmful; deprivation, on the other hand, can cause distress to animals. … Thus, when arranging schedules of deprivation the experimenter should consider the animal's normal eating and drinking habits and its metabolic requirements; a short period of deprivation for one species may be unacceptably long for another. When using deprivation or aversive stimulation, the investigator should ascertain that there is no alternative way of motivating the animal that is consistent with the aims of the experiment, and that the levels of deprivation used are no greater than necessary to achieve the goals of the experiment (BPS 2012: 8).

Anaesthesia, analgesia and euthanasia: After conducting surgical procedures, close attention should be given to proper post-operative care in order to minimise preparatory stress and residual effects. Regular and frequent post-operative monitoring of the animal's condition is essential, and it is a requirement of the personal licence that if at any time an animal is found to be suffering severe pain or distress that cannot be alleviated it must be killed humanely using an approved technique. Unless specifically contra-indicated by the experimental design, procedures that are likely to cause pain or discomfort should be performed only on animals that have been adequately anaesthetised, and analgesics should be used before and after such procedures to minimise pain and distress whenever possible (BPS 2012: 10).

VALIDITY

Types of validity

There are several types of validity that may concern a psychologist conducting research. Validity generally concerns itself with looking at whether the study measured what it was supposed to measure. Table 1.1 highlights some of the main types of validity.

Type	Description
Ecological	Ecological validity has been the subject of great debate. There are two strands that psychologists analyse to make an overall judgement on levels of ecological validity in a study: • The environment in which the study is set is the first consideration. If it is artificial and not truly reflecting a real-life situation then a study is said to have low ecological validity. If it mirrors a real-life situation then it is said to have high ecological validity. • Behaviour is the second consideration when analysing ecological validity. Some psychologists argue that the level ecological validity is simply "the degree to which the behaviour of the subjects in the laboratory corresponds to their behaviour in the natural environment" (Breakwell *et al* 1995: 221). According to this view, ecological validity is more to do with the behaviour of the participant than the setting itself. It may be worth noting that the term "mundane realism" is increasingly used in psychology. This tends to refer to the reality of the task set for participants in any study. For example, the task of reading a word list then trying to recall the words is not something commonly done in everyday life. The task would have low mundane realism. However, an activity such as reading social media and then having a conversation about how you felt is something many people do in everyday life. A task reflecting this would have high mundane realism.
Criterion	Criterion validity is a way of assessing the validity of a task by comparing the results with another measure. There are two main types of criterion: concurrent and predictive. • A concurrent criterion is used when a new test and its results are compared to a standard measure that already exists for that behaviour or skill. An example would be when developing a new intelligence test. Researchers might ask: Are results from the new test similar to those gained from well-established measures such as the Weschler Adult Intelligence Scale or the Stanford-Binet Test? If so, the new measure would be said to have high concurrent validity. If not, it would be said to have low concurrent validity. • A predictive criterion is a test used to see whether a prediction can be made of what is likely to happen in the future. Using the example of an intelligence test, it could be used as a predictor for academic success. People could take the intelligence test and have their scores recorded. Then they could sit Cambridge International Examinations AS Level Psychology examinations and have their results compared to the original intelligence test scores. If the A grade students scored highest on the intelligence test whereas the E grade students scored the lowest, then the intelligence test is said to have some predictive validity. If there is no pattern then it is said to have low predictive validity.
Construct	This looks at whether a test or task given in a study reflects any theoretical constructs it was based on. Using an intelligence test as an example again, the questions used and range of factors being tested must be justified in terms of what a theory expects a person to show in terms of intelligent behaviours or responses.
Population	This refers to how well the sample used in the study can be extrapolated to the target population and then the population as a whole.

▲ **Table 1.1** Types of validity

Subjectivity and objectivity

When researchers run a study, they need to think about what data will be collected and then how to analyse it and draw appropriate conclusions. One aspect that may affect the conclusions drawn is subjectivity or objectivity.

Subjectivity refers to analysing data by judging it from your own personal opinion and feelings. Qualitative data, when analysed, has to have some degree of subjectivity as there are no statistics associated with it. An example would be interpreting a dream someone told you about. You can attempt to interpret it using symbols or your knowledge of the person but this analysis would simply be based on your personal opinion. Someone else may give a completely different analysis based on his or her opinion. Therefore, when you are interpreting data from your own perspective, you are being subjective.

Objectivity refers to analysing data based on fact with no need to use personal judgements. This means that all potential sources of bias are minimised. For example, let's say participants are asked to complete a task as quickly as possible. Participant A completes it in 20 seconds whereas participant B completes it in 40 seconds. From an objective perspective, participant A is faster; in fact *twice as fast*. This conclusion is based on fact and *no* personal opinions are needed.

Demand characteristics

Hayes defined demand characteristics as "those aspects of a psychological study (or other artificial situation) which exert an implicit pressure on people to act in ways that are expected of them" (2000: 369). Therefore, they are the features of a study that somehow inform the participants about the true aim and this influences their behaviour *independently* of the IV. While Hayes noted the *implicit* nature of the "pressure" when a repeated measures design is used, the characteristics can be *explicit* if the tasks only differ on one crucial aspect.

Generalisability

This is about the extent to which results or the findings from a study can be transferred to situations or people who were not originally studied. These can take the following forms:

▶ Population validity: can the findings be transferred to the TP from which the sample has been drawn from *or* those not represented in the sample?

▶ Ecological validity: can the findings be transferred to situations away from the situation or setting the study took place in?

RELIABILITY

Reliability generally concerns itself with consistency over time and whether replicating a study would produce similar results. There are several types of reliability, as highlighted below.

Inter-rater or observer

This is a test of the consistency between observers when watching the same behaviours shown by the same participants. Independent observers are briefed to observe the behaviours of the same participants. This usually happens as a pilot study *before* the real data collection. A time period for the observation is agreed, as well as the recording method (e.g. the observation may be continual as in time sampling or observers might record what the participant was doing at, say, 10 seconds, 20 seconds, 30 seconds, etc.). After the task, the two observers' records are compared for consistency. One crude way of doing this is simply to compare the two in terms of the frequency of different behaviours shown to see if they are approximately the same. A more objective way is to conduct correlational analyses on the data to see the strength of the correlation between the two (or more) observers' records. However, the correlation only shows the degree of similarity, overall, between the observers' records. It does not tell us that they recorded the frequency of exactly the same behaviours. One way around this could be to train observers by having them watch pre-recorded sequences of behaviours so that they can replay an event and agree whether the behaviour was shown or not.

Test-retest analysis

This is a test of consistency of a questionnaire-based measure (e.g. an attitude). When a questionnaire is devised using techniques that generate quantitative data, a test-retest reliability analysis can be conducted to test whether the questionnaire is a reliable measure. Researchers would follow these steps:

1. Create a questionnaire that generates numerical data.

2. Allow a group of participants to complete the questionnaire.

3. After a set time frame (usually greater than two weeks), get the *same* participants to complete the *same* questionnaire.

4. Correlate the overall scores for the two time points and see whether a positive correlation occurs. This can even be assessed question by question but it is usually on total scores. If a strong positive correlation occurs then the questionnaire is said to be a reliable measure.

DATA ANALYSIS

Measures of central tendency and spread

A measure of central tendency (sometimes called a measure of average) represents how data clusters around a central point in the data set. It is supposed to represent a typical score from the collected data. A measure of spread (sometimes called a measure of dispersion) gives an index of how spread the data is around a measure of central tendency.

Measures of central tendency

Mean

The mean is usually called the average but there are another two types of average that we will look at here (see below). The mean is also called the *arithmetic mean*. To calculate this we must complete the following procedure:

1. Add up all of the scores we have collected to form our data set.

2. Divide this total by the *number* of scores that we have just added up.

Let's look at an example.

We measured the height of ten people and the results were as follows (in centimetres):

158   163   165   165   165   168   170   170   170   175

First, we add up all of the scores:

158 +   163 +   165 +   165 +   165 +   168 +

170 +   170 +   170 +   175

Next, we divide the total score by the number of scores, which is 10.

$\frac{1669}{10} = 166.9$. The mean height is 166.9 centimetres.

Median

This measure of average is the *middlemost score*. That is, when data has been placed in rank order from the smallest number to the largest number (including every repetition of a score), the median is the score that lies in the middle of the data set. To calculate a median, follow these steps:

1. Rank the data from the smallest number to the largest number.

2. Eliminate one score from the lowest end of the ranked data and one score from the highest end of the ranked data (called a pair of scores).

3. Continue eliminating these pairs of scores until either one or two scores are left. If there is an *odd number of scores* left in the data set you should be left with just one number. This is the median. If there is an *even number of scores* left in the data set you should be left with two numbers. In this case, you must complete step 4 below.

4. Add up the two remaining numbers and divide the total by 2. This is the median. Let's look at an example.

The following are questionnaire scores generated from a Likert-type scale.

11   13   13   13   15   17   17   17   18   19   19

The median is 17. Now, recalculate with an extra score:

11   13   13   13   13   15   17   17   17   18   19   19

The two remaining numbers are 15 and 17. If we now execute step 4, we get:

15 + 17 = 32. We then divide this by 2 to get $\frac{32}{2} = 16$. The median score is 16.

Mode

This measure of average is the *most common score* in the data set. Therefore, on inspecting the data set you can discover the mode by seeing which score or value is represented the most times. If two scores are equally represented then we call the distribution of scores *bi-modal*. If there are three modes then it is *tri-modal*, and so on. The best way of calculating the mode is to draw up a frequency table and see which score has the highest frequency, for example as shown in Table 1.2.

Shoe colour choice in males	Frequency
Brown	10
Green	15
Blue	18
Black	27
White	17
Red	4

▲ **Table 1.2** Frequency table for males' choice of shoe colour

From the frequency column we can easily conclude that the modal shoe colour for this data set is black.

When is it most appropriate to use each measure of average?

Each particular measure of average and measure of dispersion cannot be used on any data collected. That is, the mode, median and mean for the data are not simply calculated and all reported on every occasion (this also applies to the measures of dispersion). Table 1.3 shows that the type of measure of average and measure of dispersion used depends on the type (level) of data collected.

Level of measurement	Appropriate measure of average
Nominal: categories of data (e.g. favourite subject)	Mode
Ordinal: numerical data on a scale devised by the researcher (e.g. a happiness index)	Median
Interval/ratio: numerical data measured on a universal scale (e.g. height, weight)	Mean

▲ **Table 1.3** Measure of average appropriate for different levels of data

Measures of spread

Range

This measure of spread is used in conjunction with the *median* but can be used with any continuous data. It is the simplest to calculate as follows:

1. Rank the data from the smallest to the largest number (as for calculating the median).

2. Subtract the smallest number from the highest number then add 1.

This is used when the data is at least ordinal.

Standard deviation

This measure of spread is used in conjunction with the *mean*. This measure is the spread of data around the mean point. It is the most stringent measure of dispersion as it uses all the data in the calculation.

It is easier to interpret a standard deviation if you have two or more data sets to compare. For example, say that you have timed males and females on their ability to solve a maze. Your results are as follows.

Females	Males
Mean = 68.4 seconds	Mean = 69.3 seconds
Standard deviation = 3.9 seconds	Standard deviation = 10.4 seconds

The means are similar so, on average, females and males solve mazes in roughly the same time. However, the standard deviation is telling us that the results for females have less spread around the mean than the results for males. This is because, for the results for females, the standard deviation is smaller. Many of the females would have completed the maze around the mean time of 68.4 seconds. However, for the males the data set is much more spread out. Therefore, there were some males who were much slower than the 69.3 seconds average to solve the maze but there were some males who solved it much faster.

This measure of spread is normally used when the data is interval/ratio.

NORMAL DISTRIBUTION

Normal distribution is sometimes referred to as a bell-shaped curve; that is, the data is symmetrical around the central point of the data. If a data set is normally distributed then the mean, median and mode are *all the same value*.

Normal distribution looks like this.

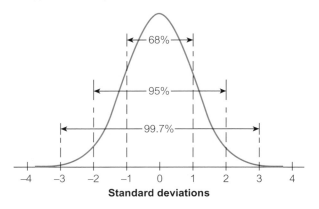

Therefore, 68 per cent of the data set is between one standard deviation less and one standard deviation more than the central point (the mean, median and mode).

Plotting of data
Bar chart

These are usually used for *nominal* data (results in named categories) or for plotting the average scores for the groups of data collected. The x-axis (horizontal axis) should always have the categories of data while the y-axis (vertical axis) should always have the frequency of occurrences or the average value that is to be represented.

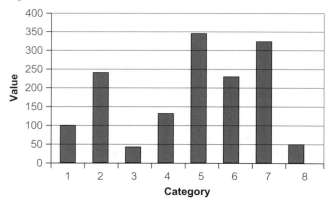

To plot a bar chart follow these steps:

▶ Enter the categories of data collected (e.g. favourite animal, or a score on a happiness scale) along the x-axis.

▶ On the y-axis, write the frequency that each category was recorded.

▶ Ensure that there are gaps between each bar because the bars represent *separate* categories.

> **CHALLENGE YOURSELF**
> People were asked what their favourite colour was. Their answers were blue, red, black, blue, green, pink, green, red, red, red, blue, black, yellow, blue, green, green, pink, blue, blue, brown.
> From this data set, draw a bar chart.
> What does your bar chart show?

Histogram

These are usually used when the data is continuous (on a numerical scale) and is plotted on the x-axis (horizontal axis). The y-axis (vertical axis) should always be used for the frequency of occurrences.

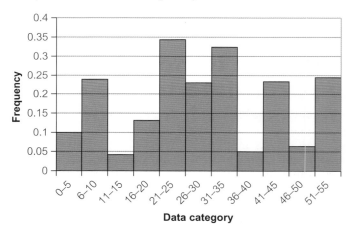

To plot a histogram follow these steps:

▶ Choose an appropriate width for each bar along the x-axis. Try to keep them exactly the same; for example, if you are entering the speed of completing a task use 1–5 seconds (s), 6–10 s, 11–15 s, 16-20 s, and so on.

▶ On the y-axis, enter the frequency at which data fell within the width of each bar on the x-axis.

Scattergraph

Sometimes these are referred to as scatterplots or scattergrams. These are used for plotting *correlations*, the relationship between two numerical measures. From these, it is clear what type of correlation has been found. The x-axis (horizontal axis) should represent one of the numerical measures and the y-axis (vertical axis) should represent the other.

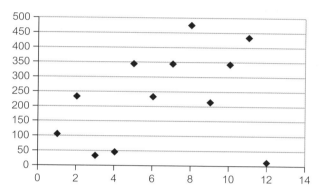

To plot a scattergraph, in the example below of participants' scores in two psychology tests, these steps would need to be followed:

- Enter the participant's first score along the x-axis.
- Enter the participant's second score along the y-axis.
- Each cross placed on the scattergraph represents a participant's pair of scores, so find a participant's score on the x-axis and then move up to that person's score on the y-axis and place a cross.

THE GOLDEN RULES OF PLOTTING DATA

The following are guidelines that should be applied every time data is to be plotted:

- Tabulate the data either as a frequency tally chart or where each participant's score on one variable for the scattergraph is next to the score on the other variable.

- Choose an appropriate graph for the type of data you have and the information that you are intending to get across to the reader with the graph.

- Label the axes fully and clearly. For example, if you are representing age groups on the x-axis, state whether the age is in years or months.

- Give the graph an appropriate title. Anyone should be able to read the title and know what the graph is representing.

- Interpret the graph as part of the data analysis. Graphs are not just to fill the space in a report, they should be used as part of your report.

6 Design a case study to examine why a child has a phobia of grass.

7 Design an observation (you choose the type) to test whether children are more playful in the morning or the afternoon.

8 Design a correlational study to test whether there is a relationship between the number of hours studied for an examination and the result gained in the examination.

ISSUES AND DEBATES FOR AS LEVEL

THE APPLICATION OF PSYCHOLOGY TO EVERYDAY LIFE

Some people argue that if studies and ideas from psychology cannot be used in everyday life then they are not useful. All psychologists have to consider this before they complete a study. Once a study has been published, other psychologists may evaluate its usefulness. This can be positive or negative. A study may only have been conducted on one sex so it may not be useful in explaining the behaviour of the opposite sex. The extent to which something is useful is debating how the findings can be used (or not used) in everyday life.

Strength of conducting useful research	Problems with conducting useful research
The main advantage is that it is can be used to improve human behaviour in some way. For example, if we find a better way to treat a mental illness then it is useful to society as a whole.	Studies might be unethical to gain more valid results. Studies need to be high in ecological validity to be of more use to society but this can be quite difficult if they are conducted in a laboratory, for instance.

INDIVIDUAL AND SITUATIONAL EXPLANATIONS

Individual explanations account for behaviours using factors from within the person (called dispositional factors, such as personality). Situational explanations account for behaviours using factors from the external environment (situations that people find themselves in).

Strengths of this debate	Problems with this debate
The findings can be very useful to society as a whole. If we find out which behaviours are down to individuals and which are down to the situations we find ourselves in, then we can help explain human behaviour more clearly. If psychologists find that there is an interaction between both sides of the debate then this is useful too.	It is not always easy to separate out individual and situational factors. Studies might be unethical to gain more valid results. Studies need high ecological validity to be of more use to this debate but this can be difficult if they take place in a laboratory, for instance.

NATURE VERSUS NURTURE

Nature refers to behaviours that are thought to be hard-wired into people pre-birth (innate or genetic). Nurture refers to behaviours that are thought to develop through the lifetime of the person. Therefore, nature tends to be based on biological factors whereas nurture tends to be based on social and psychological factors.

Strengths of this debate	Problems with this debate
The findings can be very useful to society as a whole. If we find out which behaviours come from nature and which from nurture, we can help to explain behaviour more clearly. If there is an interaction between both sides of the debate this is useful too.	It is not always easy to separate out what is nature and what is nurture. If behaviour is seen to be purely down to nature (genetics) this can be very socially sensitive. Sections of society could use this to undertake a "eugenic" movement to get rid of people with "inferior genes". This is clearly unacceptable. Studies might be unethical in order to gain more valid results.

THE USE OF CHILDREN IN PSYCHOLOGICAL RESEARCH

There are specific rules about using children in psychological research:

▶ Children aged under 16 cannot give their own informed consent to take part in a study.

▶ Children aged under 16 must get parental permission to participate in studies or *loco parentis* permission (e.g. someone who looks after them in a nursery or school).

There are other issues that may surround the use of children in research that are not linked to ethical concerns. These include the following:

▶ There must be use of appropriate language to ensure that children used as participants in research *understand* what they are doing.

▶ Some psychologists believe that children are *less* susceptible to demand characteristics.

▶ Children may get bored quicker and tired faster than adults so this needs to be considered when designing tasks in studies.

THE USE OF ANIMALS IN PSYCHOLOGICAL RESEARCH

There are ethical guidelines and rules for using animals in psychological research. The main ones are as follows:

▶ The law – psychologists must work within the law about protecting animals.

▶ Number of animals – this should be a kept to the minimum amount to make statistical analysis meaningful.

▶ Social environment – social species should be kept together and non-social species kept apart.

▶ Caging – housing in cages should not lead to overcrowding and increased stress levels.

Strength	Weakness
We can conduct research on animals that we cannot do on humans for ethical reasons.	Due to the differences in physiological and psychological "make-ups" of animals and humans it can be difficult to generalise from animal studies to human behaviour.

See pages 16–17 for more in-depth coverage of ethical guidelines in relation to the use of animals in psychological research.

3 APPROACHES TO PSYCHOLOGY

There are many different ways in which psychologists try to explain human and animal behaviour. The approaches psychologists use form the discipline of psychology. However, these approaches differ widely from each other. This chapter will cover how psychologists use these different approaches to try to explain behaviour. There are four approaches that you are expected to know about. This section looks at each in turn, highlighting their general assumptions, the main research methodology they use and which studies from AS Level fit into each one.

BIOLOGICAL PSYCHOLOGY

Physiological psychologists are interested in how our biology affects our psychology. They look, for example, at the role that genetics, brain function, hormones and neurotransmitters have on our behaviour. Many physiological psychologists believe that our behaviour can be explained via biological mechanisms more so than psychological mechanisms. However, others believe that there may be an interaction between the two. Areas of interest include origins of mental disorders, treatments of mental disorders, sleep, circadian rhythms and localisation of brain function (that is, which parts of the brain are responsible for different behaviours).

The AS Level studies that are listed in the Cambridge International Examinations syllabus under this section are:

▶ Canli *et al* (brain scans and emotions)

▶ Dement and Kleitman (sleep and dreams)

▶ Schachter and Singer (two factors in emotion).

The main research methods used in this approach are laboratory experiments and brain scanning techniques.

These are the two main assumptions that you are expected to know:

▶ Behaviour, cognitions and emotions can be explained in terms of the working of the brain and the effect of hormones.

▶ Similarities and differences between people can be understood in terms of the biological factors and their interaction with other factors.

COGNITIVE PSYCHOLOGY

Cognitive psychologists are interested in how we process information. They look into how we input information, then how we process that information and finally how we retrieve and/or use it. Some cognitive psychologists believe that the brain works like a computer following the procedure of input-process/storage-output. Areas of interest include memory and forgetting, perception, language and attention.

The AS Level studies that are listed in the Cambridge International Examinations syllabus under this section are:

▶ Andrade (doodling)

▶ Baron-Cohen *et al* (eyes test)

▶ Laney *et al* (false memory).

The main research method used in this approach is laboratory experiments.

These are the two main assumptions that you are expected to know:

▶ Behaviour and emotions can be explained in terms of the role of cognitive processes such as attention, language, thinking and memory.

▶ Similarities and differences between people can be understood in terms of individual patterns of cognition.

LEARNING APPROACH

Behaviourist psychologists are interested in ways in which humans and animals learn. They look into general laws that can apply to all species and how the experiences we have mould our behaviour over time. There are three main areas within this perspective:

▶ learning by the consequences of our behaviour (operant conditioning)

▶ learning through association (classical conditioning)

▶ learning through observation, imitation and modelling (social learning).

Strict behaviourism follows the idea that we should "observe the observable" and not examine mental processes, as they cannot be directly seen. Behaviours can be directly seen so we have objective measures of behaviour. Areas of interest include behaviour modification, therapies for mental health disorders, therapies for prisoners, etc. and development of behaviours such aggression.

The AS Level studies that are listed in the Cambridge International Examinations syllabus under this section are:

▶ Bandura, Ross and Ross (aggression)

▶ Saavedra and Silverman (button phobia)

▶ Pepperberg (parrot learning).

The main research method used in this approach is laboratory experiments.

These are the two main assumptions that you are expected to know:

▶ Conditioning helps to explain changes in behaviour.

▶ Social learning helps to explain changes in behaviour.

SOCIAL PSYCHOLOGY

Social psychologists are interested in how we "work" in the social world. They look at how individuals interact with each other and how we interact in groups. Therefore, they look at the individual as an individual but also as a group member and see how this affects behaviour. They also examine how the role of culture and society affects our behaviour. Areas of interest include prejudice, obedience and conformity.

The AS studies that are listed in the Cambridge International Examinations syllabus under this section are:

▶ Milgram (obedience)

▶ Piliavin, Rodin and Piliavin (subway Samaritans)

▶ Yamamoto, Humle and Tanaka (chimpanzee helping).

The main research methods used in this approach are questionnaires and interviews.

These are the two main assumptions that you are expected to know:

▶ Behaviour, cognitions and emotions can be influenced by other individuals.

▶ Behaviour, cognitions and emotions can be influenced by groups and social contexts.

4 CANLI *et al*

Research date: 2000

BACKGROUND

There appears to be a link between the amygdala and emotional experiences in humans and animals. Studies using brain imaging have shown correlations between the level of amygdala activation and subsequent declarative memory recall (facts and events). However, correlational studies do not show cause and effect, only that there is some form of relationship. The researchers noted that the correlations could be for any of these reasons:

▶ Some individuals are simply more responsive to emotional experiences.

▶ During scanning some people were simply in an enhanced state of emotion.

▶ The amygdala responds in a dynamic way to moment-to-moment subjective emotional experiences.

Therefore, an experiment was needed to test the connection between amygdala activation and emotional-based long-term memory recall.

THE PSYCHOLOGY BEING INVESTIGATED

The study wanted to examine any potential link between amygdala activation in the brain and long-term emotional memories. Through this study, the researchers also wanted to show other psychologists that event-related functional Magnetic Resonance Imagery (fMRI) scanning techniques can help us to understand emotional behaviour. An fMRI is a non-invasive brain scanning technique that uses the same principle as a Magnetic Resonance Imagery (MRI) scan. That is, it uses radio waves coupled with a strong magnetic field to create a very detailed image of the brain. However, an fMRI looks at blood flow in the brain during mental activity rather than just the brain's structure. Therefore, it is classed as a functional scan rather than a structural scan. The scanner traces the journey of strong oxygenated blood around the brain as we know that areas of high activity receive more oxygenated blood. All of this is called the blood-oxygen-level-dependent (BOLD) signal. The scanner maps all of the activity and produces a map of squares called voxels which represent thousands of neurons. The pictures are colour coded to show the intensity of activity.

 ASK YOURSELF
What do you think causes our emotions? Could they be linked to specific parts of the brain?

AIM

1. To investigate whether an area of the brain called the amygdala is sensitive to different levels of intensity to emotions based on subjective emotional experiences.

2. To investigate whether the degree of emotional intensity affects the role of the amygdala in aiding memory recall of stimuli classed as being "emotional".

METHOD
Participants

Ten right-handed, healthy, female volunteers were recruited. Females were chosen as they are more likely to report intense emotional experiences. Also, females have shown that they exhibit more physiological reactivity in accordance to valence judgments than men.

Design and procedure
Behavioural procedures

During a functional magnetic resonance imaging (fMRI) scan, participants were shown slides of 96 scenes, each with a normative rating for valence (emotional value) and arousal, from the International Affective Picture System stimuli set. The scenes ranged from highly negative (rating of 1.17) to neutral (rating of 5.44) for valence. They were also rated from tranquil (rating of 1.97) to highly arousing (rating of 7.63) for arousal. The scenes were randomised across participants. The scenes were shown for 2.88 seconds with an interval of 12.96 seconds before the next one appeared. In this time participants were asked to fixate on a cross on the screen. They were asked to look at the entire scene for all of the time it was presented and as soon as the cross appeared, by pressing the relevant button with their right hand, they had to rate the scene on a scale from 0 = not emotionally intense at all to 3 = extremely emotionally intense.

Three weeks after the scans had taken place, participants were given an unexpected recognition test. They viewed all of the scenes they had previously seen along with 48 new ones (foils). These foils matched the valence and arousal scores of the original scenes. During the recognition test, participants were asked whether they had seen the slide before. If they said "yes" they were asked whether they remembered the scene with certainty (coded as remembered) or had a less certain feeling of familiarity (coded as familiar). The number of forgotten scenes was also recorded.

The fMRI

During all scans the participant's head movement was minimised via a bite-bar. For the structural image eight slices were obtained for each participant. The anterior slice was 7 millimetres anterior to the amygdala. For the functional image, 11 frames were captured per trial per participant. Each frame was assigned either as a baseline image (frames 1, 2, 10 and 11) or an activation image (frames 5, 6, 7 and 8).

 TEST YOURSELF
Draw a flow diagram for the behavioural procedures stage of the study then get someone to ask you questions about it.

RESULTS

The main results were as follows:

▶ Participants' ratings of emotional intensity reflected the valence and arousal ratings of the scenes.

▶ Amygdala activation was significantly correlated with higher ratings of experienced emotional intensity. This is shown in Figure 4.1.

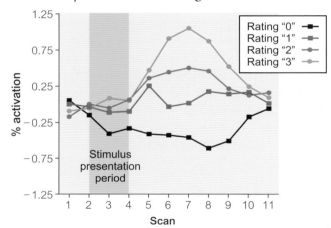

▲ **Figure 4.1** A time course plot showing average signal intensity in response to scenes that were rated in emotional intensity from 0 (least intense) to 3 (most intense)

Source: Based on Canli *et al* (2000: 2)

Participants' ratings of emotional intensity were similarly distributed across the 0–3 rating scale (0 = 29 per cent of scenes; 1 = 22 per cent; 2 = 24 per cent; 3 = 25 per cent).

Memory recall was significantly better for those scenes rated as emotionally intense (rated 3) than those rated 0–2 ($p < 0.05$).

Scenes rated 0–2 had similar distributions of percentage forgotten, familiar or remembered. However, those rated 3 were remembered and were familiar with a higher frequency than those rated 0–2. Figure 4.2 shows these distributions.

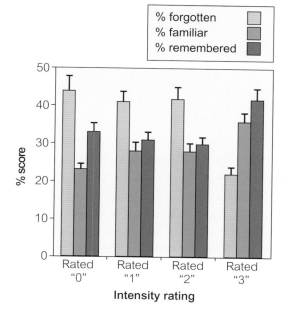

Figure 4.2 Memory performance and ratings of emotional intensity

Source: Based on Canli *et al* (2000: 2)

The degree of left (not right) amygdala activation predicted whether an individual scene would be forgotten, be familiar or be remembered. Little activation to a scene that was rated as being highly emotional was associated with forgetting that scene; intermediate activation was associated with the scene being familiar; high activation was associated with the scene being remembered.

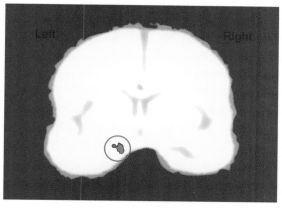

Figure 4.3 Cluster of significant correlation between amygdala activation and memory for scenes rated as emotionally intense (rated 3)

Source: Based on Canli *et al* (2000: 2)

When the left amygdala was analysed further, there was a significant correlation between its activation and the emotional intensity of the memory. The correlation became stronger the more emotional intensity was experienced (this only reached significance for those rated 3). Figure 4.4 shows the results for this.

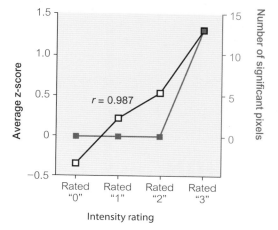

Figure 4.4 Correlation between left amygdala activation and memory for emotional items increases with greater emotional intensity

Source: Based on Canli *et al* (2000: 2)

CONCLUSION

The research team drew these main conclusions:

► The amygdala is sensitive to individually experienced emotional intensity of visual scenes.

► The activity in the left amygdala during encoding can predict subsequent memory.

► The degree to which the amygdala activation at encoding can predict subsequent memory is a function of emotional intensity.

Overall, the findings appear to suggest that the amygdala reflects moment-to-moment subjective emotional experiences.

SUMMARY

Research method (main)	Experimental
Other technique(s)	Correlational mapping; fMRI
Sample	Ten right-handed healthy females
Sampling technique	Volunteer
Experimental design	Repeated measures
IV	Intensity rating of stimuli
DV	Pixel count and percentage forgotten, familiar or remembered in the tests
Quantitative data	As above
Qualitative data	–

EVALUATION

Evaluation	General evaluation (laboratory experiments)	Related to Canli *et al*
Strength	Laboratory experiments have high levels of standardisation and so can be replicated to test for reliability.	This study had a standardised procedure including the valence scores and the length of time each picture was viewed for. This means other researchers could easily replicate this study to test for reliability.
Strength	As laboratory experiments have high levels of control, researchers can be more confident it is the IV directly affecting the DV.	As there were many controls (e.g. the valence ratings and the later unexpected recognition task), the researchers could be more confident that it was the valence of the pictures seen that was causing activity in brain areas such as the amygdala.
Weakness	In many laboratory experiments participants take part in tasks that are nothing like real-life ones, so the tasks lack mundane realism.	The task of looking at pictures for 2.88 seconds then rating emotional intensity on a scale of 0 to 3 is not an activity that the participants would come across in everyday life. Therefore, the study may lack mundane realism.

Other evaluation points include the following:

▶ Generalisability: Canli *et al* chose a specific sample of females for a particular reason. However, this means that the findings may only be representative of females. The ways in which males and females process emotional information may be different and therefore conclusions about the brain regions activated may only apply to females.

▶ Quantitative data: Canli *et al* collected a large amount of quantitative data. This has the advantage that statistical analyses to look for trends and differences are easy to conduct. However, the reasoning behind why each participant rated each picture are unknown.

▶ Correlational aspects of the study: the analyses used correlational mapping which only shows that there was a relationship between the valence of pictures and the brain activation in the amygdala. Therefore, the cause and effect argument above may not apply.

▶ Ethics – protection: participants were exposed to emotionally charged imagery which may have stressed some of them. There is no record of participants then being exposed to "happier" imagery to alleviate any negative mental state they may have found themselves in.

 CHALLENGE YOURSELF
Evaluate the study based on the sampling technique used and on its use of an fMRI scan.

ISSUES AND DEBATES

The following table discusses the Canli *et al* study in terms of the core issues and debates for AS Level.

Application to everyday life	The findings of this study may be useful for advertising agencies. If emotionally intense information is more likely to be recognised or recalled at a later date then advertisements that will appear on television or in magazines may be designed specifically to contain intense imagery.
Individual and situational explanations	Not applicable
Nature versus nurture	Some psychologists may argue that because the findings show that emotions are linked to brain function, the study supports a link to **nature**. However, as experiences were not taken into account in the study, it could still be **nurture** causing the results.
The use of children	Not applicable
The use of animals	Not applicable

CHALLENGE YOURSELF
Identify two other applications to everyday life this study could have. Explain who would benefit from these applications.

5 DEMENT AND KLEITMAN

Research date: 1957

BACKGROUND

The topics of sleep and dreaming are clearly hard to investigate because the participant is necessarily asleep and so cannot communicate with the researcher. Even when participants are awake, only self-report data can be obtained about dream content, and these alone might not be valid, as they are subjective. The study of sleep and dreaming became more scientifically rigorous with the invention of physiological techniques to measure brain activity that indicated dreaming (the electro-encephalograph, or EEG) and allowed the electrical recording of eye movements (the electro-oculogram, or EOG) rather than their direct observation. These techniques were used by Dement and Kleitman to trace the cyclical changes that occur in brain activity and eye movements during a night's sleep. The cycle alternates between a stage in which there are eye movements and several stages during which there are none.

An electro-encephalograph (EEG) detects and records tiny electrical charges associated with nerve and muscle activity. The EEG machine produces a chart (an encephalogram) that shows brain waves. These change with the frequency and amplitude (i.e. the "height", which indicates the voltage) of electrical output from the brain over time. In REM sleep, the EEG is relatively low voltage, high amplitude. In contrast, nREM sleep has either high-voltage and slow (low-amplitude) waves, or frequent "sleep spindles", which are short-lived high-voltage, high-frequency waves.

Modern EEG machines are entirely computerised, whereas Dement and Kleitman's EEG had continuously running paper. The faster the paper moved, the more detail could be recorded. The paper was usually moving at 3 or 6 millimetres per second, although a faster speed of 3 centimetres per second was used for detailed analysis.

To remember the meaning of EEG it can help to break the word down:

▶ electro (electric)

▶ encephalo (in head)

▶ graph (writing).

The same EEG electrodes and machine can also be used to record eye movements. The output – called an electro-oculogram (EOG) – indicates the presence or absence of eye movements, their size and their direction (horizontal or vertical).

THE PSYCHOLOGY BEING INVESTIGATED

In the dream or rapid eye movement (REM) sleep stage, our eyes move under the lids (hence "rapid eye movement"). In Aserinsky and Kleitman's (1955) study, participants woken from this stage were more likely to report a vivid, visual dream than participants woken from non-rapid eye movement (nREM) sleep. It is possible to separate nREM sleep into four stages (1 to 4), of which 1 is the lightest and 4 the deepest.

REM sleep resembles wakefulness in some ways: our eyes move, we often experience vivid (if bizarre) thoughts in the form of dreams, and our brains are active. However, in other ways it is very different from wakefulness: we are quite difficult to wake up, we are fairly insensitive to external stimuli, and we are paralysed. As REM sleep presents these contradictions, it is also known as paradoxical sleep.

 ASK YOURSELF
Do you remember your dreams? Are there always certain types of dreams you remember?

AIM

Overall aim: to investigate dreaming in an objective way by looking for relationships between eye movements in sleep and the dreamer's recall.

Specific aims:

1. To test whether dream recall differs between REM and nREM sleep.

2. To investigate whether there is a positive correlation between subjective estimates of dream duration and the length of the REM period.

3. To test whether eye-movement patterns are related to dream content.

METHOD

This study included several laboratory investigations with different designs. Three specific approaches were used to test the three aims above:

1. To test whether dream recall differs between REM and nREM sleep. Participants were woken either from REM or nREM sleep, but were not told which stage of sleep they had been in prior to waking. They confirmed whether they had been having a dream and, if so, described the content into a recorder.

2. To investigate whether there is a positive correlation between subjective estimates of dream duration and the length of the REM period. Participants were woken following either 5 or 15 minutes in REM sleep. They were asked to choose whether they thought they had been dreaming for 5 or 15 minutes. Longer

REM periods were also tested. Again, they gave a report of dream content and the number of words in the dream narrative was counted.

3. To test whether eye-movement patterns are related to dream content – whether these patterns represent the visual experience of the dream content or whether they are simply random movements arising from the activation of the central nervous system during dream sleep. The direction of eye movements was detected using electrodes around the eyes (EOG). Participants were woken after exhibiting a single eye-movement pattern for longer than one minute. Again, they were asked to report their dream.

Participants

Nine adult participants were used in this study (seven male and two female). Four of these were mainly used to confirm the data obtained from the five others, who were studied in detail.

Design

The researchers carried out three studies as experiments:

▶ Study 1 was a natural experiment in a laboratory setting. The levels of the IV were REM sleep/nREM sleep and the DVs were whether a dream was reported and, if so, the detail.

▶ Study 2 was a true experiment, with each participant being tested in both conditions (i.e. using repeated measures). The data were used in both experimental and correlational designs:

> **experimental** analysis – the levels of the IV were waking after 5 or 15 minutes, and the DV was the participant's choice of 5 or 15 minutes.

> **correlational** analysis – the two variables were the participant's time estimate and the number of words in the dream narrative.

▶ Study 3 was a natural experiment conducted in a laboratory (the IV of eye-movement pattern type could not be manipulated by the researchers). The DV was the report of dream content.

Procedure

The five participants studied in detail spent between 6 and 17 nights in the laboratory and were tested with 50–77 awakenings. The four participants used to confirm the findings stayed only one or two nights and were awoken between four and ten times in total. Each participant was identified by a pair of initials. Table 5.1 shows a summary of what each participant went through.

Sleep stage	REM-sleep awakenings		nREM-sleep awakenings	
	Dream recall	No recall	Dream recall	No recall
Number of times participants reported the presence or absence of a dream (DV)	152	39	11	149

▲ **Table 5.1** Instances of dream recall following awakenings from REM and nREM sleep

Source: Dement and Kleitman (1957: 340)

TEST YOURSELF
Outline how the three studies in this research were designed.

During the daytime prior to arrival at the laboratory, each participant ate normally (excluding drinks containing alcohol or caffeine). Participants arrived at the laboratory just before their normal bedtime and were fitted with electrical recording apparatus. This included electrodes attached near the eyes (to record eye movements) and on the scalp (to record brain waves). Once participants were in bed in a quiet, dark room, wires from the electrodes (which fed to the EEG in the experimenter's room) were gathered into a "pony tail" from each participant's head, to allow the person freedom of movement. The EEG ran continuously through the night to monitor participants' sleep stages and to inform the researchers when participants should be woken up. They were woken by a doorbell that was loud enough to wake them from any sleep stage. This meant that the researcher did not have to enter the room to wake participants, and so they were all treated in exactly the same way. The doorbell was rung at various times during the night and participants indicated whether they had been dreaming prior to being woken and, if so, described their dream into a voice recorder. They then returned to sleep (typically within

5 minutes). Occasionally, the researcher entered the room after a participant had finished speaking in order to ask questions. When the narrative was analysed, what was described was considered to be a dream only if there was a coherent, fairly detailed description of the content (i.e. vague, fragmentary impressions were not scored as dreams). In terms of awakenings, 21 per cent occurred in the first two hours of being asleep, 29 per cent in the second two hours, 28 per cent in the third and the remaining 22 per cent in the fourth.

The patterns of REM and nREM wakings differed between the participants. The participants with the initials PM and KC were determined randomly to eliminate any possibility of an unintentional pattern. WD was treated in the same way, although he was told that he would be woken only from dream sleep. DN was woken in a repeating pattern of three REM followed by three nREM awakenings. The waking of IR from REM or nREM was chosen by the researcher.

RESULTS

Quantitative and qualitative data were gathered in response to studies 1 and 2. Only qualitative data were gathered for study 3.

Study 1

Does dream recall differ between REM and nREM sleep?

Participants described dreams often when woken in REM but rarely from nREM sleep (although there were some individual differences). This pattern was consistent over the night. When awakened from nREM, participants tended to describe feelings (e.g. pleasantness, anxiety, detachment) but this did not relate to specific dream content.

Waking pattern did not affect recall. Specifically, WD was no less accurate despite being misled, and DN was no more accurate even though he might have guessed the pattern of awakenings. When participants were woken in high-voltage, slow-wave periods (as shown by the EEG) they often looked bewildered. They tended to state that they must have been dreaming but could remember nothing about their dream.

	Time of waking after REM stage	
	Within 8 minutes	After 8 minutes
Number of awakenings conducted	17	132
Number of dreams recalled	5	6
Percentage of occasions on which dreams recalled	29	5

▲ **Table 5.2** Number of dreams recalled following awakenings from nREM sleep immediately after, or much longer after, an REM stage

When woken from nREM sleep, participants returned to nREM and the next REM stage was not delayed. The only exception tended to be when a participant was woken in their final REM phase of the night. They then went back into REM after the awakening.

So, REM and nREM sleep differ as the vivid, visual dreams are reported only from awakenings during, or a short time after, REM sleep.

Study 2

Are subjective estimates of dream duration related to the length of the REM period?

Initially, the researchers tried to wake participants after various REM durations to ask them to estimate these durations. Although participants' responses were not wildly wrong, the task was too difficult. When asked instead whether they had been in REM sleep for 5 or 15 minutes, the participants responded more accurately. They were 88 per cent and 78 per cent accurate respectively for 5- or 15-minute REM durations. Table 5.3 shows the results for the five main participants.

S	5 Minutes		15 Minutes	
	Right	Wrong	Right	Wrong
DN	8	2	5	5
IR	11	1	7	3
KC	7	0	12	1
WD	13	1	15	1
PM	6	2	8	3
Total	45	6	47	13

▲ **Table 5.3** Results of dream-duration estimates after 5 or 15 minutes of REM

Source: Dement and Kleitman (1957: 343)

Although most of the participants were highly accurate (with only 0–3 incorrect responses), one was not. Participant DN frequently found he could recall only the end of his dream, so it seemed shorter than it actually was. Therefore, he consistently underestimated dream duration, often choosing 5 minutes instead of 15. This meant he was accurate on short REM estimates (making only two errors over ten awakenings), but inaccurate after 15 minutes' of REM (making five errors over ten awakenings).

Using REM periods over a range of durations, narratives from 152 dreams were collected. However, 26 of these could not be used as they were too poorly recorded for accurate transcription. For the remaining dreams (15–35 per participant) the number of words in the dream narrative was counted. Even though this was affected by how expressive the participant was, a significant positive correlation was found between REM duration and number of words in the narrative. The r values varied between 0.40 and 0.71 for different participants (all were significant at $p < 0.05$).

Dream narratives for very long durations (e.g. 30 or 50 minutes) were not much longer than those for 15 minutes. The participants did report, however, that they felt as though they had been dreaming for a long time, suggesting that they could not recall the early part of the dream.

Study 3

Do eye-movement patterns in REM sleep represent the visual experience of the dream?

The researchers found that participants' narratives were not sufficiently accurate to be matched exactly to the changes in eye-movement patterns over the length of an REM-sleep period. Instead, participants were woken after periods of specific eye-movement patterns (vertical, horizontal, both or little movement). A total of 35 awakenings were analysed further.

Three of the nine participants showed periods of predominantly vertical eye movements, and each was allied to a narrative about vertical movement. In one, the participant dreamed about standing at the foot of a tall cliff, using a hoist (a kind of winch or pulley). The participant reported looking up at climbers at various levels on the cliff, and down at the hoist machinery. In another dream one participant was climbing up a series of ladders and looking up and down while climbing. In a third dream a participant was playing basketball, shooting at the net and looking up to see if he had scored then looking down to pick up another ball. A single dream followed predominantly horizontal movements – the participant reported dreaming about two people throwing tomatoes at each other.

On ten occasions participants were woken after little or no eye movement. They reported either watching something in the distance or staring with their eyes fixed on a single object. In two cases the participants had been dreaming about driving. Their eyes had been very still, then made several sudden movements to the left just before being woken up. One participant reported a pedestrian standing on the left who hailed him as he drove by, and the other had been startled by a speeding car appearing to his left as he arrived at a junction.

Twenty-one awakenings followed mixed eye movements. In these instances, participants reported looking at people or objects nearby rather than far away (e.g. people fighting or talking to a group of other people).

The researchers also recorded the eye movements of people when they were awake (including the 5 original participants and 20 naïve ones). These findings confirmed that, when awake, our eyes are relatively stable when we are focused on objects in the distance, and show movements of similar amplitude to when we are dreaming of viewing nearby objects (i.e. many small but frequent and predominantly horizontal movements). Few vertical movements were recorded except when the researcher threw a ball in the air for participants to watch (and when they blinked).

Other results suggested that REM periods lasted from 3–50 minutes with an average of around 20 minutes. The amount, pattern and size of REM phases varied from period to period. The REM periods were at fairly regular intervals but individually specific. For example, participant DM averaged 1 REM phase every 70 minutes, WD 1 every 75 and KC 1 every 104. The average for the entire group was 1 REM phase every 92 minutes.

TEST YOURSELF
Outline four different results from this study.

CONCLUSION

Dement and Kleitman drew three main conclusions from this research, one in relation to each study:

1. Dreams probably (although not certainly) occur only during REM sleep, which occurs regularly throughout each night's sleep. Dreams reported when woken from nREM sleep are ones from previous REM episodes. As the REM phases are longer later in the night, dreaming is more likely at this time. Earlier research found that dreams did not occur every night. This study suggests three possible explanations for this difference:

   (a) If previous recordings were not continuous, they may have failed to catch instances of dream sleep in every participant (if short REM periods occurred between sampling intervals).

   (b) Equipment might not have detected small eye movements.

   (c) Participants in whom no dreaming was identified might have had dreams that led to few eye movements, such as those about distant or static objects.

2. It is often believed that dreams happen in an instant. If the length of REM periods is proportional to subjective estimates, this would help to confirm that the two are related and would provide some information about the rate at which dreaming progresses. The finding that the length of an REM period and its estimation by the participant are very similar shows that dreams are not instantaneous events but rather they are experienced in "real time".

3. Eye movements during REM sleep correspond to where, and at what, the dreamer is looking in the dream. This suggests that eye movements are not simply random events caused by the activation of the central nervous system during dream sleep, but are directly related to dream imagery. Furthermore, they correspond in amplitude and pattern to those we experience when awake.

SUMMARY

Research method (main)	Experimental
Other technique(s)	Observations, interviews and correlations
Sample	Nine adult participants
Sampling technique	Opportunity
Experimental design	Repeated measures
IV	Study 1: the levels of the IV were REM sleep/nREM sleep Study 2: the levels of the IV were waking after 5 or 15 minutes Study 3: the IV of eye-movement pattern type
DV	Study 1: whether a dream was reported and, if so, the detail Study 2: participants' choice of 5 or 15 minutes Study 3: the report of dream content
Quantitative data	As above
Qualitative data	Narrative of the dreams

EVALUATION

Evaluation	General evaluation (laboratory experiments)	Related to Dement and Kleitman
Strength	Laboratory experiments have high levels of standardisation and so can be replicated to test for reliability.	This study had a standardised procedure including pre-study levels of caffeine and alcohol, the doorbell sound, the EEG monitoring. This means that other researchers could easily replicate this study to test it for reliability.
Strength	As laboratory experiments have high levels of control, researchers can be more confident it is the IV directly affecting the DV.	The high level of control, so that all participants experienced the same conditions (e.g. the EEG monitoring and how data were recorded plus the pre-study levels of caffeine and alcohol) mean that for each part of the experiment, the researchers could confidently conclude cause and effect (e.g. that dream recall is affected by stage of sleep).
Weakness	As laboratory experiments take place in an artificial setting, they can lack ecological validity.	Participants had to sleep in an unusual environment (a laboratory) with electrodes on their head (EEG monitor) which is, of course, an artificial setting for them. Therefore, the study has low ecological validity.
Weakness	In many laboratory experiments participants take part in tasks that are nothing like real-life ones, so the tasks lack mundane realism.	The task of being woken up and then asking to recall dream content or estimate dream length is not a normal activity for people to engage in. Therefore, the study lacks mundane realism.

Other evaluation points include the following:

▶ Generalisability: only five people were studied in detail with four more used to confirm these findings. The small sample size could make it difficult to generalise beyond the sample. These five + four people may not represent a wide cross-section of society in terms of how we dream and what we dream about.

▶ Reductionism: the findings are all based around biological mechanisms affecting our dreaming state. Some psychologists may see this as being reductionist as there are psychological mechanisms that could be affecting dream content.

▶ Ethics – confidentiality: the researchers only used participants' initials when publishing the data to ensure that specific dreams could not be linked to individuals.

▶ Ethics – protection: as the participants were sleeping in an unnatural situation it may have altered their normal sleep patterns. The person's ability to concentrate at work or at home next day could have been affected. There was no chance to ensure a normal sleeping night before the study ended.

▶ Self-reports: as the participants had to recall dream content once woken up, the researchers could not know for sure that what participants reported was exactly what they experienced. Due to changes in brain chemistry, memories for dreams can disappear quickly once someone is in the waking state and therefore some participants may have "filled in the gaps" of their dream to make it a coherent story rather than reporting the exact dream. This could reduce the validity of the findings.

CHALLENGE YOURSELF
Evaluate this study on the use of correlations and the use of independent groups.

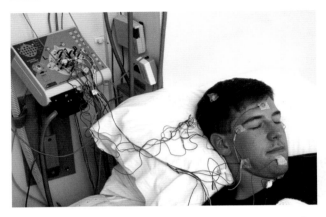

▲ **Figure 5.1** Participants in these experiments slept in a sleep laboratory attached to an EEG monitor

ISSUES AND DEBATES

The following table discusses the Dement and Kleitman study in terms of the core issues and debates for AS Level.

CHALLENGE YOURSELF
Identify two other applications to everyday life this study could have. Explain who would benefit from these applications.

Application to everyday life	The study could identify when participants were entering REM or nREM sleep. The EEG monitor that did this could help sleep scientists to identify whether a person has a disorder based around REM sleep. A person complaining of poor sleep could come into a sleep laboratory and be wired up to an EEG. The person's brain wave patterns could be monitored to see whether they were typical or atypical.
Individual and situational explanations	Not applicable
Nature versus nurture	The study could be considered to be relevant to the nature-nurture debate as it is believed that the experience of REM and n-REM sleep are universal and therefore due to nature. All participants in the study experienced both types of sleep and also the majority of dreaming took place during REM sleep. This also suggests that dreaming during REM sleep could be due to nature. However, there were individual differences between participants and this could be as a response to the environment as some of the participants had very disturbed sleep, possibly due to the uncomfortable environment of the sleep laboratory. This shows that environmental factors can also affect sleeping patterns.
The use of children	Not applicable
The use of animals	Not applicable

6 SCHACHTER AND SINGER

Research date: 1962

BACKGROUND

Early ideas that looked into emotions focused on purely physiological factors. This was based on the assumption that every emotion has a distinct physiological state. When research was conducted in the late 1800s and early 1900s, there was no real evidence for this assumption as many emotions appeared to have similar physiological bases. This allowed psychologists to begin to assess the role of psychological factors such as thoughts (cognitions) in emotions and how we experience them. Could it be that some emotions have a similar physiological basis but the way we are thinking at the time (e.g. because of what we are doing) makes us *experience* them as different emotions? Therefore, are emotions an interaction between physiological and psychological factors?

THE PSYCHOLOGY BEING INVESTIGATED

The two-factor theory of emotion forms the psychology of this study:

▶ When someone experiences an emotion, physiological arousal occurs and the person uses the immediate environment to search for emotional cues to label the physiological arousal.

▶ This can sometimes cause misinterpretations of emotions based on the physiological arousal.

▶ When the brain does not know why it feels an emotion it relies on external stimulation for cues on how to label the emotion.

ASK YOURSELF
Do you sometimes "feel" an emotion without knowing why? What do you do if this happens (e.g. how do you describe the emotion you are feeling at that time)? Do we always have to have a label for our emotions?

AIM

1. To investigate the role cognitive factors have in the experience of emotion when we are in a state of physiological arousal that has no immediate explanation (e.g. how we label that emotion).

2. When we do have an appropriate explanation for feeling a certain emotion, to see whether we always label it as the most appropriate emotion.

3. To see whether a person will react emotionally to a certain situation based on his or her physiology even if the cognitive elements of the situation remain the same.

METHOD

Participants

Participants were 184 male students from the University of Minnesota's introductory Psychology course. Around 90 per cent of students in these classes volunteered to be participants in studies. They received two extra points in their final examination for every hour they took part in an experiment. All participants were cleared by the student health service to check that they would not be harmed by the injection given in this study.

Design and procedure

As soon as participants had agreed to an injection of Suproxin (the name given to the "drug" used), they were placed into one of the four groups:

1. Epinephrine Informed (Epi Inf). Participants in this group were injected with epinephrine and told that some people feel side effects of the drug, which last no more than 20 minutes. The side effects that they were told about were hand shaking, heart pounding and feeling warm.

2. Epinephrine Ignorant (Epi Ign). The researcher injected these participants while saying that the drug was mild and harmless with no side effects.

3. Epinephrine Misinformed (Epi Mis). Participants in this group were injected with epinephrine and told that some people feel side effects of the drug, which last no more than 20 minutes. However, the side effects described were incorrect. Participants were told that feet feeling numb, and becoming itchy and developing a headache were common side effects.

4. Saline. Participants in this group were injected with a saline solution (salt) and they followed the same procedure as the Epi Ign group.

This study explored how psychological effects could help us to understand and label emotions caused by physiological mechanisms. Two conditions were used – euphoria and anger:

1. Euphoria. As soon as participants in this group had been injected, the researcher left and then returned with a confederate (a person who poses as a true participant but is an actor and is part of the study). The confederate was introduced to the participant. Both were told that they had to wait 20 minutes before beginning the "tests of vision" to allow the Suproxin to be fully absorbed by the body. The room they were in was not tidy and the researcher apologised for this. The researcher left, saying that the confederate and participant could use the paper, rubber bands, pencils and other items in the room. The confederate then completed a set procedure that was designed (it was hoped) to bring about a feeling of euphoria. He or she drew fish on a piece of scrap paper and then complained that the paper was no good so screwed it up and tried to throw it into the bin. The confederate would always miss and then try to make it into a basketball game and get the true participant involved. Using items deliberately left in the room for the purpose, the confederate would then, for example, make a paper airplane, or a slingshot from a rubber band to fire paper across the room, or try to hula hoop. If the true participant ever came up with activities the confederate could take part in, the confederate would always do so.

2. Anger. Participants in this group met the confederate in the same way as those in the euphoria condition. They were told that they needed to use the 20-minute waiting time to complete a questionnaire. Just before beginning, the confederate would tell the participant that it was unfair that the researcher had not revealed the injection beforehand and that it is difficult to refuse once you say yes to a study. At regular points when completing the questionnaire the confederate would raise issues with it. The first few questions were standard ones about non-contentious personal information, diet, etc. As the questionnaire progressed, the questions became more personal and less easy to answer. For example, respondents were asked to list childhood diseases they had caught, and the confederate would complain that he or she could never remember the details. Another question, about father's income, irritated the confederate. Subsequent questions took the form of statements such as "does not bathe or wash regularly" with respondents asked to name someone from their immediate family who most closely fitted the description. The confederate angrily crossed out these statements. Further questions included one on frequency of sexual intercourse and at this point the confederate shouted "To hell with it! I don't have to tell them all this!", then ripped up the questionnaire, threw the pieces on the floor and left the room.

 TEST YOURSELF
Outline the four conditions used in this study. What role did the confederate play in the euphoria condition?

All four of the injection conditions experienced the euphoria procedure. Three conditions experienced the anger procedure (not the Epi Mis).

Two measures of emotion were collected:

1. Observation. Although they did not know it, participants were being watched through a one-way mirror. The confederate would engage in 14 standard behaviours during the euphoria

condition. For each of these standard behaviours, the behaviour of the participant was classified into one or more of four categories: 1. Joins in with the activity; 2. Initiates a new activity that the confederate had not shown; 3. Ignores the confederate; 4. Watches the confederate. There was more than one observer to test for reliability and they agreed on 88 per cent of the observations.

For the anger condition, behaviour was coded under six categories: 1. Agrees with the confederate; 2. Disagrees with the confederate; 3. Neutral behaviour; 4. Initiates agreement or disagreement (e.g. says "I hate this kind of thing" but not as a response to the confederate); 5. Watches the confederate; 6. Ignores the confederate.

2. Self-reports. When the session with the confederate had ended, participants were asked to complete a questionnaire on which they rated how angry they felt, how good or happy they felt and whether they had felt any side effects of the drug. All of these questions used rating scales. Examples of the questions were as follows.

1. Have you experienced any palpitation (consciousness of your own heart beat)?

| Not at all (0) | A slight amount (1) | A moderate amount (2) | An intense amount (3) |

2. Did you feel any tremor (involuntary shaking of the hands, arms or legs)?

| Not at all (0) | A slight amount (1) | A moderate amount (2) | An intense amount (3) |

3. How irritated, angry or annoyed would you say you feel at present?

| I don't feel at all irritated or angry (0) | I feel a little irritated and angry (1) | I feel quite irritated and angry (2) | I feel very irritated and angry (3) | I feel extremely irritated and angry (4) |

4. How good or happy would you say you feel at present?

| I don't feel at all happy or good (0) | I feel a little happy and good (1) | I feel quite happy and good (2) | I feel very happy and good (3) | I feel extremely happy and good (4) |

Source: Schachter and Singer (1962: 387)

In addition, participants in the Epi Mis group were asked:

▸ Did you feel any numbness in your feet?
▸ Did you feel any itching sensation?
▸ Did you experience any feeling of headache?

Possible answers were rated on a 4-point scale from "not at all" to "an intense amount". Finally, all participants were asked to answer two open-ended questions on any other physical or emotional sensations they experienced during the tasks. Pulse rate was also taken twice, once just prior to the injection and then immediately after the session with the confederate.

Procedure – additional information

Participants were told that the study was about the effects of a vitamin supplement on vision. When they arrived they were taken to a private room and it was explained to them that the drug was Suproxin, the researchers were testing what effect it could have on vision and that the procedure was mild and harmless. Participants were then asked if they would agree to the injection and only one person refused. After this, a physician entered the room to give the injection. Depending on the condition that the participant had been placed in, the procedure followed the "Design" section above (e.g. if in the Epi Ign/euphoria group, the procedure reported above in the "Design" section for that group was followed).

After participants had completed the questionnaire, the researchers stated that the experiment was over. They explained the deception element of the study and how it was necessary. Then they asked if participants had been suspicious of the confederate and learned that 11 participants had been. These participants' data were eliminated from the analyses.

RESULTS

Table 6.1 shows the average pulse rating and self-rating of the different "side effects" per group.

Condition	N	Pulse		Self-rating of side effects				
		Pre	Post	Palpitation	Tremor	Numbness	Itching	Headache
Euphoria								
Epi Inf	27	85.7	88.6	1.20	1.43	0	0.16	0.32
Epi Ign	26	84.6	85.6	1.83	1.76	0.15	0	0.55
Epi Mis	26	82.9	86.0	1.27	2.00	0.06	0.08	0.23
Placebo	26	80.4	77.1	0.29	0.24	0.09	0	0.27
Anger								
Epi Inf	23	85.9	92.4	1.26	1.41	0.17	0	0.11
Epi Ign	23	85.0	96.8	1.44	1.78	0	0.06	0.21
Placebo	23	84.5	79.6	0.59	0.24	0.14	0.06	0.06

▲ **Table 6.1** The effects of the injections on bodily state

In all of the epinephrine conditions, pulse rate increased as expected. Also, those in the epinephrine groups experienced more palpitations and tremors. For five participants it was clear that the epinephrine was having no effect whatsoever and, while their data is presented in Table 6.1, the statistical analyses below did *not* include them.

When comparing groups in terms of the self-reported emotions, the following main findings emerged:

▶ Participants in the Epi Inf group were significantly less euphoric than those in the Epi Mis group.

▶ Participants in the Epi Inf group were significantly less euphoric than those in the Epi Ign group.

▶ There was no difference between the placebo and the Epi Mis group on levels of euphoria.

In terms of behavioural indications of euphoria, Table 6.2 shows the average score on an activity index (how much participants engaged in euphoric behaviours) and the number of acts they initiated.

Condition	N	Activity index	Mean number of acts initiated
Epi Inf	25	12.72	.20
Epi Ign	25	18.28	.56
Epi Mis	25	22.56	.84
Placebo	26	16.00	.54

▲ **Table 6.2** Behavioural indications of emotional state in the euphoria conditions

Source: Schachter and Singer (1962: 390)

Table 6.2 shows that the Epi Mis group engaged in the most activities and initiated more behaviours than participants in other groups. The only significant difference was between the Epi Mis and Epi Inf groups. This could be taken as these participants choosing to use psychological or behavioural cues to regulate their behaviours.

Participants also self-rated their emotional state (for the euphoria conditions only). Each participant generated a score in the following way. They subtracted the value of the point they checked on the irritation scale from the value of the point they checked on the happiness scale. Therefore, the higher the score, the happier and better the participants reported themselves to be feeling. The data is presented in Table 6.3.

Condition	N	Self-report scales
Epi Inf	25	0.98
Epi Ign	25	1.78
Epi Mis	28	1.90
Placebo	26	1.61

▲ **Table 6.3** Self-report of emotional state in the euphoria conditions

There was a significant difference between the Epi Inf versus Epi Mis conditions and also between the Epi Inf versus Epi Ign conditions.

For the anger analyses, the research team analysed both the self-report and behavioural aspects. However, more weight was placed on the self-report data. This was because the situation with the confederate would generate anger towards the researcher more than anyone else because it was the researcher who had made participants complete the questionnaire. However, even the angriest student may refrain from venting this anger as the researcher would be the person marking the student's end of term examination.

Each participant generated a score for the anger condition in the same way as scores were generated for the euphoria condition. Table 6.4 shows the average anger score from the self-report for each condition.

Condition	N	Self-report scales
Epi Inf	22	1.91
Epi Ign	22	1.39
Placebo	23	1.63

▲ **Table 6.4** Self-report of emotional state in the anger conditions

None of the groups differed significantly from each other on anger scores but the Epi Inf group showed the highest levels of self-reported anger. It should also be noted that behaviourally (through the observation) the Epi Ign group showed the most overt anger of any group on average.

Overall, the following main findings can be reported:

▶ When participants had a satisfactory explanation for their physiological state of arousal they do *not* label this state with alternative information that is available (in this case euphoria or anger).

▶ Those who were injected with epinephrine and were told exactly what they would feel, and why, did not show heightened levels of that emotion (they did not become more angry).

▶ Those who did not have adequate explanation used the current situation they were in to explain their heightened physiological state.

TEST YOURSELF
Outline three key results from this study. How useful are they? Could this study be replicated easily? Why?

CONCLUSION

There are two factors involved in our experiences of emotions: our physiological arousal or state and the information or cognitions that help us to understand the behaviour we feel. These interact and make us feel different emotions depending on the information available to help us understand the situation we find ourselves in.

SUMMARY

Research method (main)	Laboratory experiment
Other technique(s)	Questionnaire and observations
Sample	Male students from the University of Minnesota
Sampling technique	Volunteer
Experimental design	Independent groups
IV	The injection information and psychological effects (seven conditions)
DV	Measures of pulse rate, self-ratings of side effects and behaviours seen during the observation stage
Quantitative data	Coded behaviours from the observations Self-report scales used to measure emotions
Qualitative data	Two open-ended questions about other experiences during the course of the tasks

EVALUATION

Evaluation	General evaluation (laboratory experiments)	Related to Schachter and Singer
Strength	Laboratory experiments have high levels of standardisation and so can be replicated to test for reliability.	This study had a standardised procedure including the set order of the confederate's activities, what the person injecting said and did, what was injected and how the observations were set out and categorised. This means other researchers could easily replicate this study to test for reliability.
Strength	As laboratory experiments have high levels of control, researchers can be more confident it is the IV directly affecting the dependent variable DV.	As there were many controls (e.g. the instructions given to the four groups and how the confederate behaved), the researchers could be confident that it was the information provided to participants that directly affected the moods and emotions they reported.
Weakness	In many laboratory experiments participants take part in tasks that are nothing like real-life ones, so the tasks lack mundane realism.	The task of being injected with an "unknown" drug, then sitting with a confederate and attempting to complete a questionnaire is not a task that people conduct in everyday life. Therefore, the study may lack mundane realism.

This study can also be evaluated in terms of ethical issues:

▶ Deception: participants thought that they were receiving a vitamin supplement called Suproxin (when it was actually epinephrine). They also thought that the confederate was another real participant who had been injected and was completing the questionnaire.

▶ Protection: participants were injected, which could have caused physical pain. Also, as they were in situations that could bring about euphoria or anger, their psychological state on leaving the study was not the same as when they entered.

Other evaluation points include the following:

▶ Use of independent groups: the results may have been affected by participant variables as participants only took part on one of the conditions. Participants who were "naturally" more euphoric or angry could have been in the corresponding group and therefore it was not always the labelling that was affecting behaviour – participant variables could not be controlled for.

▶ Volunteers: the sample was made up of volunteer students which may not be representative of a wider population when it comes to the effects of cognitive factors on emotional behaviour. Older adults and people from other cultural backgrounds may have acted differently.

▶ Observations: there was high inter-rater reliability between the observers when watching participants' behaviour. Also, as participants were unaware of being observed it is hoped that the behaviour they showed was a valid representation of how they were reacting to the situation they were in. These aspects increase both the reliability and validity of the study.

CHALLENGE YOURSELF
Evaluate this study on the use of self-reports and the use of qualitative data.

ISSUES AND DEBATES

The following table discusses the Schachter and Singer study in terms of the core issues and debates for AS Level.

Application to everyday life	It is useful to know that people describe their feelings in terms of the cognitions available at that time, especially when people have no immediate explanation for the physiological arousal they experience. This could be useful in hospitals when patients (especially children) are given drugs that might have some side effects that are not desirable. If the patients are engaged in behaviours that might generate euphoria or happiness, this may help them to get through any short-term negative side effects. For example, the Epi Mis group showed the most euphoria when the confederate was showing euphoria too. However, there could be ethical and moral issues in deceiving patients about side effects of drugs.
Individual and situational explanations	The study appears to show a **situational** explanation for participants' behaviour. They used the situation they were in to try to understand the physiological reactions they had or thought they were having. However, these differences should be noted: • If participants experienced an unexplained state of physiological arousal, they attempted to describe or label the emotions in terms of the relevant cognitive explanations available (e.g. euphoria or anger shown by the confederate). Therefore, the situation was used to label the emotions felt – so in the euphoria condition they "felt" joy whereas in the anger condition they "felt" fury. • If participants had an appropriate explanation for the physiological arousal, they did not use situational cues to understand the arousal. For example, participants who clearly attributed their physiological state to the injection did not show any anger in the anger condition However, this is based on just three participants showing a clear attribution.
Nature versus nurture	Although the study did not focus on nature versus nurture, we can link some concepts to this issue. The study shows that there would appear to be an interaction between the two. The nature side is supported by the underlying physiological mechanisms involved in experiencing different emotions. This could be in-built (nature) or changed or developed via the environment (nurture). The cognitive component of experiencing the emotions could represent the nurture side of the argument as the environmental cues are being used to understand the current emotion a person is feeling. However, this too could be in-built in brain neurology (nature) or purely via life experiences (nurture). Overall, it would appear that both nature and nurture are supported in this study.
The use of children	Not applicable
The use of animals	Not applicable

CHALLENGE YOURSELF
Identify two other applications to everyday life this study could have. Explain who would benefit from these applications.

7 ANDRADE

Research date: 2009

BACKGROUND AND THE PSYCHOLOGY INVESTIGATED

People have been known to daydream frequently when presented with something boring. In turn, this leads to them not paying full attention to the task at hand. It is quite common for people to doodle (draw abstract or concrete symbols, patterns, figures, etc.) in ways not linked to the primary task. Prior to this study it was not known whether the act of doodling impairs attention processes by taking away resources from the primary task *or* whether it actually aids concentration towards the primary task, additionally maintaining arousal. It is common in research on attention to set participants dual tasks to monitor performance, then see which cognitive processes are needed to complete these tasks (or which processes contribute to participants failing to complete them). However, Andrade notes that if the effects of boredom are overlooked, then we cannot form any solid conclusions. Could it be that doodling actually aids concentration?

> **ASK YOURSELF**
> What do you try to do when you know you have to concentrate on something? List all the behaviours you show which you think help you to pay attention more efficiently.

AIM

To test whether doodling aided concentration in a boring task.

METHOD

Participants

Forty members of an Applied Psychology Unit participant panel at the University of Plymouth (UK) were used. They had volunteered for a different study but were recruited via opportunity sampling – once their original study had been conducted, the researcher approached them to ask if they would spend another five minutes taking part in this study. They were from the general population and aged 18–55. They were paid for participating. They were randomly assigned to either the control group (n = 20: 18 females and 2 males) or the doodling group (n = 20: 17 females and 3 males).

Design

The researcher recorded a mock telephone message using a cassette recorder. A fairly monotonous voice was used. The average speaking rate was 227 words per minute. The recording was played at a "comfortable" volume to listen to. The script included eight names of people who would be attending a party alongside the names of three people and one cat who would not attend. In addition, eight place names were mentioned. The full text appears in the original research paper.

Procedure

As participants were asked to take part in this research just after they had completed a study they had volunteered for, they were already thinking about going home. It was hoped that this would enhance the boredom of the task.

Participants were placed in one of two groups: the doodling condition or a control group. Those in the doodling condition were asked to use a pencil to shade different shapes that were 1 centimetre in diameter on a piece of A4 paper. There were ten shapes per row. Each row alternated between squares and circles. There was a left-hand side margin of 4.5 centimetres so that participants could write down any target information. Participants in the control group were given a piece of lined paper and a pencil.

Participants were led into a quiet and visually dull room. All participants were tested individually. The following instructions were read out (Andrade 2009: 2–3):

> "I am going to play you a tape. I want you to pretend that the speaker is a friend who has telephoned you to invite you to a party. The tape is rather dull but that's okay because I don't want you to remember any of it. Just write down the names of people who will definitely or probably be coming to the party (excluding yourself). Ignore the names of those who can't come. Do not write anything else."

Participants in the doodling condition were told that it did not matter how neat they were when shading their doodle or how quickly they did it. They were told that doing the shading was just to relieve the boredom of the listening task. They listened to the tape, which lasted 2.5 minutes, and wrote down the names as requested. As soon as the recording finished, the researcher collected participants' sheets and talked to them for about one minute. This included apologising for misleading them about the imminent memory test. Half of the participants were then asked to recall as many names as they could of the people who would attend the party, then the places mentioned. The other half did the reverse – they gave place names then names of people attending the party. During the debriefing after the task participants were asked whether they had suspected that they were going to be given a memory test.

TEST YOURSELF
Draw a flow diagram that shows how the participants were recruited and how the study was run.

RESULTS

Those in the doodling group shaded a mean of 36.3 shapes (range 3–110). One of the participants failed to doodle so was replaced. None of the participants in the control group doodled. Only three participants in the doodling condition and four in the control group suspected a memory test. All claimed that they had then actively tried to remember the information for the test. Table 7.1 shows the correct noting down of the eight people who were going to attend the party.

Condition	Average number of correct names written down	Number of false alarms
Doodling	7.8 (SD = 0.4)	1
Control	7.1 (SD = 1.1)	5

▲ **Table 7.1** Correct names noted during the memory test

If a response indicated a plausible mishearing (e.g. a participant had heard the name Greg instead of Craig), it was scored as being correct. New names not similar to the ones given, names of people who could not attend or responses such as "sister" were recorded as false alarms.

Each participant was given a monitoring performance score. This was calculated as the number of correct names written down *minus* the number of false alarms. A total of 15 participants in the doodling group and 9 in the control group scored maximum. Monitoring performance was significantly higher in the doodling condition (mean = 7.7, standard deviation (SD) = 0.6) than in the control condition (mean = 6.9, SD = 1.3), with $p = 0.01$.

In terms of recall, each participant generated a names score and a places score. These were scored in the same way as the monitoring performance score *except* that if a plausible mishearing was presented it had to be the same in the monitoring *and* recall phases. Table 7.2 shows these scores.

		Group	
		Control	Doodling
Names (monitored information)	Correct	4.3 (1.3)	5.3 (1.4)
	False alarms	0.4 (0.5)	0.3 (0.4)
	Memory score	**4.0 (1.5)**	**5.1 (1.7)**
Places (incidental information)	Correct	2.1 (0.9)	2.6 (1.4)
	False alarms	0.3 (0.6)	0.3 (0.4)
	Memory score	**1.8 (1.2)**	**2.4 (1.5)**

▲ **Table 7.2** Mean correct recall, false alarms and memory scores (correct minus false alarms) for names and places for the control and doodling groups (standard deviation)

Source: Andrade (2009: 3)

Overall, participants in the doodling condition recalled a mean of 7.5 pieces of correct information (names plus places) compared to 5.8 recalled by participants in the control condition. Overall, monitored names were recalled more than places (p <0.001). Recall was significantly better for participants in the doodling condition than for those in the control condition (p = 0.02). When participants who had suspected a test were removed from the analysis, there was still a significant difference (p = 0.01).

CHALLENGE YOURSELF
Plot the results of this study as a bar chart.

CONCLUSION

Andrade concluded: "Participants who performed a shape-shading task… concentrated better on a mock telephone message than participants who listened to the message with no concurrent task" (2009: 4). This was seen in both the monitoring performance task and the recall task. However, it was not clear whether the doodling led to better recall because doodlers happened to notice more of the target information or whether it actually aided memory recall by encouraging some deeper processing of the telephone message.

SUMMARY

Research method (main)	Experimental
Other technique(s)	–
Sample	40 people from an Applied Psychology Unit participant panel at the University of Plymouth (UK)
Sampling technique	Opportunity (but originally participants had come as volunteers for a different study)
Experimental design	Independent groups
IV	Doodling and control
DV	Mean correct recall, false alarms and memory scores
Quantitative data	As above
Qualitative data	–

EVALUATION

Evaluation	General evaluation (laboratory experiments)	Related to Andrade
Strength	Laboratory experiments have high levels of standardisation and so can be replicated to test for reliability.	This study had a standardised procedure including the rate of speaking and the same dimensions of paper for those in the doodling group. This means other researchers could easily replicate this study to test for reliability.
Strength	As laboratory experiments have high levels of control, researchers can be more confident it is the IV directly affecting the DV.	As there were many controls (e.g. the script and the length of time participants were talked to by the researcher before the recall test), Andrade could be confident that it was the doodling itself that was causing a change in the recall rates.
Weakness	In many laboratory experiments participants take part in tasks that are nothing like real-life ones, so the tasks lack mundane realism.	Listening to a tape recording and then having an unexpected recall test is not a usual task for people in everyday life. Therefore, the study could be low in mundane realism.

Other evaluation points include the following:

▶ Generalisibility – as the sample was from a volunteer participant panel:

  – the participants may be qualitatively different from other people (they may be more motivated than others to perform in a study)

  – the results may not reflect the population as a whole: that is, the effects of doodling may only be applicable to the sample.

▶ The use of independent measures: as different participants were used in the doodling and non-doodling conditions, participant variables may have affected some of the results. People in the doodling group may already happen to doodle a lot when they concentrate on tasks. Also, participants in that group may have just had a better memory compared to those in the non-doodling group. These possible issues reduce the validity of the findings.

Ethical issues:

▶ This study does not cause psychological harm as doodling is an everyday activity that is done by many people. In addition, the quality of the doodling was not judged by the experimenters so the participants should not have felt judged in any way. Participants in the doodling condition were told "It doesn't matter how neatly or how quickly you do this—it is just something to help relieve the boredom".

▶ There was some deception in the study as the participants were told they would not be expected to remember any of the information on the tape-recorded message. However, when it was over they were given a surprise memory test. The researchers did apologise for this test and did give a full debrief at the end of the study. This is a justifiable breach of the issue of deception as it was necessary for the study to be completed successfully and would not have affected the participants in the study.

CHALLENGE YOURSELF
Evaluate this study on demand characteristics and the use of quantitative data.

ISSUES AND DEBATES

The following table discusses the Andrade study in terms of the core issues and debates for AS Level.

Application to everyday life	The results of this study might be useful for students when they are revising for examinations. If students have a podcast to listen to or are reading notes, it could be useful for them to doodle at the same time.
Individual and situational explanations	Both sides of the argument can be seen in this study. In terms of **individual** explanations, participants may have used a similar strategy before or have a personality type that requires extra stimulation when processing information (e.g. some may be extroverts). In terms of **situational** explanations, the process of doodling in the given situation could have caused the improvement in recall rather than it being due to the individual: that is, the act of doodling is what helps people retain information.
Nature versus nurture	Not applicable
The use of children	Not applicable
The use of animals	Not applicable

CHALLENGE YOURSELF
Identify two other applications to everyday life this study could have. Explain who would benefit from these applications.

Research date: 2001

BACKGROUND

In 1997 a "Reading the mind in the eyes" test was developed to assess a concept called theory of mind. This refers to the ability to attribute mental states to oneself and other people. This test appeared to discriminate between adults with Asperger syndrome (AS) and high-functioning autistic (HFA) adults from control adults. The two former groups scored significantly worse than the control group on the test, which asked participants to look at a pair of eyes on a screen and choose, from a forced choice of emotions, which emotion the eyes best conveyed. However, the researchers were not happy with elements of the original version and wanted to "upgrade" their measure to make it better. The problems and solutions are outlined in the design section.

THE PSYCHOLOGY BEING INVESTIGATED

The main idea of the eyes test is to investigate theory of mind. The theory of mind refers to our ability to attribute mental states such as desires, belief, intentions and emotions to ourselves and others around us. It also refers to how we use this knowledge to explain and predict the actions of other people. That is, we can use the knowledge to understand that people may have different ideas and hold different emotions from us. It is believed that many people on the autistic spectrum do not have a theory of mind.

In addition, the researchers were also attempting to make the measure a more valid test of theory of mind.

ASK YOURSELF
How do you read the emotion that is conveyed by another person's face? What do you look for?

AIM

1. To test a group of adults with AS or HFA on the revised scale of the eyes test. This was to check whether the same deficits seen in the original study could be replicated.

2. To test a sample of normal adults to see whether there was a negative correlation between the scores on the eyes test and their autism spectrum quotient (AQ).

3. To test whether females scored better on the eyes test than males.

METHOD

Design

As covered in the "Background" section above, there were problems with the original version of the eyes test that needed rectifying. Table 8.1 highlights what these problems were and how the researchers redesigned the questionnaire in an attempt to overcome them.

Initially, the "correct" word and the "foils" were chosen by the first two authors of this study: Simon Baron-Cohen and Sally Wheelwright. The words were then piloted on eight judges – four male and four female. For the correct word and its foils to be used in the new eyes test, five of

Original problems	New design element (if applicable)
Forced choice between two response options meant just the narrow range of 17–25 correct responses (out of 25) to be statistically above chance. The range of scores for parents of those with AS were lower than normal but again there was a narrow range of scores to detect any real differences.	Forced choice remained but there were four response options. There were 36 pairs of eyes used rather than 25 – this gave a range of 13–36 correct responses (out of 36) to be statistically above chance. This meant that individual differences could be examined better in terms of statistics.
There were basic and complex mental states so some of the pairs of eyes were "too easy" to identify (e.g. happy, sad) and others "too hard" so it made comparisons difficult.	Only complex mental states were used.
There were some pairs of eyes that could be "solved" easily because of eye direction (e.g. noticing or ignoring).	These were deleted.
There were more female than male pairs of eyes used in the original test.	The new study used an equal amount of male and female pairs of eyes.
The possible two responses were always "semantic opposites" (e.g. happy versus sad), which made choosing between them too easy.	Semantic opposites were removed and the "foil choices" (those that were incorrect) were more similar to the correct answer.
There may have been comprehension problems with the choice of words used as the forced choice responses.	A glossary of all terms used as the choices on the eyes test was available to all participants at all times.

▲ **Table 8.1** Problems with the original study and changes made to overcome them

the eight judges had to agree with the choice. Also, if more than two judges picked a foil over the correct word, these items were replaced: a new correct word was generated with suitable foils and retested. The data from groups 2 and 3 (see below) were merged as they did not differ in performance. This was also used as a check that the correct words had some form of consensus – at least 50 per cent of this group had to select the correct word and no more than 25 per cent had to select a foil for it to be included in the final version of the eyes test. From the original 40 pairs of eyes, 36 passed these tests and were used.

The research method is a natural experiment as the IV is naturally occurring (the four groups of subjects used).

TEST YOURSELF
Outline two problems with the original version of the "Reading the mind in the eyes" test and describe how the research team tried to overcome them.

Participants

Four groups of participants were used:

1. In group 1 there were 15 males with either AS or HFA. They were recruited via a UK National Autistic Society magazine or support group. They had all been formally diagnosed.

2. There appeared to be a broad range of people in group 2. This group consisted of 122 normal adults recruited throughout adult community and education classes in Exeter or in a public library in Cambridge.

3. Participants in group 3 were all assumed to have a high intelligence quotient (IQ), as the group consisted of 103 normal adults (53 male and 50 female) who were all undergraduates at Cambridge University (71 in sciences and 32 in other subjects).

4. Group 4 consisted of 14 randomly selected adults who were matched for IQ with group 1.

Procedure

All participants, irrespective of group, completed the revised version of the eyes test. Each participant completed it individually in a quiet room. Participants in group 1 were asked to judge the gender of the person in each image. Groups 1, 3 and 4 completed a questionnaire to measure their AQ. All participants were asked to read through a glossary of terms used in the test and indicate any they were unsure of. They were reassured that they could refer to the glossary at any time during the test.

▲ **Figure 8.1** A male pair of eyes used in the test

RESULTS

Table 8.2 shows the scores gained in the new eyes test and the AQ of each group.

Group	Eyes test means (SD)	AQ means (SD)
AS/HFA adults	21.9 (6.6)	34.4 (6.0)
General population	26.2 (3.6)	N/A
Students	28.0 (3.5)	18.3 (6.6)
Matched	30.9 (3.0)	18.9 (2.9)

▲ **Table 8.2** Mean and standard deviation (in parentheses) scores for the new eyes test and AQ by group

Source: Baron-Cohen *et al* (2001: 245)

In the eyes test the AS/HFA group performed significantly worse than the other three groups. In general, females scored better than males. Unsurprisingly, the AS/HFA group scored significantly higher on the AQ than the other groups. The correlation between the eyes test and AQ was negative. The distribution of scores for the eyes test (all groups merged) formed a normal bell curve.

TEST YOURSELF
Outline two differences between the different sets of participants used in this study in terms of their performance in the eyes test.

CONCLUSION

The revised version of the eyes test could still discriminate between AS/HFA adults and controls from different sections of society as it replicated previous findings. The new eyes test appeared to overcome the initial problems of the original version and the research team stated "... this therefore validates it as a useful test with which to identify subtle impairments in social intelligence in otherwise normally intelligent adults" (Baron-Cohen *et al* 2001: 246).

SUMMARY

Research method (main)	Experimental
Other technique(s)	Questionnaire (survey)
Sample	15 males with either AS or HFA 122 normal adults recruited throughout the adult community 103 normal adults (53 male and 50 female) who were all undergraduates at Cambridge University 14 randomly selected adults who were matched for IQ with group 1
Sampling technique	Opportunity and volunteer
Experimental design	Independent groups
IV	Four groups of participants (see sample above)
DV	Scores on the eyes test and AQ
Quantitative data	As above
Qualitative data	–

EVALUATION

Evaluation	General evaluation	Related to Baron-Cohen *et al*
Strength	Comparisons can be useful as people's results are being compared on the same, standardised scale.	The revised eyes test was used for all participants. This means that all comparisons between the groups have some validity as they were compared on the same set scale using the same questions, etc.
Strength	As the measures are standardised, they are reliable because they can be used again and again to see whether they give similar results.	The revised eyes test can be used by other researchers to see whether they can replicate findings and test for reliability. Even though an older version of the eyes test was used in the original study, the new study did find reliable results in terms of performance of AS/HFA adults (there were low scores in both studies).
Weakness	There may be issues with validity. Is the test actually measuring the behaviour it is supposed to be measuring? Some psychologists, for example, believe that an IQ test does *not* measure intelligence. Instead they believe it measures someone's ability to complete an IQ test.	Some psychologists might query whether the revised eyes test is still actually measuring theory of mind traits or just the ability to complete the eyes test.
Weakness	There are further issues of validity using self-report measures with participants. Participants can misunderstand the questions, give socially desirable responses, etc.	The participants did have a one in four chance of just guessing the correct answer on the eyes test and this lowers the validity of the study. The researchers addressed the issues of misunderstanding by providing a glossary of definitions of the words used in the eyes test for the participants to read. However, it is possible that even with the definitions the participants still did not understand the words used.

There could be some evaluation based around usefulness:

▶ The main advantage is that such a study can be used to improve human behaviour in some way. As the results show that AS/HFA adults appear to lack a theory of mind, psychologists could now create therapies (or training) to help these people improve their social communication and social emotional skills to help them integrate better into society.

▶ A disadvantage of the eyes test is that it does not take into account the "full picture" of understanding emotions – in reality there are subtle cues such as body language alongside other facial cues that can

help people to understand the emotions of others. A study that assessed the same aspects as the eyes test but using a full face or a moving image with verbalisation might be even more useful to assess theory of mind.

▶ Ethics – protection: as the participants in the AS/HFA group scored poorly on the eyes test, completing it may have caused them stress. If they did not understand the emotions portrayed in the eyes the test may have been too difficult, perhaps causing distress.

ISSUES AND DEBATES

The following table discusses the Baron-Cohen *et al* study
in terms of the core issues and debates for AS Level.

Application to everyday life	Schools and educators could use the findings of this study to help AS/HFA students. These students could have extra support in helping them to understand emotions and how to read them in faces. This could help them to cope with everyday situations that involve emotions.
Individual and situational explanations	Not applicable
Nature versus nurture	The idea of whether AS/HFA can be attributed to **nature** or **nurture** is a long-standing debate with psychologists, but this study does not add to the debate.
The use of children	Not applicable
The use of animals	Not applicable

CHALLENGE YOURSELF
Identify two other applications to everyday life this study could have. Explain who would benefit from these applications.

Research date: 2008

BACKGROUND

Human memory has been manipulated in experimental studies for many years. "False memories" for events have been studied for decades to see whether people believe them. Prior to this study, psychologists had focused on false beliefs and memories for negative or neutral events and experiences. No one had looked at whether false memories could be created or implanted for positive events and experiences. Being able to demonstrate this could have far-reaching consequences. For example, for people with disorders such as phobias it would mean positive experiences could be implanted to help them overcome these disorders.

THE PSYCHOLOGY BEING INVESTIGATED

The main area being tested here is false memories. The researchers noted that people's memories of events in their own lives can be incorrect. False details about real events, and entirely false events, can be added to a person's memory storage system. From all of the stored information, people can *reconstruct* "memories" for events, for example by "filling in the gaps" and using false information that gets embedded in *actual* information.

ASK YOURSELF
Do you think people can really create false memories? Explain your answer.

AIM

1. To investigate whether positive false memories for loving asparagus can be implanted into people and then change their childhood memories of liking asparagus.

2. To investigate the consequences of implanting positive false memories in terms of the effects it has on liking asparagus and choosing asparagus.

EXPERIMENT 1

To investigate whether positive false memories for loving asparagus can be implanted into people and then change their childhood memories of liking asparagus.

METHOD

Participants

A total of 128 undergraduates were used in the study and they all received course credits for participating. Of the participants, 77 per cent were female. The mean age of participants was 20.8 years. They were randomly assigned to the "love" group (n = 63) or the control group (n = 65).

Design and procedure

Once they had arrived at the laboratory, participants were told they would be completing a series of questionnaires to help study the relationship between food preferences and personality. To limit the influence of demand characteristics, they were not told anything about false memories.

There were two main questionnaires. The first was the Food History Inventory (FHI) consisting of 24 items. The 16th item was crucial: it read "Loved asparagus the first time you tried it". All statements were rated on the same scale from 1 = definitely did not happen, to 8 = definitely did happen before the age of 10. The second was a Restaurant Questionnaire (RQ) that assessed the desire to eat 32 separate dishes. Included in this was the critical item of "sautéed asparagus spears". The questionnaire was laid out like a menu with appetisers, soups, desserts, etc. Participants had to rate how likely it was that they would order each item, regardless of price. The scale was 1 = definitely no to 8 = definitely yes. Participants completed three other questionnaires as "fillers", relating to personality, eating habits and social desirability, to disguise the true aim of the study.

Approximately one week later all participants returned. They were given false feedback about their responses to the original questionnaire. They were told (falsely) that their responses had been entered into a computer program which had generated a profile of their early childhood experiences with food. Profiles were presented as if they had been individually tailored to each participant. A section of the profile was exactly the same for everyone: "As a young child you disliked spinach, enjoyed fried foods and liked it when fellow classmates brought sweets into class." For the love group another additional critical item was added: "You loved to eat cooked asparagus." To make sure that all participants had processed these statements, all had to respond to brief questions about the sweets statement. Additionally, the love group also answered questions about asparagus. They were asked: "Imagine the setting in which this experience happened. Where were you? Who was with you?" Then, using a scale of 1 = not at all to 9 = very much, participants rated how much the experience had affected their adult personality. Following this, all participants completed the FHI and RQ again. Then two new questionnaires were completed. The first was a Food Preferences Questionnaire (FPQ) on which they had to rate 62 food items (including asparagus) on a scale of 1 = definitely don't like to eat it (for whatever reason) to 8 = definitely like to eat it. The second was a Food Costs Questionnaire (FCQ) on which, for 21 different food items, participants had to indicate

whether they would buy each item and, if so, how much they would be willing to pay for it. They had to choose one of seven statements ranging from "would never buy it" to "would buy it at $5.70". One of the food items was a 1lb (454 grams) of asparagus.

The final measure was taken via a questionnaire called Memory or belief (M/B). Participants had to respond to three items from the FHI (including the asparagus item) by choosing one of the following: (a) had a specific memory of the event; (b) had a belief that the event occurred (but no specific memory); (c) was positive that the event had not occurred.

TEST YOURSELF
Draw a flow diagram that covers the procedure for this experiment then ask someone to test you on it.

RESULTS

The main results were as follows:

▶ FHI. Excluded from the analysis were 31 participants (17 in the love group) as they were reasonably sure that they did *like* asparagus before the manipulation. The mean ratings in the love group increased 2.6 points (participants in this group were more confident that they loved asparagus). For those in the control group the increase was 0.2 points.

▶ M/B. For the love group, 22 per cent of participants indicated a memory and 35 per cent indicated a belief, leaving 43 per cent reporting that they were positive that the event had not occurred. In the control group, 12 per cent reported a memory, 28 per cent a belief and 61 per cent that the event had not occurred. This was in the predicted direction but it did not reach significance (p = 0.09).

▶ Believers versus non-believers. Believers are those who are susceptible to manipulation. If a participant rated the critical FHI item low the first time but then increased the rating the second time **and** stated memory or belief, the participant was classified as a believer. The remainder were non-believers. It was found that 48 per cent were believers. The critical FHI item rating for believers increased an average of 4.5 points and for non-believers it increased by 0.9 points. Believers were analysed again based on memory versus belief. Those who had a memory increased on average by 5.5 points and for those with a belief it was 3.6 points. This result was statistically significant (p = 0.03).

▶ Consequences of false beliefs. On the RQ, believers reported more desire to eat asparagus than the control group (p = 0.001). On the FPQ, believers reported liking asparagus significantly more than the control group (p = 0.001). Figure 9.1 shows the change in ratings for asparagus by group. For the FCQ measure, believers were willing to pay significantly more for asparagus than the control group (p = 0.02).

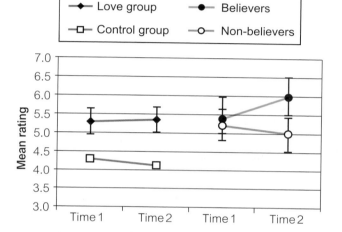

▲ **Figure 9.1** Mean rating for the item "sautéed asparagus spears" in the RQ pre- and post-manipulation in experiment 1

Source: Based on Laney *et al* (2008: 294)

CONCLUSION

According to Laney *et al* "...subjects can be led to develop positively framed false beliefs about experiences with foods, and that these beliefs can lead to increased liking of those foods." (2008: 295). The love group believers had a greater intention to eat asparagus in future in a restaurant. They also had a greater preference for asparagus. Finally, they were even willing to pay more for asparagus.

EXPERIMENT 2

To investigate the consequences of implanting positive false memories in terms of the effects it has on liking asparagus and choosing asparagus.

There were two specific aims:

1. To replicate the findings from experiment 1.

2. To examine a possible underlying mechanism of false memories by looking at whether the sight of asparagus is more appealing to people after the false manipulation about asparagus.

METHOD

Participants

Participants were 103 undergraduates from the University of Washington; 62 per cent were female and the overall mean age was 19.9 years. They received course credits for participating. They were assigned to either the love group (n = 58) or the control group (n = 45).

Design and procedure
Session 1

On arriving at the laboratory, participants were told that their data would be entered into a computer that would generate a profile of them. No cover story was given. They all completed the FHI, the FPQ and the RQ (see experiment 1). In a similar procedure to that used in experiment 1 to try to disguise the true nature of the study, researchers gave participants two "filler" questionnaires to complete. In this experiment, these were the Marlowe-Crowne Social Desirability Scale and a personality questionnaire.

Session 2

This took place one after session 1. As with experiment 1, participants were given false feedback about their responses. The critical item was in third position on their profile. It read: "You loved asparagus the first time you ate it." The control group received no information about asparagus. Those in the love group completed an elaboration exercise. They had to answer questions about their memory of this event. If they appeared to struggle to report a memory they were asked to imagine what might have happened. They were asked what age they were when the event happened, the location, what they were doing at the time and how the event made them feel. Finally, all participants produced qualitative data to the question: "What is the most important childhood, food-related event in your life that your food profile did not report?"

Participants then looked at 20 slides showing common foods such as spinach, strawberries, pizza and (the critical) asparagus. Each slide was shown for 30 seconds and was rated on four criteria:

1. how appetising participants found the food picture

2. how disgusting they found the food picture

3. whether the photograph was taken by a novice, amateur or professional photographer

4. artistic quality of the picture.

Points 1, 2 and 4 were rated on a scale of 1 = not at all to 8 = very much.

All participants then completed the FPQ, RQ and FHI. They also completed the M/B questionnaire as in experiment 1. They were then debriefed.

RESULTS

These were the main results:

▶ FHI. Both groups appeared to rate the critical asparagus item similarly before any manipulation, but differently afterwards. Thirty participants were excluded from analyses (18 in the love group and 12 in the control group) as they were reasonably sure that they loved asparagus *before* any manipulation. This left 73 participants whose data were used. For the love group, the mean confidence increased by 2.5 points (1.7 to 4.2) but it increased by only 1.07 points for the control (1.45 to 2.52). This was a significant difference (p = 0.006).

▶ Memories or beliefs? Table 9.1 highlights the main findings from this questionnaire and shows that the results went in the expected direction but just failed to reach significance (p = 0.07).

Condition	Reported "memory"	Reported "belief"	Positive it was not the case
Love	28% (n = 11)	28% (n = 11)	45% (n = 18)
Control	6% (n = 2)	38% (n = 12)	56% (n = 18)

▲ **Table 9.1** Main findings from the M/B questionnaire

Those in the love group who had a memory were compared to those who had a belief in terms of confidence about the critical event. The ratings for the critical asparagus event increased by 5.4 points in the love group and 3.5 points for those with a belief. This was a significant difference (p = 0.02). Other details were as follows:

▶ Believers versus non-believers. The same definition of believer was used here as in experiment 1. In the love group 21 participants were labelled believers. The ratings given by believers for confidence increased from a mean of 1.95 (SD = 1.12) in session 1 to 6.48 (SD = 2.02) in session 2. For non-believers the increase was from 1.42 (SD = 0.90) to just 1.68 (SD = 0.07). Males and females were equally likely to have formed a false memory.

▶ Consequences of false beliefs. The two comparison groups were the same as in experiment 1: believers and controls. Neither group's ratings changed significantly from session 1 to session 2 on the RQ. For the FPQ, believers reported more desire to eat asparagus than the control group at session 2 (p = 0.02). Table 9.2 shows the ratings given for the slides.

	Appetising		Disgusting		Artistic quality	
	M	(SD)	M	(SD)	M	(SD)
Believers	5.10[a]	(2.05)	1.81[a]	(1.57)	4.95	(2.22)
Non-believers	2.63[b]	(1.74)	3.84[b]	(2.41)	5.16	(2.09)
Controls	4.00	(2.09)	3.24[b]	(2.39)	4.76	(1.73)

▲ Table 9.2 Mean ratings of critical items after being shown the food pictures in experiment 2

Notes: All three questions asked subjects to respond on a scale of 1–8. Believers were subjects who fell sway to the manipulation. Non-believers did not fall sway. Controls were not exposed to the manipulation.

Means in the same column with the different notations are significantly different from each other at p <0.05.

Source: Laney et al (2008: 297)

Believers rated slightly more food pictures as appetising than participants in the control group (p = 0.06). Believers' ratings for how disgusting they found the food pictures were significantly lower than the control group's (p = 0.01).

CHALLENGE YOURSELF
Plot the results from experiment 2 as bar charts and draw one conclusion for every bar chart you plot.

CONCLUSION

Participants can be given positive false food beliefs that have consequences. Those who believed the false feedback were more likely to rate asparagus as being more appetising and less disgusting.

SUMMARY

Research method (main)	Experimental
Other technique(s)	Questionnaires
Sample	Undergraduates from University of California (experiment 1) and University of Washington (experiment 2)
Sampling technique	Volunteer from student pool
Experimental design	Independent groups
IV	Love group and control group; believers and non-believers
DV	Ratings on critical items on both questionnaires – comparing session 1 and session 2
Quantitative data	As above
Qualitative data	Answers to the open-ended questions about experiences with asparagus as a child

EVALUATION

Evaluation	General evaluation (laboratory experiments)	Related to Laney *et al*
Strength	Laboratory experiments have high levels of standardisation and so can be replicated to test for reliability	This study had a standardised procedure including standardised questionnaires and false feedback. This means other researchers could easily replicate this study to test for reliability.
Strength	As laboratory experiments have high levels of control, researchers can be more confident it is the IV directly affecting the DV.	As there were many controls (e.g. rating scales and the false feedback given), the researchers could be more confident that it was the false feedback that was affecting participants' liking of asparagus.
Weakness	In many laboratory experiments participants take part in tasks that are nothing like real-life ones, so the tasks lack mundane realism.	Completing questionnaires and then being given false feedback about eating habits is not a usual task for people in everyday life. Therefore, the study may lack mundane realism.

Other evaluation points include the following:

▶ Generalisability: the sample for both studies consisted of students who had volunteered to take part in the study. In terms of false memory production, the way that these students' memory systems work may be qualitatively different from the way memory systems work in other members of the population. Therefore, generalisability may be low as the sample may not be representative of a wider population in terms of false memory production.

▶ Quantitative data: the study collected a lot of quantitative data which made comparisons between the groups easier. Statistical analyses were conducted to show significant differences between the groups. The ratings regarding asparagus could easily be compared.

▶ Ethics – deception: the participants were told they would be completing a series of questionnaires to help study the relationship between food preferences and personality. However, the study was about implanting false memories of the love of asparagus, so the participants were deceived.

▶ Ethics – informed consent: it is the same argument as above; participants did not know the true aim of the study so could not give specific permission to take part in it.

▶ Use of self-reports: a lot of data were collected using questionnaires. These rely on the memory of the participants being correct but also on them telling the truth about their eating habits, etc. People may not want to reveal the full truth about certain issues so some of the findings may have questionable validity as a result. Also, the ratings for asparagus are subjective, making comparisons quite difficult.

CHALLENGE YOURSELF
Evaluate this study on the potential lasting effects of false beliefs and demand characteristics.

ISSUES AND DEBATES

The following table discusses the Laney *et al* study in terms of the core issues and debates for AS Level.

Application to everyday life	The findings of this study could be used with children labelled as "fussy eaters". For example, if children do not like fruit and/or vegetables then parents or doctors could use the same procedures as the researchers to make those children believe that they do like those types of food. This may encourage "fussy eaters" to change their habits and eat more healthily.
Individual and situational explanations	Not applicable
Nature versus nurture	Not applicable
The use of children	Not applicable
The use of animals	Not applicable

CHALLENGE YOURSELF

Identify two other applications to everyday life that this study could have. Explain who would benefit from these applications.

BANDURA, ROSS AND ROSS

Research date: 1961

BACKGROUND

This study is concerned with the tendency of children to imitate adult social behaviour, specifically aggression. Learning behaviour by imitating others is called observational learning. Several studies had already demonstrated that children are influenced by witnessing adult behaviour. However, previous studies had tended to show children repeating adult behaviour in the same situation and in the presence of the adult who modelled the behaviour. Although this suggests that children identify with adult models, it does not show whether they will go on to repeat the observed behaviour in other situations and without the adult present. One purpose of the study, therefore, was to test whether children will reproduce observed behaviour in a new situation and in the absence of the model.

This study is also concerned with the learning of gender-specific behaviours. Previous studies had shown that children are sensitive to gender-specific behaviours. For example, children see their parents as preferring gender-stereotyped behaviours. Aggression is a good example of a gendered social behaviour, being associated with masculinity.

A further purpose of this study was to investigate whether boys were more likely to imitate aggression than girls, and whether they would be more likely to imitate male than female models.

THE PSYCHOLOGY BEHIND THE STUDY

Social learning theory is being tested by the researchers in this study. To learn something in this way, someone has to go through four stages:

1. Attention. Observers must pay attention to the behaviour(s) of a role model. The role model could be the observer's parent or even a character on television. The role model must have some features that attract the observer. These can be individual factors linked to the observer only or general traits such as being friendly. The idea is that a same-sex model might have more of the relevant characteristics to be observed.

2. Retention. Observers must store the observed behaviour(s) in their long-term memory so that the information can be used again. This could be when the observer wants to imitate the observed behaviour.

3. Reproduction. Observers must feel capable of imitating the retained, observed behaviour. If they do, they may attempt to imitate the behaviour. If they do not, they may observe some more or choose never to attempt to imitate the behaviour.

4. Motivation. If observers experience vicarious reinforcement they are more likely to imitate the observed behaviour. This is when the role model has been rewarded for performing the observed

behaviour so it increases the chances that an observer will get rewarded too if he or she imitates it. Vicarious punishment can also happen where the role model gets punished for the observed behaviour. As a result, the observer is less likely to want to imitate the behaviour.

Therefore, social learning is about learning through observation and imitation. It is also "learning by proxy", which means learning indirectly through others.

ASK YOURSELF
Do you think that watching aggressive media makes someone aggressive? Are there other factors that might make someone aggressive?

AIM

Overall aim: To investigate observational learning of aggression.

Specific aims:

1. To see whether children would reproduce aggressive behaviour when the model was no longer present.

2. To look for gender differences in learning of aggression.

METHOD

Participants

There were 72 participants: 36 male and 36 female. All were selected from the nursery school of Stanford University. Ages ranged from 37 months (just over 3 years) to 69 months (5 years and 9 months). The mean age was 52 months (4 years and 4 months).

Design

This was a laboratory experiment, using a matched pairs design. The effect of three IVs was tested:

▶ the behaviour of the model – aggressive or non-aggressive

▶ the sex of the model

▶ the sex of the children.

There were eight conditions plus a control group. The children in each condition were matched for their aggression levels so that this did not become a confounding variable. This was achieved by the researcher and a nursery teacher independently rating 51 of the children on a scale of 0 to 5 for attributes such as physical aggression, verbal aggression, aggression towards inanimate objects and aggressive inhibition. Very good agreement between the two raters was achieved ($r = +0.89$). Table 10.1 gives details of the conditions in the study.

Condition	Model	Sex of model	Sex of children	n
1	Aggressive	Male	Male	6
2			Female	6
3		Female	Male	6
4			Female	6
5	Non-aggressive	Male	Male	6
6			Female	6
7		Female	Male	6
8			Female	6
Control	None	N/A	Males and females	24

▲ **Table 10.1** Conditions

Procedure

The experiment was conducted as follows:

▶ An aggressive model was shown to 12 boys and 12 girls. Six boys and six girls saw aggression modelled by a same-sex model, while the rest saw aggression modelled by an opposite-sex model.

▶ A non-aggressive model was shown to 12 boys and 12 girls. Six boys and six girls saw non-aggression modelled by a same-sex model, while the rest saw non-aggression modelled by an opposite-sex model.

▶ A control group of 12 boys and 12 girls did not see a model display any behaviour, aggressive or otherwise.

One male and one female were the role models and one female researcher conducted the study for all participants.

There were three stages.

1. Modelling the behaviour. Each child was brought individually to the experimental room. Just before entering the room, the child met the model, who was in the hallway. The researcher invited the model to come into the room and join in a game. This activity lasted for ten minutes. The child was then led to a corner of the room that looked like a play area. Once he or she was seated, the researcher showed how the child could design a picture using potato prints and stickers. The potato prints were all geometric shapes and the stickers were objects such as animals and flowers. These were chosen as previous studies had shown that children took an interest in them.

   Once the child was settled, the researcher took the model to an opposite corner of the room. This contained a small chair and table, a toy set, a mallet and a five-foot inflatable "Bobo" doll. The researcher explained that these were things for the model to play with. When the model was seated, the researcher left the room.

   In the non-aggressive conditions, the model assembled some of the toys in a quiet manner, ignoring the Bobo doll. In the aggressive conditions, the model began by assembling the toys. However, after around one minute, the model started being

aggressive towards the Bobo doll. So that the test would show that participants may well be imitating specific aggressive behaviours, the model showed a range of these. The model punched the doll; however, this is an act a child may do *without* witnessing the model. The model also raised the doll, picked up a mallet and struck the doll on its head then tossed the doll into the air and kicked it around the room. This sequence of physically aggressive acts was repeated around three times. In addition, the model also shouted verbal aggressive responses such as intentions to "sock him in the nose", "hit him down", "throw him in the air", "kick him" and "Pow!". A further two non-aggressive comments were spoken: "He keeps coming back for more" and "He sure is a tough fella". At the end of ten minutes, the researcher returned to the room, told the child to go to another games room and then said goodbye to the model.

2. Aggression arousal. All of the children were subjected to mild aggression. This was done for two reasons:

   ▶ Observation of aggressive behavior shown by others tends to *reduce* the probability of the observer showing aggression. Therefore, those in the aggressive conditions would be less likely to imitate.

   ▶ If those in the non-aggressive conditions showed little aggression after being aroused, it would indicate some inhibitory process happening.

After seeing the model in the previous room, the child entered a games room that had some attractive toys in it. These included a fire engine, a locomotive, a spinning top, a doll set and a fighter plane. The child was told that these were for him or her to play with. However, soon after the child had begun to get involved in play with the toys (usually after around two minutes), the researcher explained that these were actually her very best toys. She stated that she did not let just any child play with them and that she was going to keep these toys for other children. The child was told that he or she could play with the toys in the next room. Both the child and researcher then entered the experimental room. It should be noted that the researcher remained in the room for stage 3 as the child might refuse to be alone, but she never interacted with the child; instead, she busied herself with paperwork in the corner of the room away from the child.

3. Testing for delayed imitation. The experimental room contained toys that could allow each child to show imitative and non-imitative aggression. There were other toys that should elicit other non-aggressive forms of play. The aggressive toys included a three-foot Bobo doll, a mallet, a peg board, two dart guns and a tether ball hung from the ceiling with a face on it. The non-aggressive toys included a tea set, crayons, colouring paper, a ball, dolls, toy bears, cars, trucks and plastic farmyard animals. All of the toys were placed in the same location for every child.

The child spent around 20 minutes in the experimental room. The child's behaviour was rated on a pre-determined checklist of categories by judges through a one-way mirror. The session was divided into five-second intervals via an electronic timer. Therefore, each child had 240 behaviours recorded.

The male model rated the behaviours for all 72 children. Apart from the children he had been a model to, he never knew which condition that child was in. To assess inter-observer reliability, half of the children were observed by a second researcher who scored the children independently from the male model observer. The correlation between the two observers was greater than $r = +0.90$.

Table 10.2 shows the categories used in the observation stage of the study.

Category	Examples of behaviour in the category
Imitative physical aggression	The child: hits the Bobo doll with a mallet; sits on the doll; punches the doll on its nose; kicks the doll; tosses the doll in the air
Imitative verbal aggression	repeats any of the phrases: "sock him", "hit him down", "kick him", "throw him in the air", "Pow!"
Imitative non-aggressive verbal responses	repeats the phrases: "He keeps coming back for more" or "He sure is a tough fella"
Mallet aggression	hits an object *other than the Bobo doll* with the mallet
Sits on the Bobo doll	lays the Bobo doll on its side and sits on it, *but does not show aggression towards it*
Punches the Bobo doll	strikes, slaps, or pushes the Bobo doll aggressively
Non-imitative physical and verbal aggression	shows any physical aggression towards objects *other than the Bobo doll*; makes any hostile remarks except those in the imitative verbal aggression category
Aggressive gun play	shoots the darts or aims the gun and fires imaginary shots at objects in the room.

▲ **Table 10.2** Checklist for categories of behaviour

RESULTS

Quantitative data was recorded. This showed significant differences in levels of imitative aggression between the group that witnessed aggression and the other two groups. This was true of physical and verbal aggression.

To a lesser extent this was also true of partial imitation and non-imitative aggression. Significantly more non-aggressive play was recorded in the non-aggressive model condition. All results are shown in Table 10.3.

Response category	Experimental groups				Control group
	Aggressive		Non-aggressive		
	F model	M model	F model	M model	
Imitative physical aggression					
Female subjects	5.5	7.2	2.5	0.0	1.2
Male subjects	12.4	25.8	0.2	1.5	2.0
Imitative verbal aggression					
Female subjects	13.7	2.0	0.3	0.0	0.7
Male subjects	4.3	12.7	1.1	0.0	1.7
Mallet aggression					
Female subjects	17.2	18.7	0.5	0.5	13.1
Male subjects	15.5	28.8	18.7	6.7	13.5
Punches Bobo doll					
Female subjects	6.3	16.5	5.8	4.3	11.7
Male subjects	18.9	11.9	15.6	14.8	15.7
Non-imitative aggression					
Female subjects	21.3	8.4	7.2	1.4	6.1
Male subjects	16.2	36.7	26.1	22.3	24.6
Aggressive gun play					
Female subjects	1.8	4.5	2.6	2.5	3.7
Male subjects	7.3	15.9	8.9	16.7	14.3

▲ **Table 10.3** Results showing the mean aggressive scores for all conditions across all categories of behaviour

Source: Bandura, Ross and Ross (1961: 578)

Response category	Aggressive compared to non-aggressive model	Aggressive model compared to control	Non-aggressive model compared to control
Imitation of physical aggression	Yes. Aggressive. <0.001	Yes. Aggressive. <0.001	No
Imitation of verbal aggression	Yes. Aggressive. 0.004	Yes. Aggressive. 0.048	No
Imitation of non-aggressive verbal responses	Yes. Aggressive. 0.004	Yes. Aggressive. 0.004	No
Mallet aggression	Yes. Aggressive. 0.026	No	Yes. Control. 0.005
Sits on the Bobo doll	Yes. Aggressive. 0.018	No. Aggressive showed more but p = 0.059	No
Punches the Bobo doll	No	No	No
Physical and verbal non-imitative aggression	Yes. Aggressive. 0.026	No	No
Aggressive gun play	No	No	No

▲ **Table 10.4** Differences between the groups based solely on the behaviour of the model

Table 10.4 shows the significant differences between the groups based solely on the behaviour of the model. Each cell states whether a difference was significant, which group displayed more of the response category and gives the p value.

Table 10.4 clearly shows that participants who observed an aggressive model performed significantly more aggressive behaviours:

▶ in six of the eight response categories compared to the non-aggressive model

▶ in three of the response categories compared to the control.

The control group only showed significantly more aggressive behaviour for mallet aggression than the non-aggressive model. This was mainly due to the girls showing much more of this behaviour in the control group.

The researchers also reported these results:

▶ Around one third of the children in the aggressive conditions repeated the model's non-aggressive verbal responses. No child in the other two conditions did this.

▶ In the aggressive conditions, boys reproduced more imitative physical aggression than girls. There were no differences in terms of verbal aggression.

▶ Boys who witnessed a male aggressive model showed significantly more physical imitative aggression, more verbal imitative aggression, more non-imitative aggression and more gun play than girls who witnessed a male aggressive model.

▶ Girls who witnessed a female aggressive model showed more imitative verbal aggression and non-imitative aggression than boys who witnessed a female aggressive model. However, the results were not significant.

▶ Apart from the mallet aggression, there were no significant differences between the non-aggressive model conditions and the control group. However, this appeared to be masking some important findings. Compared to the control group, those who witnessed a non-aggressive male model (irrespective of their sex) performed *less* imitative physical aggression, *less* imitative verbal aggression, *less* mallet aggression, *less* non-imitative physical and verbal aggression and punched the Bobo doll *fewer* times.

▶ Girls spent significantly more time playing with the dolls and tea set and more time colouring than boys. Boys spent significantly more time playing with the guns.

▶ Children in the non-aggressive conditions engaged in significantly more non-aggressive play with dolls than was seen in the other two groups.

▶ Children who had observed non-aggressive models spent more than twice as much time sitting quietly (not playing with any toys) than children who had observed the aggressive model.

In summary, the key overall results were as follows:

▶ Children who had witnessed an aggressive model were significantly more aggressive themselves.

▶ Overall, there was very little difference between aggression in the control group and that in the non-aggressive modelling condition.

▶ Boys were significantly more likely to imitate aggressive male models. The difference for girls was much smaller.

▶ Boys were significantly more physically aggressive than girls. Girls were slightly more verbally aggressive.

TEST YOURSELF

Outline the sample used in the study and get someone to ask you for specific results.

CONCLUSION

Witnessing aggression in a model can be enough to produce aggression by an observer. Children selectively imitate gender-specific behaviours. Boys are more likely to imitate physical aggression, while girls are more likely to imitate verbal aggression. As the boys but not girls were more likely to imitate aggression in a same-sex model, it could be concluded – although only cautiously – that children selectively imitate same-sex models.

▲ **Figure 10.1** Children imitating the observed behaviour of adults in the study

Source: Bandura, Ross and Ross (1961)

SUMMARY

Research method (main)	Experimental
Other technique(s)	Observations
Sample	There were 72 participants: 36 male and 36 female. All were selected from the nursery school of Stanford University.
Sampling technique	Opportunity
Experimental design	Independent groups
IV	The behaviour of the model – aggressive or non-aggressive; the sex of the model; the sex of the children
DV	Amount of behaviour observed in eight categories
Quantitative data	As above
Qualitative data	Any comments noted from the children

EVALUATION

Evaluation	General evaluation (laboratory experiments)	Related to Bandura *et al*
Strength	Laboratory experiments have high levels of standardisation and so can be replicated to test for reliability.	This study had a standardised procedure including the amount of time participants watched a model for the layout of the room and which toys were available for each child. Therefore, other researchers could easily replicate this study to test it for reliability.
Strength	As laboratory experiments have high levels of control, researchers can be more confident it is the IV directly affecting the DV.	As the controls were high for both parts of the study (e.g. time watching the model, priming before entering the observation room), the researchers could be confident that it was the actions of the model that caused the children to show aggressive and non-aggressive behaviour.
Weakness	As laboratory experiments take place in an artificial setting, it is said that they can lack ecological validity.	The set-up was artificial because, especially for the first stage, the child was in an unfamiliar setting for children. As a result, it could be argued that the findings were low in ecological validity.
Weakness	In many laboratory experiments participants take part in tasks that are nothing like real-life ones, so the tasks lack mundane realism.	Some of the tasks expected of the child were not usual (e.g. sitting watching an adult play with some toys and not being involved in the play). Therefore, aspects of the study could be low in mundane realism.

Other evaluation points include the following:

▶ Quantitative data: this enabled clear comparisons of all groups to see the effect the model was having on behaviour. Therefore, conclusions could easily be drawn. However, we do not know *why* the children were acting in the ways they did as no qualitative data were collected to explore this.

▶ Ethics – protection: the children displayed aggressive behaviour and this may have continued *after* the study had ended. The children did not leave the study in the same physical or psychological state in which they entered it.

CHALLENGE YOURSELF
Evaluate this study in terms of the use of observations and the sampling technique used.

ISSUES AND DEBATES

The following table discusses the Bandura *et al* study in terms of the core issues and debates for AS Level.

Application to everyday life	The finding of this study could be used by television networks to ensure that programmes are appropriate for children. This could include ensuring that aggressive acts in a programme are limited or, alternatively, encouraging pro-social behaviour. The findings are useful for parents too. They can pick and choose which television programmes their children should watch if they know that children may imitate what they see.
Individual and situational explanations	The **situational** side of the debate is supported here. Children had been matched on individual levels of aggression already yet there were differences in imitated behaviours. Therefore, the situation that children found themselves in caused the imitated aggressive behaviours.
Nature versus nurture	Similar to the point above, children had already been matched on their levels of aggression, so the environment they found themselves in caused the imitated behaviours. Therefore, the **nurture** side of the debate is supported here.
The use of children	Some psychologists have noted that the children may have been distressed by watching the aggressive acts. They may have been psychologically harmed by witnessing the acts and by being frustrated with not being able to play with the "best" toys. Therefore, they left the experiment in a different psychological state from when they entered it. Some psychologists believe that children are less susceptible to demand characteristics than adults. In this study it was hoped that the children were showing their real behaviours when playing with the Bobo doll as they had not worked out the purpose of the study.
The use of animals	Not applicable

CHALLENGE YOURSELF
Identify two other applications to everyday life this study could have. Explain who would benefit from these applications.

11 SAAVEDRA AND SILVERMAN

Research date: 2002

BACKGROUND

There has been a lot of research by psychologists and psychiatrists into the causes and treatment of phobias. However, the role of disgust within phobias has received little attention. Disgust could interact with the fear a phobic stimulus produces to increase avoidance behaviour of that stimulus. During something called evaluative learning, the person perceives or evaluates a previously neutral object or event in a negative way (see below). Prior to this study there had been very few studies into evaluative learning in children with a specific phobia.

THE PSYCHOLOGY BEING INVESTIGATED

Evaluative learning is the key concept under investigation in this case study. It is a form of classical conditioning which is learning by association. With this type of learning, a person comes to perceive (evaluate) a previously neutral object or an event negatively. Therefore, the individual negatively evaluates the object or event *without* anticipating any threat or danger. As a result, the negative evaluation elicits a feeling of disgust rather than fear. This differs from classical conditioning (expectancy learning) as it means that the person is being cognitively

active by *thinking about disgust and consequences* rather than being a potentially passive organism.

ASK YOURSELF
List all the ways you can think of that could cause someone to develop a phobia.

AIM

There were two main aims:

1. To investigate the causes of a button phobia in a child.
2. To attempt to treat a child's phobia of buttons via targeting both disgust *and* fear responses.

METHOD

Participant

The participant was a 9-year-old Hispanic-American boy. He was part of the Child Anxiety and Phobia Program at Florida International University. The boy and his mother gave informed consent to participate in the assessment and treatment procedures of the programme. Subsequent to the follow-up process, the mother provided written consent for details of the study to be published. From the data presented to the researchers from the boy and mother (via the Anxiety Disorders Interview Schedule for *DSM-IV* Child and Parent versions), the boy met the *DSM-IV* criteria for a specific phobia of buttons.

Design and procedure

The therapy

The child was treated with an exposure-based treatment programme that tackled cognitions and behaviour. The treatment used was based on the mother providing positive reinforcement if the boy successfully completed a gradual exposure to buttons. The treatment sessions lasted about 30 minutes with the boy alone and 20 minutes with the boy and the mother. Before the first session the boy devised a disgust and fear hierarchy using a distress rating from 0–8 via a "feelings thermometer". The ratings were 2 (large denim-jean buttons), 3 (small denim-jean and clip-on denim-jean buttons), 4 (large plastic buttons – coloured and clear), 5 (hugging his mother when she wears large plastic buttons and medium, coloured plastic buttons), 6 (medium, clear plastic buttons), 7 (hugging his mother when she wears regular medium plastic buttons), 8 (small plastic buttons – coloured and clear). He was to have four sessions of behavioural exposure to the buttons using this hierarchy.

After the behavioural exposure it was planned to have seven sessions looking into the boy's disgust imagery and cognitions with a view to help him to change these over time. The sessions involved him exploring what he found disgusting about buttons alongside the researchers using self-control and cognitive strategies with him to change these thoughts.

RESULTS

The phobia began when the boy was 5 years old. In an art class he ran out of buttons to paste onto a posterboard he was creating. He went to the front of the class to get more buttons from a large bowl on the teacher's desk. His hand slipped and all of the buttons in the bowl fell on him. He said this was very distressing and since then he has avoided buttons. Initially, this avoidance did not present any real difficulties in everyday life but as time progressed it became a problem. Aspects of life such as having difficulty dressing himself, being preoccupied with button thoughts at school affecting his concentration and not touching his school uniform became more frequent. There was no evidence of any other stressors or events

that coincided with his onset of the phobia and he did not meet the criteria for a diagnosis of obsessive compulsive disorder.

By session 4, the boy had successfully completed all in vivo exposure tasks up to those with the highest distress ratings. Even though he could handle more and more buttons, his distress increased dramatically from session 2 to 3 and then from 3 to 4 (see Figure 11.1).

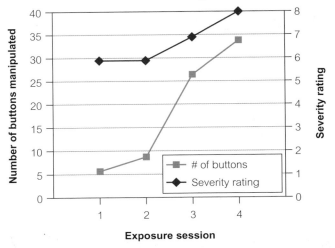

▲ **Figure 11.1** Ratings of distress relative to manipulation of buttons in treatment exposure sessions

Source: Saavedra and Silverman (2002: 1378)

In session 4, the boy's subjective ratings that had been 6 or 7 prior to the treatment were now higher. Even though the behavioural element was progressing, his distress kept increasing.

At the beginning of the seven sessions looking at disgust imagery and cognitions, the boy stated that he found buttons to be disgusting upon contact with his body and that they emitted unpleasant odours. He successfully followed the treatment regime of imagining buttons falling on him, stating how they looked, felt and smelled and explaining why. The imagery sessions progressed from using larger to smaller buttons and involved cognitive restructuring. These techniques appeared to help the boy. Two key results are worth noting:

▶ In a session where he had to imagine hundreds of buttons falling on him, before the cognitive restructuring, he rated the experience as 8 on a 0–8 scale. This rating decreased to a 5 midway through the session and ended up as 3 by the end.

▶ In a session where he had to imagine hugging his mother who was wearing a shirt with many buttons, the distress ratings went from 7 down to 4 then to 3.

He was followed up 6 and 12 months after treatment and at both times he did *not* meet the *DSM-IV* criteria for a specific phobia anymore. Also, he could wear clear plastic buttons on his school uniform shirt.

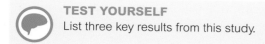

TEST YOURSELF
List three key results from this study.

CONCLUSION

It would appear that disgust plays a key role in the development and maintenance of a phobia (in this case button phobia) but a mixture of behavioural exposure and, more so, cognitive restructuring helped to eliminate the feelings of disgust, even 12 months after treatment.

SUMMARY

Research method (main)	Case study
Other technique(s)	Observations and questionnaires (rating scales)
Sample	A 9-year-old boy
Sampling technique	Opportunity
Experimental design	–
IV	–
DV	–
Quantitative data	Distress ratings and severity ratings
Qualitative data	Questions about why the boy found buttons disgusting

EVALUATION

Evaluation	General evaluation (case study)	Related to Saavedra and Silverman
Strength	When researchers focus on one individual (or unit of individuals) they can collect rich, in-depth data that has details. This makes the findings valid.	The researchers focused on just one person (the boy). He was assessed using *DSM-IV*. His feelings were assessed throughout the intervention. Therefore, a lot of data was collected to help understand the boy's phobia and how best to treat it, and this added validity to the findings.
Strength	The participant is usually studied as part of his or her everyday life, which means that the whole process tends to have some ecological validity.	It could be argued that the study has some ecological validity as the boy was in therapy and the assessment followed what could happen in a therapeutic setting.
Weakness	Generalisations are difficult when researchers focus on one individual (or unit of individuals) because the case may be unique.	The researchers only studied one individual. He could be a unique case, which would make generalising difficult as he may not represent any other person who has a button phobia.

The "Use of children" section in "Issues and debates" below can be used for evaluation purposes. Other evaluation points include the following:

▶ Ethics – informed consent: this was taken from the boy (who wanted the therapy) and from his mother. This allowed the therapy to happen and the account to be published in a journal.

▶ The ratings given by the child are subjective and there is no way of knowing whether he was telling the truth about his fears. He may have been giving lower fear and disgust ratings to get out of the therapy rather than there being a true reduction (however, this is probably not the case as he chose to undergo therapy).

ISSUES AND DEBATES

The following table discusses the Saavedra and
Silverman study in terms of the core issues and debates
for AS Level.

Application to everyday life	The findings of this study showed that the intervention therapy was a success. This means that it could be implemented with other phobic children or even adults. Using exposure-based treatment can help decrease phobias in people so could be used more often.
Individual and situational explanations	Not applicable
Nature versus nurture	The process in which the boy acquired the phobia relates to **nurture** as it was an experience in the classroom that the little boy identified as being the cause of the phobia. It is unlikely that a button phobia has gone through the process of preparedness transmission. (This process involves evolutionary ancestors passing down genetic information to make an individual "naturally" scared of certain stimuli that are dangerous and this is triggered when the person comes into contact with that stimulus.) The procedure of the therapy was set up so the boy had to unlearn his phobia, therefore also suggesting that the phobia is based around **nurture** rather than **nature**.
The use of children	The child was put under **distress** in order to complete the intervention so psychological harm happened and this goes against ethical guidelines. However, **informed consent** was taken from both the child and his mother and it would have been made clear that he would have to be exposed to buttons as part of the therapy intervention. Children may get bored quicker and tired faster than adults so this needs to be considered when designing tasks in studies. The entire therapy procedure would have been designed to counteract this for the boy so that the sessions were applicable to a child.
The use of animals	Not applicable

CHALLENGE YOURSELF
Identify two other applications to everyday life this
study could have. Explain who would benefit from
your applications.

Research date: 1987

BACKGROUND AND THE PSYCHOLOGY INVESTIGATED

Many psychologists believe that only humans possess "true language skills" alongside the ability to show a range of cognitive skills. Prior to this study, Pepperberg had reported on Alex, an African Grey parrot. It appeared from her research that he could categorise objects, count up to six and use functional phrases such as "Come here", "I want X" and "Wanna go Y". However, Pepperberg was quick to state that these do not show whether a non-human can comprehend and use abstract symbolic relationships when communicating. One cognitive skill that had been reported as being a concept not seen in non-humans is the comprehension of "same" or "different". Research by another psychologist, Premack, had shown that pigeons may understand "same" but not "different" but no other research had attempted to investigate this cognitive skill.

Premack noted that for non-humans to demonstrate comprehension of "same", two aspects must apply:

▶ They must recognise that two independent objects called A1 and A2 are *both blue* and that this is the single attribute that makes them the same.

▶ They must also recognise that this "sameness" can be "*immediately* extrapolated and *symbolically* represented not only for two other blue items, but for two novel, independent green items – B1 and

B2 – that have nothing in common with the original set of As" (Pepperberg 1987: 424).

They also need to show their comprehension of "different" in the same way.

Part of the process involved in the study used social learning. See page 64 of the Bandura *et al* study for a description of this idea.

This study was designed to test these two ways of assessing the cognitive skill of "same" or "different" comprehension.

ASK YOURSELF
Do you believe that animals are capable of thinking? In a table, set out arguments to support and to contradict this idea.

AIM

Pepperberg stated that "the present study was therefore undertaken to see if an avian subject… could use vocal labels to demonstrate symbolic comprehension of the concepts of *same* and *different*" (Pepperberg 1987: 424).

METHOD

Participant

An African Grey parrot named Alex was the sole participant in this study. He had been the focus of Pepperberg's work since June 1977. He had free access (sometimes contingent on his request such as "Wanna go X") to all parts of her laboratory for eight hours per day when the trainers were present. The trials occurred in various locations around the laboratory depending where Alex was at the time (or where he wanted to go). During his "sleeping hours" he was placed in a cage with water and a standard seed mix for parrots was available at all times. Other food, such as fresh fruit, and vegetables; nuts; and toys (e.g. keys, pieces of wood) were provided when Alex asked for them.

Design

This was an experimental case study. The following task was designed to test that Alex showed comprehension of "same" and "different":

▶ Alex was presented with two objects that could be differentiated based on three categories: colour, shape or the material it was made from. For example, he could be presented with a yellow wooden triangle and a blue wooden triangle; or a blue rawhide pentagon and a green wooden pentagon.

▶ He would then be asked either "What's same?" or "What's different?"

▶ A correct response would only be recorded if Alex vocalised the appropriate category and not the specific colour, shape or material. So, for the yellow wooden triangle and blue wooden triangle a correct response would be "colour" and not "yellow" or "blue". Therefore, there were four processes that Alex had to go through to get a correct response:

1. Attend to multiple features of two different objects.

2. From the vocal question, determine whether the response is based on sameness or difference.

3. Work out *what* is the same or different.

4. Vocally produce a category response.

To complete these processes Alex had to perform the cognitive skill of feature analysis on the objects. Previous research had simply asked non-humans to state "same" or "different" *without* a category label or performing feature analysis. For example, in these previous studies, non-humans had to only perform the following:

▶ Indicate whether the objects were the same or different and nothing else.

▶ Simply press a lever to indicate whether same or different.

▶ Recognise same pairs that were 100 per cent the same or different pairs that were 100 per cent different.

None of the above require the cognitive skills that were being tested in Alex in this study.

As Alex had already been "learning" language and concepts for around nine years prior to this study, he could already produce vocal labels in English for the items shown in Table 12.1.

Colours	Green, rose [for red], blue, yellow and grey
Shapes	Two-, three-, four- and five-cornered shapes for football-shaped, triangular, square and pentagonal shapes respectively
Materials	Paper, wood, hide [rawhide] and cork
Metallic objects	Key, chain and grate were the most noted ones

▲ **Table 12.1** Items for which Alex could produce vocal labels in English

Alex had already shown some ability to understand abstract categories. He could respond correctly to questions such as "What colour?" and "What shape?" During the course of this study he acquired labels for orange, purple and six-cornered objects. Therefore, he was at least capable of "explaining" why something was the same or different rather than merely stating "same" or "different". In addition, as he had acquired all of these labels, his responses in this experiment could not have been based just on absolute physical properties or by rote learning the answer to a given pair of objects, because the number of possible paired combinations of objects was very large. To further test his abilities, Pepperberg wanted to test Alex on novel objects that were not in his labelling repertoire. This meant he would have to *transfer* his knowledge to other objects not used in training or not presented to him before.

Training (general)

The primary technique used by Pepperberg was called a model/rival technique based on the principles of social learning. This demonstrates to the parrot the types of interactive responses desired in the study. One of the humans acts as a trainer to the second human. This trainer asks the second human questions about objects, giving praise and rewards for correct answers but showing disapproval for incorrect answers (especially ones that are similar to what Alex was making (e.g. saying "wood" instead of "green wood"). The second human is acting as a model for Alex's responses but also as a rival for the trainer's attention. The role of model/rival and trainer were frequently reversed and Alex was given the opportunity to participate in these sessions.

During any training where the purpose was to acquire a label, each correct response was rewarded with the object itself. This type of reward system gave the closest correlation between the object and the category and label that needed to be learned. In this study, the reward was the acquisition of both objects. To keep Alex's motivation levels high even with objects he did not really want, he could also choose an object as a reward if he gave the correct label – for example, if the objects were wooden triangles and he labelled them correctly but then stated "I want cork" he was given cork. If he simply stated "cork" he would not get the desired cork.

TEST YOURSELF
Draw a flow diagram that shows how the general training took place in this study.

Training (same/different)

A trainer would hold up two objects in front of the model/rival and simply ask "What's same?" or "What's different?" Both types of question and the training objects were mixed within each session of training. The objects were always red, green or blue; triangular or square; rawhide or wood. The model/rival would respond with the correct category label and be given the objects as a reward. If the model gave an incorrect category label the trainer scolded the person. When an error was presented in this phase, the objects were removed from sight, then presented again with the same question asked. The role of trainer and model/rival was then reversed. The initial training contrasted just the categories of colour and shape as Alex had already shown he could use these labels. Alex was then trained on the third label "mah-mah" (meaning matter). Sessions occurred two to four times per week and lasted from five minutes to one hour. To prevent boredom because of conducting repetitive tasks (boredom that Alex usually showed by stopping vocalisations and preening), he was

also being trained on number concepts, new labels for other objects, recognition of photographs and object permanence. Formal testing of Alex's ability was only started after he had acquired the label "mah-mah".

Procedure

Trials were carried out by secondary trainers who had never trained Alex on "same" or "different" labelling. This was used to reduce any effect of cuing from the original trainers. The "same" or "different" questioning was incorporated into other test sessions that were being conducted on Alex. On a previous day, the principal trainer would list all possible objects that could be used for testing. A student who was not involved in any training of Alex would then choose the question, from the "same" or "different" pairs and then randomly order the questions. In any given week, "same" or "different" questions were asked between one and four times. As a result, Alex or the principal trainer could never predict which questions would be asked. Testing took place over 26 months. A secondary trainer would present Alex with the objects and then ask a question (one of which could be "What's same?" or "What's different?").

The principal trainer was present wherever the trial took place but she sat with her back to Alex. She did not look at Alex during the presentation of the objects. Therefore, she never knew what was being presented. She would repeat out loud what she thought Alex had said. If that was the correct response Alex was given the objects as a reward and was praised. The same materials were never presented again during the test so there was a single "first-trial" response. If Alex answered the question incorrectly the trainer removed the objects, turned her head and emphatically said "No!". When this happened a correction procedure was used – the same objects were presented again with the same question asked until the correct response was given. Alex could learn that an incorrect response did not get the objects or his preferred choice of object. An overall test score was produced (dividing the number of correct identifications by the total number of presentations). First-trial results were also calculated. As noted before, to reduce boredom and "expectation cuing" a range of different questions covering different studies that Alex was involved in took place in any given session.

Therefore, Alex was never tested exclusively on "same" or "different" in one session and was never tested successively in one session with the same question (e.g. "What's different?").

Tests on objects that were familiar

Object pairs were presented to Alex. They were similar pairings to the ones used in the training phase but never the same. Individual objects were obviously used in more than one trial but the pairings were always novel and a specific pair would only ever be presented again if Alex gave an incorrect category label.

Transfer tests using novel objects

Alex was presented with pairs of objects that combined several attributes that had never been used in the training phase or in previous "same" or "different" questioning. For example, Alex may have been presented with a five-cornered piece of white paper. In addition, Alex was presented with totally novel objects that might not have even had a label (e.g. a pink woollen pompom). Therefore, he was exposed to objects that he did not have a label for and objects he had no experience of. Any completely new object (e.g. a toy car) was within Alex's environment (usually on a shelf) for several days prior to being used so that Alex got used to at least seeing the object to reduce any fear responses he may show.

The use of probes

A concern of Pepperberg's was that Alex might not be attending to the questions but instead merely responding to the physical characteristics of the objects themselves. By looking at the objects he could have determined the one category that was the same or different, responding with that answer. The questions used in the trials usually had only one similarity for the "same" question or one difference for the "different" question. Therefore, we cannot fully know if he was simply answering with the category label that shows one "same" or one "different" characteristic. This is why Pepperberg used probes: Alex was asked questions where the correct category label could

be two of the three labels so that the *incorrect* answer was the other label. For example, he may have been shown a green wooden triangle and a yellow wooden triangle and asked "What's same?" If he was simply responding to the physical characteristics he would say "colour" and get the answer wrong (this is the one different characteristic). If he was attending to the actual question of "same" he would give one of the other two category labels.

RESULTS

The training for Alex to acquire "colour" and "shape" as labels took four months. To acquire "mah-mah" took nine months. This was not an indication of his abilities but a product of him engaging in a range of studies at the same time. Training parrots with vocalisations that are new phonemes takes longer than training them with phonemes that are new combinations of previously learned ones. Also, the length of each session was dictated by Alex's willingness to attend.

Familiar objects

Alex scored 99 out of 129 (76.7 per cent) correct responses overall and 69 out of 99 (69.7 per cent) on first-trial only performance ($p < 0.0001$). Based on chance he should have scored 33.3 per cent. His performance on pairs consisting of objects that were no longer novel but contained a colour, shape or material he could not yet label (e.g. plastic) was 13 out of 17 (76.5 per cent) overall and 10 out of 13 (76.9 per cent) for first trials. Table 12.2 shows his performance.

Question	Correct response (number of times made)	Incorrect response (number of times made)
What's same?	Color 16	Shape 2; Matter 2
	Shape 16	Color 4; Matter 2
	Matter 16	Color 3: Shape 2
What's different?	Color 17	Shape 2: Matter 2
	Shape 16	Color 3; Matter 4
	Matter 18	Color 3: Shape 1

▲ **Table 12.2** Alex's responses to queries of "What's same?" or "What's different?" to pairs of objects that were similar but not identical to those used in training

Source: Pepperberg (1987: 427)

Transfer tests with novel objects

Alex scored 96 out of 113 (85 per cent) correct responses overall and 79 out of 96 (82.3 per cent) on first trials (p < 0.0001). When there was one novel object in a pair his score was 86 per cent and when both objects were novel it was 83 per cent. These higher percentages were not surprising to Pepperberg as she stated "... Alex received the objects themselves as his primary reward, and there was therefore some inherent incentive to pay closer attention to both of the objects and the response when these reward objects were new items that were potentially interesting to chew apart, to try to eat, or to use for preening" (Pepperberg 1987: 428). Table 12.3 shows his performance.

Question	Correct response (number of times made)	Incorrect response (number of times made)
What's same?	Color 17	Shape 1; Matter 2
	Shape 16	Color 3; Matter 1
	Matter 17	Color 3
What's different?	Color 15	Shape 1
	Shape 16	Color 1
	Matter 15	Color 3: Shape 2

▲ **Table 12.3** Alex's responses to queries of "What's same?" or "What's different?" to pairs of objects significantly different from those used in training, including objects made of colours, shapes and materials for which he might not have labels

Source: Pepperberg (1987: 428)

Probes

Alex scored 55 out of 61 (90.2 per cent) correct responses overall and 49 out of 55 (89.1 per cent) on first trials. This demonstrates he was processing the questions rather than simply the attributes of the objects. Table 12.4 shows his performance.

Question	Correct response (number of times made)	Incorrect response (number of times made)
What's same?	Color 10	Matter 1
	Shape 11	Matter 2
	Matter 11	
What's different?	Color 8	
	Shape 7	Color 1
	Matter 8	Shape 2

▲ **Table 12.4** Alex's responses to probes in order to learn whether he was responding on the basis of the experimenters' questions, and not just on physical variations in the object

Source: Pepperberg (1987: 429)

CONCLUSION

Pepperberg concluded: "The data indicate that at least one avian subject, an African Grey parrot, shows symbolic comprehension of the concept same/different" (1987: 428). Alex's scores on all tests (including first trial analyses) were significantly above chance, suggesting he understood what the questions were asking. This was shown via the probe questioning. It would therefore appear that symbolic representation, in this case of "same" or "different", is not exclusive to primates.

SUMMARY

Research method (main)	Experimental
Other technique(s)	Case study
Sample	An African Grey parrot called Alex
Sampling technique	Opportunity
Experimental design	–
IV	Whether the object is familiar or novel
DV	Whether the parrot responds correctly to the questions about "What's same?" and "What's different"?
Quantitative data	Percentage success rate on trials was measured for familiar objects and novel objects.
Qualitative data	–

EVALUATION

Evaluation	General evaluation (laboratory experiments)	Related to Pepperberg
Strength	Laboratory experiments have high levels of standardisation and so can be replicated to test for reliability	This study had a standardised procedure including the materials, colours and shapes of objects, and standardised tests. This means other researchers could easily replicate this study to test for reliability.
Weakness	In many laboratory experiments participants take part in tasks that are nothing like real-life ones, so the tasks lack mundane realism.	The task of learning "same" or "different" is not a natural task for a parrot. Therefore, the study may lack mundane realism.

This study can also be evaluated in terms of generalisability:

▶ Only Alex was used in the study and this could make generalisability difficult.

▶ Alex may be qualitatively different from other African Grey parrots. If this is the case, Alex may be unique and have skills that do not represent a wider population of African Grey parrots.

ISSUES AND DEBATES

The following table discusses the Pepperberg study in terms of the core issues and debates for AS Level.

Application to everyday life	The procedure used in this study may be useful for people who wish to or need to train animals to perform certain tasks. For example, if they use the ideas of observation and imitation, zoo keepers may be able to introduce new animals to groups more easily by encouraging role models to show the new group member what behaviours are acceptable.
Individual and situational explanations	Not applicable
Nature versus nurture	As Alex had been taught during the procedure, the study supports the **nurture** side of the debate. He was learning through both operant conditioning and social learning. He had been taught the use of labels as it was not something that came naturally to him. Therefore, it is difficult to argue that his abilities were due to **nature**.
The use of children	Not applicable
The use of animals	**Numbers**: the researchers only used one parrot in the study (the least amount of animals possible). The study still accomplished its goals despite using only one parrot. **Rewards** were used appropriately and Alex was not deprived of nutrition if he answered incorrectly. Aversive conditioning was not used in this study. Alex would be given extra food if he asked for it. **Caging**: Alex was placed in his usual cage during "sleeping hours" so he was not placed in a unusual situation throughout the study.

CHALLENGE YOURSELF
Identify two other applications to everyday life this study could have. Explain who would benefit from these applications.

13 MILGRAM

Research date: 1963

BACKGROUND

Most of the time we are told that obedience is a good thing. If your teacher tells you to get your book out or to answer a question, you might not want to do it but you probably accept that the most socially appropriate behaviour is to obey. You probably also accept that your teacher has the right to give you an instruction of this kind. However, what if you were ordered to do something that caused harm or distress to another person? This type of obedience, in which people obey orders to cause harm, is called destructive obedience. Social psychologists such as Milgram have been particularly interested in destructive obedience.

As the member of a European Jewish family that had left Europe for the United States, Milgram was profoundly affected by the atrocities committed by Nazi Germany against Jewish people and other minority groups. One of the key features of the Nazi atrocities was the extent to which people displayed destructive obedience. Many ordinary people obeyed orders that led to the systematic mass murder of minority groups, including Jews, Romanies, Communists, trade unionists and people with disabilities.

Early psychological research into the Holocaust focused on the idea that something distinctive about German culture or personality led to the high levels of conformity and obedience necessary for genocide to take place. This is known as the dispositional hypothesis. While Milgram was interested in this idea, he was also interested in the social processes that take place between individuals and within groups.

THE PSYCHOLOGY BEING INVESTIGATED

The idea that we can explain events such as the Holocaust by reference to the social processes operating in the situation, rather than the characteristics of the individuals involved, is called the situational hypothesis. This is what Milgram was testing.

Subsequent to this study he produced his agency theory. This is when we have two psychological states in certain situations:

▶ Agentic state: when we give up our free will to serve as an "agent to authority".

▶ Autonomous state: when we act on our own free will and choose whether to, say, be obedient or not.

Milgram believed that from a young age we are socialised to be obedient to authority figures. He also believed that we experience moral strain. This is when, during the agentic state, we go along with the demands of the authority figure even though we know this is wrong and do not agree with it.

> **ASK YOURSELF**
> Why do you think the Holocaust happened? Can you think of any modern-day examples of such an atrocity?

AIM

Overall aim: To investigate how obedient people would be to orders from a person in authority that would result in pain and harm to another person.

Specific aim: To see how large an electric shock a participant would give to a helpless man when ordered to by a scientist in his laboratory.

METHOD

Participants

A newspaper advertisement was used to recruit 40 men aged 20–50 (see Figure 13.1).

Public Announcement

WE WILL PAY YOU $4.00 FOR ONE HOUR OF YOUR TIME

Persons Needed for a Study of Memory

*We will pay five hundred New Haven men to help us complete a scientific study of memory and learning. The study is being done at Yale University.

*Each person who participates will be paid $4.00 (plus 50c carfare) for approximately 1 hour's time. We need you for only one hour: there are no further obligations. Your may choose the time you would like to come (evenings, weekdays, or weekends).

*No special training, education, or experience is needed. We want:

Factory workers	Businessmen	Construction workers
City employees	Clerks	Salespeople
Laborers	Professional People	White-collar workers
Barbers	Telephone workers	Others

All persons must be between the age of 20 and 50. High school and college students cannot be used.

*If you meet these qualifications. Yale University, New Haven. You will be notified later of the specific time and place of the study. We reserve the right to decline and application.

*You will be paid $4.00 (plus 50c carfare) as soon as you arrive at the laboratory.

- -

TO:
PROF. STANLEY MILGRAM, DEPARTMENT OF PSYCHOLOGY, YALE UNIVERSITY, NEW HAVEN, CONN.
I want to take part in this study of memory and learning. I am between the ages of 20 and 50. I will be paid $4.00 (plus 50c carfare) if I participate.

NAME (Please Print)..

ADDRESS..

TELEPHONE NO.. Best time to call you................................

AGE.. OCCUPATION.................................... SEX..............................

CAN YOU COME:

WEEKDAYS.. EVENINGS.............................. WEEKENDS...................

▲ **Figure 13.1** Advertisement used to recruit participants for Milgram's study

Source: Milgram (1974, 1997, 2005). *Obedience to Authority*. Pinter & Martin, London

The sample was therefore mostly a volunteer sample. Participants were from a range of backgrounds and held a range of jobs: 37.5 per cent were manual labourers, 40 per cent were white-collar workers and 22.5 per cent were professionals. All were from New Haven, Connecticut, USA. The breakdown of the sample can be seen in the Table 13.1.

Occupation	20–29 years	30–39 years	40–50 years	Percentage of total (occupations)
Workers, skilled and unskilled	4	5	6	37.5
Sales, business and white collar	3	6	7	40.0
Professional	1	5	3	22.5
Percentage of total	20	40	40	

Note: Total n = 40

▲ **Table 13.1** Distribution of age and occupation types
Source: Milgram (1963: 372)

Design

Milgram described his original study as a laboratory experiment. Technically, it might more accurately be called a pre-experiment, because it had only one condition. The results from this condition then served as a baseline for a number of variations in follow-up studies, at least 17 of which happened. Obedience was operationalised as the maximum voltage given.

Procedure

Participants were promised $4.50 for their time and it was made clear that payment was for turning up to the study, and was not conditional on completing the procedure. When each participant arrived at Yale University he was introduced to a man he believed to be another participant (called Mr Wallace; in fact, he was a confederate). The two men were then briefed on the supposed purpose of the experiment, which was described to them as to investigate the effect of punishment on learning. The experimenter was a 31-year-old biology teacher. His manner during the study was to be impassive with a somewhat stern appearance. He wore a grey technician's coat. Mr Wallace was a 47-year-old Irish-American accountant. He had been selected for the role because he was mild-mannered and likeable.

Milgram had devised a "pre-text" that would justify why electric shocks were being used. After a general introduction about punishment and learning, the following standardised text was read to both the naïve participant and the confederate.

> But actually, we know very *little* about the effect of punishment on learning, because almost no truly scientific studies have been made of it in human beings.
>
> For instance, we don't know *how much* punishment is best for learning – and we don't know how much difference it makes as to who is giving the punishment, whether an adult learns best from a younger or an older person than himself – or many things of that sort.
>
> So in this study we are bringing together a number of adults of different occupations and ages. And we're asking some of them to be teachers and some of them to be learners. We want to find out just what effect different people have on each other as teachers and learners, and what effect *punishment* will have on learning in this situation.

Source: Milgram (1963: 373)

The naïve participant and the confederate were told that one of them would play the role of teacher and the other the role of the learner. They drew slips of paper from a hat to allocate the roles, but this was rigged so that the naïve participant was *always* the teacher and the confederate was *always* the learner. They were then immediately taken to another room where the learner (Mr Wallace) was strapped into a chair. It was explained that the strapping was being used to prevent any excessive movement while being shocked. An electrode was attached to Wallace's wrist with a paste to "avoid blisters and burns". Both Wallace and the participant were shown the electric shock generator. This had a row of switches, each labelled with a voltage, rising in 15-volt intervals from 15 volts up to 450 volts. They were told that the shocks could be extremely painful but not dangerous and were each given a 45-volt shock to demonstrate.

There was a wall between the participant and Wallace, so that the participant could hear but not see Wallace. The participant read out word pairs to test Wallace on his recognition of which words went together. Each time Wallace made a mistake, the experimenter ordered the participant to give a shock. The shock got larger by 15 volts for each mistake. Wallace did not really receive shocks, but there was no way for the participant to know this. When the participant pressed one of the switches, a light corresponding to it lit up in bright red.

An electric buzzing sound was heard as it happened. Then, an electric blue light labelled "voltage energiser" flashed and a dial representing a voltage meter moved to the right.

Milgram conducted a preliminary run. Prior to this study he had noted that a procedure of reading words and giving a shock required some practice. This involved the participant being given ten words to read to the confederate. Three of these were answered correctly by Wallace; the rest of his answers were incorrect. Therefore, the participant had to administer seven shocks (up to 105 volts). Virtually all participants mastered the procedure during this preliminary run. After this, they began the "real" trial and were told that if they got to the bottom pairing on the list they were to start the list again.

At certain voltage levels, Wallace would give a pre-determined set of responses based on the ratio of three wrong answers to one correct one. In this study, there was no vocal response at all from Wallace until the shock had reached 300 volts. At this point he would pound on the wall, which could be clearly heard by the participant. From this point on, every time the participant read out the word, no answer would appear on the four-way panel. When this happened, the experimenter instructed the participant that an absence of response was to be treated as an incorrect answer and a shock should be administered. The participant was told to allow a five- to ten-second response time. If no answer was given during that time, the participant should count this as an incorrect response. Wallace repeatedly pounded the wall when the 315-volt button was pressed. However, after this voltage, he never responded to a word list, nor was he ever heard from again.

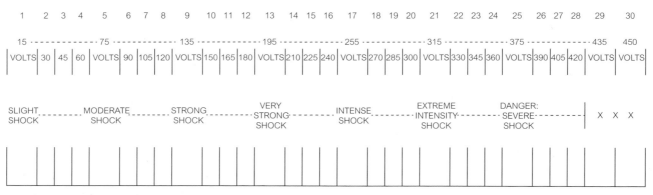

▲ **Figure 13.2** Diagram of the control panel used in the experiment

Source: Milgram (1974, 1997, 2005). *Obedience to Authority*. Pinter & Martin, London

At any point, the participant could have protested and turned to the experimenter for advice on whether he should continue giving the shocks, or simply refuse to continue. Therefore, the researcher created a series of standardised prods for the experimenter to say in an attempt to force the participant to continue. These were as follows:

▶ Prod 1 – experimenter says "Please continue" or "Please go on."

▶ Prod 2 – experimenter says "The experiment requires that you continue."

▶ Prod 3 – experimenter says "It is absolutely essential that you continue."

▶ Prod 4 – experimenter says "You have no other choice, you must go on."

The prods were always used in this sequence. If the participant refused to continue after prod 4, the experiment was terminated. The experimenter would always read the prod out in a firm but not impolite manner. Each time a participant tried to stop, the sequence was started again. There were two special prods as follows:

- If the participant asked whether the shocks could cause permanent injury the response was: "Although the shocks may be painful, there is no permanent tissue damage, so please go on." Then the usual prods were used if necessary.

- If the participant stated that he felt the confederate did not want to continue the response was: "Whether the learner likes it or not, you must go on until he has learned all the word pairs correctly. So please go on." Then the usual prods were used if necessary.

Each participant was considered to have completed the procedure either when he refused to give any more shocks (called a *defiant* participant), or when he reached the maximum voltage on the shock machine (called an *obedient* participant). Most of the trials were recorded and some photographs were taken through a one-way mirror. Notes were taken if any unusual behaviour was seen, and another observer took objective notes of any behaviours shown. The latency and duration of shocks was also measured. Participants were then interviewed and de-hoaxed. During their interview they were asked to rate on a scale of 0–14 how painful the last few shocks they gave were, then asked open-ended questions and given projective tests (designed to reveal hidden emotions and internal conflicts). They were told that the shocks were not real, that Wallace was unharmed, and that the real purpose of the study was to investigate obedience. It was the intention that each participant would leave the laboratory in a state of wellbeing.

TEST YOURSELF
Try to get the procedure down to eight "vital parts" that are essential for you to understand what the participants had to do.

RESULTS

Preliminary notions

Before Milgram conducted this study he asked 14 Yale University seniors (all psychology majors) to read a detailed description of what the study entailed. They were asked to plot a distribution of obedience for "100 Americans of diverse occupation, and ranging in age from 20 to 50 years" (Milgram, 1963: 375). All of them stated that 0–3 per cent of a sample would give the 450-volt shock. The mean was 1.2 per cent. Informally, Milgram also asked colleagues how high a shock they thought participants would give to a learner. The general consensus was that very few subjects would go beyond a "very strong shock" on the generator.

Participants accept situation

Virtually all of the participants appeared convinced that they were administering shocks to Wallace. One of the questions asked post-experiment was: "How painful to the learner were the last few shocks that you administered to him?" (Milgram 1963: 375). They had to respond on a 14-point scale ranging from 1 = not at all painful to 14 = extremely painful. The modal score was 14 with the mean being 13.42.

Signs of extreme tension

Many of the participants exhibited signs of nervousness, especially when giving the larger shocks. Qualitative data was gathered in the form of the comments and protests participants made during the procedure, and in the form of observations of their body language. Most participants showed signs of tension during the procedure. Signs included groaning, sweating, biting lips and stuttering. Fourteen giggled nervously. Three had seizures and for one of these the procedure was stopped. One observer commented (quoted in Milgram 1963: 377):

"I observed a mature and initially poised business man enter the laboratory smiling and confident. Within 20 minutes he was reduced to a twitching, stuttering wreck, who was rapidly approaching the point of nervous collapse."

When interviewed after the experiment, participants who had giggled went to great lengths to explain that they were not sadistic and that the laughter did not indicate that they enjoyed shocking the victim.

Distribution of obedience scores

Table 13.2 shows the levels of shock as described on the generator and the number of participants who administered each level as their maximum shock.

Voltage	Verbal description on the shock generator	Number of participants who gave this as their maximum shock
0–285	Slight shock, Moderate shock, Strong shock, Very Strong shock, Intense shock	0 at every voltage level
300	Intense shock	5
315	Extreme intensity shock	4
330		2
345		1
360		1
375		1
390	Danger: Severe shock	0
405		0
420		0
435	XXX	0
450		26

▲ **Table 13.2** Shock levels administered by participants

No participant stopped before shock level 20 (300 volts). Remember that at 300 volts, Wallace would pound on the wall and then never answer again. A total of 14 participants were classed as *defiant* (35 per cent of the sample) and 26 as *obedient* (65 per cent of the sample).

An example of the behaviour shown by a *defiant* participant is shown in this quote:

> "I think he's trying to communicate, he's knocking... Well, it's not fair to shock the guy... these are terrific volts. I don't think this is very humane... Oh I can't go on with this; no, this isn't right. It's a hell of an experiment. The guy is suffering in there. No, I don't want to go on. This is crazy."

Milgram 1963: 375–376.

Even when under extreme stress, many of the participants continued to give Wallace shocks. Some did express a reluctance to do so (especially beyond the 300-volt level) and showed similar behaviours to those who defied; yet they continued. There were mixed behaviours shown by those reaching the 450-volt level: some mopped their brows, others went straight for a cigarette, yet others remained calm throughout the whole procedure.

TEST YOURSELF
How generalisable are the results? How easy would it be to replicate this study? Why?

CONCLUSION

Milgram drew these main conclusions from this study:

▶ People are much more obedient to destructive orders than we might expect, and in this case considerably more than psychology students suggested in their estimates. In fact, the majority of people are quite willing to obey destructive orders.

▶ People find the experience of receiving and obeying destructive orders highly stressful. They obey in spite of their emotional responses. The situation triggers a conflict between two deeply ingrained tendencies – to obey those in authority, and not to harm people.

Results supported the situational hypothesis rather than the dispositional (individual) hypothesis.

SUMMARY

Research method (main)	Experimental
Other technique(s)	Observations, interviews and questionnaires
Sample	40 men
Sampling technique	Volunteer
Experimental design	–
IV	Strictly, an IV does not exist but Milgram could have compared the experimental procedure with the questionnaire study using psychiatrists and students.
DV	The percentage of participants who went to each voltage level
Quantitative data	As above
Qualitative data	Noted behaviours and quotes from participants

EVALUATION

Evaluation	General evaluation (laboratory experiments)	Related to Milgram
Strength	Laboratory experiments have high levels of standardisation and so can be replicated to test for reliability.	This study had a standardised procedure including the drawing of lots to be teacher or learner, the timing of when scripted responses were heard and stating that the shocks were going up in 15-volt increments. Therefore, other researchers could replicate this study to test it for reliability. Ethical guidelines may now stop this, but a study by Slater did replicate it.
Strength	As laboratory experiments have high levels of control, researchers can be more confident it is the IV directly affecting the DV.	As there were so many controls (e.g. having a "test" shock, receiving the prods at a certain time in the same order and the shock generator being the same for everyone), the researcher could conclude with confidence that it was the situation that the participants were placed in that caused the obedience levels.
Weakness	As laboratory experiments take place in an artificial setting, it is said that they can lack ecological validity.	Sitting in a laboratory in front of a shock generator is not an everyday setting that people find themselves in. Therefore, the study lacks ecological validity.
Weakness	In many laboratory experiments participants take part in tasks that are nothing like real-life ones, so the tasks lack mundane realism.	Having to give an electric shock to somebody who gets a word-pair wrong is not a task that people come across in everyday life. Therefore, the study is low in mundane realism.

The study can also be evaluated in terms of ethics. However, always take into consideration that strict ethical guidelines only came into place in 1973, so we are *retrospectively* criticising this study. Also, Milgram's preliminary notion findings did not predict what actually happened in the study.

General evaluation (ethics)	Related to Milgram
Deception	Participants thought that they were giving Wallace a real electric shock each time. Also, they were told that it was a study about memory and not obedience.
Debriefing	At the end of the study all was revealed to participants so they left knowing that they had not harmed Wallace. They were also followed up six months later to check whether they were having any psychological issues.
Right to withdraw	The prods given by the experimenter made it difficult for participants to withdraw from the study – they kept being convinced to continue even though some wanted to leave.

Other points that can be used to evaluate the study include the following:

▶ Usefulness: the study did highlight that the situation may make people behave in the way that they do rather than it being individual (dispositional). This is useful as Milgram was attempting to see (in relation to the atrocities committed during the Holocaust) whether "Germans were different" and he did not find this. All of this could begin to help explain other atrocities so we can then find ways to stop them happening.

ISSUES AND DEBATES

The following table discusses the Milgram study in terms of the core issues and debates for AS Level.

Application to everyday life	The findings of this study have been used extensively to explain why humans engage in destructive obedience. For example, ordinary people who became part of the Nazi movement in the 1930s followed out destructive orders in the Second World War from higher authority figures. Genocide, as was seen in Rwanda and the former Yugoslavia, can also be explained by the findings of this study: people will follow the orders of authority figures when placed in certain morally straining situations.
Individual and situational explanations	The **situation** that the participants found themselves in could explain the obedience rates shown. For example, it was a prestigious university, and there was always a man in a technician's coat standing behind participants. The sample was taken from the local community from a wide range of occupations, to make sure that **individual** factors would not play a role in obedience levels.
Nature versus nurture	Not applicable
The use of children	Not applicable
The use of animals	Not applicable

CHALLENGE YOURSELF
Identify two other applications to everyday life this study could have. Explain who would benefit from these applications.

14 PILIAVIN, RODIN AND PILIAVIN

Research date: 1969

BACKGROUND

This study is concerned with bystander behaviour. Bystanders are people who witness events and have to choose whether to intervene or not. There has been a lot of debate over "have-a-go heroes" who put themselves at risk to intervene and attempt to stop crimes taking place. Most of the time bystanders can help without putting themselves at risk. However, surprisingly often we do not choose to act to help people in need.

The assailant stabbed her again. 'I'm dying!' she shrieked. 'I'm dying!'

Windows were opened again, and lights went on in many apartments. The assailant got into his car and drove away. Miss Genovese staggered to her feet. A city bus, 0–10, the Lefferts Boulevard line to Kennedy International Airport, passed. It was 3:35 A.M. The assailant returned. By then, Miss Genovese had crawled to the back of the building, where the freshly painted brown doors to the apartment house held out hope for safety. The killer tried the first door; she wasn't there. At the second door, 82–62 Austin Street, he saw her slumped on the floor at the foot of the stairs. He stabbed her a third time—fatally.

Some of the details of the story as it was reported at the time have since been challenged. Given the layout of the block, it would not have been possible for anyone to have seen the whole incident, so each person would have seen just fragments of the event. Also, the area was not actually as quiet as the article implies – one neighbour said that rows between couples leaving a local bar were common late at night. Given these facts, we cannot be sure that 38 people really saw, correctly interpreted, and chose to ignore the murder. However, the Genovese murder captured the public imagination and stimulated psychological research into bystander behaviour.
Source: New York Times, 27 March 1964

1. How could you explain these events according to the individual and dispositional hypotheses?
2. What do you think you would have done?

THE PSYCHOLOGY BEING INVESTIGATED

Diffusion of responsibility

Latane and Darley (1968) proposed that the key issue in deciding whether we help or not is whether we see it as our personal responsibility to do so. One reason why groups of people do not help individuals in need is that responsibility is shared equally among the group so that each person has only a small portion of responsibility. Latane and Darley called this idea diffusion of responsibility. In a series of laboratory experiments they demonstrated that the more people who are present in an emergency, the less likely people are to help.

ASK YOURSELF
What factors would make you more or less likely to help someone who is obviously in trouble and asking for help?

AIM

The researchers wanted to extend early studies of bystander behaviour in several key ways. Their aims were:

1. To study bystander behaviour outside the laboratory, in a realistic setting where participants would have a clear view of the victim.

2. To see whether helping behaviour was affected by four variables: the victim's responsibility for being in a situation where they needed help, the race of the victim, the effect of modelling helping behaviour and the size of the group.

METHOD

Participants

An estimated total of around 4450 passengers travelled in the trains targeted by the researchers. These were all regarded by the researchers as "unsolicited participants". An average of 43 people were present in each carriage in which the procedure was conducted. An average of eight were in the immediate or "critical" area. The racial mix of passengers was estimated as 45 per cent black and 55 per cent white.

Design

The study was a field experiment carried out on trains on the New York subway. The trains chosen for use were those running between 11 a.m. and 3 p.m. during the period of 15 April to 26 June 1968. One particular stretch of track was targeted where there was a 7.5 minute gap between two stations. A single trial was a non-stop ride between 59th Street and 125th Street.

Procedure

The procedure involved a male experimenter faking collapse on a train between stops, in order to see whether he was helped by other passengers. Figure 14.1 shows the layout of the adjacent and critical areas of the subway car.

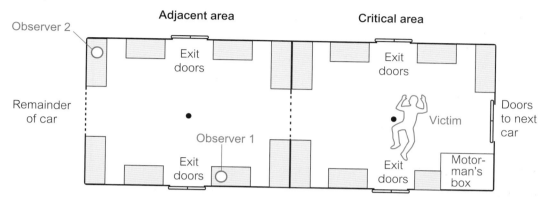

▲ **Figure 14.1** Layout of adjacent and critical areas of the subway car

Source: Based on Piliavin, Rodin and Piliavin (1969: 291)

Four IVs were manipulated in the procedure:

▶ Victim's responsibility: operationalised as carrying a cane (ill – low responsibility) or smelling of alcohol and carrying a bottle wrapped in a paper bag (drunk – high responsibility).

▶ Victim's race: operationalised as black or white.

▶ Presence of a model: operationalised as whether a male confederate; either close to or distant from the victim; helped after 70 or 150 seconds.

▶ Number of bystanders: operationalised as how many people were present in the vicinity.

For this study, four different teams were used to collect data over 103 trials. Each team consisted of four Columbia General Studies students – two males and two females. In each team the two males played the roles of victim and model helper. Each male taking the role of victim took part in both conditions used: drunk and ill. In one of the teams, the victim was black. The two females recorded the results.

For each trial, a team boarded the train using different doors. The female confederates sat outside of the critical area and recorded all data covertly. The male model and the male victim stood. The victim always stood next to a metal pole in the critical area. Shortly after the train had passed the first station (usually after around 70 seconds), the victim staggered and collapsed. Until any help was given to him, he lay on the floor looking at the ceiling.

If the victim received no help by the time the train got to the next station, the model helped him back onto his feet. At the stop, the team got off the train. The team then boarded the next train going in the other direction and repeated the procedure. Between six and eight trials were completed on a single day. All trials on a given day used the same victim condition (e.g. drunk).

The victim

All victims were males aged 26–35. Three of them were white and one was black. All dressed identically in Eisenhower jackets, old trousers and no tie. For 38 of the trials, the victim would smell of alcohol and carried a bottle of it in a brown bag. For the remaining 65 trials, the victims appeared to be sober but carried a black cane.

The model

Four males, aged 24–29, and identically dressed in casual clothes, took the role of models of helping behaviour. Four model conditions were applied to both apparently drunk and ill victims:

- Critical area – early: the model stood in the critical area and helped after 70 seconds.
- Critical area – late: the model stood in the critical area and helped after 150 seconds.
- Adjacent area – early: the model stood in the adjacent area and helped after 70 seconds.
- Adjacent area – late: the model stood in the adjacent area and helped after 150 seconds.

Whenever the model had to give assistance to the victim, he would help him into a sitting position and stay with him for the rest of the trial.

The DV – helping – was measured in terms of:

- time taken for first passenger to help
- total number of passengers who helped.

For each trial, one of the observers noted the race, sex and location of every person in the critical area. She also counted the total number of people in the subway car and recorded the total number of people who gave help, alongside their race, sex and location. The other observer recorded the race, sex and location of every person in the adjacent area. She also recorded the time taken for the first person to help. In addition, she recorded the amount of time it took someone to help *after* the model had gone to help the victim. Both of the observers recorded the comments of people in the subway car. They also attempted to get comments from the person sitting next to them.

The researchers noted that in the end there were more cane trials than drunk trials and that these were not evenly distributed across the race of the victim. Teams 1 and 2 (both white victims) began on day 1 with the cane condition. Teams 3 and 4 (one white and one black victim) began with the drunk condition. They were supposed to alternate each day. On day 4, team 2 did not do as instructed and ran cane trials instead of drunk trials as the victim did not like playing the drunk man.

TEST YOURSELF
Outline four controls used in this study. How were the participants recruited? What ethical issues are problems for this study?

RESULTS

According to researchers:

> "The victim with the cane received spontaneous help, that is, before the model acted, on 62 of the 65 trials. Even the drunk received spontaneous help on 19 of the 38 trials" (Piliavin, Rodin and Piliavin 1969: 292).

Table 14.1 shows the results of trials where help was given.

Trials	White victims		Black victims	
	Cane	Drunk	Cane	Drunk
No model	100%	100%	100%	73%
Number of trials run	54	11	8	11
Model trials	100%	77%	–	67%
Number of trials run	3	13	0	3
Total number of trials	57	24	8	14

▲ **Table 14.1** Percentage of trials on which help was given, by race and condition of victim, and total number of trials run in each condition

Piliavin, Rodin and Piliavin (1969: 292)

The differences cannot be attributable to the number of people in the carriage as the mean number for the cane trials was 45 and for the drunk trials it was 40. There was an expectation that the time taken to help spontaneously would be long (based on previous research). This was certainly not the case for the cane condition as on only 3 of the 65 trials did the model initiate help. The model was less likely to initiate help for the drunk victim.

Table 14.2 shows the data broken into two groups: trials where help was given before 70 seconds has elapsed (when the model would initiate help) and trials where help was only given after the 70 seconds had elapsed.

Trials in which help was offered:	Total number of trials		% of trial on which 1+ persons left critical area		% of trials on which 1+ comments were recorded		Mean number of comments	
	White victim	Black victim	White victim	Black victim	White victim	Black victim	White victim	Black victim
Before 70 sec.								
Cane	52	7	4%	14%	21%	0%	.27	.00
Drunk	5	4	20%	0%	80%	50%	1.00	.50
Total	57	11	5%	9%	26%	18%	.33	.18
After 70 sec.								
Cane	5	1	40%	–	60%	–	.80	–
Drunk	19	10	42%	60%	100%	70%	2.00	.90
Total	24	11	42%	64%	96%	64%	1.75	.82

▲ **Table 14.2** Time and responses to the incident

Source: Piliavin, Rodin and Piliavin (1969: 293)

It is clear that there was more spontaneous help for the cane victim than the drunk victim. When the victim was in the drunk condition, significantly more people left the critical area after 70 seconds (especially if the drunk victim was black). Also, significantly more comments were recorded from participants after 70 seconds (especially if the drunk victim was white). In 60 per cent of the 81 trials where a victim received help, it was from more than one "good Samaritan" participant irrespective of condition or race of victim. However, we do not know if the additional helpers were there to help the victim or give support to the first person who helped.

On average, 60 per cent of participants in the critical area were male. However, of the 81 spontaneous first helpers, 90 per cent were male. Therefore, men were significantly more likely to help than women ($p < 0.001$). In addition, of the 81 first helpers, 64 per cent were white but this did not differ significantly from the 55 per cent expected based on the racial distributions in the subway car. There were 65 trials where spontaneous help was given to white victims. In these cases, 68 per cent of the helpers were white. This was a significant result ($p < 0.05$). In the 16 trials where spontaneous help was given to black victims, 50 per cent of these helpers were white. Table 14.3 shows the distribution of helpers broken down by race of helper and victim.

When the victim was drunk there was mainly same-race helping. The researchers noted that this "… interesting tendency toward same-race helping only in the case of the drunk victim may reflect more empathy, sympathy, and trust toward victims of one's own racial group" (Piliavin et al 1969: 294). One reason why less help was given to the drunk victim is that the situation is potentially more dangerous than the cane situation and people may feel blame, fear and disgust towards the drunk victim.

It should also be noted that in 21 of the 103 trials, a total of 34 participants left the critical area to move away from the victim. This was seen more when the victim was drunk. In addition, they were much more likely to leave in trials where no one helped in the first 70 seconds. Even though it did not reach significance ($p < 0.08$), participants were more likely to leave the critical area if the victim was black. However, this could be because there were more trials run when the black victim was drunk compared to being in the cane condition.

Race of helper	White victims			Black victims			All victims		
	Cane	Drunk	Total	Cane	Drunk	Total	Cane	Drunk	Total
Same as victim	34	10	44	2	6	8	36	16	52
Different from victim	20	1	21	6	2	8	26	3	29
Total	54	11	65	8	8	16	62	19	81

▲ **Table 14.3** Spontaneous helping of cane and drunk by race of helper and race victim

Source: Piliavin, Rodin and Piliavin (1969: 294)

Finally, qualitative data that was recorded came mainly from female participants with comments such as "It's for men to help him", "I wish I could help him. I'm not strong enough" and "You feel so bad that you don't know what to do."

CONCLUSION

Piliavin and his colleagues admitted that the situation they set up was unusual in that their participants were trapped in a carriage with a collapsed person and therefore could not simply walk away as they could normally. Based on this study, the following occurs in this situation:

▶ A person who appears to be ill is more likely to receive help than a person who appears to be drunk.

▶ Men are more likely to help another man than women are.

▶ People are slightly more likely to help someone of their own ethnic group, especially when that person appears to be drunk.

▶ There is no strong relationship between size of group and likelihood of helping. The small correlation between group size and helping behaviour is positive rather than negative. Therefore, there is no support for diffusion of responsibility.

▶ The longer an incident goes on, the less likely people are to help (even if help is modelled), the more likely people are to leave the area, and the more likely they are to discuss the incident.

SUMMARY

Research method (main)	Field experiment
Other technique(s)	Observations
Sample	An estimated total of around 4450 passengers
Sampling technique	Opportunity
Experimental design	Independent groups
IV	• Victim's responsibility: operationalised as carrying a cane (ill – low responsibility) or smelling of alcohol and carrying a bottle wrapped in a paper bag (drunk – high responsibility). • Victim's race: operationalised as black or white. • Presence of a model: operationalised as whether a male confederate; either close to or distant from the victim; helped after 70 or 150 seconds. • Number of bystanders: operationalised as however many people were present in the vicinity.
DV	The amount of people who helped the victim, the speed it took people to help the victim
Quantitative data	As above
Qualitative data	Comments made from the passengers who witnessed the events

EVALUATION

Evaluation	General evaluation (field experiments)	Related to Piliavin *et al*
Strength	As field experiments take place in a realistic setting, it is said that they have ecological validity.	The setting was a subway train which is not artificial: travelling on these trains is a real situation that many people find themselves in daily. Even the event is something that could easily happen, so the study has ecological validity.
Strength	As participants do not know they are taking part in a study, there will be few or no demand characteristics so behaviour is more likely to be natural and valid.	As the setting is natural and no one was aware that the whole situation was staged, there was very little chance that anyone would have shown behaviour to fit the aim of the study. Therefore, the behaviour shown by participants was natural and so valid.
Weakness	Situational variables can be difficult to control so sometimes it is difficult to know whether it is the IV affecting the DV. It could be an uncontrolled variable causing the DV to change.	The positioning of people in the carriages could not be controlled for, and this is just one such example of an uncontrolled aspect. People may not have noticed the incident or may have ignored it (e.g. if they were reading) so it may not have been the type of victim affecting helping levels.
Weakness	As participants do not know they are taking part in a study, there are issues with breaking ethical guidelines such as guidelines relating to informed consent and deception.	Participants did not know they were taking part in a study – they were deceived; obviously, informed consent could not be taken from them prior to the collapse. This goes against ethical guidelines (although formal guidelines were not established at the time of the study).

Other evaluation points include the following:

▶ Usefulness: the study told us that type of victim can affect how long a person takes to help or whether a person helps at all. This could be used to educate people that in an emergency we should help others no matter who they are because the longer it takes to help, the more likely it is that the person will suffer more in the long term (especially if medical attention is required).

▶ Generalisability: it would be difficult to generalise past the sample itself as participants were all urban dwellers who were (presumably) used to travelling on a subway train. People in urban areas are more used to deindividuating (losing their sense of identity) and feeling "anonymous" whereas people who live in rural areas of even a different city might act differently.

▶ Ethics – deception: as participants did not know that they were being presented with a fake event, they believed that what they were witnessing was real, so they were deceived. Also, they did they not know they were part of a study.

▶ Ethics – informed consent: participants did not know they were part of a study, so they could not give their permission to be used in it.

▶ Ethics – protection: witnessing someone collapse can be a distressing (and some people did leave the scene quickly); participants were not protected from experiencing psychological stress.

CHALLENGE YOURSELF
Evaluate this study in terms of the use of observations and the collection of quantitative and qualitative data.

▲ What makes people help or not help people in need?

ISSUES AND DEBATES

The following table discusses the Piliavin *et al* study in terms of the core issues and debates for AS Level.

Application to everyday life	The findings of this study can be used to educate people about bystanders' intervention. To try to break stereotypes, children could be educated about helping others no matter who those in need are.
Individual and situational explanations	The results clearly show a **situational** effect as there was variation in who was helped and when. The subway train and types of victim formed the situation that participants found themselves in and this then caused certain behaviours such as helping or not helping. However, an **individual** effect might have an influence – as the sample was large and varied it might have been a certain personality type that was making people help or not help.
Nature versus nurture	Not applicable
The use of children	Not applicable
The use of animals	Not applicable

CHALLENGE YOURSELF
Identify two other applications to everyday life this study could have. Explain who would benefit from these applications.

YAMAMOTO, HUMLE AND TANAKA

Research date: 2012

BACKGROUND

We know that humans have the ability to show altruistic behaviours. Some psychologists believe this is one way in which we maintain cooperative societies. What of non-humans though? Many studies have shown us why animals may behave altruistically but at the expense of how they do it. Yamamoto and his colleagues believed that the cognitive mechanisms involved in non-human helping behaviour are not well known. By studying these we may then understand the evolution of cooperation. This is because if we are ever to deepen our understanding of this potential evolutionary behaviour, we need to know if and how animals understand the goals and intentions of others.

THE PSYCHOLOGY BEING INVESTIGATED

The main concepts under investigation in this study are:

▶ altruism – the willingness to do certain things for others even if it has a disadvantage to yourself

▶ prosocial behaviour, which refers to any action or behaviour that has the intention of helping others

▶ empathy – the ability to share someone else's emotional state by imagining what it would be like to be in that situation

▶ instrumental helping, described in this study as "help and care based on the cognitive appreciation of the need or situation of others" (Yamamoto *et al*, 2012: 3588).

ASK YOURSELF
Do you think that non-humans help each other out in the same ways as humans? Think of specific examples to enhance your answer.

AIM

1. To investigate whether chimpanzees have the ability and flexibility to help another chimpanzee depending on its specific needs.

2. The research team had noted that chimpanzees seldom help others without being asked and the team wanted to investigate this too.

METHOD

Participants

Five chimpanzees, called Ai, Cleo, Pal, Ayumu and Pan, were participants in the study. They were all socially housed at the Primate Research Institute in Kyoto University. They had all participated in previous studies about helping behaviour. They were paired with kin as follows: Ai (mother) was paired with Ayumu (juvenile); Pan (mother) was paired with Pal (juvenile); Chloe (mother – not tested in the experimental condition) was paired with Cleo (juvenile). All pairs had shown tool-giving interactions in previous research. All were labelled as experts at the tool-use tasks used in this study.

Design and procedure

The study had been approved by the Animal Care Committee at Kyoto University. The paired chimpanzees were tested in adjacent experimental booths measuring 136 × 142 centimetres and 155 × 142 centimetres; both 200 centimetres high. A hole measuring 12.5 × 35 centimetres was in the wall divider separating the two chimpanzees. It was about 1 metre above the floor. The experiment was designed so that it required the chimpanzees to select and transfer an appropriate tool to a conspecific partner so the partner could solve a task and obtain a drink of juice as a reward. The recipient chimpanzee could not reach any of the available tools in the adjoining booth. This chimpanzee could show that it wanted a tool by poking an arm through a hole in the panel that separated the two booths. The helper chimpanzee had to select a tool from a box of seven objects (e.g. a stick, a straw, a hose, a chain, a rope, a brush and a belt) to help the other chimpanzee complete the task. Only the straw or the stick could help "solve" the task to gain the juice reward. Before the experimental phase of the study, there were eight, five-minute trials (one per day) that allowed the chimpanzees to explore the seven items. Figure 15.1 shows the three conditions, which are explained below.

The researchers noted the following about the design of the study:

▶ The chimpanzees were all trained to solve the problem presented to them but no other training or shaping of behaviour had been conducted on them.

▶ The chimpanzees were allowed to communicate "naturally" to one another without symbols or any form of artificial communication techniques.

Each chimpanzee went through three tasks:

1. The first "Can see" condition. One chimpanzee was placed in a booth with a box full of seven different objects, including, for example, a stick, a straw, a brush and some paper clips connected together. Another chimpanzee was in an adjacent booth and could be seen. This chimpanzee needed to be given a tool that could help it to obtain some juice that was just out of reach. There was a hole in the wall

▲ **Figure 15.1** The first "Can see", the "Cannot see" and the second "Can see" conditions

Source: Yamamoto, Humle and Tanaka (2012: 3590)

between the two chimpanzees that objects could be passed through. The box of objects was out of reach of the chimpanzee that wanted the juice but it could put its arm through the hole to request a tool. This chimpanzee needed the stick first to reach the juice and then the straw so that it could drink the juice.

2. The "Cannot see" condition. This was the same set-up but the wall between the two booths was opaque so that the helper chimpanzee could not see what the other chimpanzee required. However, there was

a hole about 1 metre above the ground so the helper chimpanzee could, if it wanted to, stand up and look through the hole to see what the other chimpanzee required.

3. The second "Can see" condition was a repeat of the first "Can see" condition. This was used to see whether the experimental order was having an effect on object choice.

For the task to be "solved" either the straw or stick would have to be chosen and given to the other chimpanzee in the adjacent booth. The chimpanzees could communicate freely between each other during the tasks (in contrast to previous studies that allowed chimpanzees to communicate using artificial symbols called lexigrams). Before the trials took place, the chimpanzees were allowed to explore the box of tools freely with no situation to solve. In 5 per cent of these trials, a chimpanzee passed a tool through the hole.

A total of 48 trials were conducted (a random order of 24 stick-use and 24 straw-use situations) for the "Can see" condition. After this, a further 48 trials were conducted for the "Cannot see" condition. If the performance differed between these two conditions, another 48 trials of the "Can see" condition were conducted. A trial would begin when the helper chimpanzee had the box of seven items. The trial was recorded as ended when the juice was obtained or when five minutes had passed without any success in obtaining it. There were two, three or four trials per day.

All of the trials were recorded on three video cameras. An offer of a tool was counted when the helper chimpanzee held out a tool toward the recipient chimpanzee (however, for this to be counted the chimpanzees did not have to exchange the tool). Only the first tool offer was used in the analyses. Object offer was categorised in two ways: upon request (the recipient requested a tool and the helper gave one) or voluntary (the helper gave a tool with no request). If a tool was taken by the recipient without the helper knowing, it was recorded as "no offer".

TEST YOURSELF
Draw a flow diagram for the procedure of the first "Can see" condition. Ask your teacher to locate this study online. Using the link provided, watch the video footage of the study.

RESULTS

These are the results broken down for each task.

1. In the first "Can see" condition, irrespective of which object was chosen, in 90.8 per cent of trials an object from the box was offered to help solve the task. Of these object offers, 90 per cent came after the chimpanzee trying to obtain the juice had requested help (e.g. placed its hand through the hole between the two booths). Four of the chimpanzees offered the straw or stick first significantly more frequently than any other object in the box: Ai on 87.5 per cent of her trials; Cleo 97.4 per cent; Pal 93.5 per cent; Ayumu 78 per cent; all $p < 0.04$. Pan offered the brush first on 79.5 per cent of her trials. This would appear to show that the chimpanzees could distinguish between potential tools and useless objects. However, they had previous experience of the stick and straw. The first offer of a straw or stick was further analysed. When the stick was needed, the stick was offered first most often. The same pattern emerged for when a straw was needed.

2. In the "Cannot see" condition the chimpanzees offered something from the box in 95.8 per cent of trials. Of these object offers, 71.7 per cent came after a request. Four of the chimpanzees offered the straw or stick first significantly more frequently than any other object (Ai in 89.4 per cent of her trials, Cleo 88.9 per cent, Pal 100 per cent, Ayumu 93 per cent). Pan continued to offer a brush first (in 55.3 per cent of her trials). Ayumu was the only chimpanzee to look through the hole. In terms of offering the stick when the stick was needed and the straw when the straw was needed, it was virtually a 50/50 split in this condition.

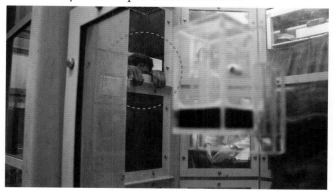

▲ **Figure 15.2** Ayumu standing up and assessing his mother's situation by peaking through the hole in the opaque panel wall separating the two booths

Source: Yamamoto, Humle and Tanaka (2012: 3591)

3. In the second "Can see" condition only three chimpanzees were tested (Ai, Cleo and Pal). In 97.4 per cent of trials something was offered from the box, with upon-request offers accounting for 79.4 per cent of all offers. As with the other trials, the stick or straw was offered most frequently first (Ai in 81.3 per cent of her trials; Cleo 95.7 per cent; Pal 100 per cent). They also gave the "correct" tool most often first (stick when stick was needed, etc.).

Figure 15.3 shows the combined results for Ai, Cleo and Pal (the chimpanzees that participated in all three tasks).

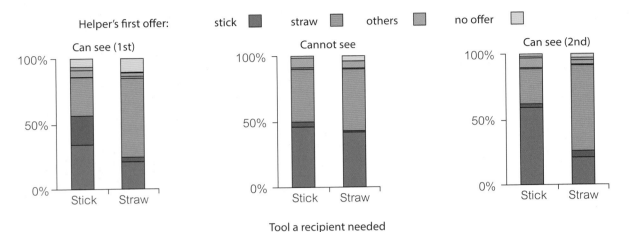

▲ **Figure 15.3** Offerings of stick or straw

Source: Based on Yamamoto, Humle and Tanaka (2012: 3590)

Finally, Table 15.1 shows each chimpanzee's first-offer ratio of stick or straw across the three tasks.

Chimpanzee	"Can see" (first)	"Cannot see"	"Can see" (second)
Ai	**0.015**	0.54	**0.008**
Cleo	**0.031**	0.61	**<0.001**
Pal	**0.008**	0.0484	**0.002**
Ayumu	**0.004**	**<0.001**	–
Pan	0.48	0.44	–

▲ **Table 15.1** Stick or straw offers by each chimpanzee across the three tasks

Values in boldface type indicate a significant difference ($p < 0.05$).

Source: Yamamoto, Humle and Tanaka (2012: 3589)

CONCLUSION

This study provides evidence for chimpanzees' flexible targeted helping based on an understanding of the needs or goals of another chimpanzee. When the chimpanzees could see what was needed they tended to select the most appropriate tool for the job. However, they still seldom helped others without a direct request.

SUMMARY

Research method (main)	Experimental
Other technique(s)	–
Sample	Chimpanzees: five mother-offspring pairings
Sampling technique	Opportunity
Experimental design	Repeated measures
IV	"Can see" and "Cannot see" conditions
DV	Proportion of trials where the stick or straw was given or not given; which tool was offered
Quantitative data	As above
Qualitative data	–

EVALUATION

Evaluation	General evaluation (laboratory experiments)	Related to Yamamoto *et al*
Strength	Laboratory experiments have high levels of standardisation and so can be replicated to test for reliability.	This study had a standardised procedure including experimental booths and the choice of items for the chimpanzees to use. This means other researchers could easily replicate this study to test for reliability.
Strength	As laboratory experiments have high levels of control, researchers can be more confident it is the IV directly affecting the DV.	As there were many controls (e.g. the tools available for use and the "Can see" and "Cannot see" procedures), the researchers could be confident that it was type of condition (whether the chimpanzees could see the objects or not) that affected their ability to choose the correct tool to complete the task.
Weakness	In many laboratory experiments participants take part in tasks that are nothing like real-life ones, so the tasks lack mundane realism.	The task of helping a fellow chimpanzee in an experimental booth with a limited amount of items is not an everyday activity for chimpanzees. Therefore, the study may lack mundane realism.

The debate about the use of animals below can also form part of the evaluation of this study. Other evaluation points include the following:

▶ The researchers used a repeated measures design. This reduces the effects of participant variables affecting the DVs as the same chimpanzees participated in all tasks. This means that the researchers could be confident it was the condition of being able to see or not see their fellow chimpanzee that affected chimpanzees' correct tool choice.

▶ Generalisability: only five chimpanzee pairings were used and they may not be representative of how all chimpanzees help each other during tasks. The chimpanzees used were bred in captivity so it might be difficult to generalise the findings to wild chimpanzees' behaviour in helping other chimpanzees, for instance.

 CHALLENGE YOURSELF
Evaluate this study in terms of validity, reliability and sampling technique.

ISSUES AND DEBATES

The following table discusses the Yamamoto *et al* study
in terms of the core issues and debates for AS Level.

Application to everyday life	The findings may be generalisable to children in terms of development and education about helping others. If children and chimpanzees take the same development path we could educate children about how we can ask other people whether they want help even if they have not directly asked us to help them.
Individual and situational explanations	Not applicable
Nature versus nurture	Not applicable
The use of children	Not applicable
The use of animals	**Numbers:** there were five pairings used in the study so the researchers probably used the least amount of chimpanzees possible to still fulfil the aims and goals of the study. **Housing:** the chimpanzees were all socially housed at the Primate Research Institute in Kyoto University. All of the chimpanzees had participated in other studies about social behaviour. **Deprivation and aversive stimuli:** none of the chimpanzees went through any procedures that deprived them of food or used aversive stimuli to train them to complete the given tasks.

CHALLENGE YOURSELF
Identify two other applications to everyday life this
study could have. Explain who would benefit from
these applications.

16 EXAM CENTRE: AS LEVEL

The questions, example answers, marks awarded and/or comments that appear in this book/CD were written by the author. In examination, the way marks would be awarded to answers like these may be different.

COMPONENT 1

Approaches, issues and debates

This component constitutes 50 per cent of the AS Level qualification and 25 per cent of the A Level qualification. You need to have studied *all* 12 core studies alongside methodology and the 5 issues and debates named in the syllabus. For the core studies, you need to know:

▶ the psychology that is being investigated

▶ the background to the study

▶ the aim(s) of the study

▶ the procedure of the study

▶ any relevant ethical issues surrounding the study

▶ the results of the study (both quantitative and qualitative where appropriate)

▶ the conclusion(s) of the study

▶ the strengths and weaknesses of the study.

In addition, you need to:

▶ know about the research method(s) used

▶ consider how each study fits into the five named issues and debates

▶ apply findings to the real world.

The five issues and debates that need to be covered (and they do not apply to all studies) are:

▶ the application of psychology to real life

▶ individual and situational explanations

▶ nature versus nurture

▶ the use of children in psychological research

▶ the use of animals in psychological research.

For more information, see pages 25–26.

The four approaches need to be covered in terms of the two main assumptions listed in the syllabus; for details see page 27.

The examination contains a range of short answer questions (which carry usually no more than 6 marks maximum) that test your knowledge of the study, how it was run, what the results mean and what were its strengths and weaknesses. There are questions that test your knowledge of the five issues and debates and how they relate to named studies. The examination is likely to end with a 10-mark evaluation-based question on one of the 12 core studies.

See the Sample Assessment Material on the Cambridge International Examinations website for an example examination. The first examination is in 2018 so from then onwards many more examination papers will become available.

This examination lasts 1 hour 30 minutes and 60 marks are available.

COMPONENT 2

Research methods

This component constitutes 50 per cent of the AS Level qualification and 25 per cent of the A Level qualification. You still need to know about the 12 core studies but you also need to know all of the research methods that are presented in that section of the syllabus. All of these can be examined so you cannot select which research methods to learn; you must learn each one.

There are three sections to the examination:

1. Section A: short-answer questions based on the core studies (22 marks)

2. Section B: scenario-based questions about an unseen study (24 marks)

3. Section C: a design-based question divided into two parts (14 marks).

Section A contains a range of short-answer questions linking the research methods section of the syllabus to the 12 core studies. You will need to show your knowledge of research methods through examples from the core studies.

Section B consists of questions based on different scenarios presented. You will have to apply your knowledge of the research methods section of the syllabus to the different scenarios, answering a series of questions.

Section C is a design-based question. You will be expected to design a study based on the given information in the question (10 marks) then make some evaluative judgment about your design (4 marks).

See the Sample Assessment Material on the Cambridge International Examinations website for an example examination. The first examination is in 2018 so from then on many more examination papers will become available.

This examination lasts 1 hour 30 minutes and 60 marks are available.

17 ISSUES AND DEBATES FOR A LEVEL

For the examination you need to know about a series of issues and debates surrounding psychology and psychological research. Five of these have already been covered at AS Level. They are:

- ▶ the application of psychology to everyday life
- ▶ individual and situational explanations
- ▶ nature versus nurture
- ▶ the use of children in psychological research
- ▶ the use of animals in psychological research.

At A Level, there are five more issues and debates that need to be covered.

CULTURAL BIAS

This refers to research being focused on one particular culture or only being applied to one particular culture. Researchers might then assume that the findings of one study relate to *all* cultures and this could clearly not be the case. In addition, researchers might only interpret results from the perspective of their own culture.

Cultural bias can only generate problems as it means that researchers may be trying to apply their cultural norms to another culture without fully appreciating how that different culture behaves. An extreme version can be when a researcher begins to derogate another culture based on his or her own cultural beliefs, which is a form of ethnocentrism.

REDUCTIONISM

This is when a psychologist believes that a complex behaviour can be explained by reducing it to one single cause or a series of component parts. For example, a researcher might state that some aspect of personality is caused only by biological mechanism. This could easily overlook social and psychological factors that could also be affecting personality. It is the opposite of holism, which is when research examines all possible angles to explain a single behaviour or set of behaviours.

Strength of reductionism	Weakness of reductionism
It allows research to be conducted that can analyse a specific area or behaviour in depth, to investigate how it affects humans.	It overlooks other factors that could be affecting the behaviour of people.

PSYCHOMETRICS

These are usually paper-and-pen tasks that literally mean "measurement of the mind". Examples are an intelligence quotient (IQ) test, an aptitude test or a test to help with educational needs. They are standardised, so people's results can be compared to a "norm" to see how intelligent they are or to what extent they have a particular personality.

Strengths of psychometrics	Problems with using psychometrics
As these tests are standardised on a large sample of people, they can be seen as being more objective and scientific. Comparisons can be *useful* as people's results are compared on the same, standardised scale. As they are standardised, they are reliable measures – we can use them again and again to see if we get similar results.	There may be issues with validity. Is the test actually measuring the behaviour it is supposed to measure? For example, some psychologists believe that an IQ test does *not* measure intelligence, but instead measures someone's ability to complete an IQ test. If tests measure specific cultural knowledge rather than the behaviour they are supposed to measure, they will be seen as ethnocentric.

DETERMINISM

This is the idea that people's actions and thoughts are totally determined by external and internal mechanisms operating on them. That is, people's behaviours and cognitions are caused (determined) by factors that make them predictable. For example, a researcher may believe that depression is caused by neurochemistry or another researcher might believe that aggression is caused by observation and imitation. Belief in determinism is the opposite to belief in free will, which argues that individuals choose their own behaviour and thoughts. Determinism is therefore about how factors outside of the individual are causing behaviours to occur (environmental determinism) or from within the individual (biological determinism).

Strength of determinism	Weakness of determinism
It allows research to take place that is focused and can unearth whether a single factor is causing a particular outcome. This can help to generate further research to see whether it is just that factor that is the cause, or a combination of factors.	It ignores the idea of free will. This is when people choose their own behaviours and thoughts based on a variety of factors. Soft determinism does state that people choose their own pathway in life, but that their behaviour is still subject to either biological or environmental pressures.

LONGITUDINAL RESEARCH

This is when the same set of participants is followed over a longer period of time to examine areas such as developmental changes. They may repeat similar tasks once per year, for example.

Strengths of longitudinal studies	Problems with longitudinal studies
These studies allow analysis of how behaviour develops over time (e.g. throughout childhood) and long-term effects (e.g. of life events on development). Individual differences between people in the study are controlled as the same people are tracked over a set amount of time. Therefore, findings are more likely to be valid.	Not all participants will want to be followed for the length of the study and will drop out (this is called "participant attrition"). This can reduce the sample size and then the generalisability and/or validity of the study as time progresses. Psychologists could become attached to participants and be subjective in their analysis of the data.

18 PSYCHOLOGY AND ABNORMALITY

All studies marked with an asterisk are not directly named in the syllabus but the information included in these studies will help the student to answer questions on the topic covered. The examination will not ask about these studies by name or ask for specific findings.

18.1 SCHIZOPHRENIA SPECTRUM AND PSYCHOTIC DISORDERS

CHARACTERISTICS OF SCHIZOPHRENIA SPECTRUM AND PSYCHOTIC DISORDERS

Definitions, types, examples and case studies of schizophrenia and psychotic disorders

Schizophrenia was first called "dementia praecox" (premature dementia) as it affects people's thoughts, emotions and behaviours. Below are the types of schizophrenia currently recognised and the characteristics that need to be shown for people to be diagnosed.

Types

Schizophrenia is an umbrella term used to outline a range of different psychotic disorders that affect thoughts, emotions and behaviours. These are the main diagnostic types:

▶ Simple – when people gradually withdraw themselves from reality.

▶ Paranoid – when people have delusional thoughts and hallucinations and may experience delusions of grandeur.

▶ Catatonic – when people have motor activity disturbances that may involve them sitting or standing in the same position for hours.

▶ Disorganised – when people have disorganised behaviour, thoughts and speech patterns. They may also experience auditory hallucinations.

▶ Undifferentiated – when an individual does not fit into one of the types above but is still experiencing affected thoughts and behaviours.

Characteristics

For a diagnosis of schizophrenia, the *Diagnostic and Statistical Manual of Mental Disorders* (DSM) outlines the following:

▶ The person shows two of the following for at least one month: delusions, hallucinations, disorganised speech, disorganised or catatonic behaviour, flattening of emotions; or continual voices in the head giving a running commentary of what is happening.

▶ The person must show social and/or occupational functioning that has declined.

▶ There must be no evidence that medical factors are causing the behaviours.

Symptoms can be split into positive and negative:

▶ Positive refers to the *addition* of certain behaviours. For example, hallucinations, delusions of grandeur or control and insertion of thoughts are all positive.

▶ Negative refers to the *removal* of certain behaviours. For example, poverty of speech, withdrawal from society and flattening of mood are all negative.

CHALLENGE YOURSELF
Find two real-life case studies of people being diagnosed with schizophrenia or living with schizophrenia.

Psychotic disorders are those mental health disorders that cause people to have atypical thoughts and perceptions about themselves and the world around them. These are disorders where people "lose touch with reality" and they tend to experience hallucinations and/or delusions.

Schizophrenia and delusional disorder

The following description and guidelines are taken from the "ICD-10 Classification of Mental and Behavioural Disorders, Clinical descriptions and diagnostic guidelines".

F22.0 Delusional disorder

This group of disorders is characterized by the development either of a single delusion or of a set of related delusions which are usually persistent and sometimes lifelong. The delusions are highly variable in content. Often they are persecutory, hypochondriacal, or grandiose, but they may be concerned with litigation or jealousy, or express a conviction that the individual's body is misshapen, or that others think that he or she smells or is homosexual. Other psychopathology is characteristically absent, but depressive symptoms may be present intermittently, and olfactory and tactile hallucinations may develop in some cases. Clear and persistent auditory hallucinations (voices), schizophrenic symptoms such as delusions of control and marked blunting of affect, and definite evidence of brain disease are all incompatible with this diagnosis. However, occasional or transitory auditory hallucinations, particularly in elderly patients, do not rule out this diagnosis, provided that they are not typically schizophrenic and form only a small part of the overall clinical picture. Onset is commonly in middle age but sometimes, particularly in the case of beliefs about having a misshapen body, in early adult life. The content of the delusion, and the timing of its emergence, can often be related to the individual's life situation, e.g. persecutory delusions in members of minorities. Apart from actions and attitudes directly related to the delusion or delusional system, affect, speech, and behaviour are normal.

Diagnostic guidelines

Delusions constitute the most conspicuous or the only clinical characteristic. They must be present for at least 3 months and be clearly personal rather than subcultural. Depressive symptoms or even a full-blown depressive episode may be present intermittently, provided that the delusions persist at times when there is no disturbance of mood. There must be no evidence of brain disease, no or only occasional auditory hallucinations, and no history of schizophrenic symptoms (delusions of control, thought broadcasting, etc.).

Source: The ICD-10 Classification of Mental and Behavioural Disorders, Clinical descriptions and diagnostic guidelines, WHO, pp. 84–85

CHALLENGE YOURSELF
Find the DSM-V criteria for the diagnosis of schizophrenia and delusional disorder. Compare it to the ICD-10 criteria.

Issues and debates tracker: Both the ICD and DSM methods of diagnosing schizophrenia may only be based on the view of one set of cultural norms (e.g. US cultural norms for DSM) so could be viewed as culturally biased. This might make it difficult to diagnose people correctly in other cultures. However, both methods have good application to everyday life as they can be used to diagnose people so that they receive the most appropriate treatment.

Symptom assessment using virtual reality (Freeman, 2008)

Freeman (2008) introduced the idea of using virtual reality (VR) to help assess the symptoms of schizophrenia shown by patients. Studies had shown that people experiencing VR show similar physiological and psychological reactions as in the real world. Freeman identified seven ways in which VR can help with schizophrenia:

1. **Symptom assessment.** VR can provide a standardised assessment of symptoms. Patients can be presented with a neutral social situation so that any paranoid thoughts are then totally unfounded. Also, patients cannot act in a way to purposefully elicit any hostile reactions as the avatar can be "programmed' not to respond. Patients' reactions to neutral avatars can help to assess the severity of paranoid delusions.

2. **Establishing symptom correlates.** VR can provide an ideal setting to monitor behavioural and physiological correlates of any symptoms. A patient's movements can easily be tracked alongside physiological measures.

3. **Identification of predictive variables.** Pre-measures of personality and behavioural aspects of schizophrenia alongside cognitive processing can be taken and then used to predict *how* patients may react to situations presented to them in VR.

4. **Identification of differential predictors.** Other predictors can be assessed to see what effect they have on patients in the VR setting (e.g. level of social anxiety or co-morbidity of psychological issues).

5. **Identifying environmental predictors.** As the VR setting can easily be manipulated, aspects of the environment can be assessed safely. For example, social paranoia may be linked to the size of the room a patient is in, so this can be manipulated to see what the "trigger size" is.

6. **Establishing causal factors.** Experimental manipulation of factors pre-VR can help determine cause and effect. For example, Freeman states that manipulating pre-anxiety levels (e.g. anxiety-inducing, anxiety-reducing and a control) can easily be implemented to see what effect this has on patients in a controlled VR environment.

7. **Developing treatment.** This can be threefold: (1) educate patients on which factors make them better or worse; (2) expose patients to persecutory fears in the VR environment in a way that is less threatening than exposure in a real-life setting; (3) help patients learn to cope with the symptoms presented – these can be tested out in a VR setting.

Strength	Weakness
The technique has good application as it could be used by practitioners to help assess the severity of a client's psychological condition.	The assessment may still lack ecological validity as it takes place in an environment that is not natural to the client.

EXPLANATIONS OF SCHIZOPHRENIA AND DELUSIONAL DISORDER

Genetic

Genetic (Gottesman and Shields, 1972, 1976)

One argument centres on whether there is an inherited (genetic) component to schizophrenia. Many reviews have taken place but those conducted by Gottesman and Shields appear to be the ones quoted the most in the field. This review looked at adoption, twin and family studies to see whether there was a potential genetic component to schizophrenia.

With studies of twins, researchers can examine monozygotic twins (MZ: identical) and dizygotic twins (DZ: non-identical) to test whether a genetic component is seen because the monozygotic twins share all of their genetic material. Therefore, if the prevalence of schizophrenia is higher in monozygotic twins (when both twins have been diagnosed with schizophrenia) this could point towards a genetic component. Five twin studies formed the review and the results are shown in Table 18.1.1.

	N pairs and probandwise concordance		
	MZ	DZ	Country
Cannon *et al*, 1998	67: 40/87 (46%)	186: 18/195 (9%)	Finland
Franzek and Beckmann, 1998	14: 11/14 (79%)	12: 2/12 (18%)	Germany
Cardno *et al*, 1999	43: 21/50 (42%)	58: 1/57 (2%)	United Kingdom
Kläning *et al*, 2016	13: 7/16 (44%)	31: 1/31 (3%)	Denmark

Representative twin studies of schizophrenia. DZ pairs are all same-gender except for inclusion of opposite-gender in Danish sample.

Note: Standard errors for small numerators will be large.

▲ **Table 18.1.1** Concordance in recent twin studies. Concordance rates are presented without age corrections.

Source: Personal Communication, © I.I. Gottesman, May 20, 2016 and used by permission

The difference between the pairwise concordance rate and probandwise concordance rate is highlighted by Gottesman and Shields as:

"… the pairwise rate expresses the degree of concordance as the percentage of all pairs in which both twins are schizophrenic, given a specified sample of twin pairs with at least one twin schizophrenic. The probandwise rate is the percentage of independently ascertained schizophrenic twins (the probands) who have a schizophrenic co-twin" (1976: 372).

The overall results do point towards a potential genetic component to schizophrenia as the probandwise rates calculated for monozygotic twins is 35–58 per cent whereas for dizygotic twins it is 9–26 per cent so there is no overlap between the rates. The general population rate is around 1.1 per cent. However, none of the rates are 100 per cent which would mean a definite genetic cause. Gottesman and Shields concluded that, even though the data points towards some form of genetic component, the external environment must play a part in the onset of schizophrenia.

They also examined adoption studies and found a trend of an increased rate of biological relatives having schizophrenia if their adopted children were also diagnosed. This was between 12.1 per cent and 18.8 per cent for the studies reviewed.

Strengths	Weakness
The study was a thorough review of the field which allowed for a somewhat objective analysis of the field at that time. The results could have been used to help understand the potential causes of schizophrenia.	As there were different studies used, it might be difficult to "truly" compare them in a review as they may have used different criteria to diagnose schizophrenia. This might mean the review is unreliable in that aspect.

Biochemical (dopamine hypothesis)

The main idea of dopamine hypothesis is that dopaminergic systems in the brain of schizophrenics are overactive. That is, their dopamine receptors are oversensitive rather than it being a higher level of dopamine that is causing their symptoms. However, there is evidence for both:

▶ When people experience amphetamine psychosis it resembles certain types of schizophrenia. This is caused by an excess of dopamine.

▶ Drug treatment (e.g. prescribing phenothiazines) does help to treat some of the symptoms of schizophrenia but these drugs can bring about symptoms similar to Parkinson's disease, which is caused by *low* levels of dopamine.

Linstroem *et al* (1999)* used a PET scan to test the dopamine hypothesis. Ten schizophrenics and ten healthy controls were injected with a radioactively labelled chemical called L-DOPA. This is used in the production of dopamine. The PET scan could trace its usage in all participants. The L-DOPA was taken up significantly faster in the schizophrenics, pointing towards them producing more dopamine.

Arakawa *et al* (2010)* noted that a drug called perospirone, which has a high affinity to D2 dopamine receptors, had an average 75 per cent usage rate which then blocked the further production of dopamine in schizophrenics.

Seeman (2011)* reviewed the field and noted that animal models of schizophrenia pointed toward elevation in levels of D2 receptors and that antipsychotics do reverse the elevation in D2 receptors but should only be used in the short term to stop other side effects.

Cognitive

One idea is that schizophrenia is caused by faulty information processing.

Cognitive (Frith, 1992)

Frith (1992) noted that schizophrenics might have a deficient "metarepresentation" system – the system that makes people able to reflect on thoughts, emotions and behaviours. It could also be linked to theory of mind (see page 52) as it controls self-awareness and how we interpret the actions of others. These are characteristics that are lacking in some schizophrenics. Also, those showing more negative symptoms might have a dysfunctional supervisory attention system. This system is responsible for generating self-initiated actions. In one study, Frith and Done (1986) reported that when participants were asked to do things such as name as many different fruits as possible, or generate as many designs for something as possible, those with schizophrenia (with negative symptoms predominant) had great difficulty in managing this.

Frith (1992) also examined a central monitoring system. This allows us to be able to understand and label actions that we do as being controlled by ourselves. Frith had noticed that in some schizophrenics inner speech may not be recognised as being self-generated. Therefore,

when they hear "voices" it is their own voice but they are unaware that it is themselves producing inner speech and believe it is someone else.

Johnson *et al* (2013)* tested the cognitive abilities of 99 schizophrenics and 77 healthy controls on a battery of cognitive tests. It was seen that the schizophrenics performed worse across all cognitive tests including those for working memory (which involves tasks such as dealing with inner speech) and that this might be the core determinant of overall cognitive impairment in schizophrenics.

CHALLENGE YOURSELF
To what extent do you feel that schizophrenia is based in nature rather than nurture? Justify your answer.

TREATMENT AND MANAGEMENT OF SCHIZOPHRENIA AND DELUSIONAL DISORDER

Biochemical

Biochemical treatment centres on using drugs to alleviate the symptoms of schizophrenia.

Davison and Neale (1997)* noted that, from the 1950s onwards, drugs classed as phenothiazines were commonly used to treat schizophrenia. They were effective as they block dopamine receptors in the brain. However, many had "extrapyramidal side effects" which resemble symptoms of neurological diseases such as Parkinsonian-type tremors, dystonia (muscular rigidity), dyskinesia (chewing movements) and akasthesia (the inability to keep still). Second-generation antipsychotics were developed to also block dopamine receptors but produce fewer side effects and there are now third-generation antipsychotics that reportedly produce even fewer side effects.

Contemporary research still shows the effectiveness of antipsychotics in treating schizophrenia. Sarkar and Grover (2013)* conducted a meta-analysis on 15 randomised controlled studies testing the effectiveness of antipsychotics on children and adolescents diagnosed with schizophrenia. It was seen that both first- and second-generation antipsychotic drugs were superior to the placebo in alleviating symptoms. Second-generation drugs were superior overall with chlozapine being the most effective of all drugs. Extrapyramidal side effects were seen more in first-generation antipsychotics while side effects that affected metabolism were seen more often in second-generation drugs.

Ehret, Sopko and Lemieux (2010)* noted that a third-generation drug called lurasidone had been shown to be effective in four separate clinical trials, reducing both positive and negative symptoms. Noted side effects had only been nausea, vomiting and dizziness. The researchers noted that drugs such as clozapine were now showing more metabolic dysfunction side effects plus bone marrow toxicity so newer drugs needed to be developed.

Keating (2013)* noted that a first-generation drug called loxapine was now being used again as an effective treatment for agitation in schizophrenic patients by getting them to inhale it as a powder. This meant a rapid onset of effect (usually around ten minutes) by using a non-invasive method that showed few side effects.

Finally, Motiwala, Siscoe and El-Mallakh (2013)* reported on the use of depot aripiprazole for schizophrenia. Depot injections are usually given deep into a muscle and allow the administration of a sustained-action drug formulation for slow release and gradual absorption, so that the active agent can act for much longer periods than is possible with standard injections. Only one study was published in a peer review journal but it was positive in terms of effectiveness and safety so in the future this method of antipsychotic drug delivery may gain momentum.

Antipsychotics (sometimes referred to as typical antipsychotics or first-generation antipsychotics) are drugs that give people extrapyramidal side effects that are "typical" (hence their name). These include movement problems similar to the symptoms of Parkinson's disease such as stiffness and peculiar walking stances. These usually occur once patients begin their course of antipsychotics.

Atypical antipsychotics do not usually cause movement-related side effects and, in theory, should produce fewer overall side effects. Longer-term issues such as tardive dyskinesia (abnormal facial, tongue and mouth movements) are also lessened using atypical antipsychotics as these drugs do not increase the production of prolactin (which happens with typical antipsychotics).

Electro-convulsive therapy (ECT)

ECT is basically a procedure where a person receives a brief application of electricity to induce a seizure. Early attempts at this were not pleasant but nowadays patients are anaesthetised and given muscle relaxants. Electrodes are fitted to specific areas of the head and a small electrical current is passed through them for no longer than one second. The seizure may last up to one minute. The patient regains consciousness in around 15 minutes. There will always be debate about whether ECT should be used for any mental health issue as clinicians and psychologists are divided on the severity of the therapy and the longer-term side effects. ECT is now mainly used for depression (see page 123), but there has been research conducted on the use of ECT with schizophrenics.

Zervas, Theleritis and Soldatos (2012)* conducted a review of the use of ECT in schizophrenia. They looked at four issues: symptom response, technical application, continuation/maintenance ECT and its combination with medication. It would appear that ECT can be quite effective with catatonic schizophrenics and in reducing paranoid delusions. There was also evidence that it may improve a person's responsiveness to medication. Lengthier courses worked well with catatonic schizophrenics. When combined with medication, ECT worked better than when only ECT was used.

Phutane *et al* (2011)* also noted that in a sample of 202 schizophrenics who had undergone ECT, the common reason why they had the ECT was to "augment pharmachotherapy" and that the main target was catatonia.

Thirthalli *et al* (2009)* studied a sample of schizophrenics split into catatonic and non-catatonic cases. The researchers reported that those who were catatonic required fewer ECT sessions to help control their symptoms.

Flamarique *et al* (2012)* studied adolescent schizophrenics. The researchers reported that participants who received ECT in conjunction with clozapine had a lower re-hospitalisation rate (7.1 per cent) compared to a group who received ECT and a different antipsychotic (58.3 per cent).

Strength	Weakness
There is evidence to suggest that ECT can be effective in helping to treat schizophrenia.	There are ethical issues in the use of the technique and long-term effects are still largely unknown.

Token economies

Token economies are based on the idea of operant conditioning (rewards and learning by consequence). Behaviour is shaped towards something desired by giving out tokens (e.g. plastic chips or a stamp) every time a relevant behaviour is shown. (See page 240–242 for an example of this in a workplace. The examples below feature medical patients as participants.)

Patients can accrue tokens and exchange them for something they would like (e.g. money or food vouchers). Therefore, patients continue to show desired behaviours as they want to earn tokens to exchange for primary reinforcers that fulfil a direct biological need such as hunger or enjoyment.

Token economy (Paul and Lentz, 1977)

Paul and Lentz (1977) set up a token economy in an institution that housed people diagnosed with schizophrenia. Patients were given tokens when they behaved appropriately and these could be exchanged for luxury items. Appropriate behaviours included participating in group therapy, self-care (e.g. bed making), appropriate socialisation and discouraging angry outbursts. A luxury item might be a cigarette and patients could earn a token to exchange for this by keeping their room neat and tidy, for instance. However, if behaviour was deemed inappropriate or rules were broken, tokens were taken away from people.

Overall, the patients who went through the token economy programme performed better than others on self-care, social care and vocational skills and, as a result, were more likely to be released from the institution earlier. There was also a reduction in the need for medication in the token economy group.

Ayllon and Azrin (1968)* introduced a token economy to a psychiatric hospital in a ward for long-stay female patients. Patients were rewarded for behaviours such as brushing their hair, making their bed and having a neat appearance. Their behaviour rapidly improved and staff morale was raised as staff were seeing more positive behaviours.

Gholipour *et al* (2012)* tested out the effectiveness of a token economy versus an exercise programme in helping people with schizophrenia. A total of 45 patients were randomly split into three groups – two treatments and a control – (therefore, there were 15 patients per group). All participants were male, had been diagnosed for at least 3 years, were between 20 and 50 years old and had no other mental health illness. Negative symptoms of schizophrenia were measured pre- and post-treatment. The average symptom scores pre- and post-treatment are shown in Table 18.1.2.

Group	Pre-treatment score	Post-treatment score
Exercise	71.07	50.47
Token economy	76.73	41.20
Control	84.67	84.87

▲ **Table 18.1.2** Average symptom scores pre- and post-treatment

Source: Gholipour *et al* (2012)

Prior to this study, Dickerson, Tenhula and Green-Paden (2005)* had conducted a review of the field. They found 13 studies and it appeared that there was evidence for the effectiveness of a token economy in increasing the adaptive behaviours of patients with schizophrenia. They noted that many studies had methodological issues that could cast doubt on findings and that long-term follow-ups were rare.

CHALLENGE YOURSELF
Find other evidence to show that token economies help people with mental health issues.

Cognitive behavioural therapy (CBT)

CBT aims to change or modify people's thoughts and beliefs and also change the way that they process information. A therapist will challenge irrational and faulty thoughts as well as behaviours that are not helping. Patients may be set tasks outside the face-to-face therapy to help challenge faulty thoughts and beliefs. For schizophrenia, the intention of CBT would be to help patients make sense of the psychotic experiences and reduce the negative effects of the condition plus any distress they may be feeling. Patients may also be given help to understand that views, thoughts and interpretations are not facts, then given help to deal with assessing them.

CBT (Sensky *et al*, 2000)

Sensky *et al* (2000) tested the potential usefulness of CBT for persistent symptoms of schizophrenia that were resistant to medication. Patients were recruited if they fitted the following criteria. They:

- were aged 16 to 60 years
- had a diagnosis of schizophrenia according to both the ICD and DSM
- had symptoms that had persisted for at least six months
- had showed no improvement for being on medication (with no evidence of poor adherence)
- did not abuse alcohol or drugs.

There were 90 qualifying participants, who were randomly assigned to one of two groups, which were:

- a manualised CBT specifically developed for schizophrenia
- a "befriending" intervention.

Both of the interventions were delivered by experienced nurses. The patients were assessed at baseline, after treatment (lasting up to nine months) and at a nine-month follow-up. An assessor who was blind to the study rated a selection of therapy sessions for quality.

Both interventions did result in a significant reduction in both negative and positive symptoms of schizophrenia alongside depression scores on the Comprehensive Psychiatric Rating Scale. However, at the nine-month follow-up, those who had received CBT continued to improve whereas the befriending group did not.

Therefore, it would appear that CBT is effective at reducing the symptoms of schizophrenia in those who have previously been resistant to antipsychotic medication.

Strength	Weakness
There was a long-term follow-up that showed the therapy to still be having a positive effect on clients.	Some of the outcome measures were from questionnaires so results could be more subjective than objective, potentially lowering the validity of findings.

Bechdolf *et al* (2005)* assessed the effectiveness of CBT versus group psychoeducation on re-hospitalisation and medication compliance up to 24 months after treatment. A total of 88 patients were randomly assigned to either group and they received 8 weeks' therapy. When followed up six months later, the CBT group were less likely to be hospitalised and be taking their medication.

At 24 months post-treatment, the CBT group had had 71 fewer days in hospital than the psychoeducational group. In a further study, Bechdolf *et al* (2010) analysed the data collected from their first study but on quality of life measures taken at six months post-treatment. Both groups reported improved quality of life but there was no significant difference between the two treatment groups.

Ng, Hui and Pau (2008)* assessed the introduction of a CBT programme in a hostel in Hong Kong for people who had become treatment-resistant to drug therapy for schizophrenia. Measures of schizophrenic symptoms, mood, insight and self-esteem were taken pre- and post-treatment. Six months after treatment there was a significant reduction in the symptoms of schizophrenia alongside an increase in self-esteem. Mood and insight remained unchanged.

Davis *et al* (2008)* noted that there had been little research into patients evaluating CBT for schizophrenia. Their study used 44 patients with schizophrenia who either underwent CBT or a support-group programme. The study lasted for six months. Irrespective of group, all patients were satisfied with the intervention they had taken part in, rating it either good or excellent. However, those in the CBT group reported higher levels of satisfaction overall especially with the quality of service and the assistance given for problem solving.

Sarin, Wallin and Widerlöv (2011)* conducted a meta-analysis on the use of CBT with schizophrenics. They concluded that there was strong evidence for CBT affecting positive, negative and general symptoms of schizophrenia compared to all other therapies. They also stated that the effects of CBT can be delayed and having 20 sessions or more is better than shorter programmes that are available.

Issues and debates tracker: All of these therapies have application to everyday life as they are useful to help control the symptoms of schizophrenia. However, a lot of studies are not longitudinal so we sometimes do not know whether the therapy works over time.

CHALLENGE YOURSELF
Design a field experiment to test whether CBT is more effective at treating schizophrenia than a placebo.

18.2 BIPOLAR AND RELATED DISORDERS

CHARACTERISTICS OF BIPOLAR AND RELATED DISORDERS

Definitions and characteristics of abnormal affect

The following description and guidelines are taken from the "ICD-10 Classification of Mental and Behavioural Disorders, Clinical descriptions and diagnostic guidelines".

Bipolar affective disorder

This disorder is characterized by repeated (i.e. at least two) episodes in which the patient's mood and activity levels are significantly disturbed, this disturbance consisting on some occasions of an elevation of mood and increased energy and activity (mania or hypomania), and on others of a lowering of mood and decreased energy and activity (depression). Characteristically, recovery is usually complete between episodes, and the incidence in the two sexes is more nearly equal than in other mood disorders. As patients who suffer only from repeated episodes of mania are comparatively rare, and resemble (in their family history, premorbid personality, age of onset, and long-term prognosis) those who also have at least occasional episodes of depression, such patients are classified as bipolar... .

Manic episodes usually begin abruptly and last for between 2 weeks and 4-5 months (median duration about 4 months). Depressions tend to last longer (median length about 6 months), though rarely for more than a year, except in the elderly. Episodes of both kinds often follow stressful life events or other mental trauma, but the presence of such stress is not essential for the diagnosis. The first episode may occur at any age from childhood to old age. The frequency of episodes and the pattern of remissions and relapses are both very variable, though remissions tend to get shorter as time goes on and depressions to become commoner and longer lasting after middle age.

Although the original concept of "manic-depressive psychosis" also included patients who suffered only from depression, the term "manic-depressive disorder or psychosis" is now used mainly as a synonym for bipolar disorder.

Source: The ICD-10 Classification of Mental and Behavioural Disorders, Clinical descriptions and diagnostic guidelines, WHO, p. 97

CHALLENGE YOURSELF
Find the DSM-V criteria for the diagnosis of abnormal affect. Compare it to the ICD-10 criteria.

Issues and debates tracker: Both the ICD and DSM methods of diagnosing abnormal affect may only be based on the view of one set of cultural norms (e.g. US cultural norms for DSM) so could be viewed as culturally biased. This might make it difficult to diagnose people correctly in other cultures. However, both methods have good application to everyday life as they can be used to diagnose people so that they receive the most appropriate treatment.

Types
Depression (unipolar) and mania (bipolar)

There are two main types of depression:

- Unipolar – this is sometimes called a major depressive episode. Symptoms for this type include having a depressed mood for most of the day, diminished pleasure in most activities undertaken, some weight loss, insomnia or hypersomnia, some psychomotor agitation, fatigue, feelings of worthlessness and a reduced ability to concentrate on tasks.

- Bipolar – this used to be referred to as manic depression. Symptoms for this type include having episodes of manic behaviour that cannot be accounted for by a physical condition, having some episode that is similar to unipolar depression (although this is not necessary for a diagnosis) and having some change in polarity.

Measures

The Beck Depression Inventory

This measure of depression is a 21-item questionnaire that covers a range of factors seen as being symptoms of depression. These include past failure, self-dislike, crying, loss of interest, irritability and tiredness or fatigue. Each statement has a 4-point scale to choose from. The points are totalled up and the higher the points, the higher the depression levels of the individual.

Figure 18.2.1 shows an excerpt from the scale.

Name: _____   Marital Status: _____   Age: _____   Sex: _____

Occupation: _____   Education: _____

Instructions: This questionnaire consists of 21 groups of statements. Please read each group of statements carefully, and then pick out the **one statement** in each group that best describes the way you have been feeling during the **past two weeks, including today.** Circle the number beside the statement you have picked. If several statements in the group seem to apply equally well, circle the highest number for that group. Be sure that you do not choose more than one statement for any group, including Item 16 (Changes in Sleeping Pattern) or Item 18 (Changes in Appetite).

1. Unhappiness

  0 I do not feel unhappy.
  1 I feel unhappy.
  2 I am unhappy.
  3 I am so unhappy that I can't stand it.

2. Changes in Activity Level

  0 I have not experienced any change in activity level.
  1 a I am somewhat more active than usual.
      b I am somewhat less active than usual.
  2 a I am a lot more active than usual.
      b I am a lot less active than usual.
  3 a I am not active most of the day.
      b I am active all of the day.

▲ **Figure 18.2.1** Excerpt from the Beck Depression Inventory

Strength	Weakness
The scale has been validated and is a long-standing measure of depression. Therefore, the result produced when a person completes it should be an accurate representation of that individual's current level of depression.	This measure of depression relies on the self-report of the individual. As the person may well be depressed, the views given as answers to the statements may not be how the person is truly feeling. Depressed people can have distorted cognitions about the world and themselves.

EXPLANATIONS OF DEPRESSION

Biological: genetic and neurochemical

The genetic argument follows the idea that depression may well run in families and be encoded in genetics.

One way of testing the idea that depression may run in families is to conduct twin studies using monozygotic (MZ: identical) and dizygotic (DZ: non-identical) twins. McGuffin *et al* (1996)* examined 214 pairs of twins where at least one of them was being treated for depression. They reported that 46 per cent of MZ and 20 per cent of DZ twins of the patients also had a diagnosis of depression. This hints at a part-genetic component for depression but a drawback is that twins tend to be brought up together and treated in the same way so we cannot rule out environmental influences.

Following on from this, Silberg *et al* (1999)* wanted to assess whether it was genetics, the environment or a combination of the two that could be causing depression. A total of 902 pairs of twins completed psychiatric interviews to assess levels of depression alongside data about life events and from parents. In general, females were diagnosed more often with depression than males. This was more marked when life events were negative. However, there were individual differences seen among the females, and those who were diagnosed with depression after a negative life event were more likely to have a twin who was also diagnosed with depression. Therefore, it would seem both genetics and the environment interact to cause depression.

Earlier studies had also shown a part-genetic component of depression. Bertelsen, Harvald and Hauge (1977)* reported that the genetic component varied depending on the type of depression. Table 18.2.1 records this.

Type of depression	Percentage chance for MZ twins	Percentage chance for DZ twins
Bipolar disorder	80	16
Severe depression (three or more episodes of depression)	59	30
Depression (fewer than three episodes of depression)	36	17

▲ **Table 18.2.1** Genetic component and type of depression

Therefore, the strongest evidence for a genetic component comes from bipolar disorder, then severe depression, followed by depression.

Kendler *et al* (1993)* estimated that the heritability rate for depression falls in the range of 41–46 per cent. In terms of a neurochemical cause, there are two neurotransmitters that have been investigated: norepinephrine and serotonin. Low levels of both of these may well be a cause of depression. Davison and Neale (1998) highlighted how certain drugs block the re-uptake of these neurotransmitters so that more of them can be used in the postsynaptic neuron. This is shown in Figure 18.2.2.

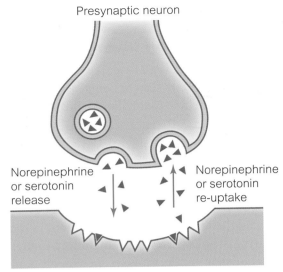

(a)

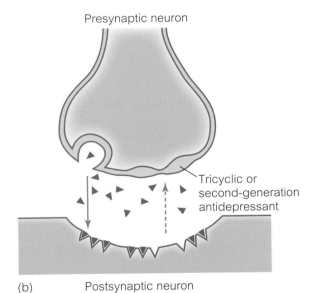

(b)

▲ **Figure 18.2.2 (a)** When a neuron releases norepinephrine or serotonin from its endings, a re-uptake mechanism begins to recapture some of the neurotransmitters before the postsynaptic neuron receives them.
(b) Antidepressant drugs called tricyclics block this re-uptake process allowing more norepinephrine or serotonin to reach the postsynaptic neuron

Biological: genetic and neurochemical (Oruc *et al*, 1998)

Oruc *et al* (1998) analysed the DNA of 42 patients diagnosed with bipolar-type disorder and compared it to 49 healthy controls. They were assessing DNA polymorphisms in the serotonin receptor 2c (5-HTR2c) and serotonin transporter (5-HTT) genes. There were no significant differences between the two groups. However, when the data was analysed by gender, an association was discovered. Females were more likely to show both polymorphisms, indicating that these variations in genetics could help to explain why females are more susceptible to bipolar disorder.

Strengths	Weakness
The measurements are objective so the findings are more likely to be valid. Also, due to this the analysis can be replicated on a different sample to test for reliability.	The results may be culturally specific (and therefore biased) as all of the sample were from Belgium. This may make generalisation difficult beyond the sample.

Cognitive

Cognitive processes (Beck, 1979)

Beck (1979) was interested in examining the irrational thought processes involved in depression. He believed that there were three factors which make people *cognitively vulnerable* to depression. The three factors in Beck's inventory are called the cognitive triad. The inventory consists of:

▶ negative view of self

▶ negative view of the world

▶ negative view of the future.

These three factors can interact with each other to make a person depressed. They will also "change" the way information is processed as they become an "automatic" way of thinking. That is, when information is being processed it is affected by all three factors so the information will be processed in a "negative way". People may simply overestimate the negative aspects of a situation, meaning they will conclude that whatever happens, something bad will come of it. Depressives may also have negative self-schemas (packets of information about themselves) that have developed since childhood by having negative experiences and/ or overly critical parents, peers or teachers. All new information that is processed will become negative as the mechanisms are all negative. As a result, depression develops.

Learned helplessness or attributional style

Learned helplessness is about individuals becoming passive because they feel they are not in control of their own life. This is caused by unpleasant experiences that they have tried to control in the past (unsuccessfully). This gives people a sense of helplessness which in turn leads to depression. The idea was based on Seligman's (1974) research on dogs. The dogs received electric shocks that they could not escape from (so they experienced lack of control) and it did not take long for them to stop trying to escape. They all became passive and appeared to accept the painful situation they were in. When in future trials there was an opportunity to escape, the dogs still did not try to do this. This is the sense of helplessness that depressives will feel if they cannot escape situations that are negative and out of their control. In addition, attribution theory could also explain depression. Weiner *et al* (1971) noted three levels of attribution that can affect people's views of their own behaviour:

1. internal (personal) or external (environmental)

2. stable or unstable

3. global or specific.

Table 18.2.2 gives an example of how the different attributional schemata can be used to explain why someone failed a psychology examination.

	Internal		External	
	Stable	**Unstable**	**Stable**	**Unstable**
Global	"I lack general intelligence for exams."	"I am really, really tired today."	"Exams are an unfair way to test my ability."	"It's an unlucky day."
Specific	"I lack the ability to pass psychology exams."	"I am fed up with studying psychology."	"The psychology exam was really unfair as it had questions I did not know the answers to."	"My psychology exam had 13 questions, which is unlucky."

▲ **Table 18.2.2** Using attributional schemata to explain examination failure

Learned helplessness or attributional style (Seligman *et al*, 1988)

Seligman *et al* (1988) assessed 39 unipolar depressives and 12 bipolar depressives for signs of learned helplessness and attributional style. They all completed the Attributional Style Questionnaire at the beginning of their cognitive therapy, at the end of their therapy and one year later. The questionnaire asks participants to make causal attributions for 12 hypothetical events (both good and bad). They then rate each cause on a 7-point scale for internality, stability and globality.

The results were as follows:

▶ A pessimistic explanatory style for negative (bad) events correlated significantly with severity of depression at all three time points. Explanatory style improved by the end of the therapy, as did depressive symptoms for the unipolar group.

▶ The pattern was also seen in bipolar depressives but the significant results were not as strong.

This study suggests that it is explanatory style (attributional style) that requires changing in depressive patients via cognitive therapy to help them improve their mental health.

Strength	Weakness
The study has good application as a therapist can assess clients for types of learned helplessness.	The measures taken were from questionnaires which could cast doubt on the validity of findings as people may not have been honest when completing them (especially as they were all diagnosed with depression).

CHALLENGE YOURSELF
To what extent do you think that abnormal affect disorders are more related to nurture than nature? Justify your answer.

TREATMENT AND MANAGEMENT OF DEPRESSION

Biological

Two examples of antidepressants that are commonly used are as follows:

▶ Selective serotonergic re-uptake inhibitors (SSRIs) – see Figure 18.2.2 on page 120 to see how re-uptake inhibitors work. Possible side effects include fatigue, headaches and insomnia.

▶ Monoamine oxidase inhibitors (MAOIs) – these work by inhibiting monamine oxidase (this breaks down neurotransmitters such as norepineprhine and serotonin) which means more serotonin and norepinephrine is available in the synapse. Possible side effects include hypertension (which is potentially fatal), dizziness and nausea.

Rucci *et al* (2011)* tested out the effectiveness of SSRIs versus interpersonal psychotherapy on suicidal thoughts in a group of 291 outpatients with major depression. Participants were randomly assigned to either treatment regime and suicidal ideation was measured using a questionnaire. The 231 patients who had shown no suicidal ideation pre-study were analysed and 32 of these did exhibit suicidal ideation during the treatment. For those on SSRIs, the time taken for these thoughts to emerge was much longer than in the psychotherapy group. Therefore, SSRIs may reduce suicidal thoughts in people with major depression.

Nakagawa *et al* (2008)* conducted a meta-analysis on the efficacy and effectiveness of a drug called milnacipran (a serotonin and norepinephrine re-uptake inhibitor) in comparison with other antidepressants. The studies selected for the analysis had to be randomised controlled trials with milnacipran compared to at least one other antidepressant. While there tended to be no differences in clinical improvement across all antidepressants, people taking antidepressants called tricyclics tended to withdraw from treatment sooner than any other drug group. There was also evidence that milnacipran may benefit patients who had adverse side effects from SSRIs and MAOIs.

Electro-convulsive therapy (ECT)

See page 114 for a description of the procedure for administering ECT.

Nordenskjold *et al* (2013)* tested the effectiveness of ECT with drug therapy compared to drug therapy alone. A total of 56 patients were randomly assigned to either 29 treatments of ECT alongside drug therapy, or drug therapy alone. The researchers measured relapse of depression within one year of completing treatment. In the group of patients just on drug therapy 61 per cent relapsed within the year compared to just 32 per cent of patients who had ECT and drug therapy.

There have been several meta-analyses testing the effectiveness of ECT. Dierckx *et al* (2012)* reviewed the field in terms of whether response to ECT differs in bipolar disorder patients versus unipolar depressed patients. A total of six studies formed their analysis. The overall remission rate was nearly 51 per cent for unipolar and over 53 per cent for bipolar disorder.

The data covered over 1000 patients. Overall, the data were encouraging as they showed similar efficacy rates for the two types of depression. Dunne and McLoughlin (2012)* reviewed the effectiveness and side effects of three types of ECT: bifrontal (BF), bilateral (BL) and unilateral (UL). Eight studies were used in the analysis. It covered data on 617 patients.

There was no difference in the effectiveness of the three types in terms of efficacy – all appeared to have some level of effectiveness. UL ECT impaired complex figure recall more than BF ECT. However, BF ECT impaired word recall more than UL ECT.

Jelovac, Kolshus and McLoughlin (2013)* reviewed relapse rates following successful ECT for major depression. Thirty-two studies were used in the analysis and all had at least a two-year follow-up. Compared to relapse rates for drug therapy (51.1 per cent 12 months following successful initial treatment with 37.7 per cent relapsing in the first six months), ECT did not fare any better, with a 37.2 per cent relapse rate in the first six months. Those who took antidepressants post-ECT had a risk of relapse half of those who took a placebo.

 CHALLENGE YOURSELF
Design a longitudinal study to investigate the effects ECT has on people with depression.

Cognitive

Cognitive restructuring (Beck, 1979)

The idea of this therapy follows Beck's cognitive triad approach to the potential causes of depression (see page 121). It is a six-stage process:

1. The therapist explains the rationale behind the therapy and what its purpose is.

2. Clients are taught how to monitor automatic negative thoughts and negative self-schemata.

3. Clients are taught to use behavioural techniques to challenge negative thoughts and information processing.

4. Therapist and client explore how negative thoughts are responded to by the client.

5. Dysfunctional beliefs are identified and challenged.

6. The therapy ends with clients having the necessary "cognitive tools" to repeat the process by themselves.

Hans and Hiller (2013)* conducted a meta-analysis on the effectiveness of CBT on adults with unipolar depression. A total of 34 studies formed the analysis and they had to assess the effectiveness of individual or group CBT as well as drop-out rates. The studies also had to have at least a six-month follow-up. It would appear that outpatient CBT was effective in reducing depressive symptoms and these were maintained at least six months after the CBT ended. The average drop-out rate was 24.63 per cent. This was reported as being quite high by the researchers but they also noted that better-quality effectiveness studies are needed to assess how good CBT truly is with depressive patients.

Cuijpers *et al* (2013)* also conducted a review examining CBT in relation to depression and comparing it to other treatments. A total of 115 studies were used and they had to be a CBT study that either had a control group or a comparison "other" treatment (e.g. psychotherapy or drug therapy). CBT was effective at reducing depression in adults but the effect size was lower when the study was classed as high quality. Therefore, the positive effects of CBT may well have been overestimated and more high-quality studies are needed.

Burns *et al* (2013)* conducted a pilot study to assess the effectiveness of CBT for women with antenatal depression. Thirty-six women who met the diagnostic criteria for depression were randomly assigned to either a CBT treatment programme or usual care. Of those who completed nine or more sessions of CBT, or completed their usual care, 68.7 per cent of the CBT group had recovered from their depression 15 weeks after treatment compared to 38.5 per cent in the usual care group.

Rational emotive behaviour therapy (REBT) (Ellis, 1962)

Ellis (1962) stated that rationality consists of thinking in ways that allow us to reach our goals; irrationality consists of thinking in ways that prevent us from reaching our goals. The idea behind the therapy follows an ABC model:

▶ **Activating event** – this is a fact, behaviour, attitude or an event.

▶ **Beliefs** – the person holds beliefs about the activating event.

▶ **Cognitive** – this is the person's cognitive response to the activating event as well as emotions.

Using the example from Table 18.2.2 (page 122) failing a psychology examination would be the A. The B that might follow could be "I am a failure" or "I hate it when I do not pass an exam" and then the C would be depression.

Szentagotai *et al* (2008)* examined the effectiveness of REBT, CBT and drug therapy for the treatment of a major depressive episode. A range of outcome measures were taken based on a questionnaire that tested three main depressive thoughts: automatic negative thoughts, dysfunctional attitudes and irrational beliefs. A general measure of depression was also taken. There were 170 participants randomly assigned to either the REBT (n = 57), CBT (n = 56) or drug therapy (n = 57) groups. In terms of depressive symptoms, there were no significant differences between the three groups but the REBT groups had an average score significantly lower than the drug therapy group. In terms of the three main depressive thoughts, all three treatments appeared to decrease these immediately post-treatment and then at follow-up.

Sava *et al* (2008)* compared REBT, CBT and the use of prozac in a sample of depressives. The participants were split into the three treatment groups and all had 14 weeks' therapy. All participants completed questions based on the Beck Depression Inventory (see page 119) prior to the therapy and then at 7 and 14 weeks post-therapy. There were no significant differences between the three groups in terms of scores on the inventory but REBT and CBT cost less for the same outcomes so these are preferred treatments.

Issues and debates tracker: All of these therapies have application to everyday life as they are useful to help control the symptoms of abnormal affect. However, a lot of studies are not longitudinal so we sometimes do not know whether the therapy works over time.

18.3 IMPULSE CONTROL DISORDERS AND NON-SUBSTANCE ADDICTIVE DISORDER

CHARACTERISTICS OF IMPULSE CONTROL DISORDERS AND NON-SUBSTANCE ADDICTIVE DISORDER

Definitions (Griffiths, 2005)

According to Griffiths (2005), there are six components to any addiction disorder:

- Salience – when the addiction becomes the single most important activity in the person's life. It dominates the person's behaviour, thoughts and feelings.

- Euphoria – the subjective experience that is felt while engaging in the addictive behaviour, like a "rush" or a "buzz".

- Tolerance – when the person has to do more of the addictive behaviour to get the same effect.

- Withdrawal – this refers to the unpleasant thoughts and physical effects felt when the person tries to stop the addictive behaviour.

- Conflict – when the person with the addiction begins to have conflicts with work colleagues, friends and family.

- Relapse – the chances of the person "going back" to the addictive behaviour are high.

Types

Kleptomania, gambling disorder and pyromania

Alongside alcoholism (abusing the use of alcohol) there are a range of impulse control disorders. They include these disorders:

- Kleptomania – when people have the urge to collect and hoard items in their homes. They may go out and steal objects even if the items have little monetary value or they could afford to buy them.

The more difficult the challenge of gaining the objects, the more thrilling and addictive it becomes.

- Compulsive gambling – when people feel the need to gamble to get a sense of euphoria especially if they win. They will continue to gamble whether they win or lose.

- Pyromania – when people deliberately start a fire because they are attracted to fires or seeing the fire service in action. They may feel a sense of arousal and satisfaction once the fire has started.

Pyromania (Burton *et al*, 2012)

Burton *et al* (2012) noted that most arsonists do not meet the DSM-V diagnostic criteria for pyromania. These criteria are shown in Table 18.3.1.

Deliberate and purposeful firesetting on more than one occasion.
Tension or affective arousal before the act.
Has a fascination with, interest in, curiosity about, or attraction to fire and its situational contexts (e.g., paraphernalia, uses, and consequences).
Pleasure, gratification, or relief when setting fires or when witnessing or participating in their aftermath.
The firesetting is not done for monetary gain, as an expression of sociopolitical ideology, to conceal criminal activity, to express anger or vengeance, to improve one's living circumstances, in response to a delusion or hallucination, or as a result of impaired judgment (e.g., in dementia, mental retardation, or substance intoxication).
The firesetting is not explained by conduct disorder, a manic episode, or antisocial personality disorder.

▲ **Table 18.3.1** DSM-IV-TR Diagnostic criteria for pyromania

Source: Burton *et al* (2012: 357)

CHALLENGE YOURSELF
Find the DSM-V criteria for the diagnosis of impulse control disorders. Compare them to the ICD-10 criteria.

Measures

Kleptomania Symptom Assessment (K-SAS)

- The K-SAS is a 12-item questionnaire that is aimed at evaluating kleptomania symptoms.

- The questions use a variety of techniques such as Likert-type scales and closed questions to help evaluate how severe each case is.

- The higher the score generated, the more severe the symptoms.

Kleptomania Symptom Assessment (K-SAS)

The following questions are aimed at evaluating kleptomania symptoms. Please **read** the questions **carefully** before you answer.

1) If you had urges to steal during the past WEEK, on average, how strong were your urges? Please circle the most appropriate number:

None	Mild	Moderate	Severe	Extreme
0	1	2	3	4

2) During the past WEEK, how many times did you experience urges to steal? Please circle the most appropriate number.

1. None
2. Once
3. Two or three times
4. Several to many times
5. Constant or near constant

3) During the past WEEK, how many hours (add up hours) were you preoccupied with your urges to steal? Please circle the most appropriate number.

None	1 hr or less	1 to 4 hr	4 to 10 hr	over 10 hr
0	1	2	3	4

4) During the past WEEK, how much were you able to control your urges? Please circle the most appropriate number.

Very much	Much	Moderate	Minimal	No control
0	1	2	3	4

5) During the past WEEK, how often did thoughts about stealing come up? Please circle the most appropriate number.

1. None
2. Once
3. Two to four times
4. Several to many times
5. Constantly or nearly constantly

6) During the past WEEK, approximately how many hours (add up hours) did you spend thinking about stealing? Please circle the most appropriate number.

None	1 hr or less	1 to 4 hr	4 to 10 hr	over 10 hr
0	1	2	3	4

7) During the past WEEK, how much were you able to control your thoughts of stealing? Please circle the most appropriate number.

Very much	Much	Moderate	Minimal	No control
0	1	2	3	4

8) During the past WEEK, on average, how much tension or excitement did you have shortly before you committed a theft? If you did not actually steal anything, please estimate how much anticipatory tension or excitement you believe you would have experienced if you had committed a theft. Please circle the most appropriate number.

None	Minimal	Moderate	Much	Very much
0	1	2	3	4

9) During the past WEEK, on average, how much excitement and pleasure did you feel when you successfully committed a theft? If you did not actually steal, please estimate how much excitement and pleasure you believe you would have experienced if you had committed a theft. Please circle the most appropriate number.

None	Minimal	Moderate	Much	Very much
0	1	2	3	4

10) During the past WEEK, how much emotional distress (mental pain or anguish, shame, guilt, embarrassment) has your stealing caused you? Please circle the most appropriate number.

None	Minimal	Moderate	Much	Very much
0	1	2	3	4

11) During the past WEEK, how much personal trouble (relationship, financial, legal, job, medical or health) has your stealing caused you? Please circle the most appropriate number.

None	Minimal	Moderate	Much	Very much
0	1	2	3	4

12) During the past WEEK, how many times did you steal? Please circle.

1. None
2. Once
3. Two or three times
4. Several to many times
5. Daily or almost daily

▲ **Figure 18.3.1** Kleptomania Symptom Assessment (K-SAS)
Source: Grant (rev. E. Corsale, MA, MFT and S. Smithstein, Psy.D.)

CAUSES OF IMPULSE CONTROL DISORDERS AND NON-SUBSTANCE ADDICTIVE DISORDER

Biochemical: dopamine

Dopamine has been linked to addiction and impulse control disorders because when it is released in the body it gives us the feelings of pleasure and satisfaction. Once these feelings become a desire, we then repeat behaviours that cause the release of dopamine and the cycle continues with repetitive behaviours. More specifically, when someone experiences an activity that is pleasurable, dopamine is released in the nucleus accumbens, which is sometimes called "the brain's pleasure centre". The sooner that an activity gives a sense of reward, the faster the nucleus produces dopamine and it produces higher levels. The entire "reward circuit" in the brain includes sources of motivation and memory alongside pleasure. Any addictive behaviour stimulates the same circuits within the brain, overloading it with dopamine. Vroon *et al* (2010)* reported that when participants were given a dopamine agonist (it activates dopamine receptors), impulsive choice increased, reaction times became faster and participants showed fewer decision conflicts compared to a control group. One drawback is that participants had Parkinson's disease so whether this can be related to people with impulse control disorder needs investigating.

CHALLENGE YOURSELF
To what extent do you feel that the dopamine hypothesis is deterministic? Justify your answer.

Behavioural: positive reinforcement

This follows the idea of rewards. When an action is followed by a pleasurable outcome, the person is more likely to engage in that behaviour again. For example, if an addictive behaviour or impulse control behaviour is followed by a positive outcome (e.g. feeling a sense of arousal when setting fire to a house or winning on a fruit machine), the person is likely to repeat the behaviour.

This can then be linked to the "reward" of a dopamine release within the brain (see above). Therefore, the release of dopamine is the outcome of engaging in an impulse control disorder behaviour, increasing the probability that the person will engage in that behaviour again.

Cognitive

Feeling-state theory (Miller, 2010)

Miller (2010) introduced the feeling-state theory for impulse control disorders. The main idea is based around state-dependent memories. Impulse control disorders are created when positive feelings, linked to certain objects, activities or events, form these state-dependent memories. This combination of feelings and objects, activities or events form a "feeling-state" in the individual. Miller defines this feeling-state as "… the entire psycho-physiological arousal of the body and its connections with the memory of a specific behaviour. In other words, the feeling-state is a unit that is composed of the feelings (sensations, emotions, and thoughts…) associated with the behaviour plus the memory of the behaviour itself" (2010: 4). Miller uses the example of a gambler – the thoughts or feelings of "I'm a winner!" combined with the memory of the event could easily create a gambling compulsion, especially if the two are linked several times. However, there can be many feeling-state links that can contribute to an impulse control disorder.

Figures 18.3.2 and 18.3.3 illustrate Miller's theory.

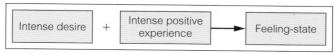
▲ **Figure 18.3.2** Creation of a feeling-state
Source: Miller (2010: 5)

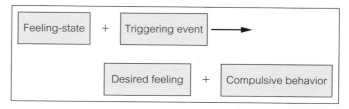
▲ **Figure 18.3.3** Activation of the compulsive disorder
Source: Miller (2010: 5)

Issues and debates tracker: These causes of impulse control disorder can be seen as reductionist as each one only looks at the cause from one angle. Also, all of these can be seen as deterministic as they are all predicting that impulse control disorders are determined by either internal or external mechanisms.

TREATING AND MANAGING IMPULSE CONTROL DISORDERS AND NON-SUBSTANCE ADDICTIVE DISORDER

Biochemical

Biochemical (Grant *et al*, 2008)

Grant *et al* (2008) acknowledged that opiate antagonists had shown some positive outcomes when used to help treat pathological gambling. However, no study had attempted to examine why individual differences occur in outcome. A total of 284 participants (48.2 per cent women) with a diagnosis of pathological gambling formed the sample group. There were two double-blind placebo-controlled trials. One was a 16-week trial with participants taking the drug nalmefene and the other was an 18-week trial using naltrexone.

A "positive" response to the treatment was measured as a 35 per cent reduction in scores on a scale measuring pathological gambling symptoms. The strongest factor associated with a positive response was a positive family history of alcoholism. Those who were on the highest dosage of drug who had more intense urges to gamble were also more likely to show a positive response. For participants receiving the placebo, those who were younger were more likely to show a positive response.

Strength	Weakness
The study used a double-blind procedure so there were no experimenter effects that could have affected the outcome measures. Therefore, the findings should be valid.	The outcome measures were collected via questionnaires so the researchers could not be sure that the participants were telling the full truth. This may reduce the validity of the findings.

Cognitive-behavioural

Covert sensitisation (Glover)

Glover (1985) reported on a case study of a female kleptomaniac who was treated using covert sensitisation. The 56-year-old female had been shoplifting for 14 years, mainly for "non-purposive" goods. For example, she stole baby shoes even though she did not have a baby to give them to. She tended to wake up every morning and think about stealing and, even though she felt a strong resistance to these thoughts, would give into them during her lunch break.

She wanted therapy, and on initial interview appeared very motivated to treat her kleptomania. She did not want to use imagery of her being caught or apprehended for stealing as she had tried to use that herself and it was never successful. She and the therapist debated what imagery should be used as part of the covert sensitisation therapy. They agreed on using the imagery of vomiting and nausea to be paired with the process of stealing goods. The four sessions worked as follows:

▶ In the first three sessions she had to imagine herself approaching something in a supermarket that she would steal. The closer she got to the product she was wanting to steal, the more nausea she had to imagine. She then had to imagine vomiting as she picked up the product. Finally, she had to imagine other shoppers watching her as she vomited.

▶ In the final session, she had to continue feeling more nauseous as she approached the product but imagine it all stopping once she put the product back on the shelf and left the supermarket.

▶ Muscle relaxation techniques were used during all sessions. She was also interested in self-hypnosis so this was also used in sessions three and four.

▶ After each session she was asked to complete homework of rehearsing the imagined scenes several times per day. When she had to go shopping she was asked to make a list of specific items to buy and not take her usual shopping bag, which she always used for shoplifting.

The therapy lasted eight weeks, as each session happened fortnightly. She reported that her thoughts of shoplifting decreased over time but she did relapse twice, stealing minor items from four different shops. There were follow-up sessions every three months and during these it became apparent that she was finding it easier to go shopping alone and not steal. At a final 19-month follow-up session she appeared more confident and cheery and had only relapsed once. She believed that the covert sensitisation using the nausea imagery had helped her overcome the kleptomania.

Strength	Weakness
The case study has real-world application: therapists can choose to use convert sensitisation to help other people overcome kleptomania.	As it was a case study it may be difficult to generalise the actual procedures to other kleptomaniacs. The woman in this example said that she could visualise the scenes very clearly and this helped. Other people may not be able to do this so it might not be an appropriate treatment for them.

Imaginal desensitisation (Blaszczynski and Nower, 2002)

Blaszczynski and Nower (2002) reported on the role of imaginal desensitisation for helping people with impulse control disorders including pathological gambling, kleptomania and compulsive buying. The technique allows clients to be taught brief progressive muscle relaxation methods. According to Blaszczynksi and Nower, there should be six steps used in a "treatment sequence":

1. Initiating the urge. Clients must begin to re-enact, mentally, a scene where they begin to have the urge to engage in some impulsive behaviour such as gambling. As this is happening, brief relaxation instructions are given to help the client relax.

> The following is a sample script for conducting Progressive Muscle Relaxation (PMR) for use in the office or on tape:
>
> Make yourself comfortable in a chair. Close your eyes and clear your mind of any thoughts or images and focus attention on your breathing … [pause] … Take a deep breath and let it out slowly … [pause] …. Just breathing easily and gently now, no effort, breathing as you normally would. Now, as you breathe out, I want you to say to yourself, 'relax.'
>
> Source: Blaszczynski and Nower (2002: 11)

2. Planning to follow through on the urge. Clients must then visualise the "trip" to the place where the impulsive behaviour usually takes place such as a bingo hall or a favourite shop. Again, relaxation instructions are read out as this is happening

3. Arriving at the venue. Clients must then imagine, in detail, what it feels like to arrive at the venue where they are going to engage in their compulsive behaviour. As with the other steps, brief relaxation instructions are given.

4. Generating arousal and excitement with the behaviour. This allows clients to imagine a certain scenario where they are getting ready to fully engage in the impulsive behaviour. In the example of gambling, this may include them choosing their favourite roulette wheel or fruit machine and imagining getting money ready to use. As usual, brief relaxation instructions are given.

5. Having "second thoughts" about the behaviour. This is when clients are asked to imagine looking around the venue and seeing people who look discouraging. Clients also must become aware of how they feel if they lose or are caught. Brief relaxation instructions are read out again.

6. Decreasing the attractiveness of the behaviour. In this final step, clients have to imagine all of the negative outcomes that could possibly happen as a result of engaging in the impulse control behaviour. They must then visualise themselves walking away from the venue having *not* engaged in the impulsive behaviour.

Alongside this, each client completes a Trigger Monitoring Table so that these behaviours can be used during the visualisation sessions. Figure 18.3.4 shows an example.

The following is a table designed to identify situations that trigger your urges to engage in troublesome behaviours. Whenever you encounter a stressor or other situation that makes you want to [behaviour], please note that situation on the sheet below. In addition, indicate on a scale of "1" to "10," with "1" being "lowest" and "10" being "highest," the various feelings you felt upon initially encountering the situation. In addition, write a brief quote of the thought(s) that went through your head when you had those feelings. Finally, identify on the same scale the feelings you experience when you first thought of [behaviour] as a way of dealing with the situation.

Trigger Monitoring Table

Situation	Feelings before planning the behaviour Scale 1 (low)–10 (high)	Thoughts before planning the behaviour	Feelings when planning the behaviour
"Coworkers leaving at the end of a work-day"	*Lonely = 8* *Anxious = 5*	*"I don't want to go home again alone"*	*Excited = 10* *Happy = 8*

▲ **Figure 18.3.4** Example Trigger Monitoring Table

Source: Blaszczynski and Nower (2002: 10)

The recommendation is for clients to do some of this at home too. Successful interventions are based on about 15 sessions spread over one week.

Strength	Weakness
It has good application as therapists can use the techniques to help clients control their impulses better.	It relies on people being able to visualise (rather than actually behaving) and some clients may not be able to do this well, so the technique might not be good for everyone with impulse control issues.

Impulse control therapy (Miller, 2010)

Miller (2010) proposed impulse control therapy. This targets two factors:

▶ Cognitive change – this is about targeting the "rationalisations" that an addict has and the distorted thinking patterns. Once these are identified as being the ones that the patient uses to justify his or her out-of-control behaviours, the therapist can begin working on changing them. This helps to re-process the patient's feeling-states.

▶ Behavioural change – once a feeling-state has been re-processed, the destructive behaviour usually disappears without any other intervention being necessary. Patients then usually find other, more appropriate, behaviours to obtain the desired feeling they *used* to get from impulse control-led behaviours.

Miller (2010) produced a 12-step guide for impulse control therapy, which is shown in Table 18.3.2.

FIRST SESSION	
1	Obtain history, frequency, and context of compulsive behavior.
2	Identify the specific aspect of the compulsive behavior that has the most emotional intensity associated with it.
3	Identify the specific positive feeling linked with the compulsive behavior, along with its rating on the PFS.
4	Locate and identify any physical sensations created by the positive feelings.
5	The client combines an image of performing the (a) compulsive behavior (b) the positive feeling and (c) physical sensations.
6	Eye movement sets are performed while the client focuses on material (e.g. memory, feeling, image, sensation, thought) that was elicited during the prior set.
7	When the PFS is ≤1, identify the related NC and use the PC, SUDS, emotions, VOC, and body location according to the standard EMDR protocol (unlike the standard protocol, no specific memory is identified and no visual image is used).
HOMEWORK	
8	Between sessions, homework is given to evaluate the progress of therapy and to elicit any other positive feelings related to the compulsive behavior.
SECOND SESSION	
9	In the second session, the compulsive behavior is re-evaluated for both the feeling identified in the first session as well as identifying other positive feelings related to the ICD.
10	If necessary, steps 2 to 8 are performed again.
11	Continue the re-evaluation and processing in further sessions until the person's drive toward the compulsive behavior has been changed.
12	When it appears that all the FSs have been processed, the negative belief that was created as a result of the compulsive behavior is determined. Use the standard EMDR protocol for processing.

Notes: PFS = positive feelings scale; NC = negative cognition; PC = positive cognition; SUDS = subjective units of disturbance scale; VOC = validity of cognition scale; EMDR = eye movement desensitisation and reprocessing; ICD = impulsive-control disorder; FS = feeling-state.

▲ **Table 18.3.2** Impulse control therapy in 12 steps

Source: Miller (2004: 6)

Issues and debates tracker: All of these therapies have application to everyday life as they are useful to help control the symptoms of impulse control disorder. However, a lot of studies are not longitudinal so we sometimes do not know whether the therapy works over time.

CHALLENGE YOURSELF
To what extent do you feel that biological treatments are the best way to cure people of impulse control disorders? Justify your answer.

18.4 ANXIETY DISORDERS

CHARACTERISTICS OF ANXIETY DISORDERS

The following description and guidelines are taken from the "ICD-10 Classification of Mental and Behavioural Disorders, Clinical descriptions and diagnostic guidelines".

F41.1 Generalized anxiety disorder

The essential feature is anxiety, which is generalized and persistent but not restricted to, or even strongly predominating in, any particular environmental circumstances (i.e. it is "free-floating"). As in other anxiety disorders the dominant symptoms are highly variable, but complaints of continuous feelings of nervousness, trembling, muscular tension, sweating, lightheadedness, palpitations, dizziness, and epigastric discomfort are common. Fears that the sufferer or a relative will shortly become ill or have an accident are often expressed, together with a variety of other worries and forebodings. This disorder is more common in women, and often related to chronic environmental stress. Its course is variable but tends to be fluctuating and chronic.

Diagnostic guidelines

The sufferer must have primary symptoms of anxiety most days for at least several weeks at a time, and usually for several months. These symptoms should usually involve elements of:

(a) apprehension (worries about future misfortunes, feeling "on edge", difficulty in concentrating, etc.);
(b) motor tension (restless fidgeting, tension headaches, trembling, inability to relax); and
(c) autonomic overactivity (lightheadedness, sweating, tachycardia or tachypnoea, epigastric discomfort, dizziness, dry mouth, etc.).

Source: The ICD-10 Classification of Mental and Behavioural Disorders, Clinical descriptions and diagnostic guidelines, WHO, pp. 115–116

 CHALLENGE YOURSELF
Find the DSM-V criteria for the diagnosis of anxiety disorders. Compare it to the ICD-10 criteria.

Types
Agoraphobia and specific phobias (blood phobia, animal phobia, button phobia)

▶ Agoraphobia is the intense fear of open spaces and/or public areas. For example, a person may fear leaving the house.

▶ Blood phobias are those which involve the sight of blood, or activities linked to blood (e.g. use of needles).

▶ Animal phobias are those where the fear of any type of animal is irrational (e.g. a fear of pigeons).

▶ For a case study of a phobia, refer to the one you studied at AS Level: Saavedra and Silverman (button phobia, see page 73–76).

Measures
The Blood-injection Phobia Inventory (BIPI)

The Blood-injection Phobia Inventory (BIPI) is a questionnaire that initially had 50 items on it that covered a range of situations related to blood and injection phobias:

▶ 32 situations related to blood, injections and the dentist

▶ 5 situations related to animal blood

▶ 4 situations related to the colour red

▶ 5 situations about agoraphobia to see whether it produces a similar phobic response

▶ 4 situations about social anxiety to see if whether produces a similar phobic response.

It also measures the frequency of symptoms, on a scale ranging from 0 = Never to 3 = Always, of a patient's different type of reactions to the situations (cognitive, physiological, behavioural). It also measures situational anxiety as well as anticipatory anxiety. An excerpt from the BIPI is shown in Figure 18.4.1.

Items of the proposed version of the BIPI

Below is a list of situations where you can find yourself and that could create distress, tension, etc. to you. The objective is to evaluate the different reactions that occur to you in each of the described situations.

The task is to rate from 0 to 3, the frequency of each symptom. Use the following scale:

3 = Always	2 = Almost always
1 = Sometimes	0 = Never

The procedure is the following: Read each of the situations shown on the left side, and then score from 0 to 3 each symptom that is listed in the top of the page.

Blood-injection Phobia Inventory (BIPI)

	Cognitive responses	Physiological responses	Behavioural responses
Symptoms+	I don't think I will be able to bear the situation.	My heartbeat speeds up.	I avoid going. I avoid it.
	I think that "something bad is going to happen to me."	My palms or armpits sweat.	My legs and/or hands shake.
	I perceive that not much time will go by before I get dizzy.	My muscles start to tense.	I escape from the situation immediately.
	I feel I confused, disoriented.	I feel that I am getting dizzy.	I shift around in my seat nervously, etc.
	I think people will notice how distressed I feel.	I breathe more quickly.	My words don't come out fluidly or my voice is uneven.
	I don't think I'll know how to react.	I feel a cold sweat all over my body.	Score total situation
	I remember past experiences and anticipate panic.	I feel more blood pumping in my body.	
	I think I'm going to faint.	I feel my face is hot.	
	I must get out of here before I make a fool of myself.	I get pale.	
	I think I should have avoided the situation, because this feeling is nothing new to me.	I faint.	
		I feel a lump in my throat.	
		I feel stomach discomfort.	

Situations

1. When I see an injured person after an accident, bleeding in the road or on TV.
2. When I see blood on my arm or finger after pricking myself with a needle.
3. When I get an intravenous injection.
4. When I see a laboratory tube with blood.
5. When I hear a conversation about blood.
6. When I think I have to accompany a relative to have a blood test or to cure an open wound.
7. When I see another person getting an intramuscular injection.
8. When I describe to another person an experience or situation involving blood.
9. When I think that the nurse has to insert the needle in my vein to extract my blood.
10. If I see an operation or surgical intervention.

Score total symptom

TOTAL

▲ **Figure 18.4.1** Excerpt from the BIPI

Source: Borda Mas, López Jiménez and Pérez San Gregorio (2010: 69–70)

Generalised Anxiety Disorder Assessment (GAD-7)

This is a seven-item questionnaire used to measure the severity of generalised anxiety disorder. The higher the score out of 21 generated, the more severe the generalised anxiety disorder.

PLEASE PRINT IN BLACK PEN

Patient's Full Name	Date of Birth	NHS Number

Generalised Anxiety Disorder Assessment (GAD-7)

This easy to use self-administered patient questionnaire is used as a screening tool and severity measure for generalised anxiety disorder.

In the past 2 weeks how often have you been bothered by any of the following problems:

1. Feeling nervous, anxious or on edge?
- [ ] Not at all
- [ ] Several days
- [ ] More than half the days
- [ ] Nearly every day

2. Not being able to stop or control worrying?
- [ ] Not at all
- [ ] Several days
- [ ] More than half the days
- [ ] Nearly every day

3. Worrying too much about different things?
- [ ] Not at all
- [ ] Several days
- [ ] More than half the days
- [ ] Nearly every day

4. Trouble relaxing?
- [ ] Not at all
- [ ] Several days
- [ ] More than half the days
- [ ] Nearly every day

5. Being so restless that it is hard to sit still?
- [ ] Not at all
- [ ] Several days
- [ ] More than half the days
- [ ] Nearly every day

6. Becoming easily annoyed or irritable?
- [ ] Not at all
- [ ] Several days
- [ ] More than half the days
- [ ] Nearly every day

7. Feeling afraid as if something awful might happen?
- [ ] Not at all
- [ ] Several days
- [ ] More than half the days
- [ ] Nearly every day

Total =   /21

The GAD-7 score is calculated by assigning scores of 0, 1, 2 and 3 to the response categories of "not at all", "several days", "more than half the days", and "nearly every day" respectively, and adding together the scores for the seven questions.
Scores of 5, 10 and 15 are taken as the cut-off points for mild, moderate and severe anxiety, respectively.

Assessor Name Signature	Date Time	Designation

version 1
March 2012   page 1 of 1

▲ **Figure 18.4.2** Generalised Anxiety Disorder Assessment (GAD-7) version 1 (March 2012)

EXPLANATIONS OF PHOBIAS

Behavioural (classical conditioning)

Classical conditioning is all about learning through association. It is a form of conditioning where the organism (be it human or animal) associates an *unconditional stimulus* with a *neutral stimulus*. After repeated associations, the organism then responds to the neutral stimulus (now called a *conditioned stimulus*) without having the *unconditional stimulus* present anymore. Figure 18.4.3 shows what happens in classical conditioning.

In their study of Little Albert, Watson and Rayner (1920) were interested in two aims:

"1. Can we condition fear of an animal (e.g. a white rat) by visually presenting it and simultaneously striking a steel bar?

2. If such a conditioned emotional response can be established, will there be a transfer to other animals or objects?" (Watson and Rayner, 1920).

At approximately nine months of age, Little Albert was presented with a range of stimuli (e.g. a white rat, a rabbit, a dog, a monkey). Albert showed no fear towards any of the objects. When Albert reached 11 months and 3 days old, the experimental procedure began to test the first aim. Albert was presented with a white rat again and as before he showed no fear. However, as Albert reached out to touch the rat, Watson struck an iron bar immediately behind Albert's head. Albert "jumped violently and fell forward, burying his face in the mattress" (1920: 4).

Albert tried to approach the rat again but as soon as he got close the iron bar was struck. After the two associations of the rat and loud noise the rat was taken away.

Seven days later, the researchers wanted to see whether his experience with the loud noise had made Alfred fearful of white rats. He was very wary around the rat and did not really want to play with it or touch it. When he did reach for it the loud noise was made, the same as in the previous week. This was done five times during the session. So, in total, Albert experienced the loud noise and white rat occurring together on seven occasions. Finally, the rat was presented by itself and Albert began to cry and crawled away rapidly. This was the first time he had cried during the study in response to the rat.

Over the next month Albert's reactions to a range of objects were observed. He was still fearful of the white rat. He showed negative reactions to a rabbit being placed in front of him and a fur coat (made from seal skin). He did not really like cotton wool but the shock was not the same as it was with the rabbit or fur coat. He even began to fear a Santa Claus mask.

His experiences can be explained via the mechanisms of classical conditioning, as shown in Figure 18.4.3.

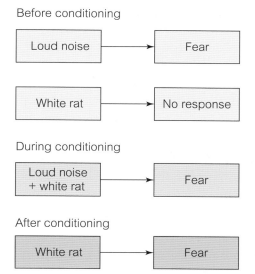

▲ **Figure 18.4.3** Classical conditioning of Little Albert

Classical conditioning may be able to explain why we form some of our phobias:

▶ *Generalisation* occurs when we produce a conditioned response to a stimulus that is *similar* but not the same as the conditioned stimulus. For example, we may produce a fear response to wasps. We could *generalise* this fear to other flying insects such as bees and hornets.

▶ *Extinction* occurs when the conditioned stimulus no longer produces the conditioned response. This could be because the conditioned stimulus has no longer been paired with the unconditional stimulus. So, for example with a person who fears wasps, over time the conditioned response of fear disappears in the presence of the conditioned stimulus of the wasp.

Psychoanalytic

Freud was the first psychodynamic psychologist who attempted to explain how people acquire a phobia. A phobia is a defence against any anxiety produced by any repressed impulses from the id. This fear is then transferred to an object, person or situation that has some sort of "symbolic" connection to the anxiety. The person then becomes fearful of that, rather than the repressed id impulses. This avoidance means the person can function psychologically by not having to focus mental energy onto the repressed conflicts he or she is having.

Freud used the case study of Little Hans to show how this can happen. When Hans was 4 years old, he developed a phobia of horses. Specifically, he was afraid that a white horse would bite him. When reporting this to Freud, Hans' father noted that the fear of horses seemed to relate to their large penises. At around the same time as the phobia of horses developed, a conflict developed between Hans and his father. Hans had been in the habit for some time of getting into his parents' bed in the morning and cuddling his mother. However, his father began to object to this. Hans' phobia worsened to the extent that he would not leave the family house.

Freud interpreted the case as an example of the Oedipus Complex. More specific details are as follows:

▶ Horses represented Hans' father. White horses with black nosebands were the most feared because they resembled the moustached father. Horses also made good father symbols because they have large penises.

▶ The anxiety Hans felt was really castration anxiety triggered by his mother's threat to cut off his "widdler" and fear of his father caused by his banishing Hans from the parental bed.

The "children fantasy" represents a relatively friendly resolution of the Oedipus Complex. In this fantasy Hans replaces his father as his mother's main love object, but the father still has a role as grandfather.

Biomedical or genetic

Blood and injection phobias (Öst, 1992)

Öst (1992) investigated two groups of patients who had been diagnosed with a "simple phobia" via DSM: blood phobic patients (n = 81) and injection phobic

patients (n = 59). Participants in each group were asked whether they had a first-degree relative who had the same phobia. In the blood phobic group, 61 per cent of participants reported this, compared to only 29 per cent of patients in the injection phobic group.

The pattern continued when participants were asked about whether they would faint in their phobic situation: 77 per cent of the blood phobic group reported this compared to 48 per cent in the injection phobic group. However, there were no differences between the two groups regarding:

▶ history of actually fainting in the phobia situation

▶ age of onset

▶ marital status

▶ occupational status

▶ age at which they received treatment.

Overall, there were more similarities than differences between the two groups and Öst believed that the blood and injection phobia should not be seen as separate. Also, due to the large percentage of people who had a first-degree relative with the same phobia, Öst believed that the cause may well be genetic.

CHALLENGE YOURSELF
What else might be causing the blood and injection phobias in this study other than genetics? Justify your answer.

Could it be that we are pre-programmed to fear certain objects that may be potentially harmful? That is, are there certain objects or things that we are expected to be frightened of so we are biologically prepared to fear them? This theory could help us to explain fears that are not totally irrational (e.g. fear of snakes – they can be dangerous). Seligman (1971)* proposed the idea that we have evolved to be frightened of fear-relevant stimuli. So, we fear objects and things that might be of a survival threat in evolutionary terms (Mineka and Öhman, 2002)*. We have fear-relevant stimuli such as snakes that we may be "prepared" to fear. We also have fear-irrelevant stimuli such as flowers that we are not "prepared" to fear.

One study into this used rhesus monkeys as the participants not humans. Cook and Mineka (1989)* wanted to see if the monkeys could become phobic of objects such as a crocodile, a flower, a snake or a rabbit even though they had never seen the object before. A group of rhesus monkeys was split into four groups and each group only saw one of the objects. The researchers controlled what the monkeys saw as they watched a video. The researchers used the technique of splicing the video so that each monkey saw the same rhesus monkey being scared of the object that its group had been assigned. For example, one monkey saw another monkey on the video being scared of the crocodile. The next monkey saw the same monkey on the video but this time the monkey was scared by the flower. Each monkey was then tested on its fear towards the object. The monkeys in the crocodile and snake groups showed fear towards a toy crocodile and a toy snake. However, when the other two groups were shown their "feared object" (e.g. the flower or the rabbit), they did not show any fear. The researchers took this as showing that the monkeys were already prepared to fear the dangerous objects but not the neutral objects.

Could it be that we are born fearful of certain objects? This takes the idea of preparedness further by saying that certain phobias are encoded into our genetic make-up (DNA) and passed down through generations.

Fredrikson, Annas and Wik (1997)* examined 158 phobic females who were scared of snakes or spiders. The participants had to report on their family history of their phobia. The researchers discovered that 37 per cent of the participants' mothers and 7 per cent of their fathers also had the same phobia. This seemed to support the idea that the phobic women had inherited their phobia. However, the researchers asked participants another question about what had happened: they asked whether participants had experienced direct exposure to the phobic stimulus (they had been frightened by the phobic object directly) or had experienced indirect exposure to the phobic stimulus (they had seen someone else being phobic towards the object). Indirect exposure was the most common for snakes – 45 per cent of participants – and for spiders it was 27 per cent. So, even though it looked as if the phobia was caused by genetics, nearly half of the snake-phobic participants could have their phobia explained via social learning.

Cognitive

The view of cognitive psychologists is that phobias being caused by the anxiety is linked to the phobic being more likely to:

▶ attend to negative stimuli

▶ believe that negative events are much more likely to happen in the future than other events.

Cognitive (DiNardo *et al*, 1988)

DiNardo *et al* (1988) researched the potential causes and maintenance of dog phobias. Initially, 790 female students of introductory psychology completed the Fear Survey Schedule. Responses to the item about fear of dogs on this survey were used to recruit potential participants. Those answering "much" or "very much" to the dog item were classed as being fearful of dogs. (Those who answered "not at all" were classed as not fearing dogs.) However, the final selection of participants for each group was based around a behavioural approach test. All potential participants rated their anxiety on a scale of 0–8 when approached step-by-step by a black Labrador with a handler. If a participant's score was always less than 2, the person was accepted into the study's non-fearful group. If a participant's average score was greater than 2, or the participant refused to touch the dog, the person was accepted into the fearful group.

A structured interview was undertaken by all participants (fearful group: n = 16, non-fearful group: n = 21). Information about frightening experiences with dogs was recorded, as well as experiences involving pain. Participants were asked about their perception of the probability that harm would happen when encountering a dog. Potential conditioning causes of the dog fears were split into S-S (those that involved pain) and S-R (those that did not involve pain). Table 18.4.1 highlights the main results.

	Ss				
	Fearful (16)		Non-fearful (21)		
	N	(%)	N	(%)	
Conditioning event					
S-S	6	(38)	8	(38)	
S-R	2	(13)	5	(24)	
Both	1	(06)	1	(05)	
None	7	(44)	7	(33)	$\chi^2 = 0.42^a$
Expected consequences					
Fear	16	(100)	3	(14)	$\chi^2 = 26.7^b$
Harm	16	(100)	2	(10)	$\chi^2 = 29.75^b$
Mean subjective probability					
Fear	0.78		0.02		$F = 194.5^b$
Harm	0.55		0.02		$F = 65.2^b$

[a]$P > 0.50$; [b]$P < 0.001$.

▲ **Table 18.4.1** Factors associated with dog fears

Source: DiNardo *et al* (1988: 242)

As Table 18.4.1 shows, in both groups the majority of conditioning events were S-S and, overall, there was no significant difference between the two groups based on the different conditioning events. However, there was a significant difference between the two groups: the fearful group expected a fearful situation and harm from an encounter with a dog. Therefore, it would seem that dog phobia is maintained by the belief (cognition) that harm is about to happen.

Strength	Weakness
The screening of using the questionnaire and the behavioural measurement ensured that the two groups were labelled correctly. This increases the validity of the study as it ensured there was a fearful and a non-fearful group.	The sample consisted only of females. There may be an issue in generalising the findings to a male population as males may have different S-S and S-R experiences and may think differently when it comes to expecting fear and harm when encountering dogs.

Kindt and Brosschot (1997)* conducted a study to test cognitive biases in people with arachnophobia. They created a Stroop-type test where participants had to read out the colour of the ink of spider-related words or pictures. Those who claimed to be arachnophobic took significantly longer to name the ink colour of the spider-related words compared to a control group. This hints at phobics having an automatic cognitive process of attending to phobias stimuli for longer than usual.

Issues and debates tracker: These causes of anxiety disorders can be seen as reductionist as each one only looks at the cause from one angle. Also, all of these can be seen as deterministic as they are all predicting that anxiety disorders are determined by either internal or external mechanisms.

TREATMENT AND MANAGEMENT OF ANXIETY DISORDERS

Systematic desensitisation (Wolpe, 1958)

If we look at the case of Little Albert again (see page 135), it can be clearly seen that the conditioned stimulus of the white rat elicited the conditioned response of fear. The phobia had been *learned*.

Systematic desensitisation works on the idea that the phobia can then be *unlearned*. The end point should recondition the patient so that the conditioned stimulus (which will be the phobic stimulus) produces a conditioned response of relaxation and not fear.

In the systematic desensistisation therapy developed by Wolpe (1958), the first step is to teach patients relaxation skills so that they understand what it feels like to have relaxed muscles. This should enable patients to recreate this feeling in a variety of situations including when confronted with their phobic stimulus.

Second, the patient produces an anxiety or fear hierarchy to work through with the therapist. A simple hierarchy, for use by a person fearful of snakes, would be as follows:

1. This is the least anxious situation – looking at a cartoon snake in a children's book.

2. The person looks at a picture of a real snake in a book.

3. The person watches a snake on a wildlife programme.

4. A snake is in the same room as the person but in a cage.

5. The snake is in the same room as the person and out of the cage.

6. The person is within 3 feet of the snake.

7. The person touches the snake.

8. This is the most anxious situation – the person lets the snake go around his or her neck.

Patients can only move to a higher stage of the hierarchy once each stage has been successfully completed; that is, the patient is showing signs of relaxation in relation to a specific stage on the hierarchy (e.g. for stage 2 above it would be when looking at a book; for stage 7, when touching the snake).

Figure 18.4.4 shows the principles of classical conditioning linked to systematic desensitisation.

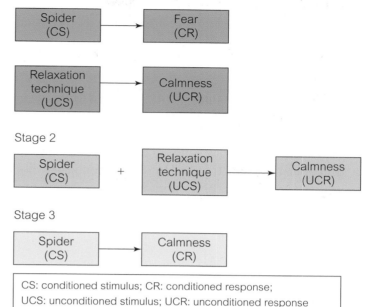

CS: conditioned stimulus; CR: conditioned response; UCS: unconditioned stimulus; UCR: unconditioned response

▲ **Figure 18.4.4** Principles of classical conditioning linked to systematic desensitisation

You can see from Figure 18.4.4 that in the conditioning phase there are competing responses of fear and relaxation. This is called reciprocal inhibition whereby it is impossible to experience both emotions at the same time. The idea is to promote the relaxation response more than the fear response. If the patient is feeling more fear than relaxation then that stage of the hierarchy is stopped until the patient feels relaxed again and is willing to have another go.

There have been many studies that support the use of systematic desensitisation to treat phobias and fears.

Capafons, Sosa and Avero (1998)* reported that for their 20 patients with a fear of flying who had several sessions progressing up their anxiety hierarchy became much less fearful of flying after the study ended. However, as with most studies in this area, there was no follow-up to see whether the fear reduction had lasted.

Zettle (2003)* showed that systematic desensitisation can be applied to people who fear mathematics. Twenty-four college students underwent treatment for six weeks (split between systematic desensitisation and a different therapy) and had to rate their anxieties towards mathematics before, during and after the treatment. Anxiety decreased markedly for those who completed their systematic desensitisation even though their mathematics ability never changed.

Ventis, Higbee and Murdock (2001)* found that both relaxation techniques and simply laughing at the phobic stimulus were effective in reducing the fear in arachnophobics. All participants had been matched on fear: some progressed up their hierarchy with relaxation and others by laughing. However, no follow-up sessions were conducted by Zettle or by Ventis, Higbee and Murdock.

Applied tension (Öst, 1989)

Applied muscle tension is a technique developed by Öst in the 1980s. It was developed to help people with blood and injury phobias. They had to repeatedly contract the major muscle groups of the arms and legs to decrease vagovasal (fainting) reactions when highly anxious. This technique has been reported to increase cerebral blood flow.

Öst (1989) reported on a study of 30 patients who had a phobia of blood, wounds and/or injuries. They were treated with applied tension, applied relaxation or a combination of the two for five, nine or ten sessions respectively. Success was measured via self-reports, behavioural assessment and physiological measures. These were taken before treatment, after treatment and at six months post-treatment. All of the groups significantly improved throughout the treatment intervention and at the six-month follow-up session. A total of 73 per cent of the patients were clinically improved at the end of the treatment and 77 per cent at the follow-up session. While there were no significant differences between the groups, many measures showed a trend in favour of the applied tension method. Öst noted that the applied tension is completed in half the time of the other two treatments so should be considered for people with blood phobia and related phobias.

Strength	Weakness
The technique has good application as it was successful in the study and therefore therapists may choose to use it with the clients to help them overcome a specific phobia.	The sample size was relatively small so it might be difficult to generalise the findings beyond the sample. The study needs replicating.

Ditto *et al* (2003)* tested the effectiveness of applied tension with people who were phobic of giving blood (having fear of needles, etc.). A total of 605 donors were randomly assigned to one of three groups: applied tension, a no-treatment control or a placebo control. Participants in the applied tension group watched an instructional video that taught them how to contract and relax the main muscle groups in the arms and legs. Participants in the placebo control watched the video but they were not told to use the technique. Those in the applied tension group reported significantly fewer phobic symptoms about being blood donors and actually produced more full quotas of blood than participants in the other two groups. They were also more likely to recommend blood donation to a friend as a result. However, there were no differences across the three groups on the probability that they would give blood again.

Holly, Balegh and Ditto (2011)* examined the role of applied tension on anxiety in people giving blood. Participants were 70 people randomly assigned to either a control group or the experimental group. Those in the experimental group were taught applied tension before watching a video that showed someone giving blood. The females in the applied tension group showed significant reduction in vasovagal symptoms (especially in those who reported high fear of needles). This was backed up with physiological data that showed it was decreased anxiety that brought about the reduction in vasovagal reactions.

CBT

See pages 115–117 for a description of how CBT works. There have been numerous studies assessing the effectiveness of CBT in relation to phobias.

Lilliecreutz, Josefsson and Sydsjö (2010)* tested the effectiveness of CBT for blood and injection phobias in pregnant women.

A total of 30 women, who had been diagnosed with the phobias, took part in the study. They took part in two sessions of CBT. The comparison groups were 46 pregnant women who received no CBT and 70 healthy pregnant women. The CBT group showed significant reductions in their anxiety levels (measured by the Injection Phobia Scale – Anxiety) after each CBT session. This continued after the birth of their child. Therefore, CBT is effective in these situations and in this study it appeared to be sustained up to three months after childbirth.

Melfsen *et al* (2011)* examined the effectiveness of using CBT for socially phobic children. A total of 44 children who were diagnosed with social phobia were randomly assigned to a CBT condition or a "waiting-list" condition. The main outcome measure was clinical improvement but other aspects were measured (e.g. coping ability, dysfunctional cognitions and frequency of interactions). There were significant differences between the groups post-therapy, with those in the CBT group being more likely to be free from their previous diagnosis of social phobia.

In addition, Andrews, Davies and Titov (2011)* tested out the effectiveness of face-to-face versus Internet-based CBT for people with social phobias. The researchers randomly assigned 70 participants to either group. Both groups made significant progress relating to symptoms and disability measures. However, the total amount of time that the therapist was required differed markedly: 18 minutes for the Internet-based CBT whereas it was 240 minutes for the usual CBT. Therefore, Internet-based CBT would be more cost-effective in areas where healthcare budgets are limited.

Galvao-de Almeida *et al* (2013)* reviewed the impact that CBT had on people with phobias. However,

all studies in the review had to have functional neuroimaging measures as part of them. A total of six studies met the inclusion criteria for the review. It would appear that people who underwent CBT had significant "deactivations" in the amygdale, thalamus and hippocampal regions of the brain. Therefore, CBT appears to directly affect brain functions linked to anxiety.

CBT (Öst and Westling, 1995)

Öst and Westling (1995) tested the effectiveness of using CBT against using applied relaxation (AR) to treat panic disorder. The patient group (n = 38) had all been diagnosed with panic disorder using the *Diagnostic and Statistical Manual of Mental Disorders* (*DSM*). All of the patients were assessed via an independent rater, self-report scales and observations before and after treatment as well as at a one-year follow-up. All patients had an individual session (CBT or AR) each week for 12 weeks.

Both of the treatment groups showed large improvements at the end of treatment and at the one-year follow-up. There were no significant differences between the two groups but the results did favour CBT. At end of treatment, 65 per cent of the AR group and 74 per cent of the CBT group were panic-free and after one year this was 82 per cent for the AR group and 89 per cent for the CBT group.

Strength	Weakness
There was a long-term follow-up procedure to show that the positive effects of the CBT lasted.	Some of the outcome measures were using self-report scales so some of the participants may not have told the truth (they may have given socially desirable answers) which could reduce the validity of the findings.

18.5 OBSESSIVE-COMPULSIVE AND RELATED DISORDERS

CHARACTERISTICS OF OBSESSIVE-COMPULSIVE AND RELATED DISORDERS

Types

Common obsessions, common compulsions, hoarding and body dysmorphic disorder (BDD)

There are many common obsessions that people with obsessive-compulsive disorder (OCD) experience. These include intrusive and persistent thoughts, doubts, worries, images, etc. They are unwanted and somewhat disturbing and can easily affect the person's life. This makes them very difficult to ignore. For example, the people affected could be:

- worrying that everything around them is contaminated with harmful germs
- worrying that a terrible event will happen if they don't check something repeatedly
- worrying that they will catch the latest disease that is being reported on the news.

There are also many common compulsions that people with OCD experience. These are the repetitive physical behaviours and actions (or mental repetition) that are performed over and over again. They may include:

- excessive washing of hands
- checking that items in the house are displayed in the "correct order"
- checking that light switches are off and that electrical plug sockets are off
- mentally counting to a certain number as it "neutralises" the obsessional thought.

Hoarding is a relatively new disorder. This is when people acquire an excessive amount of items in their home and store them but not in a systematic way. This clutter gets in the way of their everyday life and most of the items cannot be found if they are needed for use. The amount of items can mean people cannot access certain rooms in their house. They may become very distressed if someone tries to tidy up, even though most of the items are of no monetary value (e.g. there may be hundreds of old drink cartons or empty tissue boxes).

Body dismorphic disorder (BDD) is an anxiety disorder that causes people to have a distorted view of their body and appearance. They spend a lot of time worrying about their appearance and believe "minor flaws" will be spotted by other people and become a major issue. This disorder must not be confused with people being vain. People with BDD have anxiety about their appearance. According to the NHS in the United Kingdom,

"a person with BDD may:

- constantly compare their looks to other people's
- spend a long time in front of a mirror, but at other times avoid mirrors altogether
- spend a long time concealing what they believe is a defect
- become distressed by a particular area of their body (most commonly their face)
- feel anxious when around other people and avoid social situations
- be very secretive and reluctant to seek help, because they believe others will see them as vain or self-obsessed
- seek medical treatment for the perceived defect – for example, they may have cosmetic surgery, which is unlikely to relieve their distress
- excessively diet and exercise".

Source: http://www.nhs.uk/Conditions/body-dysmorphia/Pages/Introduction.aspx)

Case study

Rapoport (1989) reported on a boy called Charles in his book *The Boy who Couldn't Stop Washing*. At the age of 12, Charles began to wash obsessively. For some time he managed to keep this action under control but then spent more and more of his school day washing. Eventually, he washed so often that he had to leave school. The ritual was always the same: he would hold the soap in his right hand and put it under a running tap for one minute. He would then transfer the soap to his left hand away from the tap for another minute. He would repeat this for about one hour. He would then wash for about another two hours before getting dressed. At first, his mother discouraged him but, seeing how upset Charles became, she began to clean items in the house with alcohol and then stopped people from visiting as they had "germs" and it would upset Charles. Rapoport wanted Charles to have an EEG but the boy refused. Charles found stickiness to be "terrible" like a "disease". He had drug therapy and his symptoms disappeared for around one year. He developed a tolerance for the drug, but then he engaged in his OCD behaviour in the evening only, so as not to disrupt his day.

Measures

Maudsley Obsessive-Compulsive Inventory (MOCI)

The Maudsley Obsessive-Compulsive Inventory (MOCI) is a 30-item scale. It has two major sub-scales and two minor ones:

- Major: Checking and Cleaning
- Minor: Slowness and Doubting.

Each of the 30 items is answered with "True" or "False". Some of the items are reversed and some of them feature on more than one of the sub-scales. The total number of items for each sub-scale are:

- Checking – 9 items
- Cleaning – 11 items
- Slowness – 7 items
- Doubting – 7 items.

A practitioner can calculate an overall score and a score for each sub-scale to help individuals pinpoint the main features of their OCD. Example items include the following.

1.	I frequently have to check things (e.g. gas or water taps, doors, etc.) several times.	TRUE	FALSE
2.	My hands do not feel dirty after touching money.	TRUE	FALSE
3.	I do not stick to a very strict routine when doing ordinary things.	TRUE	FALSE
4.	I tend to get behind in my work because I repeat things over and over again.	TRUE	FALSE

Source: Hodgson and Rachman (1977: 395)

Strength	Weakness
The scale went through rigorous validity and reliability testing to ensure that it does measure OCD symptoms and that it is consistent over time.	The questionnaire relies on a patient's honesty. Patients may not want to admit to certain behaviours and thoughts when completing a questionnaire, so the overall score may not be a true representation of the OCD symptoms.

The Yale-Brown Obsessive Compulsive Scale (Y-BOCS)

The Y-BOCS is a very popular measure used in many studies. There are two parts to the measurement and it is used as a semi-structured interview technique:

- The symptom checklist is a list of 67 symptoms for OCD and the interviewer notes whether each symptom is current, past or absent (in the latter case it is not recorded). This helps the interviewer determine whether a group of clustered symptoms exists (the list is divided into groups such as aggressive obsessions, sexual obsessions, contamination obsessions, checking compulsions, ordering compulsions and cleaning or washing compulsions). An example is shown in Figure 18.5.1.

- The Y-BOCS itself consists of 19 items that the interviewee completes during the interview based on responses and observations. An example question is shown in Figure 18.5.1.

Symptom checklist

CLEANING/WASHING COMPULSIONS

	Current	Past	Examples
43. Excessive or ritualised hand washing	☐	☐	Washing your hands many times a day or for long periods of time after touching, or thinking you have touched, a contaminated object. This may include washing the entire length of your arm.
44. Excessive or ritualised showering, bathing, tooth brushing, grooming or toilet routine	☐	☐	Taking showers or baths or performing other bathroom routines that may last for several hours. If the sequence is interrupted the entire process may have to be restarted.
45. Excessive or ritualised cleaning of household items or other animate objects	☐	☐	Excessive cleaning of faucets, toilets, floors, kitchen counters or kitchen utensils.

2. INTERFERENCE DUE TO OBSESSIVE THOUGHTS

0 = None.
1 = Mild, slight interference with social or occupational activities, but overall performance not impaired.
2 = Moderate, definite interference with social or occupational performance, but still manageable.
3 = Severe, causes substantial impairment in social or occupational performance.
4 = Extreme, incapacitating.

Q: How much do your obsessive thoughts interfere with your social or work (or role) functioning? Is there anything that you don't do because of them? [If not currently working, determine how much performance would be affected if the patient were employed.]

☐ 0
☐ 1
☐ 2
☐ 3
☐ 4

▲ **Figure 18.5.1** Excerpt from the Y-BOCS symptom checklist and an example question

As you can see, there is a part-script for this question alongside how to score it. The scores are transferred to a grid that measures obsessions, compulsions and other aspects of the condition.

A person is given an obsessions score out of 20 and a compulsion score out of 20. Then nine other items are noted on the 1–4 scale for severity.

There is also a children's version of the scale.

> **Issues and debates tracker:** These scales have good application to everyday life as they can be used to help monitor the OCD of patients to see whether a treatment is working or not. Seeing a reduction in scores, for instance, could be a good indicator that a treatment is working for a patient.

EXPLANATIONS OF OCD

Biomedical (genetic, biochemical and neurological)

In terms of a neurological explanation, OCD is quite complex. There appears to be an interaction between certain areas of the brain such as the orbitofrontal cortex, the anterior cingulate cortex, the striatum, the thalamus, the caudate nucleus and the basal ganglia. These structures all communicate in the brain and deal with our "primitive" emotions such aggression, sexuality and bodily functions. Usually these circuits activate after certain activities. For example, after someone goes to the toilet it gives the person an urge to wash his or her hands. However, once the hand washing has been completed, the circuit activity dies down and the person continues with the next task. This does not appear to happen in people with OCD; the circuits do not "die down" enough which leads to complications in communication between these areas of the brain. This then stimulates the person to keep having the urge to wash his or her hands constantly. As these parts of the brain are "primitive" there is no reasoning that can take place: once it fires, the action has to be thought about and then acted upon. Therefore, the rational parts of the brain act upon the primitive urges, causing obsessions and compulsions.

CHALLENGE YOURSELF
Research the functioning of the parts of the brain mentioned above.

There is some evidence to suggest that OCD could be genetic. Ozomaro *et al* (2013)* noted that the SLITRK1 gene appears to be linked to some aspects of OCD. They examined 381 individuals with OCD and 356 control participants. They discovered three novel variants on this gene present in seven of the OCD individuals and concluded that the SLITRK1 and variants need more research but currently they appear linked to OCD.

Taj *et al* (2013)* researched another candidate gene called DRD4 (dopamine D4 receptor). A total of 173 individuals with OCD were compared to 201 healthy controls. They completed a range of questionnaires that measured OCD and mental health and all were genotyped for the DRD4 gene and variants. It was revealed that the 7R allele frequency was higher in the OCD group (especially so for females), suggesting another potential genetic cause for OCD.

Humble *et al* (2011)* wanted to test whether the neuropeptide oxytocin was correlated with OCD symptoms as previous studies had hinted at this. Even though the researchers were testing whether SSRIs affect oxytocin, the main result they reported was that, at baseline, levels of oxytocin were positively correlated with OCD symptoms as measured by the Y-BOCS.

Those with early onset OCD had the highest levels of oxytocin. Finally, reduced levels of serotonin may be linked to OCD and the drugs used in the studies do affect serotonin levels (see the treatment section of OCD on pages 146–148).

Strength	Weakness
The measures taken to test this idea are objective and scientific, which means that they are more likely to be valid.	The idea is reductionist as it does not take into account other factors that may cause OCD such as cognitions or psychodynamic ideas.

Behavioural

The behavioural aspect is linked to the compulsions that people perform during OCD. Psychologists consider it to be a learned behaviour that is being reinforced by the consequences of performing the compulsions. For example, if a compulsive behaviour ends in a favourable outcome (e.g. reductions of anxiety or hands are now free of germs) then this is positive reinforcement. As we know, positive reinforcers increase the probability of repeating that behaviour again. For example, if the end goal of a compulsion is to have arranged clothes in some form of order and this reduces anxiety and also fulfils the compulsion to have things in order, then two reinforcement mechanisms are working here: negative (removal of anxiety) and positive (clothes are now arranged in order).

Cognitive

The cognitive aspect of this is linked to the obsessive thoughts that OCD individuals have. It would appear that these thoughts increase with levels of stress. In an everyday situation most people can learn to control these but people with OCD tend to have thoughts that are more vivid and elicit greater concern. Psychologists believe that this could be due to childhood experiences that have taught these people that some thoughts are dangerous and unacceptable and this has affected their information-processing networks. When new information is being processed, it is affected by these processing networks and generates anxiety and stress that can only be alleviated with compulsive behaviours.

Psychodynamic

OCD is caused by instinctual forces (driven by the id in the unconscious) that are not under full control due to traumatic experiences in the anal stage of psychosexual development. The person with OCD is therefore fixated in the anal stage. It is the battle between the id's desires and the superego's morals that can cause OCD as the ego (and its defence mechanisms) fail to control either. Obsessive thoughts may be generated by the id (e.g. to be messy and out of control) but the ego uses defence mechanisms to counteract this by making the person behave in a way that is completely opposite to that (e.g. being neat and orderly). This defence mechanism is called reaction formation. For example, if a child has a traumatic experience while potty training (e.g. if the child is harshly treated for being messy) then the obsessive thoughts of being neat and tidy re-emerge in adolescence and adulthood. The person develops OCD as a result because any thoughts of being messy cause great anxiety because of those early unresolved traumatic experiences.

CHALLENGE YOURSELF
To what extent do you feel that the cause of OCD is more nature than nurture? Justify your answer.

TREATMENT AND MANAGEMENT OF OCD AND RELATED DISORDERS

Biomedical

SSRIs

Selvi et al (2011)* studied the effects that two "extra" drugs had on OCD patients who had not responded successfully to just taking SSRIs (see page 120 on how re-uptake inhibitors work). The initial part of the study assessed 90 patients with OCD to assess that just taking SSRIs *did not* work on reducing symptoms. The researchers chose 41 patients from this part of the study and randomly assigned them to either the risperidone (n = 21) or aripiprazole (n = 20) group. They were then given these drugs too for eight further weeks. The researchers measured success by a patient having a 35 per cent or more reduction in scores on the Y-BOCS. In the aripiprazole group 50 per cent of participants did reduce their scores by at least this, as did 72.2 per cent of the risperidone group. Therefore, risperidone appears to be more effective at treating OCD when SSRIs fail by themselves.

Another study by Askari et al (2012)* examined the effectiveness of using granisetron in conjunction with fluvoxamine (an SSRI). Participants were people aged 18–60 who were diagnosed with OCD via DSM-IV-TR. They were randomly assigned to either a granisetron or placebo group. They received 1 milligram of their "drug" every 12 hours for 8 weeks. All patients were assessed using the Y-BOCS at baseline then at weeks two, four, six and eight. Outcomes were measured in the following ways:

▸ A partial response was a minimum 25 per cent reduction in Y-BOCS scores.

▸ A complete response was a minimum 35 per cent reduction in Y-BOCS scores.

▸ Remission was scoring 16 or less on the Y-BOCS.

By week 8, 100 per cent of the granisetron group had scored a complete response and 90 per cent had met the remission criterion. Only 35 per cent of patients in the placebo group managed the same. There were no differences in the tolerance levels of both groups to the "drugs". Therefore, it would appear that the additional drug helped people with OCD reduce their symptoms.

Psychological

Cognitive (Lovell *et al*, 2006)

Lovell et al (2006) tested the effectiveness of a telephone administered CBT for the treatment of OCD. A total of 72 patients who had a primary diagnosis of OCD that could not be attributable to biological causes were randomly assigned to one of two groups (with only 65 completing the entire study):

▸ Group 1 participated in a telephone-administered CBT programme.

▸ Group 2 participated in the same CBT programme, but face to face.

Figure 18.5.2 is a flowchart of the procedure of the study.

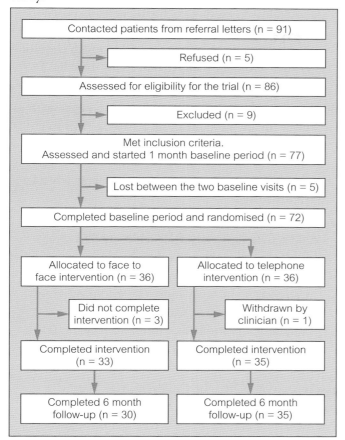

▲ **Figure 18.5.2** Flow of participants through the trial

Source: Lovell *et al* (2006: 4)

The face-to-face programme consisted of ten one-hour sessions. The first session explained the graded exposure and response prevention. It was also used to help create a hierarchy of fear so that weekly targets could be set. Participants were encouraged to practise their targets for at least one hour per day. The telephone group had one face-to-face session with the therapist as above and then eight more weekly sessions lasting 30 minutes each. Their final session was face to face.

There were three main outcome measures taken at baseline, immediately after the treatment programme had ended then at one, three and six months post-treatment:

▶ scores on the Y-BOCS

▶ scores on the Beck Depression Inventory

▶ client satisfaction.

Figure 18.5.3 shows the progression of scores over time for the first two measures.

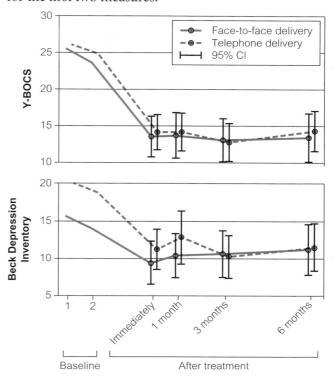

▲ **Figure 18.5.3** Scores for Y-BOCS and Beck Depression Inventory from first baseline visit to six months of follow-up

Source: Lovell *et al* (2006: 5)

The scores on both measures reduced significantly immediately after the programme had ended and continued at six months post-treatment. Clients in both groups were equally satisfied with their experiences. Therefore, it was concluded that CBT delivered by telephone was equivalent to face-to-face programmes in terms of outcomes and satisfaction.

Strength	Weakness
The study has application as it was successful so a therapist can choose to use these techniques with a client who shows OCD.	The outcome measures were self-reports so the researchers did not know whether the participants were being truthful or giving more socially desirable answers. This could reduce the validity of the findings.

Exposure and response prevention (Lehmkuhl *et al*, 2008)

Lehmkuhl *et al* (2008) reported on a case study of a 12-year-old boy with autism who was also diagnosed with OCD. The researchers used exposure and response prevention (ERP) to help the boy with his OCD. ERP programmes for OCD usually have three components:

1. Information is gathered about any symptoms.

2. ERP is initiated and led by a therapist.

3. There is generalisation and relapse training.

The therapy also involves gradual exposure, in vivo, to the feared stimuli based on a hierarchy of fear. The response prevention involves the patient blocking or refraining from engaging in any rituals during the exposure to the feared stimuli.

Jason (a pseudonym) was a 12-year-old boy who had been diagnosed with high functioning autism since he was 2 years old. At age 11 years 9 months he began developing ritualistic behaviours that were based around fears of contamination (overuse of hand sanitisers, avoidance of items such as door knobs and repeatedly checking the expiration dates on food). The symptoms began to interfere with everyday functioning. For example, at school his teachers noticed that he would not turn the pages of a book or sit comfortably in his chair. Jason went through ten 50-minute therapy sessions over a period of 16 weeks. The entire procedure was adapted to take into account his autism:

▶ The first two sessions ran as follows. The first session introduced Jason to the therapy and allowed him to construct his hierarchy of fear to work with. He had difficulties in identifying his obsessional thoughts. In session two, the therapist exposed Jason to situations based on his hierarchy of fear in the hospital. For example, he had to touch elevator buttons and door handles repeatedly until he habituated to the anxiety.

▶ For the next six sessions, each session began with a review of any homework set for Jason. This might have included giving out papers in class or using contaminated items at home. The researchers also reviewed Jason's use of coping statements when he felt distressed.

▶ In the penultimate session, Jason and his parents told the therapist that they felt there had been a significant decrease in Jason's distress levels and number of symptoms linked to his OCD. He was participating in many more classroom activities too. The final session was used to answer any remaining questions that Jason or his parents had about the treatment and what to do after the treatment phase had ended.

Jason had completed the Children's Y-BOS at pre- and post-treatment. The initial score was 18 (showing moderately severe OCD) but this had reduced to a score of 3 immediately after session ten (normal range). This score was maintained at a three-month follow-up meeting. Therefore, it would appear that ERP was successful in helping Jason with his OCD.

Strength	Weakness
As this was a case study, in-depth information was recorded, meaning that the data are rich and should be valid.	As it was a case study, generalisation may be difficult as Jason may be a unique case for whom the therapy worked.

Issues and debates tracker: All of these therapies have application to everyday life as they are useful to help control the symptoms of OCD. However, a lot of studies are not longitudinal so researchers sometimes do not know whether the therapy works over time.

CHALLENGE YOURSELF
Design a study that tests the effectiveness of two different treatments for OCD.

HOW TO EVALUATE: ABNORMALITY

For the 10-mark question in paper 3, you will be asked to evaluate one of the topics covered in this section. Below are three examples of the types of evaluation point you *could* write in the examination.

You should aim to make a range of evaluation points for the 10-mark question.

TREATMENT OF SCHIZOPHRENIA

Biological

Research into the treatment of schizophrenia has some *ethical* issues. For example, the use of ECT involves fitting electrodes to specific areas of the head and a small electrical current is passed through them for no longer than one second. The seizure may last up to one minute and the patient regains consciousness in around 15 minutes. The argument is whether a person truly understands what the procedure involves if they have a serious mental health issue that affects thought processes, such as schizophrenia. With any long-term memory problems unknown after using ECT, is it fair to give the treatment to patients who may not understand this? However, research has shown that ECT is a *useful* treatment for schizophrenia. Thirthalli *et al* (2009) reported that in a sample of schizophrenics (split into catatonic and non-catatonic), those who were catatonic required fewer ECT sessions to help control their symptoms. Therefore, ECT may be a more useful treatment for patients with catatonic

schizophrenia than for patients with other types. However, biological treatments for schizophrenia are *reductionist*. They are based on the idea that we need to treat the biology of the condition (e.g. excess dopamine) without tackling the psychological elements of the disorder. It ignores aspects such as schizophrenia being caused by faulty information processing. Frith (1992) noted that schizophrenics might have a deficient "metarepresentation" system. This would deal with being able to reflect on thoughts, emotions and behaviours. Therefore, a different treatment might be more appropriate.

EXPLANATIONS FOR PHOBIAS

Behavioural

There is *evidence* that supports the behavioural explanation for anxiety disorders that took place under controlled conditions. Watson and Rayner (1920) successfully created a phobia in little Albert by banging a metal bar behind him every time he was in the presence of a white rat. After a few trials, just showing him the rat caused him to cry and be fearful of it. As this was a study conducted under controlled conditions it means it can be replicated and tested for reliability. However, this would not happen due to *ethical* reasons as it would cause immense stress to the child. The behavioural explanation can be said to be *reductionist* as it ignores other factors that could be causing a phobia. For example, it could be that we are pre-programmed to fear certain objects that may be potentially harmful: there are certain objects or things that we are *expected* to be frightened of so we are *biologically prepared* to fear them. This can explain why we fear certain objects we have never even seen – the fear is encoded in our genetic history. For classical conditioning to explain a fear we have to have direct contact with the phobic stimulus.

TREATMENT FOR OBSESSIONS AND COMPULSIONS

Cognitive

There is some evidence that CBT is a *useful* therapy for OCD. For example, Reynolds *et al* (2013) wanted to investigate whether involving parents in their child's CBT for OCD was more effective than when children received CBT by themselves. Patients received up to 14 sessions of CBT in the trial. The main outcome was an analysis in the reduction of scores on the Y-BOCS. Both ways of delivering CBT were equally effective in reducing the severity of OCD. This is useful to know as it gives a child a choice of having CBT with or without the parent being present. Also, this can be linked to the *nature versus nurture* debate. If treatments are based on what causes OCD, then if a psychological treatment is effective it shows that OCD may be based more on nurture than nature. It could be ways in which people process information that need treating to help with OCD, rather than the nature approach of affecting the biology of patients by getting them to take drugs for their OCD.

20 CONSUMER PSYCHOLOGY

20.1 THE PHYSICAL ENVIRONMENT

RETAIL AND LEISURE ENVIRONMENT DESIGN

Retail store architecture (Turley and Milliman, 2000)

Turley and Milliman (2000) reviewed the literature about atmospheric effects on shopping behaviour. They noted five key atmospheric variables that could help predict shopping behaviour, which are:

- external variables (e.g. entrances, colour of building)
- general interior variables (e.g. music, width of aisles)
- layout and design variables (e.g. grouping of merchandise, furniture)
- point-of-purchase and decoration variables (e.g. signs and cards, price displays)
- human variables (e.g. employees' uniforms, crowding).

Table 20.1.1 lists more examples of the five types of atmospheric variable.

External variables	General interior variables	Layout and design variables	Point-of-purchase and decoration variables	Human variables
Exterior signs	Flooring and carpeting	Space design and allocation	Point-of-purchase displays	Employee characteristics
Entrances	Color schemes	Placement of merchandise	Signs and cards	Employee uniforms
Exterior display windows	Lighting	Grouping of merchandise	Degrees and certificates	Crowding
Height of building	Music	Work station placement	Pictures	Customer characteristics
Size of building	PA usage	Placement of equipment	Artwork	Privacy
Color of building	Scents	Placement of cash registers	Product displays	
Surrounding stores	Tobacco smoke	Waiting areas	Usage instructions	
Lawns and gardens	Width of aisles	Waiting rooms	Price displays	
Address and location	Wall composition	Department locations	Teletext	
Architectural style	Paint and wall paper	Traffic flow		
Surrounding area	Ceiling composition	Racks and cases		
Parking availability	Merchandise	Waiting queues		
Congestion and traffic	Temperature	Furniture		
Exterior walls	Cleanliness	Dead areas		

▲ **Table 20.1.1** Examples of the researchers' five types of variable

Source: Turley and Milliman (2000: 194)

These were the main review findings for each type of variable:

▶ External variables. The prototypicality of a store (how much the same stores from a chain look the same), exterior window displays, parking and perceived quality of location all successfully predicted shopping behaviour.

▶ General interior variables. Overall perception of the general interior of a shop predicts the probability that someone will shop there. The role of music has been extensively studied (see pages 155–156 for examples) and how it affects sales, and consumers' arousal and positive experiences while shopping. However, these experiences can be mediated by consumers' age and music preference, and the volume of the music. When odours and aromas are filtered into shops it appears to affect purchasing rates, the time consumers spent in store and pleasant feelings while there (see page 158 for a study on smell).

▶ Layout and design variables. Unplanned purchases are higher when consumers have low knowledge of products and no time pressure. Power aisles appear to be successful where a shop has a small number of different products in one aisle used to display large quantities of each of those products. Apparently, it conveys that those products are on offer at discount prices so they are more likely to be bought.

▶ Point-of-purchase and decoration variables. The effect of shelf space has been examined but the findings are mixed. It is believed that products placed at eye level or just below will be chosen first, but there is only limited evidence that this occurs. Point-of-sale displays can entice shoppers to buy more of a product as they stand and wait to be served.

▶ Human variables. Perceived crowding in a shop has been reported to have a negative effect on shopping experiences so fewer goods are purchased. Crowding stops people from browsing and comparing products.

 CHALLENGE YOURSELF
Using the information from the Turley and Milliman study, design a shop that sells perfumes, beauty products and homeware supplies.

Leisure environments (Finlay *et al*, 2006)

Finlay *et al* (2006) examined the influence of physical design of gambling venues on emotion. As people left a casino in Las Vegas, they were asked to participate in the study. A total of 48 agreed (26 male). Two or three participants were grouped with a researcher and then taken to four different casinos in succession. These casinos had two main designs: Kranes's playground macro design and Friedman's gaming macro design.

▲ **Figure 20.1.1** Kranes's playground macro design for a casino

Source: Finlay *et al* (2006: 574)

▲ **Figure 20.1.2** Friedman's gaming macro design

Source: Finlay *et al* (2006: 575)

In each casino, participants were given $5 each to spend on whatever they wanted to during a 30-minute period. They then completed a range of questionnaires used to assess the psychological effects of each casino. These included scales on pleasure, arousal and perceptions of the casino. The main findings included these points:

▶ Pleasure was significantly related to overall restoration of the casino (pleasant imagery present), coherence (organised and user-friendly casino) and complexity (more elaborate settings and visibly rich).

▶ Pleasure ratings were higher for Kranes-type designs. Arousal ratings were higher for Freidman-type designs. Overall restoration scores were higher for the Kranes-type designs. This was also true for coherence scores.

Strength	Weakness
The study has ecological validity as it took place in an actual casino.	The study used questionnaires to measure pleasure and arousal so the data could be seen as being subjective.

CHALLENGE YOURSELF
Design a laboratory experiment to test whether the Kranes-type design or the Friedman-type design is preferred by people who have never been in a casino before.

Store interior design (Vrechopoulos *et al*, 2004)

Store layout and interior design can be crucial in terms of whether shoppers enjoy the experience of shopping and so buy more products. A study by Vrechopoulos *et al* (2004) focused on store layout used in grocery retail in the UK and Greece, where three main types of store layout are used. These are:

▶ grid store layout

▶ freeform store layout

▶ racetrack store layout.

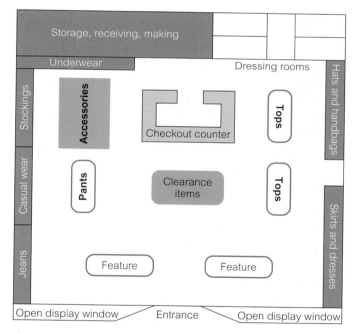

▲ **Figure 20.1.4** Freeform store layout

Source: Levy and Weitz (2001) reproduced in Vrechopoulos *et al* (2004: 14)

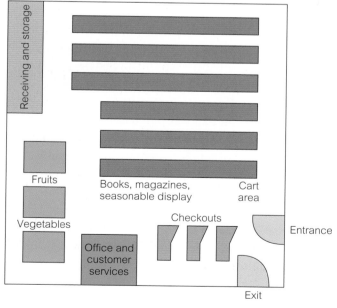

▲ **Figure 20.1.3** Grid store layout

Source: Levy and Weitz (2001) reproduced in Vrechopoulos *et al* (2004: 14)

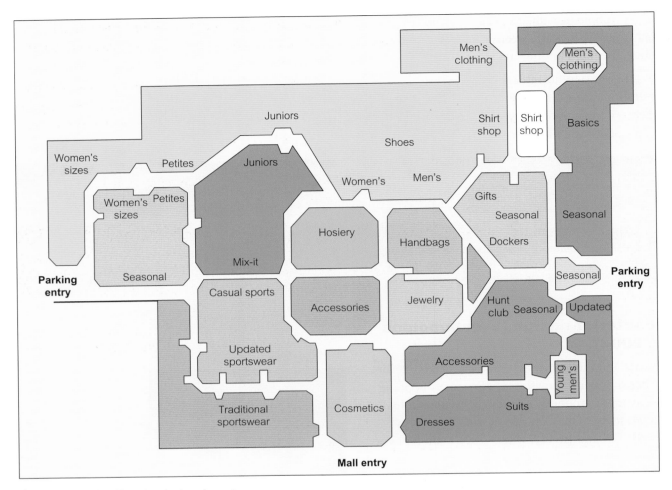

▲ **Figure 20.1.5** Racetrack store layout

Source: Levy and Weitz (2001) reproduced in
Vrechopoulos *et al* (2004: 15)

To test which layouts affect shopping behaviour, this study used a virtual store layout giving participants certain tasks to complete. Four main hypotheses were tested:

1. Consumers perceive the grid layout as more useful for conducting planned purchases than freeform or racetrack layouts.

2. Consumers perceive virtual stores using freeform layout as easier to use than stores employing the grid or racetrack layouts.

3. The racetrack layout offers more entertainment for consumers during the shopping activity.

4. Consumers spend more shopping time in the freeform layout.

The three different store designs were created into virtual stores. Real customers were given tasks to perform in just one of them, hence the design was independent measures. The same experiment was run in the UK and in Greece. There were 60 participants per country, split equally between the three design layouts. Each participant was given a budget of £20 (UK) or 12 000 drachma (Greece) to make purchases in the stores. Any product that was purchased by a participant was subsequently purchased "for real" and delivered to the participant. There were many internationally known brands in the stores (e.g. Pringles®, Heineken®) and also some local produce. The sample was drawn from Internet shoppers and experienced Internet users. A stratified sample was drawn to cover the main occupations of academics, students, employees, business executives and researchers from Brunel and Athens universities. DVs included time spent in the shop and questionnaires that measured aspects such as perceived usefulness, ease of use and entertainment.

There was no statistical difference between the UK and Greek participants so data was merged. The main results were as follows:

1. Participants perceived the freeform layout as significantly more useful in finding their shopping as the other two designs. Therefore, hypothesis 1 was rejected.

2. Participants perceived the grid layout as significantly easier to use than the other two designs. Therefore, hypothesis 2 was rejected.

3. Participants perceived the freeform layout to be the most entertaining. Therefore, hypothesis 3 was rejected.

4. The layout significantly affected time spent shopping. However, the only key difference was that participants spent longer in the racetrack design than in the grid design. Therefore, hypothesis 4 was rejected.

Therefore, it would appear that conventional retail theory about store layout does not apply to online virtual shopping.

Strength	Weakness
The study was standardised so would be easy to replicate to test for reliability.	There were only 20 participants per layout group so generalisability may be an issue due to individual differences.

Issues and debates tracker: These ideas are supporting the situational argument as they are stating that the layout of a shop will affect shopping habits rather than the individuals themselves. To investigate the latter, the researchers would have had to look at aspects of personality and individual differences and this was not done in this study. The ideas may be reductionist as the researchers focused on one aspect of shopping behaviour rather than looking at both the shopper and the environment.

CHALLENGE YOURSELF
To what extent do you feel that this study is culturally biased? Justify your answer.

SOUND AND CONSUMER BEHAVIOUR

Music in restaurants (North *et al*, 2003)

North *et al* (2003) wanted to investigate the effects of different types of music on spending in a restaurant. A total of 393 customers who ate in a restaurant were participants in the study. Gender was balanced and none of the restaurant's customers knew that they were taking part in a study. During the study, 142 participants were exposed to pop music (in 49 parties), 120 to classical music (in 44 parties) and 131 to no music (in 48 parties). The design was independent measures. The DVs were spending on starters, main courses, desserts, coffee, bar drinks, wine, total amount spent on food, total amount spent on drink and total overall spend. The restaurant served *á la carte* food at prices above market average. These were the main significant results:

▶ The amounts spent on starters and coffee, the total food bill and the total spend were significantly higher when classical music was played compared to both pop and no music.

▶ For the remainder of the items, people did spend more on *all other* DVs but they were statistically significant.

This study has implications for restaurants in terms of what music they play and how this could increase turnover.

Strength	Weakness
The study has good application as restaurants can use it to improve their turnover.	Independent groups design was used so individual differences may be playing a role in affecting the DV.

Music in open-air markets (Guéguen *et al*, 2007)

Guéguen *et al* (2007) wanted to test the effect that background noise (in this case music) had on consumer behaviour, for example the length of time people spent browsing a market stall. The researchers conducted their field experiment in an open-air marketplace in

France. Participants were 154 men and 86 women aged 30–60 years, who were "randomly" selected from people who visited the experimental stall.

The music selected for use in the study was pre-tested for sound quality and for a style that would be associated with the selling of products, in this example a variety of trinkets and toys. The music selected was joyful (sonatina) and the experiment took place in a medium-sized French town across two Saturday mornings.

There were three confederates (all 20-year-old females) who acted as if they owned the stall selling trinkets and toys, which were all priced at less than €10. Participants were randomly assigned to the music condition or no music condition. If participants were chosen for the music condition, as soon as they began to browse the stall one of the confederates would turn on the music.

For both conditions, the confederate had to time how long participants spent browsing. If a participant bought anything, the confederate waited for the customer to leave before checking how much he or she had spent.

Only the confederate who selected the customer knew who the participant in the study was. The three confederates took it in turns to be the experimenter and the seller.

The main results were as follows:

▶ When music was played, people stayed longer at the stall compared to when no music was played (5.27 minutes versus 3.72 minutes, p < .001).

▶ More customers bought one or more articles when music was played compared to the no music condition (18.3 per cent versus 10.0 per cent, p < .07).

▶ When music was played, customers spent an average of €6.34 whereas in the no music condition the amount was only €5.67 (p > .20).

Therefore, it would appear that playing music on a stall made customers browse for longer, buy more items and spend more money.

Background noise and food perception (Woods *et al*, 2010)

Woods *et al* (2010) investigated the effects of auditory background noise on the perception of "gustatory food properties" (e.g. sugar and salt levels), food crunchiness and food liking. They ran two experiments.

Experiment 1

A total of 48 students (39 female) from Manchester University in the UK volunteered to participate in the study. The age range was 19–39 years. Five participants were smokers and five reported mild symptoms of a common cold. While being recruited, participants were told that the study involved assessing foods on different attributes. All gave informed consent to take part. The food stimuli were:

▶ savoury: Pringles® Original Salted Crisps (crunchy) and Cathedral City® Mini Mild Cheese (soft)

▶ sweet: Sainsbury's Nice Biscuits (crunchy) and Sainsbury's All Butter Mini Flapjacks (soft)

▶ distractor: Carr's® Water crackers (these are neither salty nor sweet).

Participants were given bite-sized pieces of all of the food samples. During the trials, participants wore headphones that presented them with white noise that was either 45–55 decibels (quiet) or 75–85 decibels (loud). For baseline ratings, no noise was played. A repeated measures design was used as all participants ate and rated all food types under the different sound conditions. They had to sit with their eyes closed. A researcher held a paper plate containing one of the foods and made it touch the participant's fingers to let the participant know that the trial had started. Participants rated saltiness, sweetness and liking (given in a random order) on a labelled magnitude scale with responses measured to the nearest millimetre. Each participant went through 25 trials. After each food was consumed, the participant took a sip of water. To control for other individual differences, scores were generated by subtracting the baseline rating from the quiet or loud ratings given.

Statistical analysis showed that level of sound did affect people's perceptions of sweetness and saltiness. Both of these were rated lower in the loud condition compared to the quiet condition. There was no effect of "hardness" on perceptions; background noise affected ratings for both crunchy and soft food.

Experiment 2

A total of 34 students (19 female) from Manchester University in the UK volunteered to take part in this experiment. Their ages ranged from 20 to 49 years and none of them had food allergies. The study was run in the same way as experiment 1 but this time the researchers were also testing whether liking of background noise also has an effect on perception of sugar and salt levels. The food stimuli were:

- sweet: berry and caramel flavoured rice cakes
- savoury: salt and vinegar flavoured plus Marmite® flavoured rice cakes
- distractor: organic rice cakes, cream and chive flavoured rice cakes, sweet chilli rice cakes and softened rice cakes.

Again, a repeated measures design was used with sound (no sound, quiet sound, loud sound) and food type (savoury, sweet) as the main factors. Measures this time were flavoursomeness, crunchiness and liking, again all based on labelled magnitude scales.

Sound had a significant effect on crunchiness. In the loud condition, participants rated their food as significantly crunchier than in the quiet condition. There was no effect of noise on flavoursomeness. In the loud condition, there was a correlation between liking of food and liking of the background noise for the Marmite® stimuli only.

Therefore, the main conclusions were:

- perception of saltiness and sweetness diminished when the food samples were eaten in the presence of loud music
- food was perceived to be crunchier if eaten while listening to loud music
- the effect of noise on the liking of food correlated with liking of the particular noise.

Strength	Weakness
The procedure for the study was standardised so it can be replicated and tested for reliability.	The sample sizes for each study were small, meaning that individual differences may affect the generalisabilty of findings.

LIGHTING, COLOUR AND SMELL

Models of effects of ambience: pleasure-arousal and cognition-emotion models

The pleasure-arousal model (normally referred to as the pleasure-arousal-dominance or PAD model; Mehrabian, 1996) looks at individual differences in temperament. There is a key difference in individual differences that this model is based on:

- Emotional states are those that are short-lived and vary dramatically across situations such as being in a favourite shop.
- Temperament refers to those elements of a personality that are stable over time and situation.

This model is based around three main personality traits:

- State pleasure–displeasure: these traits are positive versus negative affective states such as relaxation and love versus cruelty and boredom.
- State arousal–non-arousal: these traits are based around levels of arousal such as concentration and alertness versus sleep and boredom.

- State dominance–submissiveness: these traits are based around aspects such as feeling in control versus not feeling in control at all.

All of these can be measured on a personality scale and an individual's overall profile is then plotted on a triangular graph to see how much of each PAD the person has.

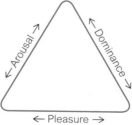

▲ **Figure 20.1.6** Three faces of emotion: a representation of the pleasure–arousal–dominance emotional state

Source: Mehrabian (1996: 264)

CHALLENGE YOURSELF
Explain how you think each of the PAD dimensions might predict how someone will react to a new shop opening in your local mall.

The cognition-emotion model (Lazarus, 1991) is based around how consumers judge the environmental stimuli around them. This judgment can be based on conscious or unconscious decision-making processes. The assessment of the stimuli must be linked to what the consumer has in terms of his or her own experiences and goals for any emotion to happen. For example, if a goal was to go out and find the perfect pair of shoes and the shoes were found, positive emotions such as elation will be experienced. However, if the right shoes were not found, despair and anger may result. Consumers use their cognitive resources to form beliefs about products and/or shopping experiences and these affect how they feel about them. Therefore, this is an information-processing model.

Lighting and colour in retail stores (Kutlu *et al*, 2013)

Kutlu *et al* (2013) aimed to find out brand identity in interior design, specifically looking at the effects of colour and lighting. A total of 121 consumers ranging from 15–60 years of age completed a questionnaire to evaluate a store image based on its colour scheme, which used a light colour. The main findings were that:

▶ 31.7 per cent of participants believed that the colour scheme was relaxing

▶ 24 per cent believed it was pleasing

▶ 20.6 per cent believed it was lively

▶ 23.1 per cent believed it was boring

▶ There was a direct correlation between luminance and store image: the lower the illuminance (which made the surroundings feel "personal") the more expensive or exclusive the participants found the store.

CHALLENGE YOURSELF
Design a study that tests how different colour schemes affect the perception of a clothes shop.

Effects of odour on shopper arousal and emotion (Chebat and Michon, 2003)

Chebat and Michon (2003) wanted to test the effects of ambient scents in a shopping mall. They tested a variety of hypotheses (11 in total) to assess how scents in a Canadian shopping mall affected people's perceptions. Data were collected over two consecutive weeks. In the first week, there was no odour control in the mall but in the second week a light citrus scent was vaporised in the mall's main corridor. Ten diffusers emitted the citrus smell for three seconds every six minutes. The scent was of a concentration to be noticed but not bother people. Participants were asked to complete a questionnaire about their shopping trip. A total of 145 people completed the questionnaire after being exposed to the scent and 447 formed the control group. Measures taken included pleasure, arousal, mall perception, perception of product quality and overall spending. The main findings included the following:

▶ The scent appeared to have a mediating effect on mood, which in turn positively affected perception of the shopping environment and product quality.

▶ Mood by itself contributed little to overall spending.

▶ Consumer spending is more likely to occur via cognitive processes than by mood alone.

Therefore, retailers ought to consider using light scents to entice shoppers into their stores as it gives the area a sense of quality.

CHALLENGE YOURSELF
The owners of a shopping mall want your help. They are trying to get more consumers to visit their mall and need to know the best ways in which to do this. Write a report for them, based on psychology evidence, which may help them increase the number of consumers who visit.

20.2 THE PSYCHOLOGICAL ENVIRONMENT

ASK YOURSELF
How do you find your way to and from your local shopping centre? How did you learn the route? What do you do when you have to visit a new shopping centre?

ENVIRONMENTAL INFLUENCES ON CONSUMERS

Cognitive maps of retail locations (Mackay and Olshavsky, 1975)

Mackay and Olshavsky (1975) investigated cognitive maps of retail locations. They wanted to compare two ways of measuring cognitive maps:

- Graphic – for example, participants have to draw lines between pairs of points on a map so this can be transposed to make a one-dimensional map.
- Multidimensional scaling (MDS) – a person uses a variety of spatial stimuli to create an internal map of an area.

A total of 78 supermarket shoppers formed the sample who were entering one of eight supermarkets in Indiana. Each participant had to:

- be the main shopper
- use that supermarket as his or her main shop of choice
- travel to the supermarket by car
- have heard of the other seven supermarkets.

Participants were all asked to draw a map of their departure point and of the eight supermarkets used in the study. They were free to draw these maps in as much detail as they wanted to.

These were the main results:

- Neither the hand-drawn nor the MDS maps were substantially closer to the actual map of either the departure point to home or the internal layout of the supermarkets.

- However, when individual maps were analysed the hand-drawn maps were closer to the actual maps than the MDS-generated ones.

Crowding in retail environments (Machleit *et al*, 2000)

In a series of studies, Machleit *et al* (2000) examined whether perceived crowding affects consumers' satisfaction levels while shopping. The points below relate to two of these studies. For the first study, 722 undergraduate and postgraduate marketing students completed a retrospective survey. They were asked to complete it after their next shopping trip (irrespective of whether they bought anything or not). They had to name the store, shopping centre or mall they had visited and then answer questions as follows:

- They were asked to rate perceived crowding on a Likert-type scale. Human crowding and spatial crowding were both measured.
- Satisfaction was measured via items on a 7-point scale.
- Emotions were measured in two different ways: using ten emotion types as noted by Izard where participants rate adjectives; then via pleasure and arousal questions (based on semantic differentials)
- Participants were asked about prior expectations of crowding. For example, when they went shopping were they expecting more or fewer shoppers than usual?
- Their intolerance of crowding was investigated.

Results (from study 1 only)

- Increased perceptions of crowding resulted in decreased positive feelings and increased negative feelings. The effect was stronger for spatial crowding compared to human crowding.
- Perceived human crowding did not significantly affect feelings of arousal.
- If the shopper found the store to be spatially crowded, the excitement of shopping decreased.
- Feelings of surprise significantly increase when the shopper experiences human crowding.
- The strongest negative emotions linked to spatial crowding were anger, disgust and contempt.
- Higher levels of perceived crowding (both human and spatial) were correlated to lower levels of satisfaction.
- Females tolerate crowding more than males (although this was not statistically significant).

Therefore, it would appear that both spatial and human crowding affect a shopper's experiences.

Strength	Weakness
There was a large, diverse sample so generalisability beyond the sample is likely to be possible.	Measures were taken using questionnaires, meaning the results could be more subjective than objective and so casting doubt on their validity.

Shopper movement patterns (Gil *et al*, 2009)

Gil *et al* (2009) tested shopper movement patterns in a supermarket. They focused on three questions:

1. How and to what extent does the spatial configuration of store layout have an impact on shoppers' behaviour?

2. Do any of the groups of shoppers express distinctive use of space or distinctive shopping behaviours?

3. Can we identify distinctive movement patterns of shoppers? If so, are those patterns associated with certain groups of shoppers?

The researchers collected data from over 480 customers by interviewing them and tracking their movements around a supermarket. This data was then used to profile shoppers based on their demographics and behaviour in the supermarket. Participants were approached just before they entered the supermarket. Details of their basic demographics were taken and they then were given a coloured tab to wear so they could be identified on exit (and followed easily via CCTV footage). On exit, they were interviewed about the aim of their trip, satisfaction, money spent, whether they had a list, etc.

The researchers identified four movement cluster patterns across the participants. These are shown in Figure 20.2.1.

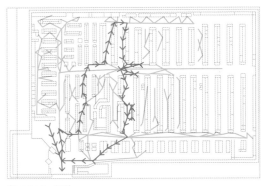

Short trip (32)

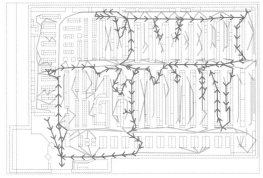

Round trip (173)

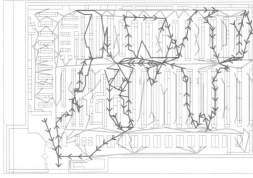

Central trip (110)

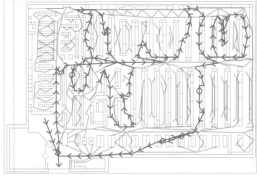

Wave trip (166)

▲ **Figure 20.2.1** Plans representing each of the four movement pattern clusters

Notes: For each movement pattern cluster, the "medoid" is identified, that is the most representative trace of the cluster closest to its centre. Each plan shows the combined level of movement from all traces in the cluster with varying intensity, overlaid with the medoid, where the arrows indicate the direction of movement.

Source: Gil *et al* (2009: 036:6)

The researchers then created "shopper DNA" profiles based on 12 different attributes. These are shown in Table 20.2.1.

Attributes	0	1	2	3	4	5	6
Gender	Male	Female					
Age group	–	18–24	25–34	35–44	45–54	55–64	65 and over
Group size	–	Alone	Two	Three	Four	Five	Six or more
Carrier type	None	Basket	Shallow trolley	Deep trolley			
Frequency of visit	–	First time	Regularly	Occasionally			
Shopping mission	–	Main	Top-up	Tonight	For now	Non-food	
Shopping list	–	Yes	No				
Attitude to promotions	–	Always	Familiar	Familiar	Never		
Satisfaction	–	Very satisfied	Satisfied	Neither	Dissatisfied	Very dissatisfied	
Shopping duration	–	<10 min	<20 min	<30 min	<45 min	45 min or more	
Walking speed	–	Slow	Medium	Fast			
Duration of interactions	–	Short	Medium	Long			

▲ **Table 20.2.1** Shopper profile attributes

Source: Gil *et al* (2009: 036:7)

From these attributes, four distinct "shopper DNA" profiles were reported, as shown in Figure 20.2.2.

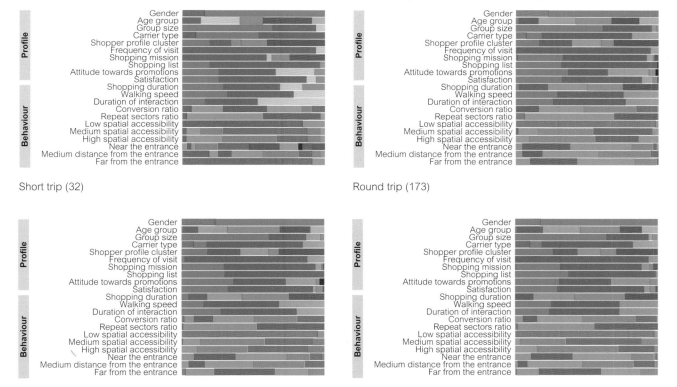

Short trip (32)

Round trip (173)

Central trip (110)

Wave trip (166)

▲ **Figure 20.2.2** "Shopper DNA" profile of each movement pattern cluster. Each band represents the percentage share of shoppers with a particular attribute according to the researchers' classification, apart from the "short trip" cluster, that has unique share of carrier types, shopping mission and shopping duration.

Source: Gil *et al* (2009: 8)

As shown in Figure 20.2.3, the researchers also analysed data to produce five different types of shopper based on movement habits.

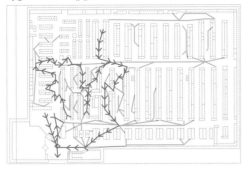

The specialist (19)

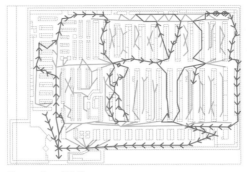

The native (161)

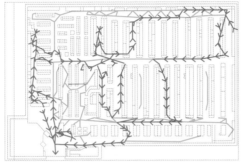

The tourist (101)

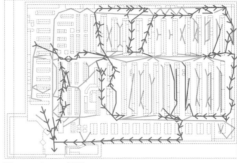

The explorer (67)

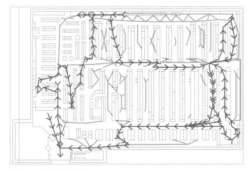

The raider (113)

▲ **Figure 20.2.3** Plans representing each of the five spatial behaviour types, with the level of movement from all traces in the cluster displayed with varying intensity, overlaid by the "medoid", with the arrows indicating the direction of movement

Source: Gil *et al* (2009: 036:10)

Finally, the researchers produced "shopper DNA" profiles for these five types of shopper, as shown in Figure 20.2.4.

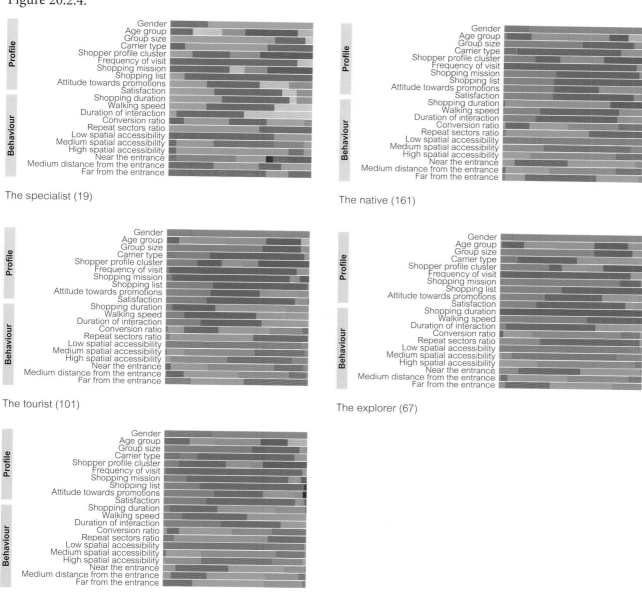

The specialist (19)

The native (161)

The tourist (101)

The explorer (67)

The raider (113)

▲ **Figure 20.2.4** "Shopper DNA" profile of each spatial behaviour cluster

Source: Gil *et al* (2009: 036:12)

The researchers concluded that "… distinct clusters of shopping strategy defined in terms of characteristic search trail through the store, and that these correlate with specific shopper profiles" (Gil *et al*, 036:1).

MENU DESIGN PSYCHOLOGY

Eye movement patterns, framing and common menu mistakes (Pavesic, 2005)

Pavesic (2005) noted common mistakes restaurants make with their menu designs:

▶ There is inadequate management commitment to menu design: the managers of a restaurant do not treat their menu design with the same diligence as other capital investment in their business. Investment in an eye-catching design is cost-effective.

▶ The menu is hard to read. This may be because the font size is too small, font colours make the menu difficult to read or pages have too much text.

▶ Prices are overemphasized. For example, all the prices are in the same column so customers can easily compare them and go for the cheapest option.

▶ The menu represents poor salesmanship because it fails to emphasise the products the restaurant wants to sell.

▶ There is poor use of space on the menu. This might include not utilising the front and back covers for generic information (e.g. opening times, address and the history of the restaurant). Pavesic collected over 1000 restaurant menus and noted that around 25 per cent have no identifying feature that links them to a specific restaurant.

▶ The menu is incongruent: it does not match the décor of the restaurant or what the restaurant is selling in terms of quality of food.

▶ The menu is too large. The size of the menu needs to take into account the size of the table. A very large menu is awkward to handle.

Pavesic also noted that, on average, a customer will look over a menu for only 109 seconds so any message needs to be portrayed in such a way that a customer quickly notices offers, prices, meal deals, etc. Pavesic noted typical eye movements over a menu that are quite "standard" in customers. This is shown in Figure 20.2.5.

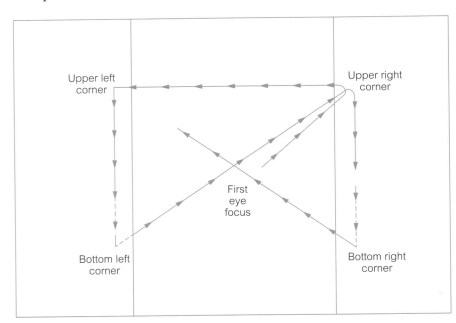

▲ **Figure 20.2.5** Typical eye movement over a three-panel, two-fold menu

Source: Pavesic (2005: 40)

Pavesic stated that "eye magnets" can be used to stop this standard pattern happening by having sections of the menu that look different from the rest to catch people's attention. He proposed that these sections are used sparingly so not to diminish their effectiveness. He noted two other design features that are effective: highlighting or using arrows, and using borders or graphics. Examples are shown in Figures 20.2.6 and 20.2.7.

Figure 20.2.6

Source: Pavesic (2005: 39)

Western   Bacon 'n Cheese
Or, tell us how you'd like it, with any of these ingredients: ham, cheese, bacon, onion and green pepper.

Sambo's Country Breakfast
Two fresh eggs, cooked your way, with bacon or sausage or ham slice and six pancakes, or hash browns and buttered toast and jelly.

The BLT Classic

The Sandwich Board
$1.99

The BLT Classic
With three strips of bacon, lettuce and three slices of tomato on toasted whole wheat bread.
Fish Fry
Breaded filet of fish on a New England-style bun with lettuce, tartar sauce and lemon wedge.
Tuna Salad
Piled high on a roll with lettuce and tomato slices.

$2.49

Hot Roast Beef
Premium top round of beef, roasted in our own ovens, served open-faced with gravy.
Pastrami
A delicious combination of pastrami, Swiss cheese, tomato and sliced onion on toasted rye bread.
Chicken Italiano
Deep-fried chicken patty, Swiss cheese and Marinara sauce on a grilled sesame bun.
The French Dip
Our own oven-roasted premium top round of beef French roll with cup au jus.
Hot Ham 'n Cheese
Shaved ham, American cheese and tomato slice mustard, pickles and lettuce on a French roll.
Hot Turkey
Sliced breast of turkey on two slices of bread with gravy.

For just 50¢ extra you can enjoy any of the Sandwich Board lunches with French fries or cottage fries.

The Calorie Corner
$2.99

The Dieter
Broiled luncheon ground beef with cottage cheese, melba toast and tomato slices.
Tuna Tomato
Tuna salad in a tomato cup, served on a bed of lettuce with

▲ **Figure 20.2.7**
Source: Pavesic (2005: 43)

Strength	Weakness
The review has good application as restaurants can improve their menu designs as a result.	The study reflects only Pavesic's views on menu design so is subjective.

Primacy, recency and menu item position (Dayan and Bar-Hillel, 2011)

Dayan and Bar-Hillel (2011) conducted two studies that examined the effect on food orders of manipulating the position of foods on a restaurant menu.

Study 1

A total of 240 students from Hebrew University, Jerusalem, Israel (aged 19–35 years; 52 per cent female) were recruited from around the campus. They were randomly assigned to one of four conditions:

1. Baseline menu
2. Mirror menu: a reverse of the base menu
3. Inside-out baseline menu: formed by turning the middle items of the base menu to the extremes and the extremes to the middle
4. Inside-out mirror menu: a reverse of the inside-out base menu.

The menus had four appetisers, ten entrées, six soft drinks and eight desserts. Table 20.2.2 shows the format of each menu.

Baseline menu:	A1, A2, A3, A4	E1, E2, E3, E4, E5, E6, E7, E8, E9, E10
	S1, S2, S3, S4, S5, S6	D1, D2, D3, D4, D5, D6, D7, D8
Mirror menu:	A4, A3, A2, A1	E10, E9, E8, E7, E6, E5, E4, E3, E2, E1
	S6, S5, S4, S3, S2, S1	D8, D7, D6, D5, D4, D3, D2, D1
Inside-Out base:	A2, A1, A4, A3	E5, E4, E3, E2, E1, E10, E9, E8, E7, E6
	S3, S2, S1, S6, S5, S4	D4, D3, D2, D1, D8, D7, D6, D5
Inside-Out mirror:	A3, A4, A1, A2	E6, E7, E8, E9, E10, E1, E2, E3, E4, E5
	S4, S5, S6, S1, S2, S3	D5, D6, D7, D8, D1, D2, D3, D4

▲ **Table 20.2.2** Item order in the four menus:
A = appetisers, E = entrées, S = soft drinks, D = desserts

Source: Dayan and Bar-Hillel (2011: 334)

Each participant was given the menu and asked to choose one item from each category. The findings are given in Figure 20.2.8.

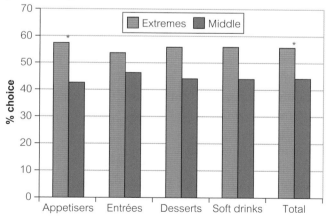

* indicates p <.05, two tailed

▲ **Figure 20.2.8** The mean percentage of choices made when an item was on the top or bottom versus in the middle of its food category, sorted by category type

Source: Dayan and Bar-Hillel (2011: 335)

Figure 20.2.8 shows that, especially for appetisers, participants chose items from the "extremes" of the list over those in the middle irrespective of the menu they were given.

Study 2

The research team noted that for study 1 the choices were made under controlled conditions. They wanted to test the results of study 1 in a real café in Tel Aviv. This study focused on three categories from the real menu: coffee with alcohol, soft drinks and desserts. There was a baseline menu that the café already used and then an inside-out baseline menu was also produced. These menus alternated daily for 15 days. The researchers analysed 459 baseline menu purchases and 492 inside-out baseline menu purchases. The findings are shown in Figure 20.2.9.

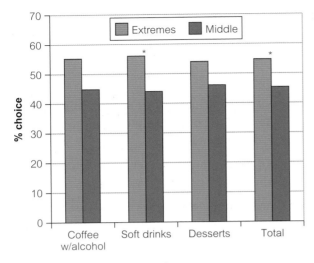

* indicates p <.05, two tailed

▲ **Figure 20.2.9** The mean percentage of choices made when an item was on the top or bottom versus in the middle of its food category, sorted by category type (study 2)

Source: Dayan and Bar-Hillel (2011: 340)

In both the laboratory study and the field study, people were more likely to choose products at the beginning or end of a list (showing primacy-recency effect) than those in the middle of a list on a menu.

Strength	Weakness
The procedure was standardised so the study can be replicated and tested for reliability.	The sample was from one university so generalising beyond the sample may be difficult.

 CHALLENGE YOURSELF
Design a menu, based on what you have learned so far, for a new restaurant that offers a three course meal with five starters, five main dishes and five desserts. Justify all of your design decisions.

Sensory perception and food name (Wansink, van Ittersum and Painter, 2005)

Wansink, van Ittersum and Painter (2005) tested whether descriptions of food on a menu affected perceptions of that food after eating it. The idea was that labelling food items with a "richer" description could affect how people perceive the food in terms of taste and quality. In this study, the researchers tested a range of hypotheses to see whether favourable descriptions of food affected

post-consumption sensory ratings, evaluations of the food eaten and comments about the food.

A cafeteria in a major US university was used as the setting. Six of the most popular dishes consumed on its menu were chosen and their descriptions were manipulated. The descriptions were altered slightly so that during any one lunch session, two of the foods had a regular or basic label, two had a more descriptive label and two were not offered. These were the labels (Wansink *et al*, 2005: 7):

▶ "Traditional Cajun red beans with rice" versus "Red beans with rice"

▶ "Succulent Italian seafood filet" versus "Seafood filet"

▶ "Tender grilled chicken" versus "Grilled chicken"

▶ "Homestyle chicken Parmesan" versus "Chicken Parmesan"

▶ "Satin chocolate pudding" versus "Chocolate pudding"

▶ "Grandma's zucchini cookies" versus "Zucchini cookies".

Anyone who selected one of the target foods was handed a one-page questionnaire by the person at the cash register. A total of 140 participants were given a questionnaire and 98 per cent completed it. The age range of participants was 23–74 years.

These three crucial items were included on the 9-point Likert scale that was used:

1. The items were appealing to the eye.

2. The item tasted good.

3. After finishing this menu item, I felt comfortably full and satisfied.

There was also space for participants to write any comments about the food.

The main results were as follows:

▶ For the three crucial items, all were rated significantly higher on average when the food had the descriptive label compared to the regular name.

▶ People believed their dish contained more calories on average if the descriptive label had been used.

▶ Those who ate food when the label was descriptive generated significantly more positive comments about the food (see Figure 20.2.10).

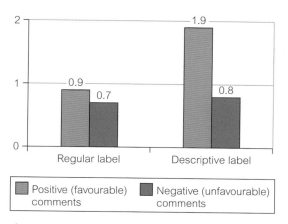

Positive (favourable) comments
Negative (unfavourable) comments

▲ **Figure 20.2.10** How descriptive labels influence the valence of open-ended feedback

Source: Wansink, van Ittersum and Painter (2005: 18)

It would seem that a simple task of adding a few descriptive words to a dish on a menu can positively affect how diners perceive the food.

> **Issues and debates tracker:** All of the findings have good application to everyday life as the ideas can be used by restaurants, for example, to increase the amount of customers visiting, potentially increasing profits. However, some of the ideas may be culturally specific and therefore it may be difficult to apply all the findings to restaurants or eating habits in different cultures.

PERSONAL SPACE

Bell *et al* (1996) define personal space as a "… portable, invisible boundary surrounding us, into which others may not trespass. It regulates how closely we interact with others, moves with us, and expands and contracts according to the situation in which we find ourselves" (1996: 275).

Hall (1963) distinguished between zones of personal space, which the researcher called "spatial zones", based around interpersonal relationships we may have.

Theories of personal space

Overload, arousal and behaviour constraint

Overload theory suggests we maintain an optimal personal space in situations. This prevents us from being bombarded with too much sensory information.

Overstimulation needs to be avoided or it can be quite difficult to cope with that situation. This is because we are too busy trying to process all of the information at once.

Arousal theory suggests that we get aroused when people invade our personal space. We try to make sense of this sudden arousal and this then dictates how much space we require. An example would be a first date. We may feel good or we may feel nervous. Both of these situations will arouse us. However, if we feel good we may require less personal space than if we feel nervous.

Behaviour constraint theory suggests that we all require a level of personal space or we feel that our behavioural freedom has been taken away. This can happen when people get too close to us.

Space at restaurant tables (Robson et al, 2011)

Robson *et al* (2011) wanted to investigate how personal space may affect people's "comfort" while they are dining in a restaurant. The study used a web-based questionnaire. The first part of the survey gathered demographic information alongside any experiences participants may have had in the restaurant business. The second part of the survey measured emotional, intentional and anticipated behavioural reactions to one of three images of tables for two placed at distances of 6, 12 or 24 inches away from each other.

▲ **Figure 20.2.11** Example of visual prompt (6-inch table spacing shown)

Source: Robson *et al* (2011: 255)

The questions asked were designed to invoke three different dining scenarios:

▶ meeting for business purposes

▶ friendship meeting

▶ romantic date.

The distances were based on Hall's zones of personal space. As there were three distances and three scenarios, there were nine conditions that participants were randomly allocated to. The questionnaire had 32 statements that used a 7-point Likert scale. Of the 32 statements, 12 were from the Stress Arousal Check List. The other items covered things such as perceived control, physical and sensory privacy, goal blocking and general comfort. A total of 1013 completed questionnaires were used in the analyses. The key findings were as follows:

▶ For pleasure, stress, control and comfort there was a significant difference between these ratings and distances in the expected direction.

▶ Close table spacing made respondents feel "less private", less likely to have a positive meal experience and more likely to be dissatisfied with the table given to them.

▶ Being seated 6 inches away from the next table made people more concerned with disturbing others or being overheard during a meal.

▶ Figure 20.2.12 shows the results for the stress measures.

▶ Figure 20.2.13 shows that comfort ratings were affected most by scenario.

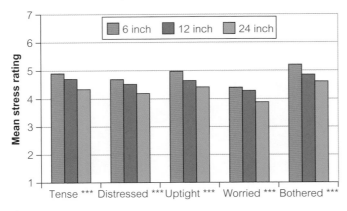

▲ **Figure 20.2.12** Results for stress measures

Source: Robson *et al* (2011: 257)

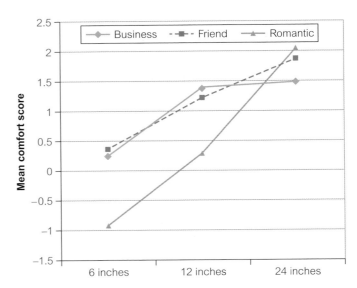

▲ **Figure 20.2.13** Comfort ratings by table spacing and scenario

Source: Robson *et al* (2011: 259)

This study seems to indicate that table distances and reasons for dining do affect the quality of experiences when eating in a restaurant.

Strength	Weakness
A large, diverse sample was used, making generalisation beyond the sample easier.	The measures were from questionnaires which can be subjective so this casts doubt on the validity of findings.

 CHALLENGE YOURSELF
Design a study using a self-report technique that investigates spacing at restaurant tables.

Defending place in a queue, Milgram *et al*, 1986)

Milgram *et al* (1986) assessed how people defend their place in a queue. Prior to the study the researchers had noted three distinguishing features of a queue:

▶ It regulates the sequence in which people are served in shop or gain access to services.

▶ The order of a queue has a distinctive spatial format.

▶ Maintenance of the queue depends on a "shared knowledge of the standards of behaviour appropriate to that queue" (Milgram *et al*, 1986: 683).

The researchers created an experiment that studied queue intrusions in 129 waiting lines, mainly at a railroad ticket counter. The queues were of an average length of six people (excluding confederates). The confederate always calmly approached a point between the third and fourth person in a queue and remarked in a neutral tone: "Excuse me, I'd like to get in there". Before anyone could respond the confederate entered the queue at that point. If the confederate was asked to leave the queue the person did so, otherwise he or she would remain there for one minute before leaving voluntarily. Three female and two male intruders were used. The number of intruders varied too: either one or two. "Buffers" were also used – these were confederates who occupied a position between the point of intrusion and the next naïve queuer. There were six experimental conditions, as shown in Figure 20.2.14.

Head   *−2 −1 0 +1 +2 +3 +4 +5*   *End*

              |

         Intrusion
          point

▲ **Figure 20.2.14**

    Source: Milgram *et al* (1986: 684)

The main results were as follows:

▶ Physical action (e.g. tugging a sleeve, putting hands on shoulders) occurred in 10.1 per cent of queues.

▶ Verbal objections were quite common. Examples included "Excuse me, you have to go to the back of the line", "No way! The line's back there. We've all been waiting and have trains to catch", "Are you making a line here?!" This happened in 21.7 per cent of queues.

▶ In 14.7 per cent of queues, non-verbal objections occurred, such as hostile stares and gestures.

Condition	No. of lines	No. of intruders	No. of buffers	No. of lines in which objections occurred	% of lines in which objections occurred
1	22	1	0	12	54.0
2	24	1	1	6	25.0
3	20	1	2	1	5.0
4	23	2	0	21	91.3
5	20	2	1	5	25.0
6	20	2	2	6	30.0

▲ **Table 20.2.3** Objections to intrusions in six experimental conditions

    Source: Milgram *et al* (1986: 685)

Figure 20.2.15 shows the percentage of people objecting according to their position in the line.

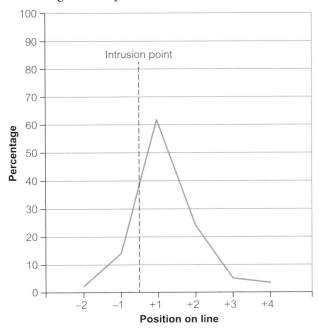

▲ **Figure 20.2.15**

    Source: Milgram *et al* (1986: 686)

Table 20.2.4 shows the effects of the buffers on objections.

Condition	% − 2	% − 1	I	% + 1	% + 2	% + 3	% + 4
			Position in line				
1	4.5 (1/22)	22.7 (5/22)		36.4 (8/22)	14.3 (2/14)	0.0 (0/9)	0.0 (0/7)
2	0.0 (0/22)	12.5 (3/24)		Buf	16.7 (4/24)	0.0 (0/15)	0.0 (0/9)
3	0.0 (0/18)	5.0 (1/20)		Buf	Buf	0.0 (0/20)	0.0 (0/18)
4	4.3 (1/23)	21.7 (5/23)		86.9 (20/23)	43.5 (10/23)	9.1 (2/22)	0.0 (0/20)
5	0.0 (0/18)	10.0 (2/20)		Buf	20.0 (4/20)	0.0 (0/15)	0.0 (0/4)
6	0.0 (0/18)	10.0 (2/20)		Buf	Buf	15.0 (3/20)	11.8 (2/17)
Total	1.7 (2/121)	14.0 (18/129)		62.2 (28/45)	24.7 (20/81)	5.0 (5/101)	2.7 (2/75)

Note: The figures in parentheses show the exact number of persons for each position on which the percentage figures are based. I = intrusion point. Buf = buffer (a confederate who passively occupied a position between the point of intrusion and the next naïve queuer).

▲ **Table 20.2.4** Spatial distribution of responses to intrusions: percentage and number of persons objecting according to position in line

Source: Milgram *et al* (1986: 685)

Therefore, we can conclude that people will object to an intrusion within a queue, but these objections are limited to mild physical action, verbal objections or non-verbal gestures, most often from people immediately behind the person who has intruded.

Strength	Weakness
The study has some ecological validity as it took place in a natural setting.	Some of the verbalisations may not have been recorded correctly.

20.3 CONSUMER DECISION MAKING

MODELS, STRATEGIES AND THEORIES

Models
Utility, satisficing, prospect

▶ The utility model proposes that consumers make decisions based on the expected outcomes of their decisions. Consumers are viewed as rational humans who can estimate outcomes to maximise their wellbeing.

▶ The satisficing model proposes that consumers get to approximately where they want to go and then stop any decision making. For example, when trying to find a new apartment potential buyers might simply evaluate possibilities that are a certain distance from a desired location and then stop.

▶ The prospect model proposes two main elements involved in decision making: value and endowment. The value relates to potential gains and losses of purchase, while the endowment refers to when an item is perceived as being more precious if you own it rather than someone else.

Strategies
Compensatory, non-compensatory, partially compensatory

▶ Compensatory strategies are seen when consumers allow a higher value of one attribute of a purchase to compensate for a lesser value. An example could be when buying a car. The miles per gallon might be excellent at the expense of generous leg room in the back.

▶ Non-compensatory strategies can take three forms:

– Satisficing: the first product under evaluation by the consumer meets all cut-off values and is then purchased.

– Elimination by aspects: each product is assessed from the bottom of a hierarchy to the top where those not meeting a level are eliminated until one is left.

– Lexigraphic: the consumer assesses products on the most important attribute first. If a product meets the standard it is selected immediately.

▶ Partially compensatory strategies can take two forms:

– Majority of conforming decisions: two products are compared across all relevant attributes and the winner is retained. This is then pitted against another product and another winner is declared. The last product is then purchased.

– Frequency of good and bad features: all products are assessed simultaneously across all relevant attributes and the one that has the largest number of good features is purchased.

 CHALLENGE YOURSELF
Design a study using a self-report technique that tests the three models above.

Marketing theories

Consideration and involvement (Richarme, 2005)

Consideration theory refers to a situation when consumers have to decide if they wish to buy something or go somewhere. The consumer will not create a list of all potential products or places but will instead create a shortlist of items to choose from when making his or her decision. The person picks from this list what to buy or where to go. A range of cognitive factors affect what appears on the shortlist so different products or places might appear each time the list is made.

Involvement theory states that the amount of cognitive effort required to make a decision is directly correlated with the level of importance that the person places on buying a certain product. An example could be comparing the amount of effort it takes to decide which packet of mints to buy compared to purchasing a new car. The amount of effort is not necessarily linked to the price of the product but more its impact on the consumer's quality of life.

CHOICE HEURISTICS

Availability, representativeness

A heuristic is a "mental shortcut" that allows us to make a series of decisions quickly. There are two main types:

▶ Availability – this shortcut helps us to make a quick decision based on how easy it is to bring something to our consciousness. It relies on how easily and quickly we can find information to help us make a judgment on our shopping. For example, if we have just heard that there has been a recall on a product made by Sony, we might not go and buy a different Sony product as a result.

▶ Representativeness – this shortcut helps us to make a decision based on comparing available information with a mental "prototype" (sometimes stereotype) we have about a product. For example, we might have a prototype that all Apple products are excellent so we use this to help us make a decision about purchasing other Apple products even if we have never bought, say, a laptop before.

Anchoring and purchasing decisions (Wansink, Kent and Hoch, 1998)

Wansink, Kent and Hoch (1998) investigated what makes consumers buy a certain amount of units. The researchers used a series of field and laboratory experiments.

Study 1

The aim of the first study was to test whether supermarket multiple-unit pricing increased sales. An example of multiple-unit pricing is "On sale – 6 for $3" whereas an example of single-unit pricing is "On sale – 50 cents each". This study was conducted over a one-week period. In 86 different stores, 13 products were put on sale using either single-unit or multiple-unit pricing. Sales were recorded and any increase in sales from baseline was noted.

Product	Level of discount	Form of price expression	Percentage change in unit sales		
			Single unit	Multiple unit	p-value
Bathroom tissue	15%	1/50¢ versus 4/$2.00	+57	+97	.02
Candy	9%	1/50¢ versus 2/$1.00	+24	+25	n.s.
Cereal (Breakfast)	33%	1/$1.99 versus 2/$3.98	+133	+137	n.s.
Cookies	44%	1/$1.67 versus 2/$3.34	+306	+372	.01
Frozen dinners	12%	1/$2.49 versus 2/$5.00	+33	+70	.003
Frozen dinners	20%	1/$2.50 versus 2/$5.00	+133	+195	.0001
Frozen entrees	26%	1/$1.25 versus 2/$2.50	+133	+156	.02
Paper towels	31%	1/75¢ versus 2/$1.50	+403	+565	.001
Soap (3-bar packs)	15%	1/$1.99 versus 2/$3.98	+48	+30	n.s.
Soft Drinks (2 liters)	17%	1/$1.49 versus 2/$3.00	+33	+66	.01
Soup (Canned)	20%	1/$1.33 versus 3/$4.00	+200	+248	.01
Soup (Canned)	17%	1/50¢ versus 2/$1.00	+108	+112	n.s.
Tuna (Canned)	18%	1/65¢ versus 2/$1.30	+36	+66	.004
	21%		+125%	+165%	.0001

▲ **Table 20.3.1** The impact of multiple-unit pricing on supermarket sales

Source: Wansink, Kent and Hoch (1998: 73)

Overall, multiple-unit pricing increased sales by, on average, 32 per cent in all stores. For 12 of the products, multiple-unit pricing increased sales. Nine of these were significant increases compared to the single-unit figures.

Study 2

The aim of the second study was to test whether high purchase-quantity limits increased sales. Three supermarkets in Sioux City, Iowa, USA, ran an offer over three consecutive evenings. The offer was a (modest) 12 per cent discount on Campbell's® soup (which made the price 79 cents per can rather than 89 cents). However, on each evening a different limit was imposed on the number of cans consumers could buy:

▶ On the first evening there was no limit on the amount of cans a person could purchase.

▶ On the second evening, each customer could only buy four cans.

▶ On the third evening, each customer could only buy 12 cans.

The supermarkets used were all of a similar size and had a similar shopper volume. A total of 914 shoppers passed the display and the researchers simply noted how many cans consumers placed in their basket or trolley. Those with no purchase limits bought 3.3 cans on average, compared to 3.5 cans when the limit was 4 cans, and 7 cans when the limit was 12 cans.

The bar charts in Figure 20.3.1 show the frequency of purchasing across the three conditions.

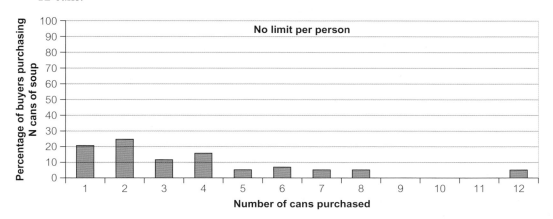

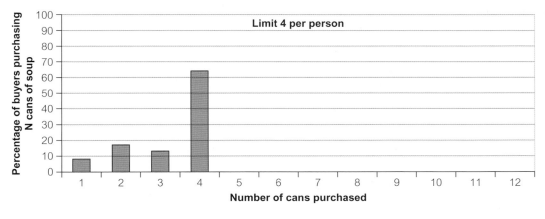

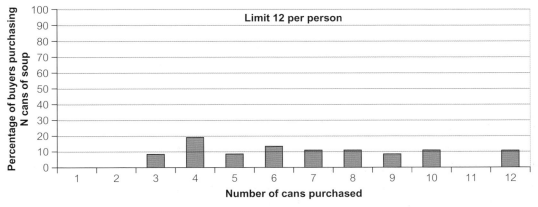

▲ **Figure 20.3.1** How purchase-quantity limits influence canned soup purchases

Source: Wansink, Kent and Hoch (1998: 75)

Studies 3 and 4

These studies examined "selling anchors" so see whether they affected purchasing. One hundred and twenty undergraduates were offered six well-known products at one of three price levels:

▶ an actual convenience store price

▶ a 20 per cent discount

▶ a 40 per cent discount.

In addition, participants were given one of two selling claims (called "anchors"). For example:

▶ "Snickers® bars – buy some for your freezer."

▶ "Snickers® bars – buy 18 for your freezer."

The results are shown in Figure 20.3.2.

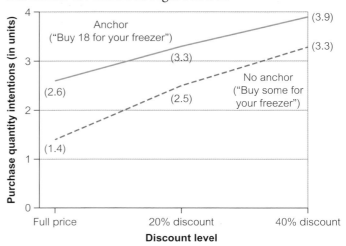

▲ **Figure 20.3.2** The impact of suggestive selling anchors and discounts

Source: Wansink, Kent and Hoch (1998: 76)

As Figure 20.3.2 shows, when a specific anchor was used, sales increased across all discount levels.

In the final study, it was found that using an "expansion anchor" (e.g. "This has 101 uses!") increased sale intentions across a range of purchase-quantity limits.

Overall, from their studies the researchers concluded the applications shown in Table 20.3.2.

	Anchor-based promotions			
	Multiple-unit pricing	**Purchase-quantity limits**	**Suggestive selling**	**Expansion anchors**
Executions	3 for $1.97	Limit of 12 per person	Grab 6 for studying	101 uses!
	12 for the price of 10	Limit of 1 per visit	Buy 8 and save a trip	Buy a month's worth
	Baker's dozen for $2.99	4 per person per day	Buy 12 for your freezer	Buy for all your friends
Implementation considerations	Discounts of 10–20% can increase sales while protecting margins.	Very low limits increase purchase incidence; high limits increase purchase quantities.	Anchor-based sales suggestions may work without a corresponding sales promotion.	Advertisements, packages, and POP materials can increase purchase quantities by stimulating thoughts of new uses.
	The larger and more expensive the product, the lower the suggested number should be.	To avoid truncating sales, set limits of at least two times higher than the typical quantity bought on deal.	Suggestive selling can be most effective with familiar, inexpensive items, such as snacks and drinks.	Expansion anchors can be used in advertising campaigns and without a sales promotion.

▲ **Table 20.3.2** Executing and improving anchor-based promotions

Source: Wansink, Kent and Hoch (1998: 79)

Strength	Weakness
The study has good application as shop owners can use the findings to increase their sales.	The study only took place in one supermarket in the United States, so generalisability beyond the study may prove difficult.

CHALLENGE YOURSELF

Next time you visit a supermarket, note real-life examples of the techniques mentioned in the study.

Pre-cognitive decisions (Knutson *et al*, 2007)

Knutson *et al* (2007) investigated neural predictors of purchases. A total of 40 participants were selected for the study. However, six had to be eliminated as they did not purchase enough items and a further eight could not be used due to excessive movements during the brain scanning phase of the study. Therefore, 26 participants were used in the final analyses. They were paid $20 per hour for the time they spent taking part in the study.

Each participant went through the same procedure. This is shown in Figure 20.3.3.

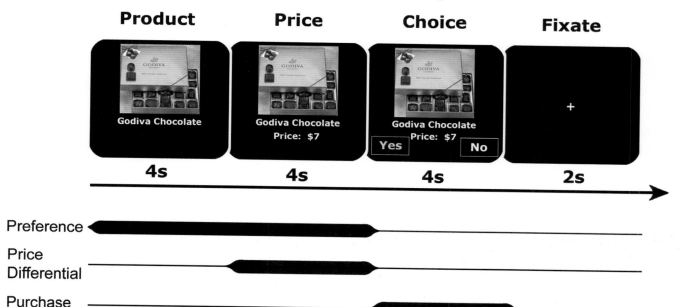

▲ **Figure 20.3.3** Shop task trial structure and regressors

Notes: For task structure, subjects saw a labelled product (product period; 4 seconds), saw the product's price (price period; 4 seconds), and then chose either to purchase the product or not (by selecting either "yes" or "no" presented randomly on the right or left side of the screen; choice period; 4 seconds), before fixating on a crosshair (2 seconds) prior to the onset of the next trial.

Source: Knutson *et al* (2007: 148)

All of the participants had $20 to spend during the sessions. While going through the procedure, all of them underwent an fMRI scan. This enabled the researchers to pinpoint what neural activity was occurring when the participant saw the product, then was given a price and then was asked to decide on a purchase.

Figure 20.3.4 shows the activities of three regions of the brain that the researchers were interested in: nucleus accumbens (NAcc), mesial prefrontal cortex (MPFC) and the insula.

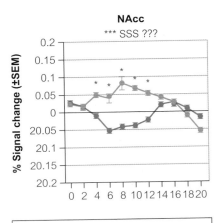
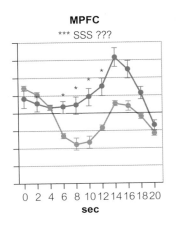
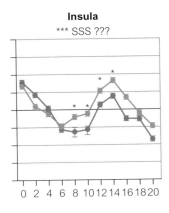

▲ **Figure 20.3.4** Activation time courses. Left to right: bilateral NAcc activation time courses for trials in which products were subsequently purchased versus not; bilateral MPFC activation time courses; and right insula activation time courses (white, predicted divergence; ***, product period; \$\$\$, price period; ???, choice period.

Source: Knutson *et al* (2007: 149)

Preference for the product was correlated with activation in the NAcc. That is, the NAcc was more activated during the product and price periods of the task. MPFC activation was positively correlated with price differentials (e.g. a participant thought the product was "well priced") during the price period but it was deactivated if the person felt the pricing was excessive. Purchasing of the product was correlated with *deactivation* of the insula while perceived excessive prices activated this region.

The researchers concluded: "These findings suggest that the activation of distinct neural circuits related to anticipatory affect preceded and supports consumers' purchasing decisions" (Knutson *et al*, 2007: 149).

Strength	Weakness
The study had a standardised procedure so it can easily be replicated and tested for reliability.	Only 26 participants were used in the final analyses, so generalisability beyond the sample may be difficult.

Issues and debates tracker: These ideas have good application to everyday life as they can be used by shops to increase turnover and sales. A shop, when introducing a new product, can utilise the ideas of anchoring and availability, for example, to expose consumers to that product.

INTUITIVE THINKING AND ITS IMPERFECTIONS

Thinking fast and thinking slow; system 1 and system 2 (Shleifer, 2012)

Shleifer (2012) reviewed the work of Kahneman and the idea of system 1 and system 2 thinking:

▶ System 1 involves thinking fast. People who are system 1 thinkers are intuitive, automatic, unconscious and effortless thinkers. They answer questions quickly through recognising resemblances and using associations.

▶ System 2 involves thinking slow. People who are system 2 thinkers are conscious, slow, controlled, deliberate, effortful, suspicious and lazy.

Most people use system 1 thinking patterns but certain circumstances may make them use system 2. Shleifer highlighted this with an example from Kahneman.

"An individual has been described by a neighbor as follows: 'Steve is very shy and withdrawn, invariably helpful but with very little interest in people or in the world of reality. A meek and tidy soul, he has a need for order and structure, and a passion for detail.' Is Steve more likely to be a librarian or a farmer?"

Source: Shleifer (2012: 3)

Shleifer notes that virtually everyone would choose librarian because associative memory links the "tale" to the job. System 1 thinking prevails. However, system 2 rarely engages even though it might be useful in this scenario. People do not take the time to assess facts such as: there are five times as many farmers in the United States as there are librarians; there are far more male farmers than male librarians.

CHALLENGE YOURSELF
Design a study that tests whether a person is a system 1 or a system 2 thinker.

Choice blindness (Hall *et al*, 2010)

Hall *et al* (2010) investigated the phenomenon of choice blindness in a naturalistic setting. Choice blindness refers to when people fail to recognise that something they have just tasted or smelt (as in this study) has been changed. A total of 180 consumers (118 female) at a supermarket in Lund, Sweden were participants in the study. The age range was 16–80 years. They were recruited as they passed a tasting venue that was set up with an researcher resembling an "independent consultant" within the supermarket.

Three pairs of jams and three pairs of teas were used in the study. Using a 10-point scale of 1 = "very different" and 10 = "very similar", independent participants had already rated the pairs for similarity so that the pairs were towards the mid-point of 5 for "difference". The pairings were:

▶ jams: blackcurrant/blueberry; ginger/lime; cinnamon-apple/grapefruit

▶ teas: apple pie/honey; caramel and cream/cinnamon; Pernod (anise)/mango.

Participants were told that the taste test was for a quality control study. The procedure is shown in Figure 20.3.5.

▲ **Figure 20.3.5** A step-by-step illustration of a manipulated choice trial in the jam condition. **(A)** Participants sample the first jam. **(B)** The researcher secures the lid back on and flips the jar upside down while putting it back on the table. The jar looks normal, but it is lidded at both ends, and with a divider inside, containing one of the included samples at each end. **(C)** Participants sample the second jam. **(D)** The researcher performs the same flipping manoeuvre with the second jar. **(E)** Participants indicate which jam they prefer. **(F)** Participants sample the chosen jam a second time, but since the containers have been flipped they now receive the alternative they did not prefer.

Source: Hall *et al* (2010: 55)

Each participant sampled a pair of jams and a pair of teas. After tasting the jams and then smelling the teas, participants had to rate each on a 10-point scale from 1 "not at all good" to 10 "very good". Once they had tasted or smelled the second of each pairing, they were asked which they preferred and offered a second taste or smell of their preferred option. After they had sampled the supposed preferred option they were asked if they had thought anything was odd or unusual. Their responses were noted and if they had detected something had changed it was classified in one of three ways:

▶ Concurrent detection: when participants immediately noticed that they had not been presented with their preferred option.

▶ Retrospective detection: when participants, either before or after debriefing, noticed the manipulation.

▶ Sensory-change detection: when participants noticed some subtle change (even if they did not consciously notice the manipulation) by saying that the taste or smell was sweeter, weaker, stronger, etc.

The rates of detection for each pairing is shown in Figure 20.3.6.

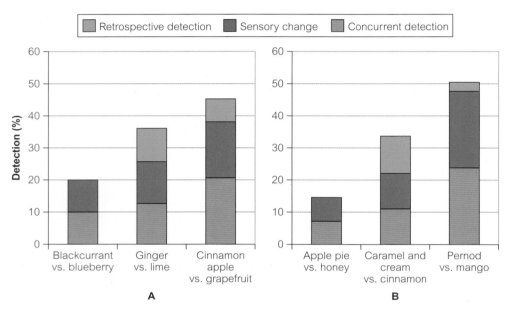

▲ **Figure 20.3.6** Detection for each pairing ("A" for jam; "B" for tea)

Source: Hall *et al* (2010: 58)

Overall, no more than one-third of all manipulation trials were detected by the participants. Therefore, in the majority of cases, the participants were blind to the manipulation that had happened and could not detect it. Also, in around two-thirds of the trial where detection happened it was not a conscious reaction.

Strength	Weakness
There were many controls in place so the research team could be confident it was the IV directly affecting the DV.	The sample was only from one area of Sweden so the results may be culturally biased and may not apply to other nationalities.

Advertising and false memory (Braun LaTour *et al*, 2004)

Braun-LaTour *et al* (2004) aimed to investigate how post-experience advertising could influence recollection of events in a series of three studies. Two of these studies are described below.

Study 1

This experiment tested whether true and false autobiographical advertising would be processed and then influence memories. The expectation was that false information about experiences at Disneyland would change what consumers could recall. That is, those who recognised the false information would be *less* likely to form false memories of an event. A total of 66 undergraduates (32 female) were randomly assigned to one of two conditions:

▶ being shown a "truthful" advertisement that featured a probable event when visiting Disneyland: shaking hands with Mickey Mouse

▶ being shown a "false" advertisement that featured shaking hands with Bugs Bunny (he is a Warner Bros character so would never be at Disneyland).

The advertisements were handed out as part of a questionnaire during a lecture. Participants were simply told to read and evaluate the advertisement. They had to rate their attitude, affect and the likelihood of visiting Disneyland in the future. They were then asked to recall their own past experiences of visiting Disneyland and whether they had seen certain characters there. Participants who had visited Disneyland had to write about their earliest recollection of visiting the site. Once they had completed the questionnaires, they were all debriefed about the nature of the false information.

Two independent judges coded participants' reactions to the advertisements and their recall statements about visiting Disneyland. They specifically coded:

- the number of words used in the recollection
- whether participants' reactions to the advertisement were personal or concentrated towards critiquing the advertisement
- whether participants noticed that Bugs Bunny did not belong at Disneyland
- how many items in the advertisement were mentioned in a participant's recollection.

There were just two results that reached significance:

- Shaking hands with Bugs Bunny: 22 per cent of the "false" group but only 7 per cent of the "true" group claimed to have shaken his hand at Disneyland.
- Confident ratings about meeting Bugs Bunny: participants in the "false" group rated this $\frac{2.3}{8}$ while those in the "true" group only rated it $\frac{1.3}{8}$.

This shows that post-event false information can affect later recall of an event.

Study 2

This study varied the way the false information was presented. It was either presented pictorially, verbally or both. A total of 100 participants (56 male) were randomly assigned to one of the three conditions and shown an advertisement. All three advertisements were "false" as they suggested Bugs Bunny is associated with Disney:

- The pictorial condition had a picture of Bugs Bunny at the bottom of the advertisement.

- The verbal condition had a headline of "Bugs Says It's Time to Remember the Magic".
- The both condition had a combination of the above.

The same procedure was used as in study 1.

There was a "picture superiority" effect. The two conditions that contained pictures resulted in the largest number of false memories: 48 per cent in the pictorial condition; 17 per cent in the verbal condition; 32 in the both condition. Therefore, only the pictorial versus verbal condition was statistically significant.

There were more "Bugs detectors" in the verbal condition: 31 per cent, compared to 12 per cent in the pictorial condition and 8 per cent in the both condition. The researchers could analyse any differences between "Bugs detectors" and participants who had created a false memory. There were some clear significant differences:

- More participants in the false memory group had personal responses to the advertisement (75 per cent compared to just 6 per cent).
- Participants in the '"Bugs detector" group had more negative affect and less positive affect compared to those in the false memory group.
- Those in the "Bugs detector" group had more negative attitudes towards the advertisement.
- Participants in the false memory group were more likely to want to visit Disneyland after the study.
- However, the memories recalled between the groups did *not* differ on length, clarity, emotional importance or personal importance.

Strength	Weakness
The procedure was standardised so the study can easily be replicated and tested for reliability.	Some of the measures relied on people's memories of events that had happened to them. These memories may not be accurate, which casts doubt on the validity of the findings from the study.

20.4 THE PRODUCT

PACKAGING, POSITIONING AND PLACEMENT

ASK YOURSELF
Do you always wrap presents for people when you give them a gift? Why do you do this? How do you feel when you receive a gift that is *not* gift wrapped?

Gift wrapping (Porublev *et al*, 2009)

Porublev *et al* (2009) conducted a qualitative study on people's perceptions of gift wrapping. Prior to the study, little research had been conducted on this topic but the researchers were aware of certain trends that had appeared in the literature:

▶ People believe that a gift should be wrapped.

▶ A gift should look like a gift.

▶ An unwrapped gift is often called a "naked gift".

The team used grounded theory for data collection and performed interpretative techniques for the analysis. Three methods of data collection were used:

▶ Observation of a Christmas gift wrap stall was carried out.

▶ There were in-depth interviews with 20 Australian participants who were 25–35 years old.

▶ Projective workshops were organised. At these workshops participants, in pairs, were asked to wrap two gifts: one for someone they were close to and one for an acquaintance. All discussions that took place were noted.

Most of the participants preferred to receive a gift that was wrapped. This was based on the "expectation of what a gift should look like". These are examples of some of the qualitative findings:

"I prefer wrapped. I like the reveal. I think all gifts are good, don't get me wrong, I like a gift under any circumstances, but it does mean somebody's taken a little bit of extra time and put extra thought into it" (Tammy).

"I'd be more embarrassed by a gift that was unwrapped than no gift at all" (Katya).

"People have always received gifts that are wrapped and therefore I think a lot of people would do it without even thinking about it... it's a tradition in our society where you give me a gift there's an expectation that you'll wrap it therefore signifying that it is a gift" (Martin).

Source: Porublev *et al* (2009: 4)

During the projective workshops, 24 gifts were wrapped. All of them looked like "traditional" gifts with ribbons and bows. Figure 20.4.1 shows some examples.

▲ **Figure 20.4.1** A sample of the gifts wrapped in the projective workshops

Source: Porublev *et al* (2009: 5)

There were certain expectations about the use of gift wrap in the process of gift exchange. Gift wrapping makes it easier for gift exchange to occur as the giver and receiver can fulfil their roles without any confusion.

Strength	Weakness
Qualitative data were collected so the researchers had rich, in-depth data to analyse, potentially increasing the validity of findings.	The sample consisted of just 20 Australians so generalisability may be an issue.

Product colour and associative learning (Grossman and Wisenblit, 1999)

Grossman and Wisenblit (1999) investigated the idea that classical conditioning could be used to explain colour choices in consumers. This has implications for companies that may wish to change the colour associations of their products. The researchers reviewed the field of colour choices and consumer behaviour across a variety of topic areas:

▶ The importance of colour in marketing was investigated. Many companies hire colour consultants to help them in this area. For example, car companies tend to change their colours by 30 per cent each year and have to plan three to four years in advance to predict which colours will be "in season". Grossman and Wisenblit note that the principles of classical conditioning work here. Consumers begin to associate certain colours with certain products, producing favourable outcomes such as more frequent purchasing.

▶ Physiological responses to colour were considered. In our evolutionary past, man associated dark blue with night (passivity) and yellows and reds with sunlight (arousal). These associations are still seen in humans.

▶ The development of colour associations was investigated. Classical conditioning can explain cultural perceptions and differences in colour associations. Cultures appear to relate colours to meanings. For example, in the West green is associated with hopefulness and red with love or a revolution. In China, white is associated with righteousness and yellow with trustworthiness. Perceptions can change over time due to associations. For example, after the Second World War, Israelis disliked yellow as it represented the patches worn by concentration camp victims.

However, several years later, many Israelis saw yellow as a good colour as it represented the rebirth of the desert in their country.

▶ Colour preference depends on the product. Clothing colours that are popular tend to be blue, red and black, whereas for cars popular colours are grey, white and red. Products such as furniture tend to be bought if they are beige.

▶ Colours have meanings for consumers. The review lists examples of how certain colours work or do not work with certain products. A vitamins company produced a black container with white lettering but consumers, when asked, did not like it as they thought it looked like a bottle of poison. A laundry detergent was tested as the manufacturer wanted to add coloured specks to it:

– Blue was chosen as it signified cleanliness.

– Yellow was rejected as it was not perceived as being clean.

– Red was also rejected as it was believed to be damaging the clothing.

▶ Consumers in the Far East associate green with labels for cans of soup and yellow with confectionery packaging and soft drinks, making it difficult for companies such as Coca-Cola to make an impact there.

▶ As a result of this review, it is clear that companies need to consider the colour of their product and the colour of their packaging. They need to know the cultural associations with different colours in the cultures where they want to sell their products.

Attention and shelf position (Atalay, Onur Bodur and Rasolofoarison, 2012)

Atalay, Onur Bodur and Rasolofoarison (2012) wanted to investigate the effect of gaze on product choice. More specifically, they wanted to assess whether consumers tend to choose the option in the centre of an array of products. The idea of "horizontal centrality" was under investigation. This is when an option is chosen that is located in the centre of a horizontal line of products such as items in a vending machine. The focus on this central product is given the term "central gaze cascade effect". The researchers ran three studies to test these effects. Two of their studies are reported here.

Study 1A

The idea was to use eye-tracking equipment to see how consumers look at products before choosing. The products used were vitamins and meal replacement bars. A pre-test was conducted to remove any potential extraneous variables with the fictitious brands that the study would use. Brand names were chosen that were not similar to any already on the market. Colour choice was tested via a readability assessment and a final three colours were chosen that did not differ statistically on readability.

This study used 67 undergraduates from HEC Paris, France. They gained extra credit for participation. Four participants had to be eliminated due to technical difficulties with the eye-tracking device. This left 63 (54 per cent female) to form the final sample.

The eye-tracking device allowed participants a degree of head movement and also let them wear glasses or contact lenses if necessary. Each participant was presented with a planogram (a 3 × 3 matrix design). Each brand was placed in a column. There were three variants of each brand, counterbalanced for each participant. The brand names were Priorin, Aplecin and Labrada for the vitamins and Bega, Niran and Salus for the meal replacement bars.

Participants were asked to review each product array on the screen as if they were in a shop and press the enter key when they were ready to make a choice. As soon as the enter key was pressed, the visual display disappeared. Once this happened, participants were asked to choose what they would purchase and then complete a questionnaire evaluating the brands. The choice had to also be recorded by participants checking a box for the *position* of the product they would have bought from the 3 × 3 design. They also had to rate, on a scale of 1–9, quality of each brand, popularity of each brand and attractiveness (higher ratings were always more favourable). They then had to rate how much market share each brand probably had and how much shelf space each would be given in a store if they were the store manager. Finally, a memory test was administered in which participants had to try to recall the brand names.

The results clearly showed that horizontal centrality had an impact on visual attention towards the products. Those in the horizontal centre received more frequent eye fixations and they were looked at for longer. The real-time gazes of participants for the first and last five seconds of gazing are shown in Figure 20.4.2.

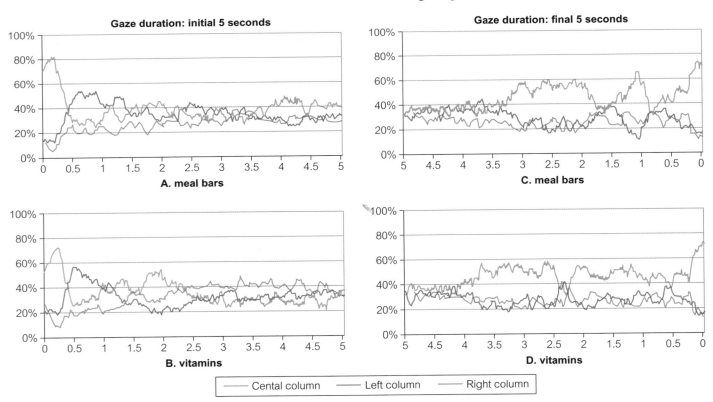

▲ **Figure 20.4.2** Likelihood of looking at each column during the initial and final five seconds

Source: Atalay, Onur Bodur and Rasolofoarison (2012)

Of the overall gazing time, the central column receives the majority of gaze time initially and towards the end.

Study 1B

This smaller study was conducted to see whether the central gaze cascade effect was due to the horizontal centrality of the brand or the centrality of the computer screen. This study simply extended on study 1A by shifting the planograms to be off-centre on the computer screen (either left or right). Another 64 participants were used in this study (57 per cent female). Participants in the study *still* fixated more on the central column, showing that the central gaze cascade effect was due to the horizontal centrality of the brand.

Strength	Weakness
The researchers employed many controls so they could be confident it was the IV directly affecting the DV.	The findings may be culturally biased as they only used participants from a small area in France. Other nationalities may not show the same effects.

Issues and debates tracker: All of these ideas have good application to everyday life. When companies are developing new products they can utilise the ideas of colour, gift wrapping and shelf position to ensure that consumers know about these products. This should increase sales and profit.

SELLING THE PRODUCT

Sales techniques

Customer focused, competitor or product focused

Within consumer psychology, there appear to be two main techniques used to help sell a product.

Customer-focused technique

The focus here is on a dialogue between someone who is selling a product and a potential customer. Even before talking about the product, a customer-focused salesperson will get to know potential customers first (e.g. their background and desires linked to the product) to show a genuine interest into why they wish to purchase. As a result, there is no standard sales pitch for all potential customers, but instead a tailored approach that makes individual customers feel that the salesperson knows something about them. According to Dale Carnegie, there are four main qualities of customer-focused salespeople:

- They will ask more questions about the customer.
- They will use a customised approach to selling rather than a "one technique fits all" approach.
- They are more interactive with the customer.
- They will generate more sales as a result.

Figure 20.4.3 shows the pathway that salespeople are likely to take if they adopt a customer-focused approach. Each stage is clearly necessary for a sale to be deemed a success and a product purchased.

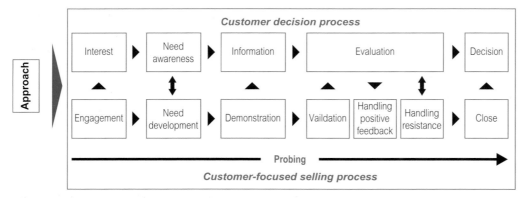

▲ **Figure 20.4.3** Customer-focused selling model

Competitor-focused or product-focused technique

This approach follows a model involving features, advantages and benefits (the FAB model):

▶ Features – this aspect should focus on the unique selling point (USP) of the product. The salesperson needs to highlight what features makes this product different from other similar products on the market.

▶ Advantages – these can form part of the USP or can be highlighted separately. The salesperson needs to highlight what advantages the product has over competitors' products.

▶ Benefits – again, these may be described as part of the USP or separated out for more impact. The salesperson needs to tell the customer all of the benefits of the product in comparison to anything else on the market.

Technical information must be kept to a minimum – unless the customer asks about it – otherwise the customer may feel overwhelmed by the amount of information and not purchase. If a team of salespeople are going to be used to launch a product, their manager should get them all involved. For example, each member of the team should think of one example of FAB, then all of these ideas can be merged into one "company policy" approach so that all salespeople are selling in the same way.

CHALLENGE YOURSELF

Watch a series of commercials that last for more than three minutes (which are sometimes called infomercials). List all of the uses of the FAB model, and how many times each commercial uses each aspect. Compare this to use of the FAB model in the short commercials (usually lasting 10–15 seconds) that are shown between programmes.

Interpersonal influence techniques: "disrupt-then-reframe" (Kardes *et al*, 2007)

Kardes *et al* (2007) wanted to test the effectiveness of the "disrupt-then-reframe" (DTR) technique on consumer behaviour. DTR follows the idea of confusing consumers with a disruptive message and then reframing the message to reduce the ambiguity caused. A series of experiments were conducted.

Experiment 1

A total of 147 participants (104 females) were randomly assigned to either a DTR condition or a reframe-only control condition. A salesperson in a supermarket approached potential participants about purchasing a box of candy:

▶ For the DTR condition the salesperson would say: "The price is now 100 eurocents (*two-second pause*)… that's 1 euro. It's a bargain!"

▶ For the reframe-only condition the salesperson would say: "The price is now 1 euro. It's a bargain!" (Kardes *et al*, 2007).

The number of boxes of candy sold was recorded. Overall, 54 per cent of participants bought at least one box of candy. However, there was a significant difference between the two groups. In the DTR group, 65 per cent of participants bought some candy compared to 44 per cent in the reframe-only group.

Experiment 2

Another study was conducted where the participants were asked to pay 3 euros to become a member of a group. The sample was 155 participants (59 per cent female). They were randomly assigned to the DTR condition or the reframe condition.

- For the DTR condition, the following script was used: "You can now become a member for half a year for 300 eurocents (*two-second pause*) that's 3 euros. That's a really small investment!"

- For the reframe only condition, the script was: "You can now become a member for half a year for 3 euros. That's a really small investment!"

Overall, 22 per cent of the participants agreed to join the group. Analysis of each condition showed that 30 per cent of participants in the DTR condition wanted to join but only 13 per cent of those in the reframe condition wanted to. This was statistically significant.

It would appear that DTR works effectively for the sales of goods but also to get people to spend money on non-tangible items such as membership of a group.

Strength	Weakness
A large sample was used for both studies, so generalising beyond the sample is a possibility.	An independent groups design was used, so individual differences may account for some of the changes in the DV, rather than the IV itself.

Ways to close a sale

Cardone (2011) proposes a 12-step approach to closing a sale, given as instructions for a salesperson:

1. Remain seated. While you are selling it is good for you to be on your feet projecting your enthusiasm, but when you are getting someone to sign something or buy the product remain seated so you are on the person's level. The process of standing up from being seated can give the impression that something has changed and the deal is off.

2. Always have a written proposal. Potential customers will only believe what they can see.

3. Communicate effectively and with clarity. Potential customers will not buy if you cannot get across all of the terms and conditions of a sale.

4. Make eye contact throughout. It should suggest that you are genuinely interested in the customer and what that person needs.

5. Always carry a pen – it is frustrating to shake hands on a deal but then not be able to sign for it.

6. Use humour but do not overuse it. It is subjective and can put a potential customer off.

7. If the potential customer appears unsure about wanting to buy, or has just said "No", ask one more time in a different way.

8. Always stay with the buyer. If more information is needed get someone to bring it to you rather than leaving the customer alone.

9. Always treat the buyer like a buyer.

10. Remain confident throughout the purchase period as it makes the customer feel valued.

11. Be positive through the purchase period too as the customer expects this.

12. Always smile.

There are other techniques that consumer psychologists believe are useful to help close a sale. Salespeople should do the following:

- Use indirect closed questions such as "Does this offer look good to you?"

- Make a list of pros and cons for buying the product but ensure that the number of pros is larger than the cons.

- Use the "possibility of lose" technique by telling the potential customer that the low price is only available today.

- Use "negative assumptions" such as "… so there is no reason not to like it". This makes the potential customer think about the product without an option to refuse.

- Follow up where possible. Customers could easily be taken aback if they receive a phone call one month after purchase asking them how the product is. They are then more likely to buy more products from that salesperson.

BUYING THE PRODUCT

Purchase decisions: theory of planned behaviour (Ajzen, 1991)

The theory of planned behaviour is based around four main concepts:

▶ attitudes towards a behaviour

▶ subjective norms about a behaviour

▶ behavioural intentions (deciding to achieve a set goal), which can relate to how hard someone is willing to try to achieve a goal

▶ perceived behavioural control (believing that you can or cannot perform a behaviour).

Figure 20.4.4 shows how these aspects could interact.

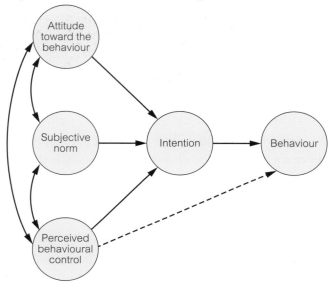

▲ **Figure 20.4.4** Theory of planned behaviour

Source: Ajzen (1991: 182)

For example, in the context of shopping behaviour, the following may happen:

▶ A person will have a an attitude such as "I love Christmas shopping" or "I really hate Christmas shopping".

▶ Subjective norms may include that it is traditional to do Christmas shopping.

▶ The intentions could be "I have a list of what I need and where to go" or "I will browse and see what I can find for people".

▶ People may already think "It is going to be so busy, so I cannot face it" or "I love the atmosphere of the shopping experience at Christmas and I will find all I need. I have all day!".

Therefore, people may go out and complete their Christmas shopping in their local mall or shopping centre, or stay at home and use the Internet to buy everything.

 CHALLENGE YOURSELF
To what extent do you think this theory is deterministic? Justify your answer.

Black box (stimulus-response) model

This model is linked to the behaviourist approach to psychology. The model follows a stimulus response format. A stimulus in the environment triggers a response from the organism. The main types of stimuli can be classed as reinforcers (rewards) and punishers. Rewards make it more likely that a person will repeat the behaviour whereas a punisher makes it less likely that a person will repeat the behaviour.

In terms of consumer behaviour, it would predict the following:

▶ Reinforcement: if people buy a product and like it, they are more likely to repeat the purchase behaviour. This can also apply to buying products manufactured by the same company.

▶ Punishment: if people buy a product and have a bad experience with it, they are less likely to purchase that product again.

Strength	Weakness
There are many studies that show people react favourably to reinforcement so this could be used by companies to ensure that their product becomes a positive stimulus.	The model cannot account for people buying products that they have no direct experience of. If they have never been rewarded for buying the product before, what makes them make the first purchase of the new product?

Consumer decision model

This model is part of the cognitive approach to consumer behaviour. The model proposes a seven-point decision process that consumers go through each time they decide to purchase a product or not to purchase it. These seven points are:

1. Need recognition: consumers need to recognise that they may need or want a product.

2. Internal information search: does the consumer have a memory for a similar product? If so, was it a good or bad product?

3. External information search: what products are available that fulfil the consumer's current needs?

4. Evaluation of alternatives: are there any alternative products that serve the same purpose?

5. Purchase: (buying the product).

6. Post-purchase reflection: how well has the product performed?

7. Divestment: getting rid of the product when it is no longer useful or is broken.

The model can be seen in Figure 20.4.5.

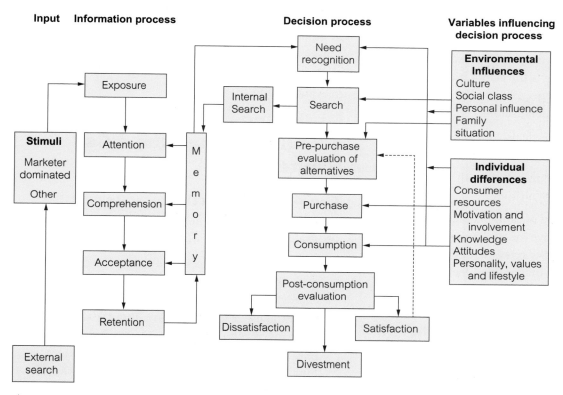

▲ **Figure 20.4.5** Consumer decision model

Source: Blackwell *et al* (2001) reproduced in Bray "Consumer behaviour theory: approaches and models", Bournemouth University: http://eprints.bournemouth.ac.uk/10107/1/Consumer_Behaviour_Theory_-_Approaches_%26_Models.pdf

Strength	Weaknesses
The model has good real-world application as manufacturers and companies can use the model to ensure that consumers pass through the seven stages to improve sales.	Some psychologists believe that there is no evidence that consumers process information in a linear way as predicted by the model. The model ignores other factors such as the roles of culture on decision making, or when people are buying a product for the first time so cannot conduct the internal information search.

20.5 ADVERTISING

TYPES OF ADVERTISING AND ADVERTISING TECHNIQUES

Advertising media (e.g. television); persuasive techniques

One theory that looks at the role of persuasive techniques in advertising is the elaboration likelihood model (Petty and Cacioppo, 1986a). The model proposes two routes for persuasion:

▶ The central route: this deals with generally strong and long-lasting changes of attitude.

▶ The peripheral route: this deals with weak and only short-lived changes of attitude.

The central route is based around people's ability to elaborate on the persuasive message presented to them. If the message is personally relevant, of perceived importance to them and makes them feel personally responsible, then people will carefully process the information presented.

The peripheral route is used if people do not feel the message is particularly relevant or of perceived importance or makes them feel responsible. In order for these messages to persuade people to "sit up and take note", the source of the information must be attractive, the person giving the message must be an expert and have credibility and there should be a limited number of arguments.

Figure 20.5.1 shows how this persuasion model works.

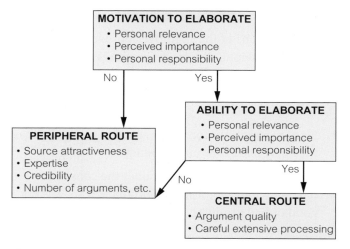

▲ **Figure 20.5.1** The elaboration likelihood model (Petty and Cacioppo, 1986a)

The Yale model of communication (see page 193) is also relevant here.

Marketing mix models: the 4 Ps (McCarthy); the 4 Cs (Lauterborn)

The 4 Ps (McCarthy)

The 4 Ps form a marketing tool that can be used by advertisers. The 4 Ps are as follows:

1. Product. McCarthy refers to this as the product mix. There is a physical product. This refers to the characteristics of the product (e.g. its dimensions, potential usage and life span). There is also the extensive product. This refers to the "added extras" (e.g. its packaging, brand name and guarantee). Finally, there is a total product. This is the overall product including emotional aspects and any values that a customer may place on it (e.g. overall perceptions of the company that could be placed onto the new product).

2. Price. The company must consider a realistic price for the product based on its potential market place. For example, is it to be sold as a multipack in a supermarket or exclusively to one shop or chain of shops?

3. Place. This refers to two main aspects. The first is the geographical location where the product may be sold. A shopping centre may be a good place to start: promotional offers can be used or the company can pay a supermarket to have the product stocked at "eye-level" for a certain amount of time. The second aspect is the way that the product will be distributed. Will the product be sold directly to the consumer (e.g. via a website only) or in a shop?

4. Promotion. This covers all of the different ways in which a company can promote its product. These include public relations, trying to obtain free publicity, actual advertising, undertaking sales promotions and cold calling potential customers.

 CHALLENGE YOURSELF
Design a new soft drink and use the 4 Ps model to create an advertising campaign for the product.

The 4 Cs (Lauterborn)

One of the main criticisms of the 4 Ps model is that is fails to understand the role of the consumer in the advertising and subsequent product purchases. Lauterborn, therefore, proposed the 4 Cs:

1. Consumer wants and needs. Products can only be sold to people who actually want to buy them so research into consumer needs is vital to success.

2. Cost to satisfy. This refers to the "overall cost" of the product that actually satisfies the needs of the consumer. Lauterborn argued that the "raw price" a product is sold at is irrelevant. All aspects need to be considered, such as the distance someone is willing to travel to buy the product, the ethical conscience a consumer has about buying or using the product and what the product would mean to a consumer if he or she owned it, or bought it and consumed it (as with food products, for example).

3. Convenience to buy. This requires research. Consumers are ever changing and although many like to purchase online (so it is important for a company to have an easy-to-navigate website), they still go out of their homes to shop. A company needs to offer a variety of ways in which consumers can purchase its products (old and new ones).

4. Communication. A company has to listen to consumers when it is launching a product. The company should ask consumers what they want and what they need. Some companies ask consumers to trial products and write reviews. All communication should be a dialogue.

 CHALLENGE YOURSELF
Go back to the soft drink you designed and advertised using the 4 Ps. Now re-launch it using the 4 Cs. What will you do differently? Which model do you prefer?

Product placement in films (Auty and Lewis, 2004)

Auty and Lewis (2004) wanted to understand the influence on children of branded products that appear on television and in movies. The researchers were interested in the role of explicit and implicit memory for product placements. The model they were testing is shown in Figure 20.5.2.

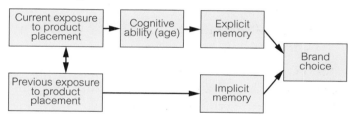

▲ **Figure 20.5.2** Working model of the effect of product placement on choice in children

Source: Auty and Lewis (2004: 701)

Participants were 48 students, who were 11–12 years old, from a secondary school in the UK, and 57 children aged 6–7. Prior permission to use the participants in the study had been obtained from their parents. Participants were then randomly assigned to one of two groups:

▶ Participants in the treatment group watched a clip lasting 1 minute 50 seconds from the film "Home Alone" where the family were having a meal. Pepsi® could be seen throughout the clip and was also mentioned, by name, by the father.

▶ Participants in the control group watched a clip of Kevin, a child superhero, eat a macaroni and cheese microwave meal (with no brand mentioned or seen in the clip). He also drank a glass of milk.

The team who led the interviews with the participants (after the participants had watched the clip) were ex-students of each school. There were four cans of drink in the interview room (two Pepsi® and two Coke®). Participants in the treatment group were told that they could have a drink and then they would be asked some "easy questions". They were then asked to describe the clip they had seen in as much detail as possible. If a participant did not mention Pepsi® in

the recall, then some general questioning was employed to see if he or she would mention a brand of cola.

Children in the control group went through the same procedure and if they did not recall the milk, they were prompted in the same way as the treatment group. Each interview lasted about five minutes. The results are shown in Table 20.5.1.

Hypothesis	N =	Supported/ Not supported	X²	Significance (p =)
H1 Children exposed to product placement in a film clip will choose a different brand when offered a choice on the same day from those who are not shown the branded film clip.	105	Supported	4.22	.040
H2 (a) There will be a difference in recall of the brand shown in a product- placement film clip between cued processors (11–12-year-olds) and limited processors (6–7-year-olds).	52	Not supported	1.47	.225
H2 (b) There will be a difference in the choice of brand between children who have correctly recalled the brand and those who do not recall the brand.	52	Not supported	0.07	.790
H3 Children who have seen the film before will make a different choice of brand from those who have not, regardless of whether or not they have been exposed to the branded clip.	105	Not supported	0.16	.683
H4 Among children who have seen the film before, those shown the brand in a film clip will choose a different brand from those who are not shown the branded film clip.	72	Supported	4.71	.030
H5 Among children who have never seen the film before, those shown the brand in a film clip will choose a different brand from those who are not shown the branded film clip.	33	Not supported	0.31	.579

▲ **Table 20.5.1** Summary of the findings

Source: Based on Auty and Lewis (2004: 702-703; 708)

As Table 20.5.1 shows, only two of the hypotheses were supported. For drink choice before the interview the split between Coke® and Pepsi® was 58:42 for the control group but 38:62 for the treatment group (in the UK the sales split is 75:25). Also, those who had been exposed to the clip before (irrespective of which condition they were in) chose Pepsi® more often (in a 33:67 split).

This led the researchers to propose a model of the effect of product placement on choice in children. Figure 20.5.3 shows this model.

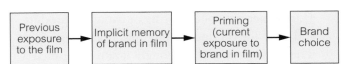

▲ **Figure 20.5.3** Suggested model of the effect of product placement on choice in children

Source: Auty and Lewis (2004: 710)

Strength	Weakness
There was a standardised procedure, meaning that the study can easily be replicated and tested for reliability.	Only children were used in the study. We cannot generalise to adults because children and adults may perceive product placements in different ways.

COMMUNICATIONS AND ADVERTISING MODELS

Changing attitudes and models of communication (source, message)

Yale model of communication

Hovland *et al* (1953) conducted many studies at Yale University which helped to form a model of persuasive communication. There are three main stages in the process:

1. Attention – the message must grab people's attention. Sound *and* visual stimuli are the most effective so using television might be better than using leaflets or the radio.

2. Comprehension – for a message to be successful it must be understood by the recipient. Messages need to be clear and concise.

3. Acceptance – the overall message has to be accepted by the recipient for behaviour change to occur. The person does not have to *believe* the message but must accept it and behave according to it for it to be persuasive communication.

There are several factors that can affect any or all of the three stages above. These include the following:

▶ The communicator – a message is more persuasive if the communicator is attractive, is similar to the recipient and is likeable.

▶ The content – it is best to cause mild fear and it is best when the message is presented verbally *and* visually. A one-sided or two-sided argument needs to be considered too.

▶ The medium – for example, the communicator needs to choose whether a television campaign would work better than a radio or leaflet campaign. If the message is simple and straightforward then conveying it via television is best; if it is complicated it is best communicated via written media.

AIDA model (Strong, 1925) and updates of it

This model, proposed by Strong (1925), is a behavioural model of advertising. It has been used to ensure that an advertisement raises awareness of a product, stimulates interest about it, raises consumers' desire for the product and makes them go out and buy it. These are the AIDA model's four stages to effective advertising:

1. **A**ttention – the advertisement needs to grab the attention of the viewers (potential consumers).

2. **I**nterest – having had the product bought to their attention, the viewers (potential consumers) should want to know more about the product.

3. **D**esire – gaining interest in the product should lead to the desire to own it.

4. **A**ction – the final stage is the action of buying the product.

All four stages are equally important and the viewer (potential consumer) needs to pass through them all for the advertisement to be deemed a success.

Strength	Weaknesses
The model has good real-world application. For example, advertising agencies can use the model to ensure that consumers pass through the four stages to improve sales.	Some psychologists (e.g. Brierley, 2002) believe that there is no evidence that consumers process information in a linear way as predicted by the model. The model ignores factors such as the roles of context and culture on consumer's thinking patterns.

One update of the AIDA model was the DAGMAR model. This stands for "Defining Advertising Goals for Measured Advertising Results". In this model there are also four stages:

1. Consumers must be aware of the product and/or organisation.

2. Consumers must comprehend what the product actually is and how they might need it.

3. They must then arrive at either a mental suspicion (not buy) or a mental conviction (to buy).

4. They must then motivate themselves to buy if necessary.

CHALLENGE YOURSELF
Create an advertisement for a new candy bar, a new car that runs on electricity and a new pair of "must have" shoes or trainers. Use the AIDA and/or DAGMAR models to help you.

Hierarchy of effects model (Lavidge and Steiner, 1961)

The hierarchy of effects model, proposed by Lavidge and Steiner (1961), has six stages. Consumers can move through several stages simultaneously. The six stages are as follows:

1. Awareness – consumers need to be aware of the existence of the product, usually as a result of advertising.

2. Knowledge – consumers need to know what the product has to offer to them.

3. Liking – consumers must develop favourable attitudes towards the product. This can be affected by past experiences with similar products or brands.

4. Preference – consumers must prefer the product to all of the competitors' offerings.

5. Conviction– consumers must have a desire to buy the product.

6. Purchase – consumers then purchase the product.

One example of moving through several stages simultaneously could be when a new fragrance is released and a consumer has previously purchased scents from the same company. As soon as a consumer is at stage 1, stages 2–5 happen at the same time until the consumer finally reaches stage 6. The consumer could reach this final stage through watching an advertisement on television or seeing the product in a shop for the first time.

Strength	Weaknesses
The model has good real-world application. For example, advertising agencies can use the model to ensure that consumers pass through the six stages so as to improve sales.	Some psychologists believe that there is no evidence that consumers process information in a linear way as predicted by the model. The model ignores factors such as the roles of context and culture on consumers' thinking patterns.

ADVERTISING APPLICATIONS

Brand recognition in children (Fischer *et al*, 1991)

Fischer *et al* (1991) were interested to see if children as young as 3–6 years of age can recognise brand logos. The sample consisted of 229 children attending preschools in Augusta and Atlanta in the United States. The children were instructed to match logos with one of 12 products that appeared on a game board. A total of 22 logos were tested, covering a range of children's products, products for adults and two cigarette brands. Other measures included having parents reporting the number of hours their children watched television each day and recording how often the children asked for products by their brand name. Table 20.5.2 highlights the success in logo recognition.

Product category	Logo	Correct product response	Recognition rate (%)
Children's brands	Disney Channel	Mickey Mouse	91.7
	"McDonald's"	Hamburger	81.7
	"Burger King"	Hamburger	79.9
	"Domino's Pizza"	Pizza	78.2
	"Coca Cola"	Glass of cola	76.0
	"Pepsi"	Glass of cola	68.6
	"Nike"	Athletic shoe	56.8
	"Walt Disney"	Mickey Mouse	48.9
	"Kellogg's"	Bowl of cereal	38.0
	"Cheerios"	Bowl of cereal	25.3
Cigarette brands	Old Joe	Cigarette	51.1
	"Marlboro" and red roof	Cigarette	32.8
	Marlboro man	Cigarette	27.9
	Camel and pyramids	Cigarette	27.1
	"Camel"	Cigarette	18.0
Adult brands	"Chevrolet"	Automobile	54.1
	"Ford"	Automobile	52.8
	Apple	Computer	29.3
	"CBS"	Television	23.1
	"NBC"	Television	21.0
	"Kodak"	Camera	17.9
	"IBM"	Computer	16.2
Surgeon General's warning		Cigarette	10.0

Quotation marks on the logo indicate that the brand name is part of the test item.

▲ **Table 20.5.2** Logos tested, correct product response and recognition rates

Source: Fischer *et al* (1991: 3146)

Across all of the products, logo recognition was highly associated with the age of the child, as shown in Figure 20.5.4.

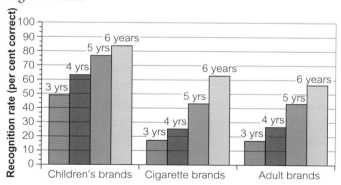

▲ **Figure 20.5.4** Logo recognition rates by years of age (yrs) for children's brands, cigarette brands and adult brands

Source: Fischer *et al* (1991: 3147)

The research team compared the recognition rates for the Disney Channel logo and Old Joe the Camel (for Camel cigarettes). Figure 20.5.5 shows the results.

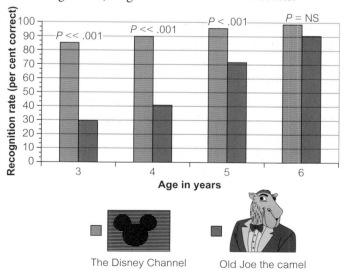

▲ **Figure 20.5.5** Logo recognition rates for the "Disney Channel" and "Old Joe the Camel" by subject age

Source: Fischer *et al* (1991: 3147)

Race and gender had no effect on logo recognition. For the 6-year-old children, there was no significant difference in logo recognition between the two logos. However, for all of the younger ages, children were more likely to recognise the Disney Channel logo than the Camel cigarettes logo.

It would appear that very young children can recall and recognise brand logos, which is a useful application for advertisers and product developers. As the older children quite easily recognised tobacco-related logos, this could be useful for health campaigns.

Strength	Weakness
The procedure was standardised so the study could easily be replicated to test for reliability.	Some of the measures relied on parents giving details about their children's behaviour (e.g. number of hours of television watched), but the parents may have given socially desirable data, making some of the findings potentially lacking in validity.

CHALLENGE YOURSELF
Design a study that tests brand recognition in adults.

Advertising and consumer personality (Synder and DeBono, 1985)

Snyder and DeBono (1985) wanted to investigate whether personality types are affected by advertising. Specifically, they wanted to investigate a personality trait called self-monitoring:

▶ High self-monitors are individuals who strive to be the person that is called for by the situation they find themselves in. They adapt their behaviours to suit that situation.

▶ Low self-monitors are people who do not attempt to mould their behaviours to suit the situation they find themselves in. Their behaviours tend to be regulated by internal mechanisms such as attitudes and feelings.

Snyder and DeBono created a series of studies to test their ideas.

Study 1

Three sets of paired magazine advertisements were created for whisky, cigarettes and coffee. The pairs of advertisements were the same except for the written message or slogan that appeared on each advertisement. One had a slogan linked to the use of the product. The other had a slogan that made a claim about the quality of the product.

The study was undertaken by 50 undergraduates. Initially they completed a self-monitoring scale and via the median were placed into one of two categories: high self-monitors or low self-monitors. The three pairs of advertisements were as follows (Snyder and DeBono 1985: 589):

▶ Two advertisements were for Canadian Club® whisky. The image-oriented slogan was "You're not just moving in, you're moving up." The product quality-oriented slogan was "When it comes to great taste, everyone draws the same conclusion."

▶ Two advertisements were for Barclay cigarettes. The image-oriented slogan was "Barclay… you can see the difference." The product quality-oriented slogan was "Barclay… you can taste the difference."

▶ The other pair of advertisements featured Irish Mocha Mint. The image-oriented slogan was "Make a chilly night become a cozy evening with Irish Mocha Mint." The product quality-oriented slogan was "Irish Mocha Mint: A delicious blend of three great flavors – coffee, chocolate and mint."

Each pair of advertisements was presented in a random order to participants. They completed a 12-item questionnaire to assess them by making them compare the two paired advertisements. The questions asked included: "Overall, which ad do you think is better?", "Which one appeals to you more?" and "Which ad do you think would be more successful?" (Snyder and DeBono, 1985: 589.)

Table 20.5.3 shows the results.

	Product		
Self-monitoring category	Canadian Club	Barclay	Irish Mocha Mint
High	6.84	5.00	7.40
Low	4.88	3.68	6.08

▲ **Table 20.5.3** Evaluations of the advertisements used in study 1

Source: Snyder and DeBono (1985: 590)

Note: Range = 0–12. Higher scores indicate greater favor-ability toward image-oriented advertisements, and lower scores indicate greater favorability toward product-quality-oriented advertisements.

Source: Snyder and DeBono (1985: 590)

Table 20.5.3 shows that the two personality types evaluate advertisements in different ways. High self-monitors rated image highly, whereas low self-monitors rated product quality highly.

Study 2

The researchers wanted to see whether the way a product is advertised affects how much someone is willing to pay for it. They asked 40 participants to complete the self-monitoring scale and then participants were assigned to one of two conditions for all three products in study 1: image-oriented advertisements or product-quality advertisements.

After participants had viewed each advertisement they were asked "How much would you be willing to pay for this product?" (Snyder and DeBono, 1985: 590.) To prevent extreme responses, there were ranges to choose from: whisky ($5–15), cigarettes ($0.50–1.50) and coffee ($2–5).

	Self-monitoring category	
Type of advertisement	High	Low
Canadian Club[a]		
Image	9.75	7.50
Quality	8.24	8.64
Barclay[b]		
Image	0.89	0.74
Quality	0.89	0.94
Irish Mocha Mint[c]		
Image	3.43	2.97
Quality	3.28	3.50

▲ **Table 20.5.4** Results from study 2: price willing to pay

Note: Dollar signs omitted.
[a] Range = $5.00–$15.00. [b] Range = $0.50–$1.50.
[c] Range = $2.00–$5.00.

Source: Snyder and DeBono (1985: 591)

Table 20.5.4 shows that for high self-monitors, favourable images were worth more money. For low self-monitors, product quality was worth paying for. This indicates that, within the same campaign, advertisers might benefit from using different advertisements in order to appeal to different personality types.

Strength	Weakness
There were many controls in the study so the researchers can be more confident that it was the IV directly affecting the DV.	Only undergraduates were used in the study so it may be difficult to generalise findings beyond the sample.

Effective slogans (Kohli *et al*, 2007)

Kohli *et al* (2007) created a seven-point procedure for writing effective slogans:

1. Keep your eye on the horizon.

The researchers recommend that advertisers have a long-term view about where they want the product to be. Slogans that are created today need to "stand the test of time" so using language that might date should be avoided. The researchers note that the BMW slogan "The Ultimate Driving Machine" is a good example.

2. Every slogan is a brand positioning tool, and it should position the brand in a clear manner. The positioning can be based on features of the product or the benefits of buying the product. Slogans can be simple. The researchers note one from Excedrin® (a "pain killer" that uses the slogan "The Headache Medicine").

3. Link the slogan to the brand.

The researchers note that the level of incorrect slogan recall is very high. Therefore, advertisers should include the brand name in the slogan.

4. Please repeat that.

According to the researchers, repetition of the slogan in any advertisement leads to better recall. Therefore, advertisers should not just use the slogan once.

5. Jingle, jangle.

Jingles can enhance memorability of a product in the short term, so they should be used.

6. Use slogans at the outset. Slogans are a fundamental component of brand identity. Therefore, when a business is advertising new products from an "old" company, a slogan should be used immediately to establish brand identity during the campaign and beyond.

7. It's okay to be creative.

Keeping it simple may not be the most effective strategy as this involves shallow processing and the consumer may well forget the advertiser's efforts. The researchers use an example of Vicks NyQuil® that uses a complex slogan of "The Nighttime, Sniffling, Sneezing, Coughing, Aching, Stuffy Head, Fever, So You Can Rest Medicine".

Source: The seven points above are based on Kohli *et al* (2007)

CHALLENGE YOURSELF
Find the advertisements for at least five different products that do not have a slogan. Create a slogan for each one.

Issues and debates tracker: All of these ideas have good application to everyday life. Companies can use the ideas of slogans and how personality affects choice to design effective advertising campaigns for new products, with the hope that this will increase sales and profits.

HOW TO EVALUATE: CONSUMER

For the 10-mark question in paper 3, you will be asked to evaluate one of the topics covered in this section. Below are three examples of the types of evaluation point you *could* write in the examination.

You should aim to make a range of evaluation points for the 10-mark question.

RETAIL DESIGN

The findings from studies have good *application*. Shops and casinos, for example, can design "better" places for people to experience, which could then increase profits and customer satisfaction. For example, Finlay *et al* discovered that pleasure was significantly related to overall restoration of the casino (pleasant imagery present), coherence (organised and user-friendly casino) and complexity (more elaborate settings and visibly rich). Therefore, when a casino needs a re-fit the owners can try to incorporate all of these designs, along with a Kranes-type design to get more people into their casino to spend money. However, many studies have small sample sizes so *generalisability* of findings might be quite difficult. In the Finlay *et al* study only 48 people were asked their opinion of casinos and the Vrechopoulos *et al* study only had 20 participants per layout group. This might mean that the findings are not that useful outside of the sample.

ENVIRONMENTAL INFLUENCES ON CONSUMERS

Many studies in this area use questionnaires to measure the outcome variables, which means that the findings *may lack some validity*. People may not be truthful in their answers on a questionnaire or they may want to give socially desirable results to make themselves look good to the researcher. For example, in the Machleit *et al* study on crowding, people had to rate perceived crowding on a Likert-type scale (human crowding and spatial crowding were both measured) and satisfaction was measured via items on a 7-point scale. These are subjective measures, which means that accurate findings may be limited as people perceive the different ratings points differently.

ADVERTISING APPLICATIONS

Many studies in this area are experimental and therefore have standardised procedures so can be *easily replicated to test for reliability*. The Fischer *et al* study used the same game with logos for all children in their study while Synder and DeBono used the same three advertisements (depending whether participants were in the image or product quality group), meaning that other researchers can replicate the same study to see whether a different sample produces similar results or not. This also has an impact on *internal validity* because through use of standardised procedure and controls, such as the advertising statements in the Snyder and DeBono study, researchers can be more confident that it is the IV directly affecting the DV with no other variables getting in the way.

22 PSYCHOLOGY AND HEALTH

All studies or comments marked with an asterisk are not directly named in the syllabus but the information included in these studies or comments will help the student to answer questions on the topic covered. The examination will not ask about these studies by name or ask for specific findings.

22.1 THE PATIENT–PRACTITIONER RELATIONSHIP

PRACTITIONER AND PATIENT INTERPERSONAL SKILLS

ASK YOURSELF

When you visit a doctor, what skills do you expect the doctor to show that make you feel more confident that he or she is giving you the best possible treatment?

Non-verbal communication (McKinstry and Wang, 1991)

McKinstry and Wang (1991) wanted to investigate whether the way in which doctors dress affects what a patient thinks of them. A total of 475 patients (67 per cent female) attending 30 doctors took part in the study. Five different locations in Lothian, Scotland were used. Participants were asked to look at eight different photographs, shown in Figure 22.1.1.

Participants were then asked: "Which doctor would you feel happiest about seeing for the first time?" They scored each example on a scale of 0–5. They were also asked to rate the confidence in the ability of each of the doctors in the photographs, alongside whether they would be unhappy seeing any of them. The final section of the questionnaire enabled participants to answer closed questions about doctors' dress codes in general and to give their attitudes towards different styles of dress.

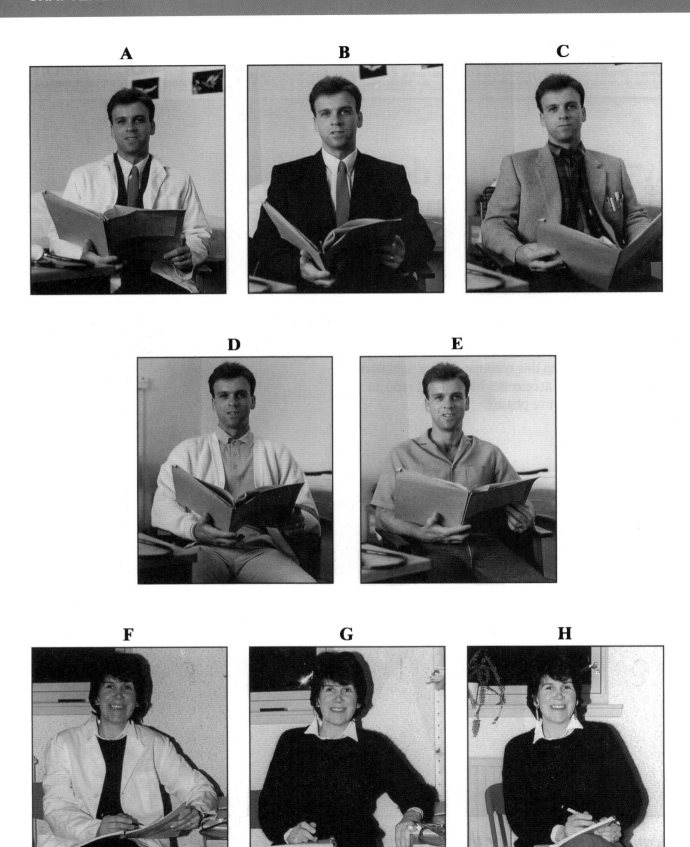

▲ **Figure 22.1.1** Photographs used in the study

Source: McKinstry and Wang (1991: 270)

The results are show in Table 22.2.1.

Number of patients								
	Male doctor wearing:					Female doctor wearing:		
Acceptability score	White coat	Suit	Tweed jkt	Cardigan	Jeans	White coat	Skirt	Trousers
5	183	238	141	76	60	263	222	104
4	122	116	120	77	44	118	194	86
3	75	46	182	96	58	56	42	166
2	47	48	22	147	76	25	13	65
1	39	19	4	31	154	7	2	20
0	9	8	6	48	83	6	2	34

▲ **Table 22.1.1** Scores for doctors in different styles of dress

Source: McKinstry and Wang (1991: 276)

The following results were statistically significant:

▶ The doctor in a smart suit was the most popular.

▶ The doctor in a cardigan and casual trousers scored significantly higher than the doctor in jeans.

▶ The informally dressed female doctor scored significantly lower than the other two female doctors.

▶ Older patients were more likely to give high scores to the male doctor in a white coat or a formal suit.

▶ Older patients were more likely to give higher scores to the female doctor in a white coat.

Of the sample, 41 per cent (n = 194) answered yes to the question: "Do you think you would have more confidence in the ability of one of these doctors (based on their appearance)?" Participants' main choices were:

▶ male: suit (n = 84), white coat (n = 74), tweed jacket (n = 22), jeans (n = 9), cardigan (n = 4)

▶ female: white coat (n = 94), skirt (n = 65), trousers (n = 13).

The final set of results is shown in Table 22.1.2.

Patients:	Percentage of respondents (n = 475)
believe male doctors should usually wear:	
white coat	15
suit	44
tie	67
would object to male doctor:	
wearing jeans	59
wearing an earring	55
having long hair	46
believe female doctors should usually wear:	
white coat	34
skirt (rather than trousers)	57
would object to female doctor:	
wearing jeans	63
wearing lots of jewellery	60

(n = total number of respondents)

▲ **Table 22.1.2** Patients' responses to questions about specific items of doctors' dress

Source: McKinstry and Wang (1991: 277)

Table 22.1.2 shows that most participants thought a male doctor should wear a tie, and a female doctor a skirt. Jeans appear to be too informal and prompted the most objections from participants, regardless of whether a male or female doctor was wearing them.

Strength	Weakness
A large, diverse sample was used in the study, making it easier to generalise beyond the sample.	The judgment was only based on appearance so could be seen as being reductionist: (several other factors also affect patients' judgments of their doctor).

CHALLENGE YOURSELF
To what extent do you feel the findings from the study are culturally biased? Justify your answer.

Verbal communications

Verbal communications are based around the speech used by a doctor to try to gain access to relevant information about a patient's condition and then the potential treatment. Medical jargon is one potential hindrance when it comes to verbal communications between doctor and patient.

Verbal communications: McKinlay (1975); Ley (1988)

McKinlay (1975) examined the comprehension of medical terminology in sample of participants who were using a maternity service in Aberdeen, Scotland. A total of 87 families were used in the study and were interviewed about the use of maternity services 4 times in an 18-month period. The fourth interview collected data on the comprehension of medical terminology used by doctors. A total of 13 words were chosen that could be misunderstood. Each word was read out and then used in the context of a sentence. An example was:

> "Rhesus: Doctors sometimes, while examining a woman who is expecting, say she's 'rhesus positive'. What are they talking about?" (McKinlay 1975: 10).

The responses were transcribed verbatim and two independent doctors scored them on the following scale:

▶ Score A: the patient did not recognise the word or understand it.

▶ Score B: the patient had an incorrect understanding of the word.

▶ Score C: the patient recognised the word but did not understand it.

▶ Score D: the patient had a good idea what the word meant.

One year after the transcripts were scored, a separate group of doctors rated each of the words on what they expected patients to understand. Patients were split into two groups for analysis: those who used the maternity services regularly ("utilisers") and those who were "underutilisers". When scoring a participant's transcript, the two doctors did not know which group the participant was in.

The main results are shown in Table 22.1.3.

	Underutilizers			Utilizers			Physicians		
	A: No Knowledge	B/C: Wrong or Vague	D: Adequate	A: No Knowledge	B/C: Wrong or Vague	D: Adequate	A: No Knowledge	B/C: Wrong or Vague	D: Adequate
Antibiotic	11.1	60.0	28.9	13.9	44.4	41.7	27.8	68.7	5.6
Breech	8.9	6.7	84.4	0.0	0.0	100.0	11.1	66.7	22.2
Enamel	8.9	40.0	51.1	8.3	30.6	61.1	27.8	44.4	27.8
Glucose	17.8	44.4	37.8	19.4	36.1	44.4	11.1	61.1	27.8
Membranes	24.4	31.1	44.4	11.1	25.0	63.9	50.0	50.0	0.0
Mucus	33.3	33.3	33.3	30.6	22.2	47.2	38.9	50.0	11.1
Navel	4.4	15.6	80.0	11.1	33.3	55.6	0.0	27.8	72.2
Protein	37.8	62.2	0.0	30.6	58.3	11.1	27.8	55.6	16.7
Purgative	57.8	28.9	13.3	72.2	13.9	13.9	16.7	44.4	38.9
Rhesus	13.3	75.6	11.1	11.1	86.1	2.8	55.6	38.9	5.6
Scanning	13.3	35.6	51.1	8.3	30.6	61.1	66.7	33.3	0.0
Sutures	48.9	6.7	44.4	50.0	11.1	38.9	61.1	33.3	5.6
Umbilicus	84.4	15.6	0.0	83.3	5.6	11.1	50.0	38.9	11.1
Total									
Respondents	45 (100.0%)			36 (100.0%)			18 (100.0%)		

▲ **Table 22.1.3** Distribution of comprehension of 13 words by two groups of patients and the comprehension expected by doctors (physicians). Results are given as percentages of the number of respondents, for each word

Source: McKinlay (1975: 6)

For nearly all of the 13 words, the utiliser group had a higher percentage for score D than the underutiliser group. Therefore, it would appear that people using medical services regularly have a better understanding of medical terminology compared to people who don't use the services as much. In addition, the study showed that the doctors consistently underestimated the level of medical terminology comprehension in their patients.

CHALLENGE YOURSELF
Compare the percentage scores for the two groups with the doctors' expectations. What conclusions can you draw?

Strength	Weakness
The transcripts were scored independently with the doctors blind to which group each participant was in. This improves the validity of the study (as the scoring was objective). It also improves the study's reliability (as the physicians agreed on which score category each transcript was given).	The sample was limited in terms of geography (Scotland) and type of participant (maternity service users). This could make it difficult to generalise findings to other cultures. It could also be difficult to generalise to people who use other specialist health services where their comprehension levels may be specific to their medical condition.

One issue that Russell (2005)* noted was that, when a doctor does use jargon, many patients are reluctant to stop the doctor and ask for clarification as they do not want to be seen as being less intellectual.

Other factors that can affect verbal communications in interactions include the following:

▶ The volume of information conveyed is a factor. Ley (1988) stated that patients tend to remember just over 50 per cent of the information given to them in a consultation.

▶ Primacy effect plays a part – patients tend to be better at remembering and recalling information from the beginning of the consultation.

▶ Patients who have some medical knowledge tend to recall more of the consultation. Patients remember and recall only what they feel is important "to them" in the consultation.

▶ Instructions are more likely to be forgotten if presented orally (which is why many are printed on drug labels).

> **Issues and debates tracker:** These studies have good application to everyday life as they can be used as part of the training for doctors to improve communication skills. This should help patients better understand their health condition and/or treatment regime.

PATIENT AND PRACTITIONER DIAGNOSIS AND STYLE

A practitioner can use differing styles to diagnose a patient. The styles differ in the way that information is collected and used to make the diagnosis.

Practitioner style

Doctor-centred and patient-centred styles (Byrne and Long 1976; Savage and Armstrong, 1990)

Byrne and Long (1976) analysed about 2500 recorded medical consultations across many countries and discovered two main "styles":

▶ The doctor-centred style meant that the doctor asked questions that were closed so that the patient could only answer "Yes" or "No". When the patient attempted to expand on answers or tried to give more information, this was mainly ignored. It would appear that the doctor wanted to make the symptom–diagnosis link with no extra communication and everything was based on "fact" rather than any discussion. Therefore, the patient was passive in the conversation.

▶ The patient-centred style meant that the doctor asked open questions so that the patient could explain and expand on answers. The doctor would try to limit the use of medical jargon to ensure that the patient understood the diagnosis and potential treatment. The doctor would encourage patients to express themselves how they wished and would ask for clarification as and when it was needed. Therefore, the patient was active in the conversation.

Savage and Armstrong (1990) conducted a study to compare the effects of "directing" and "sharing" styles of consultation on patients' satisfaction with a consultation. In an inner London general practice, 359 patients were randomly selected to receive either a direct or a sharing style of consultation. Table 22.1.4 shows the differences in style.

Part of consultation	Style of consultation	
	Directing	Sharing
Judgment on the consultation	"This is a serious problem" or	"Why do you think this has happened?"
	"I don't think this is a serious problem"	"Why do you think this has happened now?"
Diagnosis	"You are suffering from..."	"What do you think is wrong?"
Treatment	"It is essential that you take this medicine"	"What have you tried to do to help so far?"
		"What were you hoping that I would be able to do?"
		"Would you like a prescription?"
		"I think this medicine would be helpful; would you be prepared to take it?"
Prognosis	"You should be better in ... days"	"What do these symptoms or problems mean to you?"
Follow up and closure	"Come and see me in ... days"	"Are there any other problems?"
	"I don't need to see you again for this problem"	"When would you like to come and see me again?"

▲ **Table 22.1.4** Examples of directing and sharing styles of consultation by general practitioner (GP) during five parts of consultation

Source: Savage and Armstrong (1990: 969)

The GP did not know which style to adopt until the patient entered the consultation room and the GP turned over a card allocating one of the two styles. An independent observer listened to a selection of 40 recordings of the consultations and confirmed that all aspects of each consultation conformed to the style allocated on the card.

Table 22.1.5 shows results from patients who were questioned immediately after their consultation.

Assessment	Style of consultation		
	Directing	Sharing	Significance
I was able to discuss my problem well	130/157 (83)	132/154 (86)	NS
I received an excellent explanation	63/162 (39)	41/156 (26)	$x^2 = 5.7$; df = 1; p = 0.02
I perceived the general practitioner to have complete understanding	86/162 (53)	61/158 (39)	$x^2 = 6.8$; df = 1; p = 0.01
I felt greatly helped	77/162 (48)	66/156 (42)	NS
I felt much better	45/162 (28)	48/155 (31)	NS

▲ **Table 22.1.5** Effect of doctor's style of consultation on assessment of his understanding of their problem by patients immediately after consultation. Figures are numbers (percentages) of patients (n = 320).

Source: Savage and Armstrong (1990: 969)

Table 22.1.5 shows that more patients felt that an excellent explanation was given, and that the GP had a complete understanding of the problem, when the directing style was used.

The researchers also compared responses from patients who completed a questionnaire immediately after the consultation and the same one a week later:

▶ This comparison showed that 45 per cent of participants in the directing style group, but only 24 per cent of those in the sharing style group, felt they received an excellent explanation immediately after consultation. One week later these figures were 33 per cent and 17 per cent respectively.

▶ A total of 62 per cent of patients in the directing style group but only 37 per cent of those in the sharing style group felt that the GP had a complete understanding of their health issue immediately after the consultation. One week later these figures were 39 per cent and 18 per cent respectively.

It would therefore appear that a more directing style of consultation brings about more satisfaction in patients.

Strength	Weakness
The procedure was standardised, meaning that the study could easily be replicated and tested for reliability.	The participants were from one inner London practice, which might make it difficult to generalise beyond the sample used.

Practitioner diagnosis
Type I and type II errors

There are occasions where a doctor will get something wrong. Errors are classified into two types:

1. Type I error. This is when the doctor diagnoses somebody to be healthy when the patient is actually physically or psychologically ill. Many believe this to be the most serious of the two errors as the patient does not get any treatment and the condition worsens.

2. Type II error. This is when the doctor diagnoses somebody as ill when in fact the patient is healthy.

Disclosure of information

For a diagnosis to occur, the patient does have to give some information to the doctor. However, as the doctor will have an array of patients who have their own styles of communication, reaching the correct diagnosis can sometimes be quite difficult.

Sarafino (2006) noted that the patient can hinder the communication when the patient:

▶ wants to criticise the doctor or becomes angry

▶ clearly ignores what the doctor is saying

▶ insists on more tests and medication when the doctor says there is no need

▶ wants a certificate for an illness that the doctor does not believe the patient has

▶ makes sexual remarks to the doctor.

The above can stop a consultation "in its tracks". A patient may show a real concern about a condition that is only minor or show no concern for a condition that is major. The doctor still needs to get the correct information out of the patient to make a diagnosis. Different patients will describe symptoms of the same illness in vastly different ways, which can also make it difficult for the doctor to make a reliable and valid diagnosis. Sarafino (2006) noted that this may be the case as patients simply interpret symptoms differently from each other (or have a different hierarchy of what they feel are the "main symptoms" of an illness). Also, some patients may wish to "play down" symptoms that may point towards a major illness. Finally, patients may not have the requisite vocabulary to describe accurately the symptoms they are feeling.

Disclosure of information (Robinson and West, 1992)

Robinson and West (1992) assessed the amount of information given by patients at a genito-urinary clinic via a computerised interview compared to a paper questionnaire. A total of 69 patients formed the sample. Significantly more symptoms were elicited via the computerised interview. When both methods were compared to notes taken by the doctor during the treatment of these patients, significantly fewer symptoms were recorded by the doctor. When patients were asked to report prior attendance at a genito-urinary clinic, they did so more often via the computerised interview than when they completed the questionnaire and gave information for doctor's notes. Therefore, an initial computerised interview at genito-urinary clinics may be useful to gain more relevant and important information from patients.

 CHALLENGE YOURSELF
Design a study that compares the effectiveness of two different methods used to help patients disclose information about their health.

MISUSING HEALTH SERVICES

Delay

Delay in seeking treatment (Safer *et al*, 1979)

Safer *et al* (1979) devised a model after interviewing many patients that tried to explain why patients delay seeking treatment. There are three stages to this:

1. Appraisal delay – this refers to the time taken for a person to interpret a physical symptom as a potential indicator of illness. This is affected by immediate sensory information – something bleeding or making a person experience major levels of pain will be interpreted much more quickly as "something wrong" than a small pain, for instance.

2. Illness delay – this refers to the time taken between people recognising that they are ill and actually seeking some form of medical attention. This is affected by familiarity – a new and different symptom will create a faster reaction and help-seeking behaviour than an old symptom that re-occurs.

3. Utilisation delay – this refers to the time taken between deciding to seek medical attention and actually doing so. This is affected by a number of factors such as cost, how severe the pain is and whether the person feels that going to get help would cure the illness. People can easily ignore illnesses without immediate pain and therefore can have illnesses such as hypertension and cancer for more than, for example, three months before they decide to go and get medical attention and advice.

Hypochondriasis

One specific behaviour that leads to a misuse of health services is hypochondriasis. According to Sarafino (2006) it is the "tendency of individuals to worry excessively about their own health, monitor their bodily sensations closely, make frequent unfounded medical complaints, and believe they are ill despite reassurances by physicians that they are not" (2006: 250).

Hypochondriasis (Barlow and Durand, 1995)

In Barlow and Durand's (1995) book about abnormal psychology, the researchers note the following about hypochondriasis:

- It is characterised by a person's fear that he or she has some serious illness or disease.

- There is a pre-occupation with bodily symptoms, which could be something as simple as a cough or sweating. The person misinterprets these as a sign of illness and disease.

- The person believes that a health professional's judgment is incorrect. Being told he or she is healthy has only a very short-term effect on the person.

- The person visits a range of health professionals with the belief that the first one (and subsequent ones) were incorrect in their diagnosis.

- The person mistakenly believes that he or she has a disease or illness.

Hypochondriasis is potentially caused by:

- a stressful lifestyle

- being exposed to family life where there was a disproportionate amount of illness

- an attention-seeking mechanism as a person notices that other people with illnesses gain a lot of attention.

Fallon (2010)* noted three types of hypochondria:

▶ The obsessive-anxious type – when people worry that they are ill despite reassurances from a doctor that they are not. They believe that the doctor has missed something serious.

▶ The depressive type – when people either go to the doctor crying that they are about to die and that there is no point testing them, or they refuse to go to the doctor.

▶ The somatoform type – when people exhibit many of the physical symptoms of an illness and always assume it is a very serious problem. They always think they have the worst illness possible given the symptoms.

Gropalis *et al* (2013)* noted a cognitive-behavioural element to the condition. Hypochondriacs might have faulty information processing in the brain. Those who have high anxiety when it comes to health-related issues always direct their attention towards any source of health threat. They can also easily access memories of illnesses. This may make them think that certain minor symptoms are something much more serious.

Schwenzer and Mathiak (2012)* reported that the cognitive bias described here could be a "general" bias towards "less positive" views. In their study, participants without any knowledge of Chinese language characters had to guess, just by looking at the characters, whether they portrayed a positive or negative meaning. This was used to see what biases lie in processing information that is clearly not related to illness in any way. Those who had higher hypochondriasis scores on a scale rated the characters as being less positive than the people with low hypochondriasis scores. Therefore, a "general distrustful attitude towards familiar procedures should be considered in hypochondriasis" (2012: 178).

Münchausen syndrome

This syndrome was named after Karl Freidrich Hieronymus Baron von Münchhausen, who told wild tales of travels and adventure in the 1700s. The condition is a "factitious disorder" which describes symptoms that are artificially produced by the patient rather than it being a natural illness process. Turner and Reid (2002) noted the three main features as:

▶ simulated illness (artificial symptoms)

▶ pathological lying (pseudologia fantastica)

▶ wandering from place to place (peregrination).

It is an extreme form of factitious disorder accounting for about 10 per cent of all factitious disorder case studies. A generic but typical case would involve patients who have travelled to different hospitals under different names turning up and giving a factitious history of their condition. They may simulate symptoms and in some cases eat contaminated food in order to vomit or produce blood. Many illnesses are claimed and the most common are fevers, infections, bleeding and seizures. However, Turner and Reid state that these patients may go through medical procedures that do not show that they have a "real illness" and many are then "caught out" by inconsistencies in their self-reported medical histories.

In addition to Münchausen syndrome, there is Münchausen syndrome by proxy. In these instances the mother or carer of a child deliberately exaggerates and fabricates illness of the child. The caregiver may induce physical and psychological problems into the child. It is now referred to as factitious disorder by proxy. Criddle (2010) noted three levels of this syndrome:

1. Mild (symptom fabrication) – the caregiver may claim the child experiences mild symptoms of an illness the child does not have.

2. Moderate (evidence tampering) – the caregiver may go as far as manipulating laboratory specimens of the child or falsifying the medical records of the child.

3. Severe (symptom induction) – the caregiver induces an illness into the child including diarrhoea, seizures and even sepsis. These methods may also include poisoning (e.g. with insulin and salt), applying faecal matter to open wounds to infect them, and injecting urine into the child.

CASE STUDIES

Münchhausen syndrome (Aleem and Ajarim, 1995)

Aleem and Ajarim (1995) studied a 22-year-old female university student who had been referred to hospital with a potential immune deficiency. She had a painful swelling over her right breast for five days before admission. She also stated that she had previously had abdominal wall swellings that had needed medical attention on about 20 difference occasions. Her problems appeared to begin when she was 17 and suffering from amenorrhea. She had been prescribed oral contraceptives and after just a few months was showing symptoms of deep vein thrombosis. She was prescribed warfarin and was hospitalised to try to reduce the thrombosis.

Soon after this she began complaining of painful swellings in her groin. Assessment pointed towards hematoma. She had come from a supportive family. Her mother had died from breast cancer. The patient, while intelligent, lacked any real medical knowledge. The researchers' initial physical assessment revealed scarring from the previous swellings but results of a lot of other tests were "normal". An abscess had to be drained as it had failed to clear up with antibiotics. After four days of being hospitalised, the patient developed another breast lesion which became infected and needed to be surgically drained. Suspicion was now being raised by the doctors as there was no explanation for the abscess or lesions seen.

The patient underwent a psychiatric assessment but she did not know she was being assessed for potential Münchausen syndrome. She was very defensive in the assessment and "extremely rationalizing her answers" and no other psychological issues were identified.

Finally, when she was not in bed one day, nurses found a syringe full of fecal material. When she returned to her bed, one of the other patients told her what the nurses had found. She became very hostile and angry, left the hospital immediately and was lost to the follow-up procedure. She was then officially diagnosed with Münchausen syndrome.

Strength	Weakness
As this was a case study, a lot of rich, in-depth qualitative data was collected so the findings should be valid.	As it was a case study, it may be difficult to generalise as the woman may have been unique.

In another case of Münchausen syndrome Zibis *et al* (2010)* studied a 24-year-old woman who had been referred to a surgeon as she had extremely painful, stiff and swollen right hand and arm. She reported having had four previous operations on the same region. Four days into her treatment at the hospital she developed a "fever temperature" that would not react well to any drug. However, diagnostic tests could not locate any infection or fever. It was discovered that she was preheating thermometers to take her own temperature and that she was often heard punching the wall at night (presumably with her right hand). She was also seen reading medical text books about hand diseases and amputations. The medical staff stopped her treatment. Her temperature dropped back to usual levels and 20 days after taking her cast off, her arm was free of any injury.

Faida *et al* (2012)* reported a case of Münchausen syndrome involving a 40-year-old woman who had injuries to her right leg. She was complaining of arthritis of the right leg with headaches and ulcers. During her hospitalisation, her condition got worse and she could no longer walk on her right leg. Tests to examine why this could be the case showed nothing abnormal about the leg. When a standard x-ray was taken, it revealed that a sewing needle was embedded in her right calf. When the hospital staff questioned her about this she became very aggressive and denied any knowledge of it. She then attempted to jump out of the hospital window to escape but thankfully was stopped. Many of her symptoms resolved spontaneously after this incident.

 CHALLENGE YOURSELF
Write up another case study of Munchausen syndrome. Compare it for similarities and differences to the Aleem and Ajarim case study.

22.2 ADHERENCE TO MEDICAL ADVICE

TYPES OF NON-ADHERENCE AND REASONS WHY PATIENTS DON'T ADHERE

Types of non-adherence
Failure to follow treatment, failure to attend appointments and problems caused by non-adherence

Clarke (2013) noted different types of *adherence* that we can reverse to discover different types of *non-adherence*, which are:

▶ not following short-term advice (e.g. to take three pills per day, five hours apart, for one week)

▶ failing to attend a follow-up interview or a referral appointment

▶ not wanting to make a lifestyle change (e.g. to reduce then quit smoking or take more exercise)

▶ not engaging in preventative measures linked to health (e.g. using contraception).

According to Sarafino (2006), up to 40 per cent of a given population fail to adhere to the medical advice given to them. That is, two in five people do not follow their doctor's advice. In addition, the research showed the following:

▶ When medicine needs to be taken for short-term acute illness, the adherence rate climbs to 67 per cent.

▶ For longer-term chronic regimes, the figure appears to be around 50 per cent.

▶ People tend to adhere more just before or just after seeing a doctor.

▶ There appears to be very little adherence at all to any advice that involves a change in lifestyle.

Sarafino (2006) was quick to note that these are probably overestimates of non-adherence as the data are only based on people who were willing to take part in a study and then admit to non-adherence. Also, the data fails to appreciate the range of adherence as some patients will adhere to advice 100 per cent of the time but others' adherence may vary markedly from illness to illness.

Problems caused by non-adherence

When patients don't adhere to their prescribed drug regimen, several problems can occur:

▶ They may not improve their health condition.

▶ They may become ill with a different health issue because they are not taking their drugs.

▶ Drugs that have not been consumed could be around the house for others to consume (e.g. a child may think the drugs are sweets).

▶ There are financial costs when patients don't turn up for follow-up appointments and/or through not turning up they may stop someone having an appointment who needs it.

▶ Producing drugs that are then destroyed incurs financial cost.

Rational non-adherence

There are patients who choose not to adhere to medical advice as it appears rational for them to do this. By this, we mean that they have conducted a cost-benefit analysis and it appears to them "costly" to adhere to the treatment being given to them or asked of them. Laba, Brien and Jan (2012)* wanted to try to understand rational non-adherence using a community sample of patients in Australia. The patients were given a discrete choice online survey that wanted to estimate the importance of eight medication factors with regard to non-adherence. The factors were:

▶ immediate medication harm

▶ immediate medication benefit

▶ long-term medication harm

▶ long-term medication benefit

- cost
- regimen
- symptom severity
- alcohol restrictions.

Six of the factors appeared to affect choice of adherence rationally in the sample. The two that did not were symptom severity and alcohol restrictions. Therefore, rational non-adherence is a complex interaction between the six remaining factors with an overall cost-benefit analysis by individual patients finally predicting whether they will adhere or not. It was noted that when a potential health outcome was framed in terms of "side effects" the person quite rationally was more likely not to adhere than if a health outcome was framed in terms of "therapeutic benefits". Therefore, the way that the treatment is, essentially, "sold to them" affects whether patients will adhere (as rational people do not want side effects but do want therapeutic benefits).

Why patients don't adhere: rational non-adherence (Bulpitt, 1994)

Bulpitt (1994) reported that part of the idea of rational non-adherence is from a patient's risk-benefit analysis of taking or not taking prescribed medication. One issue he revealed is that the public appear to be "obsessed with risk" but rarely consider benefits. One negative piece of media about a certain medication or treatment is enough for someone to rationalise a decision *not* to take that medication if it is ever prescribed.

Bulpitt examined the risks and benefits of drug treatment for hypertension in the elderly. When reviewing two large trials for hypertensive treatments the following emerged:

- Risks included increased gout (4/1000 patients per year), increased diabetes (9/1000), increased incidences of a dry mouth and diarrhoea.

- Benefits included reduction of "stroke events" by 40 per cent and coronary events reduced by 44 per cent with a certain drug combination (the average across reviewed trials was 14 per cent).

However, with the focus on risks over benefits, people may "rationally" decide not to take certain treatments because of the potential risks while ignoring what appear to be better benefits.

CHALLENGE YOURSELF
Design a study using the self-report method that investigates reasons why people *do* adhere to medical advice.

The health belief model (Becker and Rosenstock, 1979)

The health belief model developed by Becker and Rosenstock (1979) attempts to predict when people will make rational health decisions. It assumes that people are ready to change their health-related behaviours under the following circumstances:

- Perceived vulnerability: if people believe that they are vulnerable to a health problem.

- Perceived severity: if people believe that the health problem can have serious consequences.

- Perceived benefits: if people believe that taking the necessary action can reduce any vulnerability to the health problem.

- Perceived barriers: if people believe that the costs of taking the necessary action are outweighed by the overall benefits.

- Cues to action: if people are confronted with factors that will make them want to change (e.g. reading about someone else in a similar position; feeling physically ill).

- Self-efficacy: if people believe that they can be successful in changing their behaviours to benefit their health.

- Modifying variables: these are factors such as upbringing or cultural norms that can have an effect on decision making.

Figure 22.2.1 shows how these factors interact.

CHALLENGE YOURSELF
To what extent do you feel that the health belief model is deterministic? Justify your answer.

Examine models and theories of health promotion

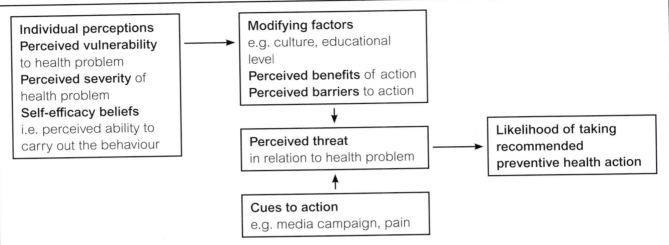

The model assumes that people make rational decisions on health-related behaviours and that people are ready to change if they:

- believe they are vulnerable to the health problem in question (**perceived vulnerability**)
- believe the health problem has serious consequences (**perceived severity**)
- believe taking action could reduce their vulnerability to the health problem (**perceived benefits**)
- believe the costs of taking action (**perceived barriers**) are outweighed by the benefits (**perceived benefits**)

- are confronted with factors (e.g. pain in the chest or a television programme) that prompt actions (**cues to action**)
- are confident that they are able to be successful in the action (**self-efficacy**) – if people believe they can stop smoking or eat healthier, they are more likely to listen to health promotion messages).

At the individual level there are **modifying variables**, i.e. individual characteristics such as culture, education level, past experiences, and motivation that can influence people's perceptions.

Quist-Paulsen and Gallefors (2003)* Randomised controlled trial to investigate smoking cessation using fear messages after heart problems

Aim The researchers wanted to see if a longer intervention including *fear arousal* could promote smoking cessation and prevent relapse.

Procedure The participants (heart patients) were randomly allocated to a treatment group and a control group. All patients were offered group counselling sessions. Patients in the control group only received group counselling. Patients in the treatment group also got personal advice from trained nurses and information material stressing the risks of continued smoking (fear arousal) and advantages of cessation. They were advised to stop smoking and nicotine

replacement was offered to those with cravings. Nurses contacted the patients in the treatment group by telephone nine times after these patients went home, to encourage cessation and stress the negative aspects of smoking on their condition.

Results In the intervention group 57 per cent of participants and in the control group 37 per cent had stopped smoking at the end of the programme.

Evaluation Using fear arousal is controversial but the researchers argue that it was justified since many more patients stopped smoking in the treatment group. The results indicate that cues to action and perceived threat can predict behavioural change. The study also provided additional help to support self-efficacy in the patients (e.g. by offering them medication to stop craving and by asking the spouses to stop smoking).

▲ **Figure 22.2.1** The health belief model
Source: (Rosenstock *et al*, 1988)

MEASURING NON-ADHERENCE

Subjective

One technique that can be used is for patients to complete self-reports with questions related to how much they are adhering to the treatment. Patients can be given booklets to record when they took certain drugs or engaged in certain behaviours that are asked of them as part of their treatment. Many psychologists are sceptical about the validity and reliability of self-reports as patients can easily lie about what they have done in terms of adhering to treatment. However, Kaplan and Simon (1990) noted that if the questions are direct and simple to answer then this technique can be used successfully to measure rates of adherence. However, patients may give socially desirable answers especially if they have *not* been adhering to the treatment prescribed to them.

Self-reports (Reikart and Droter, 1999)

Reikart and Droter (1999) investigated who participates in research on adherence to treatment in insulin-dependent diabetes. Alongside objective measures of blood sugar tests, the researchers used a series of self-reports. These included:

▶ Adherence and IDDM Questionnaire-R, to measure adherence to treatment covering aspects such as dietary behaviours, insulin adjustment and hypoglycaemia preparedness

▶ a record of demographics that enabled the team to note all relevant details (e.g. age ethnicity, disease duration and marital status of parents).

There were 94 families who participated in the study. They were split into three groups:

▶ non-consenters: families who declined to participate

▶ non-returners: families who said they would participate but didn't return the questionnaires

▶ participants: families who completed and returned their questionnaires.

The non-returners had significantly lower treatment adherence scores (the clinic staff knew who the non-returners were) and these people tested their blood sugar levels less frequently than participants. Participants and non-consenters did not differ on any measures.

Objective

Pill counting (Chung and Naya, 2000)

Chung and Naya (2000) tested compliance with treatment featuring an oral asthma medication using a device called "TrackCap™". A total of 57 patients (32 male; age range 18–55 years) formed the participant group. The treatment phase lasted 12 weeks. Participants were required to take 20 milligrams of zafirlukast twice a day. At the beginning of the study each participant was given 56 tablets, which was enough for three weeks' worth of treatment with one week's supply spare. The tablets were dispensed in screw-top bottles fitted with a TrackCap™ mechanism. Patients were scheduled to return to the hospital every three weeks so that their medication could be replenished. They were told to remove only one tablet at a time then replace the cap immediately to prevent moisture getting into their bottle of pills. They did not know that the TrackCap™ was keeping a record throughout the study. The TrackCap™ worked as follows:

▶ Each removal of the TrackCap™ was taken to indicate a single medication use.

▶ It only recognised but did not accumulate multiple openings that occurred within one minute of each other.

▶ If the cap was left off the bottle for more than 15 minutes, it was recorded as one additional event.

A total of 47 patients completed the 12 weeks of the study. Compliance or adherence was calculated in three different ways:

Percent TrackCap™ compliance was defined as follows:

$$\% \text{ Compliance} = 100 \times \frac{\text{Number of TrackCap}^{\text{TM}} \text{ events}}{\text{Number of prescribed tablets}}$$

Compliance also was estimated from returned tablet counts, with percent compliance defined as:

$$\% \text{ Compliance} = 100 \times \frac{\text{Number of dispensed tablets minus number of returned tablets}}{\text{Number of prescribed tablets}}$$

TrackCap™ adherence was the degree to which patients followed dosing instructions precisely on a daily basis and was defined as follows:

$$\% \text{ Adherence} = 100 \times \frac{\text{Number of days with 2 TrackCap}^{\text{TM}} \text{ events at least 8 h apart}}{\text{Total number of days' dosing}}$$

The median adherence rate was 71 per cent and the median compliance rate was 89 per cent. Figures 22.2.2 and 22.2.3 show the distribution of days of full adherence and distribution of compliance levels.

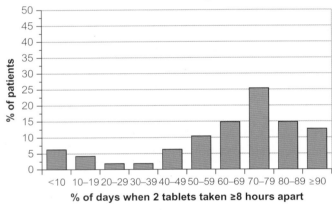

▲ Figure 22.2.2

Source: Chung and Naya (2000: 855)

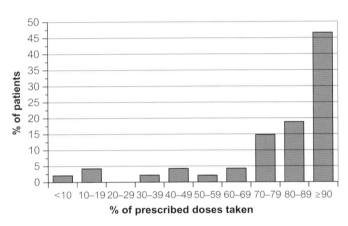

▲ Figure 22.2.3

Source: Chung and Naya (2000: 855)

Based on the tablet count method, the median compliance was 92 per cent. Overall, the TrackCap™ system could be a way of measuring both compliance and adherence to a drug-based treatment programme for people with asthma.

Strength	Weakness
The study has good application because the TrackCap™ system worked, so GPs could use it to measure how much a patient is adhering to a treatment regimen.	This system of measuring adherence is restricted to use with health conditions that require pills to be taken.

Biochemical tests

Biochemical tests can be run on the patient to measure adherence. These include urine analysis and blood tests to detect levels of the drug that the patient should have consumed.

Biochemical tests (Roth, 1987)

Some psychologists believe these are the best methods to use after reviewing the research (e.g. Roth, 1987), but biochemical tests are very expensive compared to the other options available. Also, while these tests do detect drug levels, they still do not show total adherence to a regime, only that the person has ingested enough of the drug for it to be detectable.

Roth and Caron (1978)* used an element of biochemical analysis in their study examining the accuracy of patients' statements on the consumption of an antacid used to treat peptic ulcers. Patients were given a case of 36 bottles of the antacid with measuring cups and told to take 1oz four times per day. Every so often a health professional would visit to collect empty bottles and replenish the antacid. To validate the "bottle count" as a measure of adherence, blood tests were taken to detect an inactive substance that had been placed in the antacid solution. On analysis, the mean actual intake by the sample of participants was 47 per cent but their estimated intake was 89 per cent.

Figure 22.2.4 compares the patients' estimates with the amount of bottles of antacid consumed.

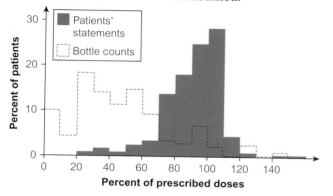

▲ **Figure 22.2.4** Histograms comparing patients' stated intake with intake estimated by bottle counts. The prescribed dose of 4oz per day is 100 per cent on the abscissa

Source: Roth and Caron (1978: 363)

Therefore, while patients believed they were consuming roughly the recommended doses of antacid, the bottle count (and blood analysis) told the doctors something very different.

CHALLENGE YOURSELF
To what extent do you feel that biochemical tests are the most effective measure of patient adherence? Justify your answer.

Repeat prescriptions

Repeat prescriptions have been a relatively new addition to the medical field with patients who are on longer-term treatment having the option of asking for the same amount of drugs again *without* having to see a doctor first. These patients simply request a repeat prescription from their local doctor's surgery and then pick up the drug. Although this means that patients have to have the motivation to do this (so the argument is that they must be adhering to the treatment), they could still obtain the drugs but not consume them (especially if the drugs are free).

Repeat prescriptions (Sherman *et al*, 2000)

Sherman *et al* (2000) wanted to assess whether using the measure of repeat prescriptions was a valid measure of adherence. A total of 116 children who had persistent asthma were used in the study. During a clinic visit, the pulmonologist interviewed the patients, caretakers, or both, to estimate levels of adherence to medication. A nurse then asked all caretakers where they tended to get medications from. The nurse then telephoned the 66 pharmacies that were identified by the caretakers and asked for data on refill histories. The information that was provided by the pharmacies was 92 per cent accurate. Adherence rates for drugs differed from 38 per cent to 72 per cent. Physicians could only identify 49 per cent of patients who had less than a 50 per cent adherence rate to medications.

The researchers concluded: "Physicians often were unable to identify patients with very poor adherence. Checking prescription refills is an accurate and practical method of identifying such patients" (Sherman *et al*, 2000: 533).

Issues and debates tracker: All of these methods have good application to everyday life. They can be effectively used to track patients' adherence to drug treatments to ensure that they are taking the correct dosage at the correct time. This can reduce wastage and also help people to get better, faster.

IMPROVING ADHERENCE

Improve practitioner style (Ley, 1988)

Ley (1988) reviewed the field of practitioner style in his book *Communicating with Patients* and came up with three sets of practical guidelines for practitioners that should help improve adherence:

▶ Satisfaction: aspects such as a shorter waiting time, listening to the patient and being friendly improved adherence.

▶ Selection content: the practitioner seeing what the patient wants to know, thinking about what he or she as a practitioner wants the patient to know and questioning via the health belief model improved adherence.

▶ Understanding and memory: aspects such as avoiding medical jargon, encouraging feedback from the patient, being specific rather than general and providing appropriate written back-up improved adherence.

Figure 22.2.5 highlights all of the factors Ley believed could be used by practitioners to improve their communication skills with patients, which in turn would improve adherence rates.

| SATISFACTION | Short waiting time
Be friendly rather than business-like
Some talk about non-medical topics
Listen to patient
Find out what worries are
Find out what expectations are — if not
    to be met say why |

| SELECTING CONTENT | What does patient want to know?
What are the patient's Health Beliefs?:
    Vulnerability
    Seriousness
    Effectiveness
    Costs and barriers
What do you want the patient to know?
Would motivating communication help:
    Fear arousal
    Sidedness? |

| UNDERSTANDING AND MEMORY | Avoid jargon
Use short words and short sentences
    — simplification
Encourage feedback
    Increase recall
    Primacy
    Stressed importance
    Explicit categorisation
    Specific rather than general
    Repetition
Written back-up
    readability
    physical format:
        letter size
        colour
        quality of print and paper |

▲ **Figure 22.2.5** Summary of ways to improve communication with patients

Source: Ley (1988: 180)

CHALLENGE YOURSELF
Produce a pack of information that can be used to train new practitioners on how to communicate with patients and improve patients' adherence to a drug treatment programme. Justify your decisions about what information your pack will include.

Behavioural techniques (Yorkley and Glenwick, 1984; Watt *et al*, 2003)

Yorkley and Glenwick (1984) evaluated a range of applied community interventions that were trying to increase immunisation in pre-school children. A total of 1133 families with immunisation-deficient children were randomly assigned to one of six groups:

▶ Group 1: General prompt (n = 195) were families who received a mailed prompt that contained general information about inoculation. It contained a standard immunisation schedule for the entire pre-school age span.

▶ Group 2: Client-specific prompt (n = 190) received a mailed prompt that told them which child or children needed which inoculations. It mentioned that the missing inoculations were going to be free of charge.

▶ Group 3: Specific prompt with increased public health clinic access (n = 185) consisted of families who received the same prompt as group 2 (the client-specific prompt) but, in addition, they received a second document about two different clinic sessions that were happening on a Wednesday night or on a Saturday. There was an added incentive of enticing parents to sign their children up so that the parents could go out for the evening or day when their children would be inoculated and looked after for free.

▶ Group 4: Specific prompt with monetary incentive (n = 183) were families who received the same prompt as group 2 (the client-specific prompt) but, in addition, group members received a second document about $175 in cash prizes if they brought their child or children to be inoculated.

▶ Group 5: Contact control (n = 189) group members received a telephone call containing information about inoculation.

▶ Group 6: No contact control (n = 191) was a group of families not contacted during the study period.

All intervention attempts (except using group 1's general prompt) produced evidence of improvement when compared to the control groups. The monetary incentive group produced the largest effect, followed by the increased access group, the specific prompt group then the general prompt group. Therefore, it would seem that a relatively inexpensive approach to increasing immunisation is to offer a monetary incentive.

Strength	Weakness
A large, diverse sample was used across all conditions, meaning that the findings are more likely to be valid and generalised beyond the sample used.	As an independent groups design was used, we cannot rule out some individual differences causing a change in the DV rather than the type of prompt.

Watt *et al* (2003) reported on a new asthma spacer called the Funhaler (see Figure 22.2.6). The study used a sample of 32 children (n = 10 males; age range 1.5–6 years; mean age 3.2 years; mean asthma duration 2.2 years). Questionnaires were completed after the use of the Breath-a-Tech (the current market leader in Australia for asthma drug dispensing) and the Funhaler.

The whistle and toy spinner (the toy element of the design) was designed to be away from the drug delivery system. In terms of adherence to the drug:

▶ 38 per cent more parents medicated their child on the previous day using the Funhaler compared to those using the standard Breath-a-Tech method

▶ 60 per cent more children adhered to the recommended dosage of four or more cycles of drug delivery with the Funhaler compared to the Breath-a-Tech method.

Therefore, it would appear that making delivery of drugs for children "more of a game", by including fun as part of the procedure, improves adherence levels.

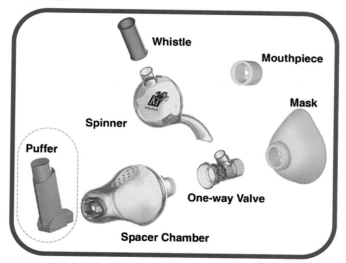

▲ **Figure 22.2.6** The Funhaler

Source: Watt et al (2003: 580)

22.3 PAIN

TYPES AND THEORIES OF PAIN

People can experience a variety of types of pain and there are theories as to why we experience pain outside of a physiological cause. All of these are covered below.

Definitions of pain

According to Sarafino (2006), pain can be a sensory and/or emotional discomfort which tends to be associated with actual tissue damage or threatened tissue damage including irritation. People's experiences of pain differ markedly but virtually every human being does experience pain in some form.

Acute and chronic organic pain

Acute pain refers to times when people experience temporary pain for about six months or less. They experience anxiety while the pain is there but this dissipates quickly once the pain begins to disappear. When pain lasts continually for more than a few months, it is referred to as chronic pain. People experiencing this will have high levels of anxiety and may well develop a sense of helplessness and depression. This is especially true if treatment is not helping. The pain interferes with daily life, thoughts and sleep patterns. For both of these types, the cause of the pain is physiological.

Psychogenic pain

Not all pain stems from physiological mechanisms. Psychogenic pain refers to episodes where there is no organic (physiological) cause of pain but the person is experiencing pain.

One controversial element of pain perception has been phantom limb pain. This is a condition whereby a patient who is an amputee still experiences pain in a limb that is not longer physically there or in a limb that has no functioning nerves in it. Yet, the pain is described in the same way as any other ache or pain that people experience daily. It does not always centre around the pain element as some amputees still feel as if they can move their phantom limb as they please. The pain symptoms can last for several months or even years and can be quite severe in nature. It is often described as shooting or burning pain or like cramp.

Theories of pain

Specificity theory (Descartes, 1664)

This was an early model of pain. It was predicted that we have a sensory system that is dedicated to pain. A series of neurons form a pathway to a dedicated pain centre in the brain. The more this pathway is used, the more intense is the pain experienced by the person. Therefore, according to this theory, pain is purely physiological and there are nerve centres in the brain that exclusively process this information. Some psychologists believe that they have evidence for certain fibres being exclusive to pain but others state that they cannot find them. There are sensory fibres in our skin that can detect heat, cold and certain pressures but these can also detect pain so the exclusivity argument is now a weak one. A more comprehensive theory is gate control.

Gate control theory (Melzack and Wall, 1965)

Melzack and Wall (1965) proposed the idea of a gate control theory of pain. Pain is detected and still picked up by sensory signals but the spinal cord plays a key role in the experience of the actual pain. The spinal cord has a mechanism in it that acts just like a gate: it is either open or closed. If it is open the pain is experienced but the spinal cord can modulate the pain level by having the gate slightly open rather than fully open. There are three main factors involved in the gate-opening process:

▶ One factor is the amount of activity in pain fibres. The more "noxious" the pain stimulus is, the more likely the gate will be opened (e.g. in someone with a severe cut).

Another factor is the amount of activity in other peripheral fibres. These are called A-beta fibres. They carry information about "low-level pain" (e.g. a scratch or a touch). When there is activity in these fibres the gate tends to close as the pain is low level and not dangerous.

Messages from the brain are also a factor. Information such as excitement and anxiety can affect how much the gate is opened or closed.

Sarafino (2006) noted conditions that can open or close the gate in the spinal cord. The gate can be opened by:

- severe injury
- anxiety, worry, depression, etc.
- focusing too much on the pain, plus boredom.

The gate can be closed by:

- medication
- positive emotions (e.g. laughing through happiness)
- rest and relaxation
- distraction from the pain.

 CHALLENGE YOURSELF
To what extent do you think the gate control theory of pain is reductionist? Justify your answer.

MEASURING PAIN

This next section will examine the different ways in which pain can be measured by a practitioner or psychologist.

Self-report measures

Self-report measures are often obtained using questionnaires that allow the person experiencing the pain to rate how severe it is. Common examples are the use of a box scale, a verbal rating scale or a Likert-type scale. Examples of these are given in Figure 22.3.1

Box scale:

No pain | 0 | 1 | 2 | 3 | 4 | 5 | 6 | 7 | 8 | 9 | 10 | Worst pain possible

Verbal rating scale:

No pain   Some pain   Considerable pain   Worst pain possible

Likert-type scale:

The example questions below would be answered using the options of:

Strongly agree, Agree, Don't know, Disagree, Strongly disagree.

1. The pain usually gets worse at night.

2. Pain relief helps me control my pain.

▲ **Figure 22.3.1** Scales for recording pain – box rating, verbal rating and Likert-type scales

Patients may also be asked to keep a pain diary, as shown in Figure 22.3.2, so the practitioner can monitor when the pain is happening and how the patient feels.

PAIN DIARY FOR:

DATE: Did you change your medication today? If yes, describe:

Pain rating scale:

| No pain | 0 | 1 | 2 | 3 | 4 | 5 | Unbearable pain |

Time	Pain rating and body position	Activity at start of pain	What medication did you take and how much?	Pain rating after 1 or 2 hours	Comments/other problems
8.30 p.m.	5/ lower back pain	Leaned over and dragged dining chair away from table	Aspirin (2)	4 – helped a little	Could stand up better
11.00 p.m.	2/ lower back dull ache	Lying flat on back in the bed	Ibuprofen (2)	1 – helped	Trouble getting to sleep: got to sleep at around 2.00 a.m.

▲ **Figure 22.3.2** Example of a pain diary

Clinical interviews

Another type of self-report can be gained through a clinical interview. This is essentially a dialogue between a psychologist and a patient. It is used to help diagnose the potential causes of pain and then come up with a plan of action to help to control or get rid of the pain. The psychologist will have a series of questions to ask the patient and will ask them when appropriate, as the situation will seem more like a conversation than an interview. The psychologist must ensure that all pre-set questions are asked but the order is not set because the psychologist will only ask questions based on the answers given by the patient. Therefore, the psychologist needs to be skilled in directing the interview by being able to ask the questions that will keep the dialogue going.

Strength	Weakness
This type of interview has good application as it allows psychologists to get a holistic view of the patients and find out all they need to know about the patients' experiences of pain. This will allow for more appropriate treatment to be given.	In clinical interviews psychologists rely on patients telling the truth and being able to describe their pain experiences accurately.

Psychometric measures and visual rating scales

The McGill Pain Questionnaire (MPQ)

One standardised psychometric measure of pain is the McGill Pain Questionnaire (MPQ). This questionnaire comes in four parts:

1. A diagram of a body is presented to the patient, who simply has to mark where the pain is located around the body.

2. There are 20 sub-classes of descriptive words from which the patient has to choose a maximum of one per class. The further down the list in each sub-class the word is, the more points it scores so that an overall pain rating index can be calculated.

Part I.   Where Is Your Pain?

Please mark on the drawing below the areas where you feel pain. Put E if external, or I if internal, near the areas which you mark. Put EI if both external and internal.

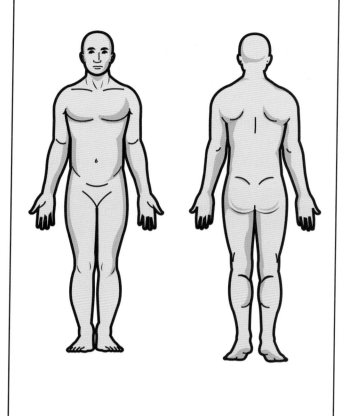

Part 2.   What Does Your Pain Feel Like?

Some of the words below describe your <u>present</u> pain. Circle <u>ONLY</u> those words that best describe it. Leave out any category that is not suitable. Use only a single word in each appropriate category – the one that applies best.

1	2	3	4
Flickering	Jumping	Pricking	Sharp
Quivering	Flashing	Boring	Cutting
Pulsing	Shooting	Drilling	Lacerating
Throbbing		Stabbing	
Beating		Lancinating	
Pounding			

5	6	7	8
Pinching	Tugging	Hot	Tingling
Pressing	Pulling	Burning	Itchy
Gnawing	Wrenching	Scalding	Smarting
Cramping		Searing	Stinging
Crushing			

9	10	11	12
Dull	Tender	Tiring	Sickening
Sore	Taut	Exhausting	Suffocating
Hurting	Rasping		
Aching	Splitting		
Heavy			

13	14	15	16
Fearful	Punishing	Wretched	Annoying
Frightful	Gruelling	Blinding	Troublesome
Terrifying	Cruel		Miserable
	Vicious		Intense
	Killing		Unbearable

17	18	19	20
Spreading	Tight	Cool	Nagging
Radiating	Numb	Cold	Nauseating
Penetrating	Drawing	Freezing	Agonizing
Piercing	Squeezing		Dreadful
	Tearing		Torturing

Part 3.   How Does Your Pain Change With Time?

1. Which word or words would you use to describe the <u>pattern</u> of your pain?

1	2	3
Continuous	Rhythmic	Brief
Steady	Periodic	Momentary
Constant	Intermittent	Transient

2. What kind of things <u>relieve</u> your pain?

3. What kind of things <u>increase</u> your pain?

Part 4.   How Strong Is Your Pain?

People agree that the following 5 words represent pain of increasing intensity. They are:

1	2	3	4	5
Mild	Discomforting	Distressing	Horrible	Excruciating

To answer each question below, write the number of the most appropriate word in the space beside the question.

1. Which word describes your pain right now? _____
2. Which word describes it at its worst? _____
3. Which word describes it when it is least? _____
4. Which word describes the worst toothache you ever had? _____
5. Which word describes the worst headache you ever had? _____
6. Which word describes the worst stomach-ache you ever had?
   _____

▲ **Figure 22.3.3** The MPQ

Source: Melzack (1975)

3. The patient has to describe the pattern of pain from three sub-classes of words and then produce some qualitative data about what things relieve but also increase the pain.

4. The final part asks the patient to rate the strength of the pain via six questions. The scores for the questions are added up to create a present pain intensity score.

Visual rating scales can come in the form of visual analogue scales as shown in Figure 22.3.4.

No pain [----------------------------] Worst pain possible

▲ **Figure 22.3.4** Visual analogue scale for recording pain

The physician can measure (with a ruler) the distance along the scale to get a numeric measure of how intense the pain is – other questions and bi-polar adjectives can be used on these scales too.

Behavioural or observational measures

The UAB Pain Behavior Scale

The University of Alabama at Birmingham (UAB) Pain Behavior Scale can be used by nurses to assess the degree of pain patients are in through observing their behaviour. The patient will be asked to perform several activities such as walking around, sitting down then standing up and the nurse rates each of these to give a total score of how much the pain is affecting the patient's behaviour. Figure 22.3.5 lists the parameters and shows the method of scoring some of them.

In addition, structured clinical sessions can also be used and these can be tailored to the pain condition a patient has. The patient can be asked to perform a series of tasks linked to their pain (e.g. if it is lower back pain one of the tasks may be to tie their shoe laces). All of the tasks are recorded for observation. A trained observer then watches the recording and scores the patient so an overall pain score can be calculated.

The UAB Pain Behavior Scale

Parameters

(1) vocal complaints verbal (2) verbal complaints non-verbal (groans, moans, gasps, etc.) (3) downtime (time spend lying down because of pain per day from 8.00 a.m. to 8.00 p.m.) (4) facial grimaces (5) standing posture (6) mobility (7) body language (clutching or rubbing site) (8) use of visible support equipment (brace, crutches, can, leaning on furniture, etc.) (9) stationary movement (ability to stay still) (10) medication use.

Total score = SUM for all 10 items

Interpretation: minimum score = 0; maximum score = 10

The higher the score the more marked the pain-associated behaviour and the greater the level of impairment.

Parameter	Points	Finding
verbal complaints	none	0
	occasional	0.5
	frequent	1
non-verbal complaints	none	0
	occasional	0.5
	frequent	1
down time	none	0
	0 to 60 minutes	0.5
	> 60 minutes	1
facial grimaces	none	0
	mild and/or infrequent	0.5
	severe and/or frequent	1
standing posture	normal	0
	mildly impaired	0.5
	distorted	1

▲ **Figure 22.3.5** The UAB Pain Behavior Scale

Pain measures for children

The Pediatric Pain Questionnaire (Varni and Thompson, 1976)

Some of the self-report scales mentioned earlier can be used with children. The visual analogue scale has been particularly successful. The box scales and verbal rating scales can also be used as long as they are written in children's language so they can easily understand them. However, one questionnaire has been developed that can be used just with children – the Pediatric Pain Questionnaire. Children have to describe their pain *in their own words* then, to help describe their pain some more, they choose as many adjectives as they want to. There is a visual analogue scale used with faces as the bi-polar ends and then, similar to the MPQ, a picture of a person so they can indicate where the pain is (see Figure 22.3.6). In addition to choosing from the faces, children are asked to pick colours to represent different levels of pain (they choose their own colours). Then they colour in the part of the body which has that colour of pain.

▲ **Figure 22.3.6** The Pediatric Pain Questionnaire

Source: Adapted from the Varni/Thompson Pediatric Pain Questionnaire: Form C (Child), unpublished manuscript. Modified for Children's Hospital and Regional Medical Center, Seattle, Washington (USA)

The Wong-Baker Scale (1987)

This scale allows a child to choose their level of pain from six different faces. First, the doctor has to establish where the pain areas are, then the child chooses the intensity of the pain using the faces shown in Figure 22.3.7.

Explain to the child that each face is for a person who feels happy because he has no pain (hurt) or sad because he has some or a lot of pain. Face 0 is very happy because he doesn't hurt at all. Face 1 hurts just a little bit. Face 2 hurts a little more. Face 3 hurts even more. Face 4 hurts a whole lot, but Face 6 hurts as much as you can imagine, although you don't have to be crying to feel this bad. Ask child to choose the face that best describes how he/she is feeling.

▲ **Figure 22.3.7** Faces rating scale

Source: Whaley and Wong (1987) reproduced in Wong and Baker (1988: 11)

Strength	Weakness
The scales have been validated on children to ensure that they are fit for purpose, so they can be used with validity and reliability.	Even though the scales may allow children to describe pain in their own words, they may find it difficult to truly express how they are feeling.

Issues and debates tracker: Most of these scales are psychometric in nature so should have been validated and also shown solid reliability. They are useful as they allow direct comparisons to other people who complete the scale but also to population norms if they have been used on a lot of people. However, in some cases the reasons for patients' pain or how they truly feel about it are not revealed because the scales simply generate numbers.

MANAGING AND CONTROLLING PAIN

Patients can manage and control their pain levels in a variety of ways. These range from biological to cognitive and alternative techniques.

Medical techniques (biochemical)

One of the main medical techniques used to control pain is the use of chemicals. Sarafino (2006) highlighted four main types available to patients:

▶ Peripherally active analgesics – these inhibit the production of certain neurochemicals that are produced as a result, for example, of tissue damage. Common examples of these drugs are aspirin and ibuprofen. Aspirin, for instance, reduces the experience of pain but also reduces inflammation that could be causing the pain.

▶ Centrally acting analgesics – these are good at reducing acute pain in the short term as they act directly on the central nervous system. Examples of these drugs are codeine and morphine.

▶ Local anaesthetics – these can be applied locally to the site of pain (or be injected) to give almost immediate relief. They block the nerve cells at the site of damage. An example of this type of drug is novocaine.

▶ Indirectly acting drugs – these are used for other conditions but can also help in pain management. For example, antidepressants can help reduce psychological aspects of depression but they can also help relieve pain.

Strength	Weakness
Techniques using chemicals are objective and biological and have been proven to work on organic pain.	There can be negative side effects.

Psychological techniques: cognitive strategies

Attention diversion, non-pain imagery and cognitive redefinition

A variety of cognitive strategies can be used to help alleviate and manage pain in patients. Cognitive behavioural therapy (CBT) can be used. The therapist needs to tackle the thinking behind the pain, the emotions involved with the pain and the behaviour seen as a result of it. The therapist can use a variety of techniques for this. These include helping patients to reduce counterproductive strategies (e.g. changing strategies that are actually making the pain worse rather than better), giving them some skills training on how to cope and training them to change their cognitions from negative to positive in terms of successful pain management.

Sarafino (2006) noted a range of other cognitive strategies that can be used with patients. These include the following:

▶ Attention diversion – this technique gets the patient to focus on something that is not linked to the pain in any way. This can include looking at a picture, singing a song, playing on a video console or having to focus on someone's voice. Distractors have to be relevant to the patient and be engrossing enough for that person. Hence, they have to be individually tailored.

▶ Imagery – this can be called guided imagery and involves patients creating a mental scene "far removed" from the current state of pain. This could be a place that is pleasant (e.g. a beach) and the therapist has to guide patients through the scene to distract them from the pain. The therapist may ask about sights and sounds, for instance. The aim is to create a "place" that cannot be linked to the pain being experienced.

Cognitive redefinition can also be used to help pain management. This is when patients can be told about what to expect, truthfully, about their pain but for them to redefine how they interpret their own pain experiences. When it comes to pain management, there are two ways that cognitive redefinition may help a patient:

▶ Coping statements – this technique allows patients to emphasise their own ability to tolerate pain. They may say to themselves "Come on, be brave, you can handle this!" or "This is going to hurt, but you are in control".

▶ Re-interpretative statements – this technique allows patients to help themselves negate any unpleasantness about their pain experiences. They may say to themselves "This is not the worst thing that will ever happen to me and it won't last long" or "Yes, this will hurt for a little while, but think of the long-term benefits".

Alternative techniques

Hypnosis, transcutaneous electrical nerve stimulation (TENS), acupuncture

A variety of alternative techniques can be used with a patient experiencing any degree of pain, including the following:

1. Hypnosis* – patients who are good hypnotic subjects could benefit from using hypnosis as part of their pain management. The hypnotist can use suggestions and imagery to help the patient cope with pain. It is common for the suggestion of analgesia (pain relief) to work on hypnotic patients as a result of their high levels of suggestibility. The hypnotist could also teach patients self-hypnosis skills so they can use hypnosis to reduce their pain when at home.

2. Transcutaneous electrical nerve stimulation (TENS) machines – these machines have electrodes which are placed either side of the source of pain. The TENS machine then sends a mild electrical current between the electrodes which, in theory, reduces the sensation of pain.

3. Acupuncture – this is an ancient Chinese practice of inserting special fine metal needles under the skin of the patient in areas chosen depending on the source of the pain. Once inserted, the needles are "twirled" or stimulated electrically. There are reportedly hundreds of insertion points for the needles depending on what could be causing the pain or which area of the body is experiencing it.

CHALLENGE YOURSELF
To what extent do you feel that the best way to manage pain is through alternative techniques? Justify your answer.

22.4 STRESS

SOURCES OF STRESS

Physiology of stress and effects on health

The physiological response to stress is controlled by two body systems:

▶ The autonomic nervous system is composed of two approximately antagonistic sub-systems, the sympathetic and parasympathetic branches. The autonomic nervous system acts rapidly to stimulate physiological changes such as breathing and heart rate as well as affecting the second element, the endocrine system.

▶ The endocrine system provides a slower communication route through the body using hormones released in response to signals from nerves or from other glands. In an emergency, the sympathetic branch of the autonomic nervous system responds quickly, preparing for "fight or flight". The sympathetic nervous system also sends impulses to the endocrine system, which responds by releasing hormones that enhance the preparation for action. This mechanism, which links the sympathetic nervous system to the adrenal medulla, is called the sympathetic adrenal medullary system.

Stress has a range of effects on health including the following:

▶ Cardiovascular problems – these can include hypertension (high blood pressure) and atherosclerosis (the build up of fat deposits in blood vessels), both of which increase the risk of having a heart attack.

▶ Gastrointestinal disorders – an increase in stomach acids can lead to ulcers and digestive problems; also, conditions such as irritable bowel syndrome can be made worse by stress.

The general adaptation syndrome (GAS) model (Selye, 1936)

Selye (1936) described the body's response to stress and began to explore the links between stress and illness. He induced stress in rats using stressors such as heat and fatigue. The rats showed the same physiological responses regardless of the nature of the stressor; they had enlarged adrenal glands and they developed stomach ulcers. Selye proposed that the body responded to any stressor by getting itself ready for action. This response has *evolved* to help the individual to deal with emergency situations such as fleeing physical danger. Selye identified three phases to the body's response to stress through which an individual passes if a stressor persists over time:

1. Alarm reaction: the body's mechanisms for dealing with danger are activated. This reaction is based around the fight or flight mechanism in animals. Physiological reactions include respiration rate increasing, heart rate increasing and blood pressure rising.

2. Resistance stage: the person struggles to cope with the stress and the body attempts to return to its previous physiological state. This happens if no more stress is experienced. However, the person is more vulnerable than before so if stress is experienced before returning to the previous state, the person will struggle to cope.

3. Exhaustion stage: if the stressor persists and the body cannot return to its previous state, physical resources become depleted, eventually leading to collapse.

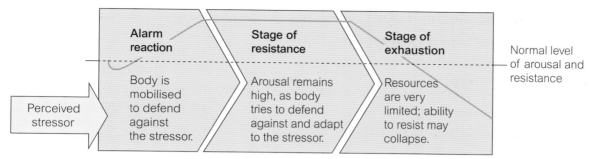

▲ **Figure 22.4.1** GAS in three phases

MAIN CAUSES OF STRESS

Work (Chandola *et al*, 2008)

Chandola *et al* (2008) wanted to investigate which biological and behavioural factors link work stress to coronary heart disease (CHD). They ran a seven-phase study using civil servants from Whitehall, London (UK). A total of 10 308 participants started the study. The phases were:

1. 1985–1988 (recruitment)

2. 1989–1990 (postal questionnaire)

3. 1991–1993 (postal questionnaire + clinical examination)

4. 1995 (postal questionnaire)

5. 1997–1999 (postal questionnaire + clinical examination)

6. 2001 (postal questionnaire)

7. 2002–2004 (postal questionnaire + clinical examination).

Work stress was measured by a job-strain questionnaire. Participants were classified as being under work stress if they reported job strain, felt job control was low and felt socially isolated at work. Various follow-up measures were taken:

▶ fatal CHD and non-fatal CHD episodes

▶ biological risk factors: waist circumference, serum triglycerides, blood pressure, antihypertensive medication, morning rise in cortisol, low heart-rate variability

▶ behavioural risk factors: alcohol, smoking, activity, diet.

By phase 7 there were 9692 participants still alive and 6484 attended the final clinical examination. The results showed that greater reports of work stress were associated with higher risk of CHD. This was true for fatal CHD, myocardial infarction and definite angina. There was an age-related effect too. Participants who were younger showed a much stronger link between work stress and CHD. Those who reported greater work stress also had poorer diets and engaged in much less physical activity. All of this led the researchers to conclude "… cumulative work stress is a risk factor for CHD…" (Chandola *et al*, 2008: 643).

Strength	Weakness
The study was longitudinal so the researchers could track developmental changes (to do with stress and work) over time.	Stress was measured using a self-report technique so some of the workers may have given socially desirable answers, which could reduce the validity of findings.

CHALLENGE YOURSELF
To what extent do you feel that the findings of the study are culturally biased? Justify your decision.

Life events (Holmes and Rahe, 1967)

Holmes and Rahe (1967) constructed a questionnaire called the Social Readjustment Rating Scale (SRRS), shown in Figure 22.4.2. The questionnaire is used to measure the amount of stress a person experiences over a certain amount of time (usually one year). Holmes and Rahe initially conducted research into how different life events are perceived in terms of how stressful they are. Each of the 43 life events were given a score out of 100, which were called the life change units (LCUs). People simply had to add up all the LCUs they had scored over one year. This generated a total of LCUs that could be used as an indicator of the level of stress experienced. The researchers noted that people who scored more than 300 LCUs in a given year were much more likely to become ill due to the amount of stress they experienced.

Rank	Life event	Mean value	Rank	Life event	Mean value
1	Death of spouse	100	23	Son or daughter leaving home	29
2	Divorce	73	24	Trouble with in-laws	29
3	Marital separation	65	25	Outstanding personal achievement	28
4	Jail term	63	26	Spouse begins or stops work	26
5	Death of close family member	63	27	Beginning or ending school	26
6	Personal injury or illness	53	28	Change in living conditions	25
7	Marriage	50	29	Revision of personal habits	24
8	Fired at work	47	30	Trouble with boss	23
9	Marital reconciliation	45	31	Change in work hours or conditions	20
10	Retirement	45	32	Change in residence	20
11	Change in health of family member	44	33	Change in schools	20
12	Pregnancy	40	34	Change in recreation	19
13	Sex difficulties	39	35	Change in church activities	19
14	Gain of new family member	39	36	Change in social activities	18
15	Business re-adjustment	39	37	Mortgage or loan less than $10 000	17
16	Change in financial state	38	38	Change in sleeping habits	16
17	Death of a close friend	37	39	Change in number of family get-togethers	15
18	Change to a different line of work	36	40	Change in eating habits	15
19	Change in number of arguments with spouse	35	41	Vacation	13
20	Mortgage over $10 000	31	42	Christmas	12
21	Foreclosure on mortgage or loan	30	43	Minor violations of the law	11
22	Change in responsibilities at work	29			

▲ **Figure 22.4.2** The SRRS questionnaire

Source: Holmes and Rahe (1967: 216)

The scale was created using the responses from 394 participants who were asked to rate the 43 life events. The life event of marriage was assigned a value of 500 and the participants were asked the following:

> "The mechanics of rating are these: Event 1, Marriage, has been given an arbitrary value of 500. As you complete each of the remaining events think to yourself, "Is this event indicative of more or less readjustment than marriage?" "Would the readjustment take longer or shorter to accomplish?" If you decide the readjustment is more intense and protracted, then choose a *proportionately larger* number and place it in the blank directly opposite the event in the column marked "VALUES." If you decide the event represents less and shorter readjustment than marriage then indicate how much less by placing *a proportionately smaller* number in the opposite blank."
>
> Source: Holmes and Rahe (1967: 213)

Personality (Friedman and Rosenman, 1974)

Friedman and Rosenman (1974) observed that their coronary patients tended to sit on the edge of their seat, leaping up frequently to enquire how much longer they would be kept waiting for their appointments. The possibility of a connection between the heart conditions and the tense, frenetic behaviour of these individuals led to the proposal of "hurry sickness", later renamed "type A behaviour" (Friedman and Rosenman, 1974).

Type A individuals tend to be highly competitive, aggressive, impatient and hostile, with a strong urge for success. Their behaviour tends to be goal-directed and performed at speed. In contrast, people with type B behaviour are relatively "laid back", lacking the urgency and drive typical of type A individuals. Some individuals do not fall clearly into either category and are termed type X. The risk of stress-related illnesses, such as coronary heart disease, is greater for type A individuals than for type B due to the physiological strains placed on the body.

See more on Friedman and Rosenman's research on pages 233–234.

MEASURES OF STRESS

Physiological measures
Recording devices and sample tests

The following are some of the techniques used to measure stress physiologically in people:

▶ Blood pressure monitors are used to measure both systolic and diastolic pressure. Each pressure is given a number and the result is written as 115/75 for example (this is an ideal reading). If a person has a reading of 185/125 then this indicates severe hypertension likely to be caused by extreme stress.

▶ Blood and urine tests can be used to measure levels of cortisol in our body. Cortisol is a stress hormone. Higher levels indicate that the body is physiologically stressed.

▶ Galvanic skin response devices have electrodes that are attached to a person's finger tips. They measure the amount of electrical resistance in the skin. Higher levels of skin response can be an indicator of autonomic nervous system arousal which is linked to stress.

Recording devices (Wang *et al*, 2005)

Wang *et al* (2005) used a functional Magnetic Resonance Imaging (fMRI) scanning device to examine cerebral blood flow in participants under psychological stress. The perfusion fMRI uses arterial spin-labelling to "follow" the pathway of stress. The study group consisted of 32 participants, 25 of whom (of average age 24.1 years; and 12 female) formed the experimental group. The other seven participants formed a control group. Within the experimental group, two participants were eliminated for having incomplete behavioural data and abnormally high salivary cortisol. None of the experimental group had a history of neurologic or psychiatric disease.

High-stress and low-stress tasks were devised as follows:

▶ For the high-stress tasks, mental arithmetic was chosen. The participants had to perform serial subtraction of 13 from a 4-digit number given to them. They had to respond verbally. As the task progressed, they were prompted to be quicker with their responses and to restart once an error occurred.

▶ Low-stress tasks were always given *before* the high-stress task. Participants had to count backwards from 1000 aloud.

The measures taken were as follows:

▶ Perfusion fMRI – there were scans in total, lasting eight minutes each, and then an anatomical scan for six minutes after all tasks had been completed.

▶ Self-report measures of stress and anxiety (on a scale of 1–9) were recorded as soon as participants entered the scanner, then after each scan had taken place.

▶ Salivary cortisol was also taken as soon as participants entered the scanner then after each scan had taken place. This was a two-minute procedure using a cotton swab.

▶ On a scale of 1–9, all participants had to rate effort, frustration and task difficulty after the low-stress then the high-stress tasks.

▶ Heart rate was also taken.

The average subjective ratings, heart rate and salivary cortisol are shown in Figure 22.4.3.

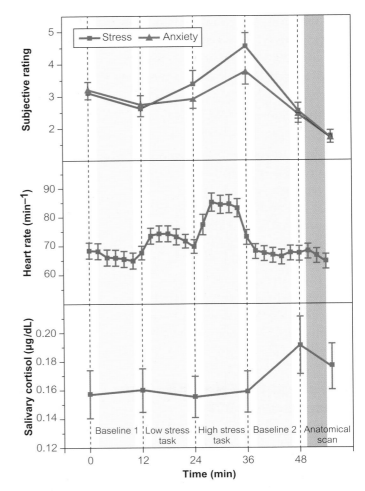

▲ **Figure 22.4.3** Average subjective ratings of stress and anxiety, heart rate, and salivary-cortisol level during the time course of the stress experiment. Time 0 indicates the start of MRI experiments. The pale columns represent the perfusion fMRI scans (each 8 minutes) and the dark column represents the anatomical scan. Behavioural ratings and salivary-cortisol samples were taken between scans, whereas heart rate was continuously recorded every 2 minutes. Note that the peak in salivary-cortisol level lags behind other measures. The error bars indicate standard error.

Source: Wang *et al* (2005: 17 805)

The ratings for the two tasks are shown in the Table 22.4.1.

Stress	Effort	Difficulty	Frustration
Low-stress task	4.4 (0.5)	3.4 (0.4)	3.4 (0.4)
High-stress task	7.0 (0.3)	6.6 (0.3)	6.1 (0.4)

Data are presented as mean (standard error).

▲ **Table 22.4.1** Self-report of effort, difficulty and frustration during the low- and high-stress tasks (scale 1–9)

Source: Wang *et al* (2005: 17 806)

Overall, the subjective stress ratings mirrored the tasks given to them. The salivary cortisol peaked ten minutes after the end of the high-stress task, which was expected due to the time lag between physiological and subsequent behavioural measures. All of the measures of the tasks were significantly higher in the high-stress task than the low-stress task.

The main results for the fMRI scans were as follows:

▶ Cerebral blood flow was positively correlated with subjective stress ratings in the ventral right prefrontal cortex and left insula/putamen area.

▶ The ventral right prefrontal cortex along with the right insula/putamen and anterior cingulate showed sustained activity after the high-stress task.

▶ Variations in the baseline cerebral blood flow in the ventral right prefrontal cortex and right orbitofrontal cortex were found to correlate with changes in salivary-cortisol levels and heart rate caused by the stress tasks.

Strength	Weakness
The measurement technique is objective and scientific, meaning that no interpretation is needed and making the findings more valid.	The act of going through an fMRI may have an effect on cerebral blood flow which could be a confounding variable – this could cause more stress.

Sample tests (Evans and Wener, 2007)

Evans and Wener (2007) used three indices of stress to examine what happens to commuters during rush hour on a crowded train. Participants were 139 adult commuters (54 per cent male) who took part in the study during their commute from New Jersey to Manhattan. All had to have been taking this route for at least 12 months to qualify for participation. Three measures were taken from each commuter:

▶ A saliva sample was taken at the end of the journey and then analysed for cortisol levels.

▶ Motivation was measured by persistence with a proofreading task and the number of errors spotted.

▶ Mood was measured using two semantic differential items (a 5-point scale was used to rate mood from "carefree" to "burdened" and from "contented" to "frustrated").

The researchers measured carriage density (by dividing the number of passengers in a car with the number of seats available) and seat density (by dividing the number of people sitting in the same row by the number of seats on that row). It was only seat density that had a significant effect on all three stress measures. The higher the density, the higher the cortisol, the fewer the errors detected and the more negative the mood.

Strength	Weakness
The Evans and Wener study has some ecological validity as the train journey was something that participants did on a regular basis.	Some of the measures were subjective via the self-report techniques so the researchers could not know whether the train journey was causing the stress, or something else was causing it.

Psychological measures

Self-report questionnaires (Holmes and Rahe, 1967; Friedman and Rosenman, 1974)

For the Holmes and Rahe (1967) scale, see page 230.

There is no set self-report measure that was used by Friedman and Rosenman (1974) but a type A structured interview has been used in some studies. However, the following was noted by Friedman and Rosenman (1974) about how to differentiate between type A and type B behaviour and it would have formed any self-report measure on the topic:

1. Type A people will forcefully note certain words in their speech and then finish off sentences quickly.

2. Type A people are always moving, walking and eating rapidly.

3. Type A people feel impatient in most scenarios they encounter. One example is that they might try to finish other people's sentences.

4. Type A people tend to be polyphasic: they frequently want to be doing two or more things at the same time.

5. Type A people will always direct a conversation towards things they like or that intrigue them.

6. Type A people will feel guilty for relaxing.

7. Type A people do not appreciate their surroundings.

8. Type A people will attempt to do more and more in less and less time.

9. If two type A people meet they do not show compassion for their similarities but challenge each other to "be the best".

10. Type A people might use repetitive gestures.

11. Type A people will give themselves praise for good work just because they have done the work faster than others have, rather than based on its quality.

CHALLENGE YOURSELF
Create a questionnaire using a Likert-type scale that would measure the degree to which someone is a type A personality.

MANAGEMENT OF STRESS

Medical techniques (biochemical)

These may focus around the use of medication to reduce the body's automatic response to stressors. There are two main types of drug that can be prescribed to people who are suffering from stress:

▶ Benzodiazapines – these are a group of drugs (including valium) that directly affect stress reactions in the central nervous system.

▶ Beta-blockers – these are a group of drugs that reduce the anxiety and blood pressure linked to stress. They act on the peripheral nervous system and block activity from ephinephrine and norepinephrine.

Drugs should only be used as a short-term, temporary measure for dealing with stress. For longer-term control, it is better to use psychological techniques to teach people new ways of coping.

Psychological techniques

Biofeedback is a technique that attemps to get people to take control of their own physiological state. Usually, people are connected to devices that measure key physiological processes such as heart rate, blood pressure, muscle tension, etc. The equipment gives individuals instant and continuous readings of these key physiological measures. The idea is that individuals take voluntary control of their physiology using the idea of rewards. If people are attempting to reduce their resting heart rate and they can see that deeper breathing and relaxation is doing this instantly then they are more likely to want to do the same next time. Sarafino (2006) noted that there is a lot of evidence for the usefulness of biofeedback techniques for stress-related illnesses such as tension headaches, even with children.

Biofeedback (Budzynski and Stoyva, 1969)

Budzynski and Stoyva (1969) investigated the role of biofeedback in muscle relaxation. They developed an instrument that did the following:

▶ It continuously tracked the level of muscle action potential.

▶ It presented the patient with instant feedback from a given muscle.

▶ The information was given as a tone that varied in pitch depending on the level of muscle activity.

▶ The feedback loop could be adjusted to shape deep muscle responses.

▶ The instrument measured the performance of an individual in terms of relaxation attempts.

The researchers trialled the instrument on 15 people to see whether operant conditioning via information feedback would shape muscle relaxation. The participants were split into three groups:

1. The experimental group. Participants in this group were told that the pitch would vary depending on the level of muscle tension in the forehead. They were told to keep the tone as low as possible.

2. The constant low tone group. Members of this group were given irrelevant feedback because the tone always remained low. They were told to relax their forehead muscles as much as possible and that the constant low tone would help them to do this.

3. The silent group. No feedback was given to participants in this group and they were simply told to relax their forehead muscles.

Participants had to lie on a bed in a dimly lit room. There were 20 trials per session which were automatically sequenced so that there was no experimenter interaction with participants during the trials.

Figure 22.4.4 shows the performances of the groups over the five sessions they all experienced.

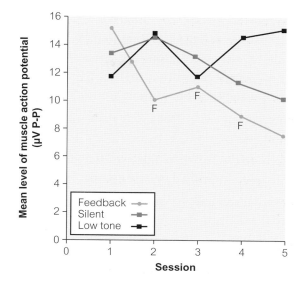

▲ **Figure 22.4.4** Mean levels of frontalis muscle action potential levels in feedback, no feedback (silent), and irrelevant feedback (low tone) groups. Each group consisted of five subjects.

Notes: "F" indicates a feedback session; uV P-P signifies microvolts peak-to-peak.

Source: Budzynski and Stoyva (1969: 233)

In terms of decrease in muscle action potential from baseline to the end of the trial:

▶ The experimental group had decreased by 50 per cent.

▶ The constant tone group by 28 per cent.

▶ The silent group by 24 per cent.

It would appear that using correct biofeedback can help people relax muscles more efficiently.

Strengths	Weakness
The procedure was standardised so that it could easily be replicated by other researchers to test for reliability. The feedback was standardised for each group. The study showed that using correct biofeedback has good application for health professionals, especially in treating people with tension headaches.	It may be difficult to make generalisations because there were only five participants in each group and they might not represent a wider population.

Imagery

Imagery can also be used to reduce stress in people: mental imagery is used to distract people from thinking about any stressors they have. In addition, they may be taught relaxation techniques to help with the distraction. These may include visual imagery to take them "away from their stressors" and deep-breathing exercises or even yoga and meditation. People using mental imagery will have to imagine a variety of situations that have nothing to do with the stresses they are currently experiencing. Ensuring that people are not focusing on current stressors allows them to calm down and take control of their own physiological state.

Imagery (Bridge *et al*, 1988)

Bridge *et al* (1988) conducted a controlled randomised trial to test the effectiveness of using imagery with women with stage I or II breast cancer (n = 145). Participants were randomly assigned to one of three groups:

▶ the control group, where they were encouraged to talk about themselves

▶ the relaxation group, where they were taught to concentrate on individual muscle groups

▶ the relaxation and imagery group, where they followed the same procedure as participants in the relaxation group, but were also taught to imagine a peaceful scene of their own choice to aid relaxation.

Participants in the two relaxation groups were given a tape recording of instructions so they could carry out relaxation sessions at home every day for 15 minutes. They had "official" sessions once per week for six weeks. Improvement in mood, depression and anxiety were measured using self-report scales. Initial scores on these measures did not differ between the three groups. However, at six weeks, the mood scores were significantly lower in the two intervention groups, with the women in the combined group being the most relaxed. Therefore, it would appear that using mental imagery can help to alleviate the stresses involved in cancer management.

Strength	Weakness
The study has good application as it shows that the technique works over time, so practitioners can ensure that patients work through the entire programme.	An independent groups design was used, meaning that some individual differences (e.g. participant variables) may have affected the outcome measures as well as the technique.

Preventing stress (Meichenbaum, 1988)

Some techniques can be used that allow people not to be affected by stress and stressors. These are called preventive measures. One that has generated a great deal of research and following by therapists is stress inoculation therapy, which was proposed by Meichenbaum. This therapy has three stages:

1. Conceptualisation phase – this is when a relationship is built between the trainer and clients. The trainer will educate clients about the nature and impact that stress has on their lives. The trainer may even show how clients may be currently making their stress worse without them even knowing they are doing it. Clients are then encouraged to see perceived stressors as being problems to be solved rather than as a negative experience. They are introduced to different coping mechanisms and strategies they can then use. They are also taught to break down stressors into short-term, intermediate and long-term coping goals.

2. Skill acquisition and rehearsal phase – this is when the elements from stage 1 have been taught and clients have to put them into practice. The skills are initially practised with the trainer in the clinic but then clients are encouraged to try them in the real world. Some of the coping mechanisms could

include relaxation training, cognitive restructuring, interpersonal communication skills and using social support to help clients in times of need.

3. Application and follow-through phase – this is when there are opportunities for clients to apply all of the coping skills to increasing levels of stressors. Additional techniques, such as imagery, modelling, role playing and rehearsal, are used in the form of "personal experiments" so that clients can show that they can cope with any level of stressor. These help to consolidate the skills they have already learned. They are also given follow-up booster sessions to ensure that the entire process is working.

The whole technique is flexible and can be a simple 20-minute session for people who are just about to go into surgery, or 40 one-hour weekly sessions for people who cannot cope with any level of stress.

Issues and debates tracker: These techniques have good application to everyday life. This is because the treatments can be used effectively to help people combat stress, which should also have a "knock on" effect of improving their overall general health. Having different techniques allows a doctor to choose the best one for the patient.

22.5 HEALTH PROMOTION

STRATEGIES FOR PROMOTING HEALTH

 ASK YOURSELF
What do you think are the best ways in which we can promote healthy eating?

Fear arousal

The idea behind fear arousal is that if you "scare people enough" they will change their thoughts and behaviour. Roberts and Russell (2002) noted that while fear-arousing methods may be effective, there are certain factors that can affect whether the person the message is aimed at does follow its advice. These are:

▶ the unpleasantness of the fear-arousing message

▶ the probability that whatever the message is warning about will occur if the person does not follow the advice given

▶ the perceived effectiveness of the recommended action portrayed in the message.

Therefore, ideally, the message should be relatively unpleasant; people must believe that what it is warning about will happen to them and that any "evasive" action will be effective.

Fear arousal (Janis and Feshbach, 1953)

Janis and Feshbach (1953) showed three groups of participants a film about dental hygiene. Each group received either a strong fear message, a moderate fear message or a minimal fear message.

The group who received the minimal fear message showed the highest level of agreement with the advice (36 per cent) compared to the strong fear group (8 per cent). Therefore, the researchers reported that only minimal fear is effective.

For details of another study on fear arousal – Cowpe (1989) – see page 273.

Persuasive communication

Yale model of communication

Hovland *et al* (1953) conducted many studies at Yale University which helped to form a model of persuasive communication. There are three main stages in the process:

1. Attention – the message must grab people's attention. Sound *and* visual stimuli are the most effective, so using television might be better than using leaflets or the radio.

2. Comprehension – for a message to be successful it must be understood by the recipient. Messages need to be clear and concise.

3. Acceptance – the overall message has to be accepted by the recipient for behaviour change to occur. The person does not have to *believe* the message but must accept it and behave according to it for it to be persuasive communication.

There are several factors that can affect any or all of the three stages above. These include the following:

▶ The communicator – a message is more persuasive if the communicator is attractive, is similar to the recipient and is likeable.

▶ The content – it is best to cause mild fear and it is best when the message is presented verbally *and* visually. A one-sided or two-sided argument needs to be considered too.

▶ The medium – for example, the communicator needs to choose whether a television campaign would work better than a radio or leaflet campaign. If the message is simple and straightforward then conveying it via television is best; if it is complicated it is best communicated by written means.

Providing information

"The Angina Plan" (Lewin *et al*, 2002)

Lewin *et al* (2002) assessed the effectiveness of "The Angina Plan", a cognitive-behavioural disease management programme. Produced for patients newly diagnosed with angina pectoris, "The Angina Plan" was a 70-page workbook and audio-taped relaxation programme. It contained information about:

- angina
- the role of frightening thoughts and misconceptions about the triggering adrenaline
- hyperventilation and panic attacks.

Before patients took the book and audio-tape away, they were given information that tackled any misconceptions they had about angina pectoris. The audio-tape was meant to be used for 20 minutes per day and a nurse followed up the patients at weeks 1, 4, 8 and 12 after they began the programme.

Surgeries in York (UK) were approached to take part in the study. Patients who were recruited were randomly assigned to a group following "The Angina Plan" or an educational session led by a practice nurse. The sample consisted of 142 patients. There were no significant differences in baseline measures. At six months, however, patients following "The Angina Plan" showed a greater reduction in anxiety, depression, the frequency of angina, the use of glyceryl trinitrate and physical limitations. They were also more likely to have changed their diet and increased their daily walking distance. Therefore, it would seem that a carefully planned intervention programme of providing information alongside self-relaxation techniques can help people with angina pectoris.

Strength	Weakness
The study has good application – following "The Angina Plan" was successful, which means other surgeries and health authorities can use it too.	Only surgeries in York were involved. It may be difficult to generalise beyond this geographical area as it could be unique.

CHALLENGE YOURSELF
To what extent do you think that the findings from the study are culturally biased? Justify your answer.

Sarafino (2006)* noted that one way in which people can engage in healthy behaviour is through information. This helps people make decisions about their own lifestyles. There are three main ways in which information can be provided:

- Mass media (e.g. television, radio, magazines and newspapers) can be used. One popular approach is for health services and the government to inform the general population about the negative consequences of certain health-related behaviours such as smoking and drinking alcohol. The following points should be considered:

  – This method appears to have limited success as many people misunderstand the messages. This is especially true if people are not all that motivated to change their behaviour anyway.

  – If people *are* motivated to change behaviour then this method of providing information can be useful.

- Sarafino (2006)* gave the example of "Cable Quit", a television show that helped people to prepare to quit unhealthy behaviours by giving out information from the first day they decided to quit. Around 17 per cent of people had still quit a year after watching the programmes.

- The Internet* – there are thousands of websites that promote healthy behaviour and allow people to track their own progress and meet others online to help motivate them to change. An advantage is that there is a wealth of information for people to look at to see *how* they can change. However, not all information will be correct or checked by health professionals.

- Medical settings* – having information displayed in a doctor's surgery or office might make people believe the messages more. As the information is in a professional setting, it could receive instant respect.

HEALTH PROMOTION IN SCHOOLS, WORKSITES AND COMMUNITIES

Schools

Schools have a good opportunity to promote healthy living to students. Lessons where students are taught about the benefits of healthy living can be part of any curriculum.

Healthy eating at school (Tapper, Horne and Lowe, 2003)

Tapper, Horne and Lowe (2003) employed three techniques to increase healthy eating (with a focus on eating fruit and vegetables) in children at school:

- Taste exposure – the more a child tastes a novel food, the more the child learns to like the taste.

- Modelling – watching a role model eat certain foods can have an impact on whether a child is likely to imitate the behaviour.

- Rewards – when used appropriately, rewards can be useful in altering behaviour. Using them can be beneficial when: they are highly desirable; they are contingent on performance; and they convey a message that they are gained for desirable behaviours.

The researchers' initial study took place in a home environment. Participants were children 5 or 6 years old who were identified as fussy eaters by their parents or carers. There were four different intervention methods:

- fruit and vegetable presentation only
- rewarded taste exposure
- peer modelling
- peer modelling with rewards.

The peer modelling was based around a video featuring the "Food Dudes". These characters were children who were slightly older than the participants and who gained super powers from eating fruit and vegetables. They were in battle against the "Junk Punks" who wanted to take over the planet by destroying all fruit and vegetables. By doing this, the "Junk Punks" would stop humans getting their "Life Force" foods of fruit and vegetables. In addition, rewards (stickers, pens, erasers, etc.) could be gained for eating set targets of fruit and vegetables. The peer modelling with rewards group showed dramatic increases in consumption of fruit and vegetables. Prior to the intervention, participants would eat only 4 per cent of fruit presented to them and 1 per cent of vegetables. After the intervention this rose to 100 per cent for fruit and 83 per cent for vegetables. A follow-up check showed that this had been sustained even when participants had not watched the video any more or received any of the rewards.

The researchers then produced a nursery school version of the "Food Dudes" with characters called Jarvis and Jess. This had a major impact on the younger children targeted, with an increase from 30 per cent to 71 per cent for fruit consumption. This was being maintained at follow-up 15 months after the intervention. A similar increase was seen for vegetables (from 34 per cent to 87 per cent consumption) and this was also maintained at follow-up.

A further study was carried out at a primary school in North Wales. The intervention process happened as described above. At break time, participants were allowed to choose whatever food they wanted. The options included fruit and vegetables but also chocolate bars, cakes and crisps. Fruit consumption rose from 28 per cent to 59 per cent while vegetable consumption rose from 8 per cent to 32 per cent. The number of other snacks being chosen fell.

Finally, the research team proposed a whole-school programme using the idea of "Food Dudes". Designed so that it could easily be implemented by school staff, this programme featured the elements described in Figure 22.5.1.

- A Food Dude video containing six 6-minute adventure episodes.
- A set of Food Dude rewards.
- A set of letters from the Food Dudes. These provide praise and encouragement and remind children of the reward contingencies.
- A Food Dude homepack to encourage children to eat fruit and vegetables in the home context as well as at school.
- A staff manual and staff briefing video to help teachers implement the programme correctly.
- A set of education support materials to help teachers meet curriculum targets using the Food Dude theme.

▲ **Figure 22.5.1** The "Food Dude" programme

Source: Tapper, Horne and Lowe (2003: 20)

A variety of schools trialled the whole-school programme and all reported significant increases in participants' consumption of fruit and vegetables at break times. The researchers gave three reasons as to why the programme was so effective:

▶ Children discovered for themselves the intrinsic rewards of eating fruit and vegetables.

▶ The programme changed the culture of the school to one where it supports the eating of fruit and vegetables as being "the norm".

▶ It changed the self-concept of children: they could label themselves as "fruit and vegetable eaters".

Strength	Weakness
The study has good application – the programme was successful, so other schools may want to introduce it.	Following the programme is time consuming. The commitment needed to make it work cannot be guaranteed in a school environment due to other pressures.

Walter *et al* (1985)* reported on a study of 22 US elementary schools. The researchers introduced a curriculum that had a focus on physical fitness and nutrition. The schools were randomly assigned either to the programme or to act as a control. The children who received the programme curriculum had lower blood pressure and cholesterol levels compared to the control children after one year. However, many schools cannot afford to hire specialists to teach such curricula.

Worksites

Reducing accidents at work: token economy (Fox, Hopkins and Anger, 1987)

Fox, Hopkins and Anger (1987) reported on the potential long-term effects of a token economy scheme on safety performances in open-pit mines. The token economy was based around the idea of trading stamps that could be redeemed at various stores in the locality. The employees earned stamps for:

▶ working without lost-time injuries

▶ being a member of a work group where all members had no lost-time injuries

▶ not being involved in equipment-damaging accidents

▶ making appropriate safety suggestions

▶ unusual behaviour that prevented an injury or an accident.

The employees could lose stamps:

▶ if they or a member of their group were injured

▶ for causing equipment damage

▶ for failing to report injuries or accidents.

The implementation of the token economy scheme had an immediate effect. There was a large reduction in the number of days lost from work due to injuries. There were also reductions in the number of lost-time injuries and the costs of accidents. Figures 22.5.2, 22.5.3 and 22.5.4 show how these improvements were sustained for years after the scheme began.

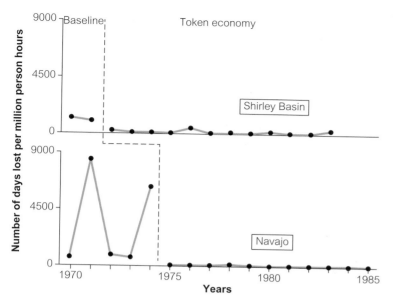

▲ **Figure 22.5.2** The yearly number of days lost from work, per million person hours worked, because of work-related injuries

Source: Fox, Hopkins and Anger (1987: 220)

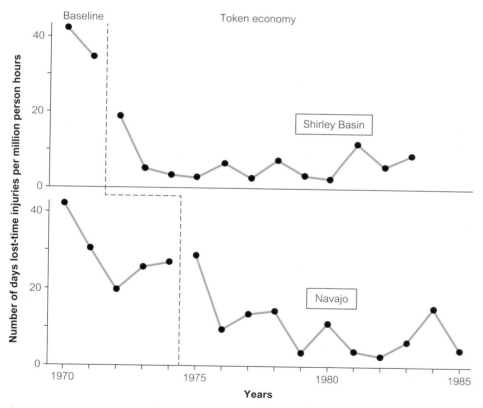

▲ **Figure 22.5.3** The yearly number of work-related injuries, per million person hours worked, requiring one or more days lost from work

Source: Fox, Hopkins and Anger (1987: 221)

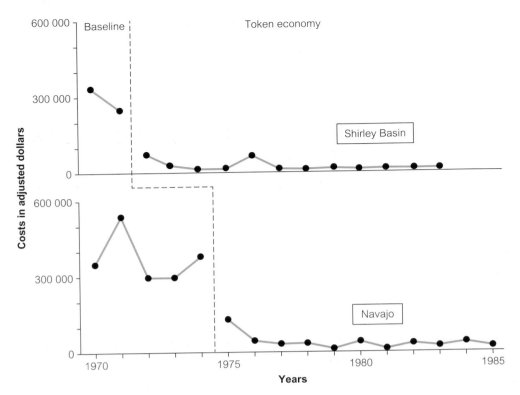

▲ **Figure 22.5.4** The yearly costs, adjusted for hours worked and inflation, resulting from accidents and injuries

Source: Fox, Hopkins and Anger (1987: 222)

In the company Johnson & Johnson there is an example of a strong worksite health promotion. In 1978 the company began the Live For Life Program which covers thousands of the company's employees. It educates people on health knowledge, how to manage stress, exercising, weight control and smoking cessation. Each employee who takes part has an initial health screening that assesses the person's current health status. Participants then take part in a lifestyle seminar that promotes healthy living. After this, employees take part in action groups led by professionals in their fields based on the initial health screening – a group on quitting smoking or weight management, for example. Employees are then followed for a year to see if they are following their programme. In addition to this, the workplace has exercise areas and nutritional food is served in its cafeterias. Studies have been conducted in the company that show employees who take part in the Live For Life Program increase their physical activity levels, decrease in weight and are more likely to quit smoking compared to employees who do not take part in the programme.

Communities

Five-cities project (Farquhar *et al*, 1985)

Farquhar *et al* (1985) reported on the Stanford five-cities project about health promotion. The researchers wanted to test the effectiveness of community-wide health education on stroke and coronary heart disease. Participants were in two treatment cities (n = 122 800) and two control cities (n = 197 500). The treatment cities received a five-year low-cost treatment intervention programme based on the principles of social learning theory, a behaviour-change model, and organisational community principles, alongside some social marketing. It was estimated that the cities were exposed to 26 hours of multichannel education. Risk factors were taken at baseline and then at three time points after the intervention had begun. After 30–64 months of the multichannel education, the following results emerged in the treatment groups:

▶ There was a significant reduction in plasma cholesterol (2 per cent).

▶ There was a 4 per cent reduction in blood pressure.

- Resting pulse rate had decreased by 3 per cent.

- Smoking rates had dropped by 13 per cent.

- Mortality risk scores had decreased by 13 per cent and coronary heart disease risk scores had decreased by 16 per cent.

Therefore, a low-cost multichannel education programme does appear to be effective in promoting healthy behaviours in the community.

Strength	Weakness
The sample size was very large and diverse, meaning that the researchers could be confident that the findings can generalise beyond the sample used.	Even though it was a "low-cost" method, local authorities and councils may still not be able to afford to implement the scheme as they have other pressures for money and funding.

INDIVIDUAL FACTORS IN CHANGING HEALTH BELIEFS

Unrealistic optimism (Weinstein, 1980)

Weinstein (1980) ran two studies that examined whether college students have unrealistic optimism about future life events.

Study 1

In this study 258 college students had to estimate their own chances of experiencing 42 different life events compared to their classmates. These were both positive (e.g. owning your own home, living past 80 years of age, receiving a good job offer after graduation) and negative (e.g. attempting suicide, being sterile, dropping out of college). Participants rated their own chances to be above average when the event was positive but below average when the event was negative. Factors such as the degree of desirability, the perceived probability of an event occurring, past personal experience and perceived controllability appeared to influence this "optimistic bias".

Study 2

Students had to list what factors they thought influenced their chances of experiencing eight future life events. When these lists were read by a second group of students, the amount of unrealistic optimism shown by this group for the same eight life events decreased significantly. Therefore, as soon as people begin to compare their likelihood with what others' perceive, any optimistic bias is reduced significantly.

Transtheoretical model (Prochaska et al, 1992)

The transtheoretical model (Prochaska et al, 1992) states that there are six stages involved in changing health-related behaviour:

1. Precontemplation: when people are not intending to change their behaviour in the foreseeable future (the Prochaska et al study states this as being in the next six months). People may find themselves in this stage when the information they are reading is ambivalent about the consequences of not changing or they have tried several times before and failed.

2. Contemplation: when people are ready to want to change their behaviour in the next six months. They are aware of more of the benefits of changing their health-related behaviour. However, they are also very aware of the cons of changing their behaviour. They may feel ambivalent about changing due to the constant battle between the benefits and cons of changing.

3. Preparation: when people are intending to change their behaviour in the immediate future (the Prochaska et al study states that this is in the next month). They may have some plan of action such as joining a gym.

4. Action: when people have made changes to their health-related behaviour in the last six months.

5. Maintenance: when people are working towards preventing any relapse in behaviour. They become more and more confident that they can continue with the necessary changes to behaviour.

6. Termination: when people have 100 per cent self-efficacy coupled with 0 per cent temptation to relapse. They find ways of coping with days and events that used to make them relapse in to unhealthy behaviours.

CHALLENGE YOURSELF
Design a longitudinal study to see if people really do go through the transtheoretical model when changing their health-related behaviour.

Health change in adolescents (Lau *et al*, 1990)

Lau *et al* (1990) investigated the role of parents and peers in preventive health beliefs and behaviour. The researchers focused on young adults' health beliefs and behaviours linked to drinking, diet, exercise and wearing seat belts in a car.

A total of 1106 students from Carnegie Mellon University, Pittsburgh (USA) were chosen as participants. Baseline questionnaires were returned by 1029 students. Of these students, 947 parents also completed questionnaires so these student-parent pairs formed the sample for analysis. The student sample was 31 per cent female, 89 per cent white and aged 15–27 years. These participants were followed for three years while at college. At year 1, the questionnaire was completed by 879 participants. This figure dropped to 635 then 532 for the next two years.

The baseline questionnaire focused on six behaviours:

▶ alcohol consumption

▶ eating habits

▶ exercise

▶ sleeping

▶ smoking

▶ wearing seat belts.

Questions focused on actual behaviours and on beliefs about health. That is, the questions asked participants about performances on a variety of preventive health behaviours alongside the efficacy of performing these behaviours.

Participants' parents were asked the same questions except those about sleeping habits and smoking. They were also asked questions about performance of the behaviours and the efficacy of performing but also about their efforts in training their children to perform them.

The results showed the following:

▶ There was a substantial change in health behaviours over the three years and peers had the strongest impact on this.

▶ Parents are much more influential than peers as a source for influencing health beliefs and behaviours.

It would appear that parents have a gradual influence on the health beliefs and behaviours of their children while they live together at home and this then persists throughout the students' first three years at college.

Strength	Weakness
The study was longitudinal, so the researchers could track developmental changes (health behaviour in this case) over time.	There was an attrition in participants, meaning that those who completed the study may have been qualitatively different in their health behaviour. This could mean that it is difficult to generalise beyond the final sample as, for example, they may have been more motivated in general.

Issues and debates tracker: This section focused on the role of the individual in health promotion. All three ideas covered place an emphasis on people changing their attitudes or beliefs about health in an attempt to improve it. However, there may be situational factors that also need to be considered, for example finance, diet and where a person lives. Considering all factors together might help people even more in reaching their health goals.

23 HOW TO EVALUATE: HEALTH

For the 10-mark question in paper 3, you will be asked to evaluate one of the topics covered in this section. Below are three examples of the types of evaluation point you *could* write in the examination.

You should aim to make a range of evaluation points for the 10-mark question.

IMPROVING ADHERENCE

There is evidence to suggest that using techniques such as simple text messaging is *useful*. Lewis *et al* (2013) reported on a scheme that sent tailored text messages to people currently undergoing HIV treatment. After being assessed prior to receiving text messages, the patients received reminder texts, answered weekly adherence texts and those who adhered to treatment received tailored messages. The adherence to medication (self-reported) improved significantly during the three months that patients were receiving the texts. Objective measures of adherence such as viral load confirmed that these patients had been adhering to treatment. Therefore, this technique is very useful at improving adherence to HIV treatment. However, using cognitive techniques such as memory intervention could be seen as *reductionist*. Comparing the human information processing system to that of a computer is reductionist. It ignores the role of emotional and social factors on how we process information. For example, Insel's six-stage technique to help people adhere to blood pressure treatment does not take into account the emotional side of a patient. Having patients go through the process of "teach – ask – wait – ask again – wait – ask again" might have the opposite of the desired effect. As the patients are having to constantly think about their blood pressure, which might be upsetting, and as they are focusing on the emotional aspect, they may then forget to take their pill!

MEASURING PAIN

One way of measuring pain is via questionnaires. This may *improve validity* because people may be more likely to reveal truthful answers in a questionnaire as it does not involve talking face to face with someone. Therefore, a patient using the McGill Pain Questionnaire may give more accurate results on where the pain is located on a picture (especially if it is in a sensitive part of the body) rather than in front of a doctor. This could lead to quicker and more effective treatment. However, patients may give *socially desirable* answers rather than giving truthful answers as they want to look good. Some people may want to appear stronger and more resistant to pain than they actually are so, again, on the McGill Pain Questionnaire people may choose descriptors that do not truly describe their actual pain feelings, but instead choose descriptors that are not "as strong". This could have an effect on receiving the most appropriate treatment.

MANAGEMENT OF STRESS

Using just medical treatment is *reductionist*. It assumes that stress is caused by biological problems and it ignores the psychological and emotional aspects of stress. Simply "masking" the biological symptoms of stress does not help to solve the cause of the stress – and this is what needs managing. Taking pills will not get rid of a major life event that is actually causing the stress in the first place. Psychological treatment is better for directly dealing with the problem that is causing stress.

24 PSYCHOLOGY AND ORGANISATIONS

All studies or comments marked with an asterisk are not directly named in the syllabus but the information included in these studies or comments will help the student to answer questions on the topic covered. The examination will not ask about these studies by name or ask for specific findings.

24.1 MOTIVATION TO WORK

NEED THEORIES

Hierarchy of needs (Malsow, 1970)

One idea from humanism that attempts to explain motivation was proposed by Maslow (1970, but based on his earlier research). He created a hierarchy of needs that starts at basic needs and moves up to higher level "meta needs". The hierarchy progresses from physiological needs to safety needs, to social needs, to esteem needs and finally to self-actualisation needs. The model is illustrated in Figure 24.1.1.

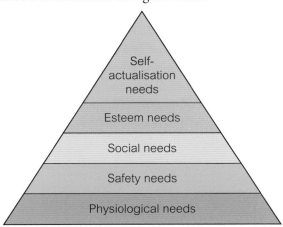

▲ **Figure 24.1.1** Maslow's hierarchy of needs

A human being must work up the hierarchy of needs to achieve self-actualisation – this is realising and reaching one's full potential. The basic (physiological) needs always have to be met (even if partially) before a person can consider working up the hierarchy towards self-actualisation. A worker has to be motivated and fulfilled at a physiological and safety level before attempting anything higher.

Greenberg and Baron (2008)* set out how this can be applied to the workplace in the following ways:

▶ To satisfy physiological needs, organisations can make sure that workers take breaks (e.g. for refreshments). Some companies, especially those where the workforce is quite sedentary in an office environment, provide exercise facilities for free. This can improve the health of workers and make them more productive.

▶ With regard to safety needs, organisations can ensure that workers have protective clothing if necessary and use specifically designed products, for example to reduce the strain of using computers and keyboards all day as part of a worker's job.

▶ To meet social needs, organisations can organise events that can build a "team spirit" into the workforce. A company may have a "family day" for everyone to get together out of the pressures of work. There is a company called The Picnic People which coordinates events to get the workforce together, for example.

▶ Esteem needs might be met through incentives organisations create such as "employee of the month" or annual awards ceremonies for the workforce. They can also award bonuses for suggestions for improvements within the organisation.

▶ Self-actualisation needs are met when organisations nurture their workforce to allow people to reach their full potential (via things such as career progression and appraisals).

Strength	Weakness
The theory is easy to test for validity as each level is clearly described.	The theory ignores other factors that might motivate people to work.

CHALLENGE YOURSELF
To what extent do you think that this theory is reductionist? Justify your answer.

ERG theory (Aldefer, 1972)

Aldefer (1972) built on the model proposed by Maslow and reduced the five main motivation levels to just three as follows:

▶ Existence needs – these are similar to what Maslow called physiological needs.

▶ Relatedness needs – these are similar to what Maslow called social needs.

▶ Growth needs – these are similar to what Maslow called self-actualisation needs.

The main difference between Maslow's idea and the ERG model is that for the latter there is no strict hierarchy. All of the needs have to be addressed at work in some form or another. The greatest motivator is when all three are being fulfilled at work. However, when one is not totally fulfilled, the worker may still feel a good sense of motivation if the other two are. An example would be gaining a pay rise when there is no current chance of being promoted; this fulfils the ER but not the G. However, the worker will still feel motivated to work.

Achievement motivation theory (McClelland, 1965)

Proposed by McClelland (1965), achievement motivation theory is based around the idea that people (and workers) are motivated by different needs and motives in different situations. There are three key

needs and motives that people are driven by and they differ from individual to individual:

▶ People have a need for achievement. This is about having the drive to succeed in a situation. Therefore, workers driven by this will love the challenge of their job. They want to get ahead in their job and be excellent performers. They like to solve immediate problems swiftly and will go for challenges that offer a moderate level of difficulty (so that they feel challenged but know the goal is achievable). They also desire feedback about their efforts so will thrive on appraisals.

▶ People have a need for power. This is about having the drive to direct others and be influential at work. Workers in this category are status driven and are more likely to be motivated by the chance to gain prestige. They will want to solve problems individually and reach appraisal goals. The drive for power can be for personal gains or organisational gains.

▶ People have a need for affiliation. This is about having the drive to be liked and accepted by fellow workers in the organisation. People driven by this prefer to work with others and get motivated by the need for friendship and interpersonal relationships. Therefore, their main motivator is on cooperative tasks.

Workers can be assessed on these three key needs and motives by taking a thematic apperception test (TAT). To do this, workers have to look at a series of ambiguous pictures that tell a story. They have to tell whatever story they feel is behind the picture and their stories are then scored on a standardised scale that represents the three key needs and motives. From these, it can be seen whether a worker is driven by achievement, power or affiliation.

Strength	Weakness
The theory has application as companies can use the information to help motivate staff via their appraisals.	The theory tends to be tested using the TAT, which is a subjective way of measuring motivation.

COGNITIVE THEORIES

Goal-setting theory (Latham and Locke, 1984)

Goal-setting theory (Latham and Locke, 1984) appears relatively straightforward: it states that performance at work is affected by the goals that a workforce is set. The setting of these goals affects people's beliefs about whether they can perform a task or not.

However, goals need to be specific to an individual or group. Simply saying "work harder" has very little effect on people as they may already feel that they are working hard. Setting specific and achievable goals allows workers to direct their attention towards achieving them while assessing how well they are doing. If workers feel that they may not reach a specified goal, they will be motivated to work harder to try to attain it. An organisation must set challenging but attainable goals, give workers the necessary equipment and support to attain the goals and give them feedback throughout the process as this will motivate them to attain each goal.

According to this theory, there are three main guidelines for setting effective goals:

► Assign specific goals. Goals have to have clarity, be measurable and achievable. An organisation cannot say "do your best" and then hope the workforce gets motivated. Research has shown that workers may find the goal challenging but this motivates them to want to achieve it.

► Assign difficult, but acceptable, performance goals. Goals that are perceived as unachievable will demotivate the workforce as will those that are seen as being "too easy". Therefore, a goal must be difficult, in order to get workers motivated, but not impossible to attain. There can be vertical stretch goals which challenge workers to achieve higher success in activities that they are currently involved with (e.g. sales). There are also horizontal stretch goals which challenge workers to perform certain tasks that are new to them.

► Provide effective feedback on goal attainment. Feedback throughout the process allows workers to know how far they are progressing and what is left to attain a goal. This keeps motivation at an optimal level. If feedback is used wisely, workers will believe even more that they can attain the goal and will be more motivated to achieve it.

Strength	Weakness
The theory has application as companies can use the information to help them set realistic goals to motivate people at work.	Not all goals are universal so it may *not* help to motivate workers if the goal is something they have no desire to achieve.

VIE (expectancy) theory (Vroom, 1964)

This theory, devised by Vroom (1964), attempts to explain motivation more from a cognitive angle. Motivation is based on three factors that are multiplicative:

▶ Valence refers to the value that workers place on any reward they believe they will receive from the organisation. The overall reward must be one that reflects the efforts put into attaining a goal and therefore be *desired*.

▶ Instrumentality refers to any perceived relationship between effort and outcome that may affect motivation. This can be based around rewards as well. If any performance or motivation is not perceived as being instrumental in bringing about a suitable reward, then it is less likely to happen – motivation will be low.

▶ Expectancy refers to any perceived relationship between effort and performance that may affect motivation. If workers do not expect their efforts to make any difference to attaining a goal then their motivation will be low. If they do feel effort brings about reward then their performance will increase as they will be motivated.

This can be expressed as an equation:

$$M = V \times I \times E$$

Therefore, motivation is determined by how the three factors interact, so if one of them is low then motivation as a whole will be low as a result. All have to be reasonably high for motivation to be high too.

Managerial applications of expectancy theory

How can the above be used by managers in an organisation to improve motivation of its workforce? Riggio (1999)* and Greenberg and Baron (2008)* highlight the following practical ways:

▶ Managers need to define any goal-based work outcome very clearly to all workers. Clarity is the key to success. All rewards and costs of performance based around these rewards must be known and be transparent.

▶ Managers should get workers involved in the setting of any goals and listen to their suggestions about ways to change jobs and roles to help attain them. This should help to increase VIE levels.

▶ For the valence element, managers should ensure that the rewards are ones that employees desire and see in a positive light. These may need to be individually specific as not all workers are motivated by the same things. Greenberg and Baron (2008)* highlight how many companies now use a "cafeteria-style benefit plan" where employees can choose their own personalised incentives from items such as pay, additional days off and lower day-care costs for their children. The valence element for workers is very high if they are striving for something *they have chosen*.

▶ Progression from performance to rewards has to be achievable. Any performance-related goal (especially if workers have some performance-related pay) has to be attainable for all. Workers whose portion of their wage is based on performance need goals that are attainable but where motivation is the key to reaching them. Greenberg and Baron (2008)* state that if there is a pay-for-performance method in the company then this should increase the instrumental motivation element of expectancy theory and motivation increases.

Equity theory (Adams, 1963)

The general idea behind this theory is that workers are motivated by a need for equity and fairness. If workers feel that they are receiving fair treatment in their workplace, they are more likely to be motivated to continue to work as they are. However, if they do not feel they are receiving fair treatment their motivation will be taken away from their work and used to try to decrease any feeling they have about inequity. There are three things that need to happen to assess the equity of a work situation:

▶ Inputs – workers assess what they are bringing to the job in terms of experience, education, effort, etc.

▶ Outcomes – these are the expectations workers have, based on their input. Outcomes include pay and conditions, getting recognition, having challenging work, etc.

▸ "Comparison others" – this is when workers compare their input–outcome ratio with other workers perceived to be roughly their equal. After doing this, workers can decide whether their current employment is equitable or not. If they decide it is inequitable, two things can happen:

– Underpayment equity: if workers feel that their pay and conditions are inferior based on a "comparison other" , they will feel that they need to find a way to stop this and regain motivation. This can be done in a variety of ways, according to Adams. Workers may increase outcomes by confronting their boss about pay and conditions, or use an appraisal to highlight the inequitable nature of their current position. They could also decrease inputs by slowing down or reducing the quality of their work. A worker could also change the "comparison other" worker to someone more appropriate.

– Overpayment equity: if workers feel that their pay and conditions are superior based on "comparison others", there is still an imbalance. As a result, workers may try harder with their input as they are receiving more pay and better conditions then the other workers. They could ask for a pay cut (but this is highly unlikely). When conducting another "comparison other" exercise they could choose someone of a higher status, believing that they are getting better conditions as managers have seen their potential.

Strength	Weakness
Studies have shown that when workers are given a "higher-status" job title even if their job has not changed, they will increase their input levels as predicted by the theory.	The theory assumes that all people are motivated by equity and inequity and, as we have seen in this section, this may not be the case.

MOTIVATORS AT WORK

Intrinsic and extrinsic motivation

Extrinsic motivation is a desire to perform a task or behaviour because it gives positive reinforcement (e.g. a reward) or it avoids some kind of punishment. In terms of the workplace, this might mean workers gain extra pay or a day off for their efforts.

Intrinsic motivation is a desire to perform a task or behaviour because it gives internal pleasure or helps to develop a skill. In terms of the workplace, people will attribute success to their own desires (autonomy) and may be interested in simply mastering a task rather than focusing on something such as extra pay.

CHALLENGE YOURSELF
Design a study that investigates whether workers prefer intrinsic or extrinsic motivators at work.

Types of reward system
Pay, bonuses, profit-sharing and performance related-pay

There are many reward systems that organisations can use with their workforce. They tend to be based around both extrinsic and intrinsic motivators. They can include the following:

▸ Pay – having some pay linked to a certain task or goal can increase the motivation of workers as they want to have more money.

▸ Bonus – offering a bonus is are quite widespread in organisations linked to sales and finance. At the end of each year (maybe after an appraisal), workers will be given a bonus payment based on the performance of themselves and the company as a whole.

▸ Profit-sharing – a certain percentage of any profit a company makes can be "ring fenced" to be shared by all workers. Therefore, everyone may be more motivated to attain goals and reach performance criteria so that there is a monetary reward.

▶ Performance-related pay – when we covered the VIE (expectancy) theory of motivation we discussed performance-related pay. In addition, sales organisations may set minimum targets which give workers basic pay and anything achieved above the target earns them commission. This should motivate workers to exceed minimum targets as they will gain a reward in the process.

Non-monetary rewards
Praise, respect, recognition, empowerment, sense of belonging

As we have seen, not all motivators have to be extrinsic. There are important intrinsic motivators in the workplace such as the following:

▶ Praise – simply gaining praise from a superior at work can motivate a worker to continue to work hard and meet targets and goals. It is a form of positive reinforcement.

▶ Respect – gaining respect from superiors and fellow colleagues is also important in an organisation. This internal feeling of "good" can motivate workers to continue to try hard at a task.

▶ Recognition – simply being recognised for any "over and above" effort can motivate a worker to continue to work hard. For example, an "employee of the month" scheme or being mentioned in a work newsletter can motivate people greatly.

▶ Empowerment – when workers succeed at a difficult task or achieve a difficult goal they may have a sense of empowerment. This may make them believe that the next task is attainable even if it looks difficult. It equips them to continually try hard at a task.

▶ Sense of belonging – making workers feel "part of the team" and that their individual efforts are appreciated can motivate them to keep trying hard and reaching even difficult goals.

> **Issues and debates tracker:** These ideas all have good application to real life. Each of the motivators could be used by a company to improve the motivation of its workforce, which in turn should increase production and profit. These could also be negotiated with workers during their appraisals so that they can get a personalised motivation programme at work.

24.2 LEADERSHIP AND MANAGEMENT

TRADITIONAL AND MODERN THEORIES OF LEADERSHIP

> **ASK YOURSELF**
>
> What makes a good leader or manager at work? List all of the traits you think make someone a good leader or manager and then see how many appear in the following theories.

Universalist and behavioural theories

This section looks at a range of psychological theories that attempt to explain what makes someone become a leader.

Universalist theories include great person theory and theories centred on charismatic and transformational leaders.

Behavioural theories include theories from Ohio State University studies (initiating structure and consideration) and University of Michigan studies (task-oriented and relationship-oriented behaviours).

Great person theory

This follows the idea that "great leaders are born, not made". Therefore, you are either a "natural" leader or not. People's natural abilities allow them to "rise to the top" of any organisation because of the skills they were born with. These leaders have special traits that allow them to progress up the managerial levels of an organisation and then lead the company effectively over time. These traits are stable and effective when they are used in a position of authority.

Charismatic and transformational leaders

Another idea is that certain leaders have the necessary charisma to become leaders. They possess first-class interpersonal skills. Charisma comes from the Greek for "gift of grace" and it means that leaders possess

a charismatic personality that allows them to lead a workforce effectively. These leaders tend to have very good public speaking skills, exude confidence, inspire people, captivate their audiences every time. As a result, the workforce is motivated to follow them and attain the goals set by them. In addition, Greenberg and Baron (2008) reviewed the field and produced a list of five "agreed" traits that charismatic leaders have:

▶ Self-confidence – they show high confidence about their own ability and the ability of their workforce to attain a goal.

▶ A vision – this usually takes the form of making working conditions or working life better.

▶ Extraordinary behaviour – they show some unusual or unconventional behaviours.

▶ Recognition as change agents – in other words, they are seen to make things happen.

▶ Environmental sensitivity – they show realism about what can be achieved given the resources they have available.

Transformational leaders, according to Riggio (1999), change how the workforce think, reason and behave. They inspire workers using six different behaviours:

▶ Identifying and articulating a vision – they excite workers with a vision for the company.

▶ Providing an appropriate model – the leaders "practise what they preach".

▶ Fostering the acceptance of group goals – cooperation between all workers is promoted and a common goal is set.

▶ Maintaining high performance expectation – excellence is encouraged and work quality is improved.

▶ Providing individualised support – the leaders will show care and concern for all individuals.

▶ Providing intellectual stimulation – the leaders will challenge workers to rethink how they do things.

Researchers at Ohio State University collected data from self-reports and observations of leaders and their workers. From this they listed over 100 different behaviours shown by leaders. They conducted a factor analysis on the data (this looks for relationships between variables and clusters similar ones together) and found that there are just two broad categories of leaders:

- Initiating structure – this includes assigning specific tasks to people, defining groups of workers, creating and meeting deadlines and ensuring that workers are working to a set standard.

- Consideration – this is shown by leaders who have a genuine concern for the feelings of workers and their attitudes. The leaders establish rapport with workers while showing them trust and respect. They will listen to workers more often than the other category of leaders and try to boost the self-confidence of their workforce.

Researchers at the University of Michigan examined many leaders of large organisations and also found two main types of behaviour in these leaders:

- Task-oriented behaviours – these were behaviours that focused on the actual task being conducted. The leaders are more concerned with setting up some structures within an organisation such as targets, standards, supervising workers and achieving goals.

- Relationship-oriented behaviours – these were behaviours that had a focus on the wellbeing of the workforce. The leaders would look at interpersonal relationships between worker and worker, plus worker and manager. They would also take the time to understand the feelings of their workforce.

The researchers concluded that the relationship-oriented behaviours were more effective at motivating a workforce than task-oriented ones.

Adaptive leadership (Heifetz, 1997)

Heifetz (1997) proposed the idea of adaptive leadership. Leaders have to mobilise their workforce to tackle whatever challenges happen and to then make them thrive. This can be done via being an adaptive leader, according to Heifetz. These are the basic assumptions of this idea:

- Leadership is about change that enables the workforce to thrive.

- Any change has to be built on the past.

- Organisational change can only happen through experimentation.

- Leadership relies on diversity.

- Adaptive leadership can involve displacing, re-regulating and rearranging "old" structure in an organisation.

- Adaptive changes will take time.

To be an adaptive leader, the person must meet the following conditions:

- Get rid of the broken system's illusions that it is not broken

- Differentiate between technical problems and adaptive challenges.

- Distinguish leadership from authority.

- Learn to live in a "productive" zone even if it causes short-term disequilibrium.

- Observe, then interpret, then intervene.

- Engage above and below the neck.

- Connect to purpose.

There are other tips that Heifetz notes that can help someone to become an adaptive leader:

- Don't do it alone. Involve others in the organisation and distribute responsibilities according to each worker's strengths.

- Remember that the best way to learn is through life experiences.

- Resist leaping into action and try to stay reflective at all times.

- Make difficult choices but enjoy the experience.

Strength	Weakness
The theory has application as managers can train certain workers to become adaptive leaders.	The theory is subjective and has not been tested objectively by other researchers.

Three levels of leadership (Scouller, 2011)

Scouller (2011) proposed a model of leadership that has three levels. These are as follows:

- Public leadership is about the actions a leader takes in a group setting. These could be, for example, actions taken during meetings or trying to influence management. "Togetherness building" is a technique that can be used. This encourages group-wide trust and respect while developing an atmosphere in which it is "natural" for individuals to want to perform to their highest standard. This also nurtures the sharing of information and wanting to help colleagues.

- Private leadership is about how an individual handles group members. To achieve private leadership the leader needs to get to know people individually. Each member of a group needs to have individual targets to help support any group task that is set. The leaders need to help review individual task performances at appraisal, giving group members targets to help improve their performance where necessary. Selecting appropriate people for the job is part of this level of leadership, as is removing people who do not fulfil their roles or who underperform consistently.

- Personal leadership is about leaders' psychological, moral and technical development that can affect their presence within a company and their behaviour. Therefore, it is about self-awareness, the progression to self-mastery and technical competence (and updating knowledge) where applicable. It requires leaders to have a sense of connection with employees around them. It is the inner core of leadership.

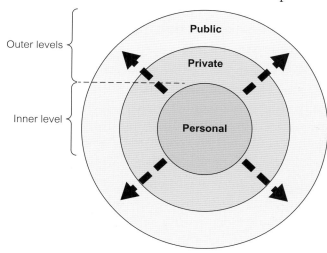

▲ **Figure 24.2.1** The three levels of leadership model

Source: Scouller (2011: 36)

Scouller (2011) believes that personal leadership is the most powerful of the three. He likens it to a pebble hitting the water where the personal leadership is the point of entry and this then "ripples out" to the private and the public leadership levels. If the "pebble" is positive, the ripples will be positive too. However, if the "pebble" is negative then the ripples will also be negative.

CHALLENGE YOURSELF

Design a study to find out which type of Scouller's leadership levels is most common in a company.

LEADERSHIP STYLE AND EFFECTIVENESS

Effectiveness: contingency theory (Fiedler, 1976)

This theory, proposed by Fiedler (1976), looks at the interaction between the style of leadership that leaders adopt and the situation that they find themselves in. For a leader to be effective in the workplace, the leader's style must fit with the amount of authority, power and control the leader is given in the organisation. There are various steps to assess whether a leader will be effective in a workplace:

- Completion of the least preferred co-worker (LPC) questionnaire – leaders complete a questionnaire about the person with whom they can work least well. They rate them on bi-polar adjectives such as boring/interesting and frustrating/helpful. From this, leaders can be seen as being either task-oriented (so they give harsh ratings to fellow workers) or relationship-oriented (so they give favourable ratings even though the person is the least preferred).

- Leader–member relations – this is measured by getting the workforce to assess the leaders on how well liked they are, etc.

- Task structure – this measures how well a particular work task is structured with well-defined goals.

- Position power – this looks at company policy and examines how leaders can hire and fire, discipline and reward workers.

The ideal situation for a leader to thrive is when the leader–member relations are positive, the task is very well structured and the leader has strong position powers.

Riggio (1999) notes that a task-oriented leader is most effective when the situation is at the extremes: either highly favourable or highly unfavourable. In highly favourable situations, teams are already well established, as are power positions and task structure, so the leader simply "slots in". In highly unfavourable situations, the leader can give a failing project the necessary structure and drive to succeed. Relationship-oriented leaders appear more effective in the middle-ground projects that need more support and coaching than goal setting.

Situational leadership (Hersey and Blanchard, 1988)

Hersey and Blanchard (1988) proposed the theory of situational leadership, which is also based around the task and relationship behaviour. This theory looks at styles that work depending on whether there are low or high task controls and/or low or high relationship aspects of the task. Therefore, there are four different types of situation in the workplace. These are as follows:

▶ Low relationship but high task – these are situations where workers need structure and direction from their leader to achieve a set goal but require very little emotional support to do so. The best behaviour for the leader is *telling* the workforce what to do.

▶ High relationship and high task – these are situations where workers need both structure and emotional support. They need help improving a skill with set guidelines and need the emotional support to do it. The best behaviour for the leader is *selling* the idea to the workforce.

▶ High relationship but low task – these are situations where workers need very little guidance on *what* to do but need a lot of emotional support to achieve it. The best behaviour for the leader is *participating* with the workforce on the task.

▶ Low relationship and low task – these are situations where workers are already able to perform the task and are willing to do so. The best behaviour for the leader is *delegating* the workload across the workforce.

Styles of leader behaviour

Permissive and autocratic styles (Muczyk and Reimann, 1987)

Muczyk and Reimann (1987) based their theory of leadership on two styles – permissive and autocratic – that can be combined to assess how a leader may be acting. In permissive leadership, workers are not told how to do their jobs and autocratic leadership means that workers are not allowed to participate in any decision making. Therefore, there can be four combinations:

▶ Permissive and autocratic – leaders will make decisions by themselves and let the workers "get on with it".

▶ Permissive but not autocratic – leaders will make decisions with others involved and will then let the workers "get on with it".

▶ Not permissive but autocratic – leaders will make decisions by themselves and then closely monitor how the workers are performing on the task.

▶ Not permissive or autocratic – leaders will make decisions with others involved and will closely monitor how the workers are performing on the task.

Strength	Weakness
The theory has application as different types of leader can be identified and used best within an organisation.	The theory could be reductionist as it only looks at factors in a given situation, overlooking other important leadership skills.

LEADERS AND FOLLOWERS

Leader–member exchange model (Danserau, 1994)

It would appear that the theories we have presented so far are based on the ideas that every leader treats every member of his or her workforce equally and in the same way every time. This is clearly not the case in reality. Danserau (1994) proposed the leader–member exchange (LMX) model, which looks into this issue.

Leaders form different relationships with their workforce early on in any process and, based on very limited information, classify workers into two distinct groups. The favoured ones (be it because they follow the same ideals as the leader or are seen as hard workers, etc.) form part of the "in group". There is then, by default, an "out group" which consists of workers that do not "fit in" with what the leader wants (be it because of a personality clash or that they are perceived to not be hard workers, etc.). Obviously, the in group will get more attention and praise and recognition compared to the out group. This can demotivate the latter group considerably while those in the in group get bolstered.

Riggio (1999) noted that an LMX can be of low quality where the leader has a very negative view of the out group and the out group does not see the leader as effective. An LMX can also be of high quality where the leader has a very positive view of his or her in group and that in group sees the leader as being encouraging and motivated.

Individualised leadership model (Danserau, 1995)

Danserau (1995) expanded his ideas into an individualised leadership model. There was one single mechanism which appears to secure leadership status: provide support for a subordinate's feelings of self-worth. Data from the United States and other countries indicated that if the leader shows an absence of support for the subordinate's feelings of self-worth then that leader will find it extremely difficult to become a "true" leader and run a satisfying team. Therefore, a leader needs to vary his or her efforts within and between groups depending on an assessment of the teams' worth. In other words, he or she must become an "individualised" leader.

Followership: qualities and types (Kelley, 1988)

Kelley (1988) noted five styles of followership:

- Alienated. These include people who are passive but independent. They have been effective before but may have experienced a lot of setbacks. They are capable in their jobs but always focus on the problems within an organisation. They remain cynical and do not contribute to any problem solving.

- Effective. These are people who are active and critical thinkers. They have the courage to initiate change (or help someone else who is initiating it). They are open to taking risks. They always serve the best interests of the organisation. They always work towards having a positive impact in any task given to them.

- Passive. These are people who are passive and uncritical thinkers. They lack any initiative and have no sense of responsibility. They always require supervision and always let the leader "do the thinking" for them.

- Conformist. These people tend to be active but dependent thinkers. They happily carry out orders. They willingly participate in tasks. They are overly concerned with avoiding conflict.

- Pragmatic survivor. These people can have the qualities of the other four styles. They will change their style to suit the situation they find themselves in as long as it benefits them directly. They tend to avoid risk taking though.

The styles can be categorised on two dimensions:

- critical versus dependent thinking
- passive versus active behaviour.

Figure 24.2.2 shows the placing of each style on the two dimensions.

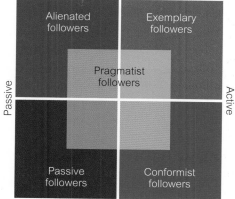

▲ **Figure 24.2.2** Two dimensions of followership style

Source: Based on Kelley (1988)

> **Issues and debates tracker:** Some of these theories focus on how an individual who already possesses the necessary skills to lead a team at work goes on to become a manager. Therefore, such theories favour the individual side of the individual-situational debate. However, it could be argued that the people have become leaders due to their experiences in the workplace and these have made them the leaders they are now. This would favour a situational explanation.

Measuring leadership: Leadership Practices Inventory (Kouzes and Posner, 1987)

Kouzes and Posner (1987) created the Leadership Practices Inventory (LPI) to allow leaders to see which of five core styles they think they use in their everyday working environment. The researchers called the five styles:

1. Model the way
2. Inspire a shared vision
3. Challenge the process
4. Enable others to act
5. Encourage the heart.

An individual completes an inventory of 30 items that cover these five core styles using the response scale shown in Table 24.2.1.

RESPONSE SCALE	1 – Almost never	3 – Seldom	5 – Occasionally	7 – Fairly often	9 – Very frequently
	2 – Rarely	4 – Once in a while	6 – Sometimes	8 – Usually	10 – Almost always

▲ **Table 24.2.1** Response scale used in this study

Source: Kouzes and Posner (2013: 1)

The inventory is also completed by a range of people in the organisation including managers and co-workers or via a direct report. Averages across all other raters is also calculated.

A Five Practices Data Summary sheet is produced, as shown in Table 24.2.2.

	SELF	AVG	INDIVIDUAL OBSERVERS								
			M1	D1	D2	D3	D4	C1	C2	C3	O1
1. Model the way	53	**45.8**	51	51	55	50	25	47	42	45	46
2. Inspire a shared vision	45	**45.2**	47	49	48	54	31	45	42	42	49
3. Challenge the process	54	**49.2**	49	54	58	54	29	48	51	44	56
4. Enable others to act	53	**49.0**	50	49	56	54	32	48	47	51	54
5. Encourage the heart	39	**40.6**	47	36	35	47	26	49	38	39	48

▲ **Table 24.2.2** Five Practices Data Summary

Source: Kouzes and Posner (2013: 2)

Also, a Leadership Behaviour Ranking chart is produced. An example is shown in Figure 24.2.3.

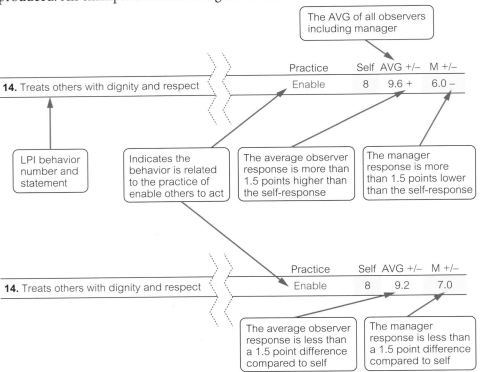

▲ **Figure 24.2.3** Leadership behaviour ranking

Source: Kouzes and Posner (2013: 4)

Alongside many other charts and graphs, a full list ranking all 30 items based on the average score across *all* respondents is given, showing the most to least frequent leadership behaviours. Table 24.2.3 shows some examples.

MOST FREQUENT

		PRACTICE	SELF	AVG +/−	M +/−
14.	Treats others with dignity and respect	Enable	10	9.6	10.0
4.	Develops cooperative relationships among the people he/she works with	Enable	8	8.4	8.0
8.	Challenges people to try out new and innovative ways to do their work	Challenge	9	7.9	8.0
26.	Is clear about his/her philosophy of leadership	Model	8	7.6	8.0
5.	Praises people for a job well done	Encourage	6	7.1	8.0 +
16.	Asks for feedback on how his/her actions affect other people's performance	Model	7	5.0 −	7.0

LEAST FREQUENT

▲ **Table 24.2.3** Examples of leadership behaviour ranking

Source: Kouzes and Posner (2013: 5)

This analysis can give leaders a clearer and more objective appraisal, helping them to pinpoint strengths and weaknesses of their current leadership qualities and behaviours. They may then wish to improve some of the weaknesses as necessary to fit in more with the ethos of their employer.

Strength	Weakness
The tool has good application as it can be used in an organisation to analyse what types of leader work there and then people can be given jobs that fit their skills.	The measurement is based on self-report and people may not always be honest about their own and others' behaviours.

CHALLENGE YOURSELF
To what extent do you think that the LPI is deterministic? Justify your answer.

24.3 GROUP BEHAVIOUR IN ORGANISATIONS

GROUP DEVELOPMENT AND ROLES

The dynamics of a group can be assessed when we look at how groups form in organisations. Tuckman and Jensen (1977)* noted a five-stage formation process:

1. Forming – members of a group get to know each other and ground rules are established in terms of conversations and appropriate behaviours. These are based around the job (the reason) that they are working but also around aspects relating to social skills (e.g. hierarchy).

2. Storming – this stage is characterised by group conflict. Members may want to resist any authority from whoever becomes the "group leader" and there may be conflict between equals too (e.g. personality clash). If nothing can be resolved then the group dissipates. If the conflict can be overcome then the leadership stage is accepted and the group can move on.

3. Norming – this involves the group becoming more cohesive. Identification as a group member becomes stronger and the unit begins to work well on tasks. Group members begin to feel more comfortable in sharing feelings and responsibilities plus ways in which goals can be met. This stage is complete when all group members accept a common set of expectations of group behaviour.

4. Performing – the group is now set to work as a cohesive unit on tasks and to attain any goal or goals set. The group energy is diverted towards completing tasks to a high standard. The leader is now fully accepted.

5. Adjourning –there may be no longer any need for the group once the goals have been attained, so the group dissipates. This can happen abruptly (e.g. as a charity event ends) or take longer (e.g. new goals are formed that only some members of the group want to attain).

Some psychologists disagree about the nature of group formation and cohesiveness and that the order may differ between groups. This is tackled in a theory called punctuated-equilibrium model. There are just two phases that any group in an organisation goes through:

1. Phase 1 is when group members define who they are and what they want to achieve (e.g. goals). This phase usually lasts around 50 per cent of the group's entire lifetime so new ideas tend not to be acted upon and the group is in a state of "equilibrium" moving slowly towards its target.

2. Phase 2 is entered suddenly, when the group has a "midlife crisis" and members realise that they will not achieve their goal. They recognise that they must change their outlook and pathway towards a target so they can take on new ideas and work harder to attain any goals. They move into a state of "punctuating" to cope with these changes.

Group development (Tuckman, 1965)

Tuckman (1965) proposed a four-stage developmental procedure linked to the formation of groups:

1. Orientation to the task. Group members must identify the task and then work out how best to use the group to solve it or work through it. They must decide on which type of information will be needed for the task.

2. Intra-group conflict. Group members may begin to show their individuality by becoming hostile to other group members. This can easily polarise the group.

3. Development of group cohesion. The group accepts individual differences within it. Group members then "re-unite" as a force to work on the task given to them.

4. Functional role-relatedness. Group members finally begin to tackle the task given to them, utilising the different strengths they have.

Team roles (Belbin, 1981)

Belbin (1981) proposed that there are nine different roles that people can take within a team. Each role category has certain strengths but also "allowable weaknesses".

People can be in more than one team role. The roles are as follows:

1. **Plant.** These workers are creative, imaginative and can solve difficult problems in a team. Their allowable weaknesses include not being able to communicate effectively as they get too pre-occupied in the task.

2. **Specialist.** These workers are dedicated, self-motivated and provide much-needed knowledge and skills that could be rare. Their allowable weaknesses include sometimes dwelling on the technicalities of a task and so slowing the whole process down.

3. **Monitor evaluator.** These workers are strategic, seek opinions from all team members and are accurate judges. Their allowable weaknesses include possibly lacking drive and the ability to inspire members of the team.

4. **Implementer.** These workers are reliable, efficient and can easily turn ideas into practical action. Their allowable weaknesses include being somewhat inflexible and maybe too slow to respond to changing ideas.

5. **Shaper.** These workers are challenging and thrive on pressure. They are not afraid to take risks to complete a task. Their allowable weaknesses include being easily provoked into negative action and they may often offend the feelings of team members.

6. **Completer finisher.** These workers are anxious, conscientious and are good at finding errors. They deliver projects on time every time. Their allowable weaknesses include worrying too much about tasks and being reluctant to delegate work within a team.

7. **Teamworker.** These workers are cooperative, perceptive and somewhat diplomatic. They listen to other members of the team and try to avoid any friction. Their allowable weaknesses include being indecisive at crucial moments in a team task.

8. **Coordinator.** These workers are mature, confident and good at being a chairperson of a team. They clarify goals and delegate tasks well within a team. Their allowable weaknesses include being manipulative at times and loading too much work onto other team members.

9. **Resource investigator.** These workers are extravert and enthusiastic about tasks. They like to explore opportunities for the team. Their allowable weaknesses include being overly optimistic at times and quickly losing enthusiasm if a task is not going well.

All of these types are measurable according to Belbin. He developed the Belbin Team Inventory (sometimes referred to as the Belbin Self-Perception Inventory or the Belbin Test) to show which category or categories workers fall into within a company.

Measuring team roles: the Belbin Team Inventory

The Belbin Team Inventory is a questionnaire (self-report) used to allow workers to answer a series of questions that then allocates them to one or several of the Belbin Team roles outlined above.

The original inventory was split into eight sections featuring scenarios. For each of the sections there are eight answers that workers must read through and then tick a statement that describes themselves in that scenario. They can tick as many statements as they wish. Once they have completed a section, participants have to allocate a total of 10 points across all of the items they have ticked to represent how often they think they react in that way. Obviously, if only one tick is present that item is given 10 points. However, if more than one tick appears, participants have to divide the 10 points between the items, ensuring that the total never exceeds 10 for that section.

Once a participant has completed all eight sections, the points are transferred to the final grid which allows a total score to be generated for each of the team roles.

Note that there were only eight categories on the original scale as "Specialist" was added at a later date.

Strength	Weakness
The scale can be used to identify what type or types of team member a worker is, so that the person can be allocated particular tasks that require his or her skills. Therefore, it has real-life application.	As the scale is a self-report, we have to rely on workers being honest about their points allocation. Some results may not be valid as workers may want to look better than they really are.

Issues and debates tracker: These ideas have good usefulness in everyday working life. Managers can measure and assess the team styles of their workers. This allows them to place their workers into the best teams possible for a variety of tasks. This could then increase production and work satisfaction for employees as they are being used to their best abilities.

DECISION MAKING

The decision-making process (Wedley and Field, 1983)

Wedley and Field (1983) devised a comprehensive model of decision making based on decision methods and decision styles. A number of processes occur which has the outcome of either a leadership decision being made or a group decision.

The decision methods are as follows:

▶ Individual interactions (II). These involve face-to-face discussions with individuals in an organisation. These interactions are used to gather information.

▶ Interacting group method (IG). This is when groups get together to interact while making decisions. For example, these could be committee meetings or a regular Monday morning meeting.

▶ Nominal group method (NG). This is a set process. People generate their ideas privately without any discussion. Each idea is presented in turn to the group. Then there is a discussion forum to clarify (but not criticise) any of the ideas. Finally, all of the individuals rank the ideas in order to come to an overall group rating.

▶ Delphi Group Method (DG). The group participants never directly interact. Through a series of anonymous questioning periods, people submit questions to a central administrator. The administrator edits the ideas for clarity, reformulates the problem being discussed and then feeds back the ideas to the workforce, who begin the process of questioning again.

The decision styles are as follows:

▶ Autocratic style (A1). The leader does not gather any information from other people.

▶ Autocratic style (with information from others) (A2).

▶ Consultative style (individually with each person) (C1).

▶ Consultative style (with a group) (C2).

▶ Group style (G2). This involves purely group interactions to help make decisions.

Figure 24.3.1 shows the model proposed by Wedley and Field to show the best routes from several situational questions to the "best outcome method".

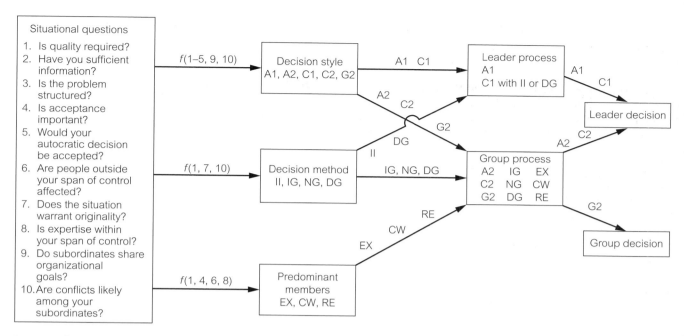

Situational questions

1. Is quality required?
2. Have you sufficient information?
3. Is the problem structured?
4. Is acceptance important?
5. Would your autocratic decision be accepted?
6. Are people outside your span of control affected?
7. Does the situation warrant originality?
8. Is expertise within your span of control?
9. Do subordinates share organizational goals?
10. Are conflicts likely among your subordinates?

$f(1–5, 9, 10)$

Decision style
A1, A2, C1, C2, G2

$f(1, 7, 10)$

Decision method
II, IG, NG, DG

$f(1, 4, 6, 8)$

Predominant members
EX, CW, RE

A1   C1

A2

C2

DG

II

IG, NG, DG

RE

CW

EX

Leader process
A1
C1 with II or DG

G2

Group process
A2   IG   EX
C2   NG   CW
G2   DG   RE

A1

C1

A2

C2

G2

Leader decision

Group decision

Note: Other codes are EX (expert members in the group), CW (co-workers involved) and RE (representative membership of the group).

▲ **Figure 24.3.1** Model of the predecison process

Wedley and Field (1984: 699)

Strength	Weakness
The theory may have good application as an organisation can identify which group process is happening and ensure that it is the best one for the task.	The data relies on questionnaires and people submitting their ideas. People may not be honest or not feel confident enough to tell the truth in the "anonymous" phase.

CHALLENGE YOURSELF

To what extent do you think that the Wedley and Field decision methods are reductionist? Justify your answer.

Groupthink

Groupthink (Janis, 1971) and strategies to avoid groupthink

There may be other situations when a group decision may appear to be a good idea but it truly is not. There are two things that can happen to make the decision-making process go wrong: groupthink and group polarisation.

Groupthink is what happens when a highly cohesive group where all members respect each other's viewpoints comes to consensus on a decision too quickly without any critical evaluation. The group then makes a very poor decision as a result.

Riggio (1999) notes eight symptoms of groupthink:

▶ Illusion of invulnerability – as the group is so cohesive the members see themselves as powerful and invincible. They then fail to spot poorly made decisions.

▶ Illusion of morality – all group members see themselves as the "good guys" who can do nothing wrong.

▶ Shared negative stereotypes – group members hold common beliefs.

263

▶ Collective rationalisations – group members easily dismiss any negative information that goes against their decision with no thought.

▶ Self-censorship – group members suppress any desire to be critical.

▶ Illusion of unanimity – group members can easily (and mistakenly) believe that the decision was a consensus.

▶ Direct conformity pressure – all those showing doubts have pressure applied to them to join the majority view.

▶ Mindguards – some of the group members buffer any negativity away from the group's decision.

Another factor that can adversely affect group decision making is group polarisation. This refers to when groups make "riskier" decisions compared to those made by individuals. Group polarisation follows the idea that, after discussion, people begin to hold even stronger views about a decision. For example, imagine that certain members of the group want to sell off part of a company and after discussing the issue they feel even more strongly about wanting to sell. However, there may be some people in the group who do not want to sell. After discussion, they feel even more strongly about not selling. They "polarise" towards a stronger position than before discussion. This shift towards the polar end of a decision is called a "risky shift" as the group will then attempt to take the riskier option if a consensus can be reached (or just a majority one). Therefore, the majority may win but then take a more extreme view of the decision. However, some psychologists state that group polarisation can still happen even with a "cautious risk" – the group may still polarise after discussion but not in an extreme way.

Avoiding groupthink

Greenberg and Baron (2008) noted four different ways in which groupthink can be avoided:

▶ Promote open enquiry. A group leader could question all decisions made in order to get the group to think again and not go for the first, easy option. Leaders should also encourage members to question and be sceptical so that all decisions are thoroughly assessed.

▶ Use subgroups. Split the members of the main group up and set them exactly the same decision-making tasks. Get them to present their findings; differences between the subgroups can be discussed to form an overall group decision. If the subgroups agree then you can safely say that groupthink has not generated that decision.

▶ Admit shortcomings. You need to get members of the group to be critical and point out any *potential* flaws or limitations of the decisions being made. This should allow the group as a whole to discuss these to ensure that group members have not simply decided on the easiest option.

▶ Hold second-chance meetings. Allow group members to digest the original decision then get them back for a second meeting so they can discuss anything that is worrying them about the decision. This allows "freshness" to be resumed; if a decision task is tiring group members they will go for the easy option. Having two "fresh" attempts at the decision should reduce the probability of groupthink.

Cognitive limitations and errors (Forsyth, 2006)

Forsyth (2006) discusses the potential cognitive limitation and errors made by groups during decision-making processes. Prior to meetings, during meetings and after meetings, people have to think about ideas and potential consequences either by themselves and/or as part of a decision-making group. Forsyth notes the three types of "sin" committed during group decision making, based on the work of MacCoun and Kramer in the mid 1990s:

▶ Sins of commission involve misusing information.

▶ Sins of omission involve overlooking information.

▶ Sins of imprecision involve relying inappropriately on mental "rules of thumb" or heuristics that are inappropriate.

Sins of commission have four sub-types:

► Belief perseverance: when people rely too much on information that has already been reviewed by others and deemed inaccurate.

► Sunk cost bias: when people are reluctant to abandon a course of "thinking action" once an investment has been made (even if it is clearly not the best option).

► Extra-evidentiary bias: when people use information that they have been explicitly told to ignore.

► Hindsight bias: when people overestimate the accuracy of their knowledge of an outcome

Sins of omission have two sub-types:

► Base-rate bias: when people fail to attend to information about general tendencies.

► Fundamental attribution error: when people attribute the cause of behaviours to dispositional factors while overlooking potential situational factors.

Sins of imprecision have three sub-types:

► Availability heuristic: when people base their decisions on information that is readily available and do not hunt for other useful information.

► Conjunctive bias: when people fail to recognise that the probability of two events occurring together will always be less than the probability of just one of those events occurring.

► Representativeness heuristic: when people excessively rely on salient but misleading aspects of a problem.

In addition, Forsyth notes that a confirmation bias can also cause errors in thinking within groups. This is when we have the tendency to seek out information that confirms our beliefs rather than disconfirms. This can become a major issue if individuals within a group continue to do this if it means that a unified solution cannot be reached. Forsyth noted research that showed that this bias is seen much more in a homogenous group than when individuals make decisions or when there are dissenters in the group.

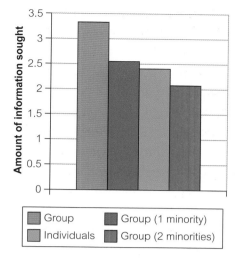

▲ **Figure 24.3.2** The magnitude of the confirmation bias in groups and individuals.

Notes: "Individuals, when they must make a decision, tend to seek out information that supports their initial preferences. This tendency is even stronger in groups, for groups showed a stronger preference for confirming information. Groups that include two members who initially disagree with the position taken by the majority of members, however, are somewhat *less* biased than individuals."

Source: Forsyth (2006: 332)

GROUP CONFLICT

There may be times in any organisation where there is group conflict. There are different types of conflict:

► Intra-group conflict is when people within the same group conflict and this interferes with the pathway towards a goal.

► Inter-group conflict is when there is conflict between different groups within an organisation.

► Inter-individual conflict is when two individuals within a group or organisation have a dispute.

Levels and causes of group conflict
Organisational and interpersonal

There can be any number of reasons why group conflict can happen within an organisation. According to Riggio (1999), there appear to be two broad categories of group conflict:

▶ Organisational factors form one broad category. For example, status differences within an organisation might cause friction. There could be conflict between people about the best pathway towards a goal. There may be a lack of resources such as money, supplies or staff which can cause conflict too. Also, when there are groups that form a "chain of events" for a task to be completed, there are many opportunities for things to go wrong and hence conflict occurs.

▶ Interpersonal reasons make up the other broad category. These are things such as the personal qualities of two workers "clashing", meaning they do not cooperate on tasks. It may be that individuals simply cannot get along with each other or due to a failed task may never want to work with each other again. Sometimes, if the conflict is between two heads of different departments, this can escalate into conflict between those departments as a result.

Positive and negative effects of conflict

Conflict that occurs within an organisation can have both negative and positive effects:

▶ There could be the following negative effects. Group cohesiveness may diminish as people do not get on. Communication can be inhibited as a result of people not talking. Workers may no longer trust each other due to conflict. Constant "bickering" can reduce productivity and goal attainment.

▶ Here are some examples of positive effects. Conflict may get group members to rethink what they are doing. This improves creativity and innovation (and reduces the problems of groupthink). Workers may become less complacent with their

work if conflict is occurring. If it means that the whole workforce is listened to and consulted then productivity may increase as all workers feel "part of the organisation".

Managing group conflict (Thomas, 1976)

Thomas (quoted in Riggio, 1992) identified five different strategies that can be used to manage group conflict in an organisation:

▶ Competition – individuals may persist in conflict until someone wins and someone loses and then the conflict, apparently, diminishes within the groups these individuals are from.

▶ Accommodation – this involves making a "sacrifice" in order to reduce conflict and can help to cut losses and save the relationship between the two groups in conflict.

▶ Compromise – each group under conflict must give up something to help resolve the conflict. This can only be achieved if both sides can lose things that are comparable.

▶ Collaboration – the groups need to work together to overcome the conflict as long as resources are not scarce.

▶ Avoidance – this involves suppressing the conflict or withdrawing from the conflict completely. Neither side can truly resolve the conflict; the differences are still there and have not been worked through. This strategy can be used if the conflict is so aggressive that both sides need to "cool off".

Another technique might be for managers to create a superordinate goal. This is a goal that the conflicting groups are willing to work for together. This will focus them away from the original conflict. Also, managers can use their authority to call a vote on the conflict situation. As a result, the majority of workers will "win" the conflict and managers then have to deal with the losing workers. Managers could also create opportunities for both groups to get a better understanding of one another through workshops, discussion and presentations.

> **CHALLENGE YOURSELF**
> You have been asked to help out a company that is experiencing group conflict. What advice would you give to the managers of the company as to the best ways they can manage group conflict? Justify your answer.

24.4 ORGANISATIONAL WORK CONDITIONS

PHYSICAL AND PSYCHOLOGICAL WORK CONDITIONS

Physical

The Hawthorne studies (Wikstrom and Bendix, 2000)

In this review, Wikstrom and Bendix looked at what the original (1920s) Hawthorne studies actually showed. The "Hawthorne effect" is a psychological term that refers to the effect when people know they are taking part in a study: they may change their behaviour as a result of being observed. As a result, any behavioural changes may be due to this effect rather than any manipulation such as an IV. Therefore, findings from such studies could be questionable.

The original studies into the Hawthorne effect were brought about by the managers of the Hawthorne Plant in Chicago, USA in the 1920s. They wanted to test the effects of lighting on the productivity of their staff. They systematically reduced the illumination levels for the experimental group, whereas the control had constant illumination. Workers in both groups increased their productivity levels over time (inspecting parts, winding coils and assembling relays). When the light "resembled moonlight levels" the workers in the experimental group began to complain that the light levels were affecting their work.

Light levels did not appear to affect productivity. However, as the workers knew they were in a study, it could have been this that made them work "better" and therefore the light levels did not have the desired effect.

Wikstrom and Bendix concluded that while the original studies may have shown the Hawthorne effect, many subsequent studies probably haven't and they listed other factors that might be affecting the productivity of workers during a study:

- relief from a harsh supervisor
- having positive attention for their work
- having rest pauses different from a normal work session
- higher income
- thinking they may be influencing work procedures.

Psychological

Bullying at work (Einarsen, 1999)

Einarsen (1999) reviewed the nature and cause of bullying at work. There appear to be five types of behaviour that can be classified as bullying:

- work-related bullying, which can include changing work tasks or making them too difficult to perform
- social isolation
- personal attacks or some form of attack on someone's personal life
- verbal threats
- physical violence or the threat of it.

In terms of bullying at work, surveys tend to show that there are three main reasons behind it:

- competition concerning status and job positions
- envy
- the aggressors being uncertain about themselves.

When surveys have asked people which one of the above they think is the main reason for bullying at work, around 67 per cent have answered "envy". However, Einarsen notes that there are also four factors that appear to be common in eliciting harassment at work:

- deficiencies in work design (e.g. having a heavy workload compared to an "equal" colleague)
- deficiencies in leadership behaviour (e.g. a lack of constructive leadership and too much destructive leadership; also, predatory bullying may already be a common trait seen in leaders at a company)
- a socially exposed position of the victim
- a low moral standard within the department.

CHALLENGE YOURSELF
Design a study that investigates bullying at work.

Open-plan offices (Oldham and Brass, 1979)

Oldham and Brass (1979) studied changes in employees' reactions to work when they were moved from a conventional office to an open-plan office (one without interior walls or partitions). The setting was a newspaper organisation with 21 different job roles, ranging from reporter and copy-editor to receptionist and clerk. At the beginning of the study, all employees worked in conventional offices and the company had been contemplating moving to an open-plan design for some years. There were three "waves" of data collection:

1. T1 was approximately eight weeks before the planned move.

2. T2 was nine weeks after the move to an open-plan office.

3. T3 was 18 weeks after the move to an open-plan office.

The same questionnaire was given to employees at each time point. The researchers measured aspects of the job such as autonomy, skill variety, task identity, task significance and task feedback. Aspects such as intra-departmental and inter-departmental interaction were also measured. A measure of concentration was

also taken. In addition, outcome measures were taken relating to:

▶ work satisfaction

▶ interpersonal satisfaction

▶ internal work motivation.

A total of 140 non-supervisory members of the company were invited to take part in the study and 128 participated. They were split into the following groups:

1. The experimental group (n = 76) were employees who moved to the open-plan office and completed measures at T1, T2 and T3.

2. The non-equivalent control group (n = 5) were members of the pressroom who did not move. They completed all measures at T1, T2 and T3.

3. The quasi-control group (n = 26) were chosen "at random" and moved to the open-plan office but only completed measures at T2 and T3.

At T2 and T3, groups 1 and 3 did not differ significantly on all but one measure – supervisory feedback – meaning that the exposure to the measures at T1 was not responsible for any of the changes seen at T2 and T3. Therefore, the researchers focused on the experimental group to see whether the three main measures changed over time. The results showed significant changes, as shown in Table 24.4.1.

Variables	Internal consistency reliability	1	2	3	4	5	6	7	8	9	10	11	12	13	14	15
1 Work satisfaction	.86															
2 Interpersonal satisfaction	.85	.67														
3 Internal motivation	.82	.48	.38													

▲ **Table 24.4.1** Median internal consistency reliabilities and intercorrelations among all variables (n = 76)

Source: Oldham and Brass (1979: 278)

Table 24.4.1 shows that all measures decreased over time, meaning that the workers became less satisfied with work, experienced less interpersonal satisfaction at work and also reported less internal work motivation. Therefore, it would appear that open-plan offices do not

help in giving workers satisfaction and motivation to perform their daily tasks. This may be due to a change in job characteristics accompanying the move to an open-plan office.

Strength	Weakness
The study followed a standardised procedure so it can be easily replicated to test for reliability.	The study used just one company changing its offices so generalisation is difficult.

> **Issues and debates tracker:** These ideas have good real-life application because they can be used to improve the quality of people's working life. Assessment of open-plan offices can be used to see whether this layout is appropriate for a particular company. At appraisals workers may wish to confide in managers about potential bullying at work. Investigating such issues should help to improve the working conditions of many people.

TEMPORAL CONDITIONS OF WORK ENVIRONMENT

Temporal conditions refer to the time conditions in which people work. There are many different work patterns that people follow around the world, from the 9 a.m. to 5 p.m. work pattern, to shift-workers' hours, to those "on call". Below we look at some of the options an organisation has when choosing the temporal conditions for its workers.

Shift work

Rapid rotation (metropolitan rota and continental rota) and slow rotation

Shift work refers to when a worker does not do the same work pattern each week. Workers need to alternate the times they work so that an organisation can, say, operate on a 24-hour basis. Workers alternating between day and night shifts is a good example. However, more organisations run a rotation of three shifts per day: day shift (typically 6 a.m. to 2 p.m.), afternoon or twilight shift (2 p.m. to 10 p.m.) and night shift (10 p.m. to 6 a.m.). Therefore, workers need to change their "working day". There are different options that an organisation can use for this:

▶ Rapid rotation – these are frequent shift changes that workers have to follow. There are two types:

  – A metropolitan rota is where workers complete two day shifts, then two twilight shifts, then two night shifts. This is then followed by two days off work.

  – A continental rota is where workers complete two day shifts, two twilight shifts, three night shifts, two days off work, two day shifts, three twilight shifts, two night shifts, then three days off work. After this, the rotation begins again.

▶ Slow rotation – these are infrequent changes of shift that workers have to follow. For example, they may work day shifts for three weeks or more, have a few days off, then work night shifts for three weeks or more. This type of shift pattern allows workers' circadian rhythm (their daily rhythm of sleep and wake) to adapt to a particular shift rather then it being "out of sync" with work patterns, which can happen on a rapid rotation. Circadian rhythms need time to adapt to a change in shift pattern. If they do not there can be long-term health implications and some studies have even suggested that people who work shifts have higher rates of mortality. Also, when working at night, workers are attempting to go against their biological clock. During the night, humans are expected to sleep so our cognitive functioning decreases. This means we are more prone to accidents and making errors on tasks at night.

CHALLENGE YOURSELF
Design a field experiment that investigates whether the metropolitan rota or the continental rota is seen as being better by workers in a company.

Slow rotation theory (Pheasant, 1991)

Pheasant (1991) notes that the slow rotation theory is adopted by some companies. The idea behind this is that because physiologically it takes time to adapt to night work, workers should change their shift patterns as rarely as possible. This will allow their physiological mechanism time to adapt to new patterns of work. Permanent night shift work is preferable to working to metropolitan or continental rotas as there is minimal change to a person's daily (circadian) rhythms. However, as soon as workers have a series of "rest days" the adapted circadian rhythm for night work is lost as people will have lifestyle behaviours they wish to conduct during the day (e.g. shopping, going to the gym).

Effects of shift work on health (Knutsson, 2003)

Knutsson (2003) reviewed the effects of shift work on health. Here are the main findings given under the headings of six health issues:

▶ *Mortality* There was no evidence to suggest that shift work directly affects mortality rates.

▶ *Gastrointestinal diseases* These are much more common in shift workers than in day workers. Common complaints include changes to bowel habits, and ulcers.

▶ *Cardiovascular disease* Shift workers had a 40 per cent excess risk of developing cardiovascular disease compared to day workers. Factors such as work schedules, noise and chemical compounds used at work also affected cardiovascular disease rates.

▶ *Cancer* Knutsson states "…. there is no conclusive evidence that night work *per se* increases the risk of cancer" (2003: 105).

▶ *Diabetes and metabolic disturbances* Studies have shown that concentrations of potassium, uric acid, glucose, cholesterol and total lipids increase during night work. However, they do return to typical levels upon return to day work. Some studies have indicated that the prevalence of diabetes increases with more and more exposure to shift work.

▶ *Pregnancy.* There is some evidence to suggest that shift work leads to low birth weight and increased spontaneous abortion.

The review also suggested a pathway between shift work and disease. This is shown in Figure 24.4.1 Therefore, it would appear that shift work can have detrimental effects on health.

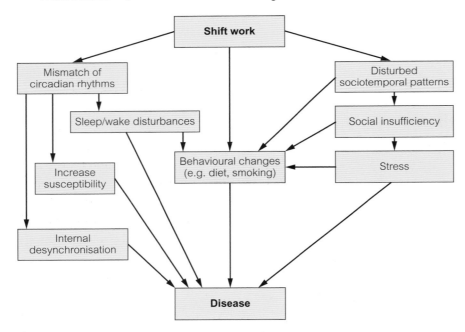

▲ **Figure 24.4.1** Disease mechanisms in shift workers

Source: Based on Knutsson (2003: 106)

Shift work and accidents (Gold *et al*, 1992)

Gold *et al* (1992) examined the effect shift work had on sleep and accidents related to sleepiness in hospital nurses. The sample was of female nurses (n = 878) in a US hospital in Massachusetts. Participants completed a self-administered questionnaire that covered:

▶ current shift work patterns

▶ quality of sleep

▶ alcohol usage

▶ medication

▶ use of sleeping aids and/or drugs

▶ nodding off at work and while driving to and from work

▶ accidents, errors and "near-misses".

The nurses were split into different work schedule categories, as shown in Table 24.4.2.

Day/evening (n = 336): Within a month, working ≥ 4 day or evening shifts but no night shifts.
Night (n = 69): Within a month, working ≥ 8 night shifts and no day/evening shifts.
Rotator (n = 119): Within a month, working ≥ 4 day or evening shifts and ≥ 4 night shifts.
Day/evening, occasional night (n = 61): Within a month, working ≥ 4 day or evening shifts and 1–3 night shifts.
Night, occasional day/evening (n = 14): Within a month, working ≥ 8 night shifts and 1–3 day or evening shifts.
Part-time rotator (n = 17): Within a month, working 4–7 night shifts and 0–3 day or evening shifts.

▲ **Table 24.4.2** Work schedule categories of nurses surveyed

Source: Gold *et al* (1992: 1012)

A total of 687 questionnaires were used in the analyses. The patterns of sleep are shown in Figure 24.4.2.

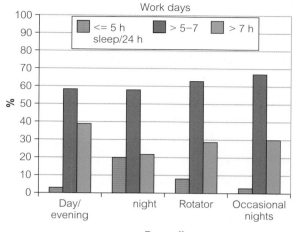

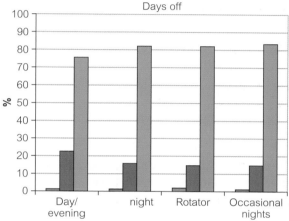

Notes: Only 3 per cent of day/evening nurses slept ≤5 hours/24 hours on work days, as compared to 8 per cent of rotators and 20 per cent of night nurses. Less than 50 per cent of nurses from each of the work schedules slept >7 hours/24 hours on work days. On days-off greater than 75 per cent of nurses from each of the work schedules slept >7 hours/24 hours.

▲ **Figure 24.4.2** Hours of sleep per 24 hours on work days and on days-off by category of work schedule

Gold *et al* (1992: 1012)

These were some of the other key results:

▶ Rotators and night nurses reported fewer hours of sleep than the other groups.

▶ Night workers were 1.8 times more likely to report poor-quality sleep compared to day/evening nurses. This rose to 2.8 times more likely for rotators.

▶ Nodding off at work occurred at least once per week for 35.3 per cent of rotators, 32.4 per cent of night nurses and 20.7 per cent of day/night nurses.

▶ Compared to the day/night group, rotators were 3.9 times more likely and night nurses 3.6 times more likely to nod off driving to and from work.

▶ Two confounding variables were reported that could affect the type of relationship between shift work,

accidents and type of accident: nurses who had worked for less than a year were more likely to have had an accident and an age of 35 years or younger predicted near-miss car accidents.

▶ Reporting any kind of accident was twice as high for rotators compared to day/night nurses.

It would appear that sleep deprivation that affects circadian rhythms during rotating shift work is clearly associated with errors in job performance and with accidents.

Strength	Weakness
A large, diverse sample was used in the hospital so it is likely that the findings can be generalised beyond the sample and have some validity.	The data was collected through questionnaires and participants may not have remembered things correctly or been honest in their answers, potentially lowering the validity of the findings.

HEALTH AND SAFETY

Accidents at work
Errors and accidents in operator-machine systems

Operator-machine systems are those where human workers have to interact with machinery to do their job. We will look at visual and auditory displays and controls. With technological advances still happening at a rapid pace, organisational psychologists need to help companies with the design of machinery to make the job more efficient but also to stop errors and accidents from occurring.

Visual displays*

There are three types of visual display that can be used in organisational machinery:

▶ Quantitative – these are displays that project numbers giving data – temperature, time, speed, etc. Digital displays have taken over from "clock-like" displays as they are much easier to read and fewer errors occur.

▶ Qualitative – these are displays that allow for a judgment using words as the tool. For example, a piece of machinery may not project temperature as a number but have sections simply labelled "cold", "normal" and "hot" – workers can then judge what to do based on this information.

▶ Check-reading – these are simpler displays where the information is limited but highly useful. For example, there may be a simple on-off button, or a light that comes on when something is not working correctly (or is working correctly).

Auditory displays*

In addition to a variety of visual displays noted above, auditory displays can be used. Buzzers, bells or a constant pitched sound can alert workers to a potential problem or that a job is completed in a production line. Workers no longer have to be looking at a display to know what is happening; the sound tells them. The type of noise needs to be what Riggio (1999) called "psychologically effective". That is, a really loud blaring horn or repetitive short beeps are usually perceived as danger so a worker will be alerted to something that is occurring.

Riggio (1999) noted when it was better to use either visual displays or auditory displays:

▶ It is better to use visual displays when a message is complex, a permanent message is needed, the work area is noisy, the workers' jobs involve reading information from displays, etc.

▶ It is better to use auditory displays when a message is simple, the work area is too dark to see a visual display, workers need to move about as part of their jobs, the message is urgent, information is continually changing, etc.

When a worker and machine are interacting, it is inevitable that at some point an error will be made.

According to Riggio (1999), this can happen in four different ways:

- An error of omission is made. This refers to a failure to do something (e.g. a worker may fail to switch something on or off).

- An error of commission is made. This refers to performing a task incorrectly (e.g. a worker may simply not follow an instruction).

- An error of sequence is made. This refers to not following a set procedure for a task (e.g. a worker may work out of sequence, causing an error).

- An error of timing is made. This refers to performing a task too slowly or too quickly (e.g. a worker may press a button too quickly on a machine or not quickly enough to turn it off).

There are other factors which may well affect workers and cause them to perform a task incorrectly:

- There may be lack of training on using a piece of equipment or the manual may be too complicated to understand.

- Some workers have a personality trait called accident proneness – the way they coordinate themselves both physically and psychologically makes them more likely to have an accident or make an error.

- Fatigue may be a factor. Workers who are having to cover a night shift are more likely to have accidents or make an error as they are working against their natural circadian rhythm – between 1 a.m. and 4 a.m. the human body is in a "cognitive dip" as the body is primed for sleep not, for example, working machinery.

Reducing accidents at work: token economy (Fox *et al*, 1987)

Fox *et al* (1987) investigated use of a token economy to improve safety in the work place. See pages 240–242.

Safety promotion campaigns (Cowpe, 1989)

There have been several safety promotion campaigns that have used psychological principles. One of these was devised by Cowpe (1989). Chip pan fires during a period in the 1970s were the biggest cause of domestic fires in the UK (31 per cent) causing damage costing over £8 million. An advertising campaign was created to educate people on how to cope with a chip pan fire at home.

The television advertisement campaign consisted of two 60-second commercials screened from 1976–1982. Both of them showed viewers what causes a chip pan fire and more importantly what to do to put it out (turn off the heat, cover the pan with a damp cloth, leave the pan to cool down). The commercials were shown in ten television regions in the UK. They were always shown between January and April.

Data was collected by analysing statistics from fire brigades and two consumer surveys – one in 1973and another in 1983. The main results were as follows:

- There was a decline in all television regions that showed the advertisements from 7 per cent in the Central region to 25 per cent in the Granada region.

- The first set of statistics in 1976 showed that the campaign's effects had diminished by August.

- In 1982, regions that did not show the advertisements still had a decrease in chip pan fires (6 per cent) but this dropped to 2 per cent six months later and then increased by 1 per cent after a further four months.

- If a region showed both advertisements then chip pan fires reduced by 9 per cent. However, in regions that only showed one of the two advertisements, the reduction was 19 per cent (showing that overexposure can reduce the impact of the advertisements).

- It was calculated that the campaign saved over £1 million pounds in property damage.

- The consumer surveys showed that there was an increase in awareness. For example, in the Yorkshire region, awareness increased from 62 per cent to 90 per cent after the first advertisement was shown and this increased to 96 per cent by the end of the campaign.

Therefore, it would appear that television advertising can promote safety effectively.

Strength	Weakness
The study was longitudinal in nature so any developmental changes (and behavioural changes) could easily be tracked.	The campaign tackles a behaviour that is culturally specific and therefore the overall findings may be culturally biased and not apply to other risky behaviours in other cultures.

24.5 SATISFACTION AT WORK

THEORIES OF JOB SATISFACTION

Two-factor theory (Herzberg, 1959)

Herzberg proposed the two-factor theory of job satisfaction. He believed that job satisfaction and job dissatisfaction are two *independent things* when it comes to the workplace. Prior to this, many psychologists believed there was a continuum from being satisfied to being dissatisfied at work. Herzberg surveyed many workers and asked them what made them feel especially bad or good about their job. He analysed the contents of these surveys and concluded that there are two main factors at work:

▶ Motivators – these are related to the content of the actual job and include:

   – level of responsibility within the job

   – how much workers had already achieved in the job

   – what recognition workers had received while doing the job

   – the content of work within the job

   – how much they had advanced (or could advance) within the job

   – how much they felt they had grown with the job.

These have to be *present* to achieve job satisfaction.

▶ Hygienes – these are related to the context of the job and include:

   – how company policies and administration affect the job

   – what level of supervision workers have in the job

   – what interpersonal relations are like within the job

   – what the working conditions are like within the job

   – salary.

These have to be *absent* or *negative* for job dissatisfaction to occur.

Therefore, workers need a range of motivators to be present to be satisfied with their job but when hygiene factors are absent this leads to dissatisfaction. Riggio (1999) notes that other organisational psychologists have tried to replicate Herzberg's findings but they keep failing to find these two distinct factors.

Job characteristics theory (Hackman and Oldham (1976)

Hackman and Oldham (1976) introduced us to the job characteristics model. Personnel staff, managers, leaders, etc. can use it to devise and create jobs that will appeal to workers and keep them motivated. There are five critical decisions that have to be incorporated into any job design:

▶ Skill variety – does the job require different activities that utilise a range of the worker's skills and talents? It should.

▶ Task identity – does the job require the completion of a whole piece of work from its inception to its completion? It should.

▶ Task significance – does the job have a real impact on the organisation or even beyond that? It should.

▶ Autonomy – does the job allow the worker some freedom in terms of planning, scheduling, carrying out tasks and organising teams? It should.

▶ Feedback – does the job allow for easily measurable feedback to assess the effectiveness of the worker? It should.

All of these added together bring about three critical psychological states, according to Hackman and Oldham (1980). Workers:

▶ experience meaningfulness at work

▶ experience responsibility in terms of the outcome of work

▶ have knowledge of the actual outcome of the job which can help employee growth.

All of this then makes workers much more motivated, their quality of work improves drastically, they become more satisfied and there is less absenteeism and fewer people leaving their job.

Figure 24.5.1 shows Hackman and Oldham's ideas about job satisfaction.

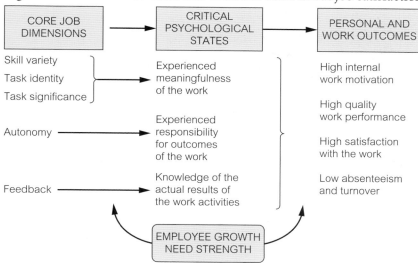

▲ **Figure 24.5.1** The job characteristics model for work motivation

Source: Hackman and Oldham (1976: 256)

Techniques for job design: enrichment, rotation and enlargement

In addition to the job characteristics model, once a job has started there are other methods that can increase workers' satisfaction and motivation. Three of these are as follows:

▶ Job enrichment – this gives workers more jobs to do that involve more tasks to perform that are of a higher level of skill and responsibility. Workers can then have greater control over their job and it makes the job more interesting. Both of these increase satisfaction and motivation. One drawback is that this may be difficult to implement across many jobs within one organisation.

▶ Job rotation – this gives workers regular changes to tasks within their role at work. There may be daily, weekly or monthly changes to the tasks that they are required to perform and this should keep them "fresh" and highly motivated throughout their working day. This increases the workers' skills base too.

▶ Job enlargement – this gives workers more tasks to do but at the same level and usually as part of a team effort. There is no more responsibility or they are not required to learn new skills, rather they perform a wider variety of differing tasks during their working day.

MEASURING JOB SATISFACTION

There are numerous ways in which workers' job satisfaction can be measured by an organisation. This allows the organisation's managers to assess how much they are allowing people to enjoy their work and be motivated.

Rating scales and questionnaires

There are some standardised rating scales and questionnaires that an organisation can use to measure the degree of satisfaction individual workers feel with their job. Two examples follow.

The Job Descriptive Index (Smith, Kendall and Hulin, 1969)

Think of your present work. What is it like most of the time? In the blank space beside each word write:		Think of the pay you get. How well does each of the following words describe your present pay? In the blank space beside each word or phrase write:		Think of the opportunities for promotion that you have now. How well does each of the following words describe them? In the blank space beside each phrase write:	
Y	for "Yes" if it describes your work	Y	for "Yes" if it describes your pay	Y	for "Yes" if it describes your opportunities for promotion
N	for "No" if it does not describe it	N	for "No" if it does not describe it	N	for "No" if it does not describe them
?	if you cannot decide	?	if you cannot decide	?	if you cannot decide

Work on present job	Present pay	Opportunities for promotion
---- Routine ---- Satisfying ---- Good	---- Income inadequate for normal expenses ---- Insecure ---- Less than I deserve	---- Dead-end job ---- Unfair promotion policy ---- Regular promotions

Think of the kind of supervision you get on your job. How well does each of the following words describe this supervision? In the blank space beside each word or phrase write:		Think of the majority of people that you work with now or the people you meet in connection with your work. How well does each of the following words describe these people? In the blank space beside each word write:		Think of your job in general. All in all, what is it like most of the time? In the blank space beside each word or phrase write:	
Y	for "Yes" if it describes the supervision you get on your job	Y	for "Yes" if it describes the people you work with	Y	for "Yes" if it describes your job
N	for "No" if it does not describe it	N	for "No" if it does not describe them	N	for "No" if it does not describe it
?	if you cannot decide	?	if you cannot decide	?	if you cannot decide

Supervisor on present job	People on present job	Job in general
---- Impolite ---- Praises good work ---- Doesn't supervise enough	---- Boring ---- Responsible ---- Intelligent	---- Undesirable ---- Better than most ---- Rotten

▲ **Figure 24.5.2** The Job Descriptive Index – the five dimensions

Source: Smith, Kendall and Hulin (quoted in Riggio, 1999)

The Job Descriptive Index is a self-report questionnaire for workers. It measures satisfaction on five dimensions: the job, supervision, pay, promotions and co-workers, as shown in Figure 24.5.2. Phrases are read and the worker has to answer "Yes", "No", or "?" if undecided. Each answer to each phrase is already assigned a numerical value based on standardisation scoring. Therefore, the worker's satisfaction can be summed for the five different dimensions to see whether all or just one or two dimensions are bringing about satisfaction or dissatisfaction.

Strength	Weakness
The questionnaire attempts to be holistic by measuring satisfaction on five different dimensions so it should have validity.	Many of the questions have fixed choices so workers may pick the one closest to their actual satisfaction rather than what they are actually feeling. This could reduce the validity of the index.

Minnesota Satisfaction Questionnaire (Weiss *et al*, 1967)

This is also a self-report questionnaire for workers. It measures satisfaction on 20 dimensions (e.g. supervisors, task variety, responsibility, promotion, potential). Each item is read and the worker has to rate how much he or she agrees with the statement on a 5-point scale from "very dissatisfied" to "very satisfied". Again, each worker generates a score overall and for each of the 20 dimensions so satisfaction and dissatisfaction can easily be identified. Examples of the 20 dimensions are given in Figure 24.5.3.

On my present job, this is how I feel about ...	Very dissatisfied	Dissatisfied	Neutral	Satisfied	Very satisfied
1 Being able to keep busy all the time	1	2	3	4	5
2 The chance to work alone on the job	1	2	3	4	5
3 The chance to do different things from time to time	1	2	3	4	5
4 The chance to be "somebody" in the community	1	2	3	4	5
5 The way my boss handles his/her workers	1	2	3	4	5
6 The competence of my supervisor in making decisions	1	2	3	4	5
7 The way my job provides for steady employment	1	2	3	4	5
8 My pay and the amount of work I do	1	2	3	4	5
9 The chances for advancement on this job	1	2	3	4	5
10 The working conditions	1	2	3	4	5
11 The way my co-workers get along with each other	1	2	3	4	5
12 The feeling of accomplishment I get from the job	1	2	3	4	5

▲ **Figure 24.5.3** Excerpt from the Minnesota Satisfaction Questionnaire

Source: Weiss *et al*: "Vocational Psychology Research", University of Minnesota, copyright 1977. Reproduced by permission.

Quality of Work Life (QWL) questionnaire (Walton, 1974)

The QWL Evaluation Scale allows workers to assess how they feel towards their job on eight different dimensions:

1. Salary (compensation) – four items
2. Working conditions – six items
3. Use of their capacities at work – five items
4. Opportunities at work – four items
5. Social integration at work – four items
6. Respecting the laws and rules at work – four items
7. The space work occupies in their life – three items
8. The social relevance and importance of their work – five items.

Each item is answered on a 5-point scale from 1 = very dissatisfied to 5 = very satisfied. Once the scale is completed, an overall score can be generated for each worker but also a score for each of the eight dimensions to see if there are areas where a worker is highly satisfied or highly dissatisfied with his or her work.

Example questions include those shown in Figure 24.5.4.

1.1 How satisfied are you with your salary (remuneration)?

Very dissatisfied	Dissatisfied	Neither satisfied nor dissatisfied	Satisfied	Very satisfied
1	2	3	4	5

3.2 Are you satisfied with the importance of the task/work/activity that you do?

Very dissatisfied	Dissatisfied	Neither satisfied nor dissatisfied	Satisfied	Very satisfied
1	2	3	4	5

4.1 How satisfied are you with your opportunity of professional growth?

Very dissatisfied	Dissatisfied	Neither satisfied nor dissatisfied	Satisfied	Very satisfied
1	2	3	4	5

5.3 Regarding your team's and colleagues' commitment to work, how do you feel?

Very dissatisfied	Dissatisfied	Neither satisfied nor dissatisfied	Satisfied	Very satisfied
1	2	3	4	5

▲ **Figure 24.5.4** QWL Evaluation Scale: example questions

Source: Reproduced in da Silva Timossi *et al* (2008: 14–16)

Strength	Weakness
The questionnaire can be useful in appraisals to show managers what is good and not so good about the working life of the employee being appraised. Therefore, it has real-life application and usefulness.	The questionnaire is a self-report measure and workers may not complete each question accurately. For example, they may want to make themselves seem better than they actually feel at work because they believe that showing negativity restricts work opportunities.

CHALLENGE YOURSELF
Design a study that looks at two different groups of workers in the same company and finds out which group are more satisfied with their job.

Issues and debates tracker: Psychometric tests are useful as they enable direct comparison of workers based on their satisfaction scores and/or workers can be tracked over time to see how satisfaction changes in the workplace. However, as a lot of the data is quantitative it does not reveal the reasons for the satisfaction or dissatisfaction shown in workers' scores.

ATTITUDES TO WORK

Job sabotage

Job sabotage is about rule breaking and workers making a conscious effort to stop themselves and others from working for an organisation. This can be caused by frustration as workers begin to feel powerless in their job. It can also be brought about as an attempt to make working conditions better, for instance to gain better wages or physical conditions in a factory. Finally, it can be an attempt to challenge authority as workers feel that their managers or leaders are not performing in *their* job. This is an extreme form of dissatisfaction so cannot be used to discover job dissatisfaction on a daily basis and in the majority of workers.

Workplace sabotage (Giacolone and Rosenfeld, 1987)

Giacolone and Rosenfeld (1987) conducted a study to investigate the reasons why workplace sabotage occurs. They used a volunteer sample of 38 workers in a factory in the United States making electrical products. A sabotage methods questionnaire was constructed. An ex-employee of the company was asked to list all of the different methods he had come across that workers had used to sabotage their workplace. A list of 29 different methods was listed. They fell into four distinct categories:

▸ work slowdowns; for example, slowing up feed and machine speed rates, disappearing "looking for parts" or carrying out management requirements word for word

▸ destruction of machinery, premises or products; for example, writing poetry on the wall of the bathroom, using glue to block tool lockers or turning on a machine then walking away so it would damage itself

▸ dishonesty; for example, using company tools to complete personal work, workers changing the time on their clocking-in card or taking tools home to use

▸ causing chaos; for example, workers calling on the union to help them at work, harassing the foreman or throwing their time cards away.

A sabotage reasons questionnaire was also constructed. The same ex-employee had to list as many reasons as he had heard where workers had attempted to justify their sabotage actions. A total of 11 reasons were given:

1. Self-defence
2. Revenge
3. "An eye for an eye"
4. To protect self from the boss or company
5. To protect a friend or family from the boss or company
6. To protect own job
7. The company deserved the sabotage
8. The company had hurt the worker in the past
9. Does not matter as no one was hurt
10. A release for the frustrations at work
11. For fun.

The participants were asked to rate each of the 29 methods on a Likert-type scale from 1 ("not at all justifiable") to 7 ("totally justifiable"). The same scale was used when rating the 11 reasons. Each participant received a total score for the reasons questionnaire. These were ranked in order and then split via the median. This was so there would be a "high reason accepter" group and a "low reason accepter" group.

The top five differences between the groups for justification for methods used were as follows (all in the direction of the high reasons group seeing these as more justifiable than other methods):

1. Attempting to scare a foreman into quitting the job
2. Setting up a foreman to get the person into trouble
3. Doing things too quickly, to ensure that the machine broke
4. Altering the dimensions of the goods being produced
5. Stealing as compensation for low wages.

In terms of the four main categories, the high reason accepters were significantly more likely to justify work slowdowns, destruction and causing chaos compared to the low reason accepters. However, there was no difference between the two groups on justifying dishonesty.

Strength	Weakness
The study was based around actual methods of sabotage and reasons for sabotage. Therefore, the findings have application to the real world. It is useful for companies to know what the motives for sabotage are, and what types of sabotage occur, to try to reduce incidences.	The study took place in a single factory producing electrical goods so these reasons and methods may only apply to this one company: generalisation may be difficult.

Job absenteeism

Job absenteeism can be categorised as voluntary and involuntary. Voluntary absenteeism refers to instances where the worker has chosen to take the time off (e.g. the worker may choose to have an extra day for a long weekend or may have errands to run such as going to the vet). Involuntary absenteeism refers to times when the worker does not choose to be off work but is absent. The main reason for this is illness. Organisations have to be prepared for a certain number of instances occurring per worker and have policies in place to deal with it (e.g. use temporary workers or use an agency to find cover workers). Voluntary absenteeism may well be a measure of job dissatisfaction but, as with withdrawal above, the reasons vary so widely that it is another low validity attempt (people may just take the odd day off to do other things but really love their job). Therefore, as Riggio (1999) points out, there are problems with using this as any measure due to the complexity of reasons that people give for voluntary absenteeism.

Absenteesim (Blau and Boal, 1987)

In addition, in studying absenteeism Blau and Boal (1987) provided another model that examined the role of the following aspects:

▶ job involvement – classified as high or low depending on how involved an employee is with the job and company

▶ organisational commitment – classified as high or low depending on how committed the employee is to the company and its vision for the future, etc.

▶ individual task-related – how well the employee works by him- or herself on tasks

▶ group maintenance-related – how well the employee works in teams.

Table 25.4.1 highlights how these aspects interact according to Blau and Boal.

Cell (describing individual)	Effort focus	Salient satisfaction focus	Label
1 High job involvement and high organizational commitment	Individual task-related = higher; group maintenance-related = higher	Work itself Future with company Pay Co-worker Supervisor	Institutionalized stars
2 High job involvement and low organizational commitment	individual task-related = higher; group maintenance-related = lower	Work itself Working conditions Pay	Lone wolves
3 Low job involvement and high organizational commitment	Individual task-related = lower; group maintenance-related = higher	Co-worker	Corporate citizens
4 Low job involvement and low organizational commitment	Individual task-related = lower; group maintenance-related = higher	Reward	Apathetic employees

▲ **Table 24.5.1** Job involvement; organisational commitment; individual task-related and group maintenance-related aspects

Source: Blau and Boal (1987: 293)

ASK YOURSELF
Which of Blau and Boal's four categories is more likely to be absent from work? Justify your choice.

Measuring organisational commitment (Mowday, Steers and Porter, 1979)

Employers could measure a person's commitment to the organisation by using the Organizational Commitment Questionnaire (OCQ) devised by Mowday, Steers and Porter (1979). This is a 15-item questionnaire with a 7-point Likert scale ranging from "strongly agree" to "strongly disagree". A copy of the OCQ is shown in Figure 24.5.5.

Organizational Commitment Questionnaire (OCQ)	
Instructions	
Listed below are a series of statements that represent possible feelings that individuals might have about the company or organization for which they work. With respect to your own feelings about the particular organization for which you are now working (company name) please indicate the degree of your agreement or disagreement with each statement by entering one of the seven alternatives below alongside statement.*	
1. I am willing to put in a great deal of effort beyond that normally expected in order to help this organization be successful.	
2. I talk up this organization to my friends as a great organization to work for.	
3. I feel very little loyalty to this organization.	(R)
4. I would accept almost any type of job assignment in order to keep working for this organization.	
5. I find that my values and the organization's values are very similar.	
6. I am proud to tell others that I am part of this organization.	
7. I could just as well be working for a different organization as long as the type of work was similar.	(R)
8. This organization really inspires the very best in me in the way of job performance.	
9. It would take very little change in my present circumstances to cause me to leave this organization.	(R)
10. I am extremely glad that I chose this organization to work for over others I was considering at the time I joined.	
11. There's not too much to be gained by sticking with this organization indefinitely.	(R)
12. Often I find it difficult to agree with this organization's policies on important matters relating to its employees.	(R)
13. I really care about the fate of this organization.	
14. For me this is the best of all possible organizations for which to work.	
15. Deciding to work for this organization was a definite mistake on my part.	(R)

* Responses to each item are measured on a 7-point scale with scale point anchors labelled:

(1) strongly disagree: (2) moderately disagree; (3) slightly disagree: (4) neither disagree nor agree: (5) slightly agree: (6) moderately agree: (7) strongly agree.

An "(R)" denotes a negatively phrased and reverse scored item.

▲ **Figure 24.5.5** The OCQ

Source: Mowday, Steers and Porter (1979: 228)

The higher the score on the OCQ, the more committed the employee is to the organisation.

HOW TO EVALUATE: ORGANISATIONS

For the 10-mark question in paper 3, you will be asked to evaluate one of the topics covered in this section. Below are three examples of the types of evaluation point you *could* write in the examination.

You should aim to make a range of evaluation points for the 10-mark question.

NEED THEORIES OF MOTIVATION

One problem with these theories is that they *generalise* without taking into account *individual differences*. For example, Maslow's hierarchy of needs suggests that we all progress up the pyramid in the same way. Individuals may, though, progress up the pyramid in different ways, as they have different motivations and needs – some people may never want to self-actualise in the workplace, instead choosing to do this through leisure activities outside of work; therefore, attempts to "involve all in the same way" may not work. The measuring of the needs as predicted by some theories, such as McClelland's achievement motivation theory, can be *subjective*. Workers can be assessed on the achievement motivation theory's three key needs and motives by taking a thematic apperception test (TAT). In the test, workers have to look at a series of ambiguous pictures that tell a story. They have to tell whatever story they feel is behind the picture and these responses are then scored. However, one member of personnel staff may score the response in a different way from someone else working in the department.

THEORIES OF LEADERSHIP AND MANAGEMENT

Many theories have good *application*, meaning that companies can use them either to find out who in the company would make a good leader, or when the company needs to train someone to become a better leader. For example, Heifetz believes that leaders should be focused on not doing things by themselves. They should involve others in the organisation and distribute responsibilities according to each worker's strengths. Therefore, potential leaders could be trained to behave in this way and be monitored to help the company create better leaders, which should improve output and profits. However, some of the theories may be *culturally biased* as they are based on the ideals of US business. Some theories may not transfer well to other cultures where hierarchies are different or where a company runs a strict manager–worker relationship based on authority rather than democratic decision making.

MEASURING JOB SATISFACTION

Many methods of measuring job satisfaction are based on questionnaires and may be more *valid* than using an interview because workers may be more likely to reveal truthful answers in a questionnaire as it does not involve talking face to face with someone. Therefore, information from the Job Descriptive Index may be more valid compared to an interview using some of the same questions. However, some workers may give *socially desirable* answers as they want to look good rather than giving truthful answers – this lowers the validity of measuring job satisfaction. Workers may want to look more satisfied about their job if a stern manager is going to read the responses, so that they appear to be enjoying their work and so they look good, especially if the process is linked to a potential promotion.

26 EXAM CENTRE: A LEVEL

The questions, example answers, marks awarded and/or comments that appear in this book/CD were written by the author. In examination, the way marks would be awarded to answers like these may be different.

COMPONENT 3

Specialist options: theory

This component constitutes 25 per cent of the A Level qualification. You will need to answer questions on the **two** options that you have been taught from the following:

▶ Psychology and abnormality

▶ Consumer psychology

▶ Psychology and health

▶ Psychology and organisations.

You will need to answer two questions for **both options** you have studied:

▶ Question 1. This question is divided into three parts (total of 12 marks).

▶ Question 2. This is a structured essay question divided into two parts (18 marks).

Question 1 is split into three parts worth 2, 4 and 6 marks each. These questions cover knowledge of studies, theories and concepts from the option (the 2-mark and 4-mark questions) and then a discussion question (a 6-mark question).

For question 2 the "describe" part carries 8 marks and the "evaluation" part with a named issue or debate carries 10 marks.

See the Sample Assessment Material on the Cambridge International Examinations website for an example examination. The first examination is in 2018 so from then on many more examination papers will become available.

This examination lasts 1 hour 30 minutes and carries 60 marks (30 marks per option).

COMPONENT 4

Specialist options: application

This component constitutes 25 per cent of the A Level qualification. You will need to answer questions on the **two** options that you have been taught from the following:

▶ Psychology and abnormality

▶ Consumer psychology

▶ Psychology and health

▶ Psychology and organisations.

This examination will be split into three sections:

1. Section A. You will answer **two** questions (**one** per option studied) from a choice of four available. Each of these questions is based on stimulus material and is divided into four parts (2 + 4 + 4 + 5 marks). In this section, 30 marks are available.

2. Section B. You will answer **one** design-based question from a choice of four. Each question is divided into two parts (10 + 8 marks) so, in this section, 18 marks are available.

3. Section C. You will be asked to write **one** essay from a choice of four. There are 12 marks available.

Section A examines your knowledge of **both** options you have studied. You must answer all questions for the **two** options you have covered at A Level. The questions test knowledge about the topic content of each option as well as research methods, and issues and debates. The last question, for which 5 marks are available, is a discussion-based question and you will be expected to form a conclusion.

Section B asks you to design a study linked to a topic area from the syllabus. You can choose which **option** you want to answer the question from. For example, you may have studied consumer psychology, and psychology and health, and choose the health question to complete in this section. You only have to answer **one full question**. For the design part of the question, 10 marks are available then the following 8-mark question asks you to explain what psychology your design is based upon.

Section C asks you to write a short essay based on a quotation. You can choose which **option** you want to answer the question from. For example, you may have studied consumer psychology, and psychology and health, and choose the health question to complete in this section. You only have to answer **one essay question**. You will need to read the quotation and then discuss the extent to which you agree with the quotation, using examples from the material you have studied for that option.

See the Sample Assessment Material on the Cambridge International Examinations website for an example examination. The first examination is in 2018 so from then on many more examination papers will become available.

This examination lasts 1 hour 30 minutes and 60 marks are available.

INDEX

Laney, C. et al: "Asparagus, a love story: healthier eating could be just a false memory away". Used by permission from *Experimental Psychology* 2008; Vol. 55(5):291–300 © 2008 Hogrefe & Huber Publishers (now Hogrefe Publishing) www.hogrefe.com DOI 10.1027/1618-3169.55.5.291.

Lovell, K. et al: "Telephone administered cognitive behaviour therapy for treatment of obsessive compulsive disorder: randomised controlled non-inferiority trial", BMJ Publishing Group Ltd, October 26, 2006. Reproduced with permission of BMJ Publishing Group Ltd.

McKinlay, J. B: "Who is really ignorant – physician or patient?" *Journal of Health and Social Behavior*. Vol. 16, number 1, 1975, pp. 3–11 American Sociological Association and J. B. McKinlay.

McKinstry, B. and Wang, J. X: "Putting on the style: what patients think of the way their doctor dresses". *British Journal of General Practice* July 1991; 41(348): 270, 275–278. Reprinted by permission.

Milgram, S: "Announcement placed in local newspapers to recruit subjects" (p. 15) from *Obedience to Authority: An Experimental View*. Copyright © 1974 by Stanley Milgram. Reprinted by permission of HarperCollins Publishers and Pinter & Martin, London.

Milgram, S: *Obedience to Authority: An Experimental View*. Copyright (c) 1974 by Stanley Milgram. Reprinted by permission of HarperCollins Publishers and Pinter & Martin, London.

Milgram, S: "Behavioral study of obedience". *Journal of Personality and Social Psychology*. Vol. 67, No. 4, 1963. Reprinted by permission.

Milgram, S: "Response to intrusion into waiting lines". *Journal of Personality and Social Psychology* Vol. 51, No. 4, 1986, pages 683 and 685, American Psychological Association. Reprinted with permission.

Miller, R: "The Feeling-State Theory of Impulse-Control Disorders and the Impulse-Control Disorder" *Traumatology* Vol. 16 (3), September 2010 2-10, American Psychological Association. Reprinted with permission.

Mowday, R. T., Steers, R.M. and Porter, L.W: "The measurement of organizational commitment". *Journal of Vocational Behavior*. Vol. 14, Issue 2, 1979. Reprinted with permission from Elsevier.

Oldham, G.R. and Brass, D.T: Table from p.278 *Administrative Science Quarterly*. Vol. 24, number 2 1979. Reprinted with permission.

Pepperberg, I. M: "Acquisition of the same/different concept by an African Grey parrot (Psittacus erithacus): learning with respect to categories of color, shape, and material". *Animal Learning & Behavior*, pp 424, 427-429 15 (4) 1987 from http://link.springer.com/article/10.3758/BF03205051#page-1. Reprinted with permission of Springer.

Piliavin, I. M., Rodin, J. and Piliavin, J: 1969. "Good Samaritanism: An underground phenomenon?" *Journal of Personality and Social Psychology, 13* (4) 289-299. http://dx.doi.org/10.1037/h0028433. Copyright © 1969 American Psychological Association. Reprinted with permission. No further reproduction or distribution is permitted without written permission from the American Psychological Association.

Porublev, E. et al: "To wrap or not wrap? What is expected? Some initial findings from a study on gift wrapping", ANZMAC: Sustainable management and marketing conference. Melbourne, Australia. December 2009. Reprinted by permission.

Richards, J. S., Nepomuceno, C., Riles, M. et al: "Assessing pain behavior: the UAB Pain Behavior Scale" published in *Pain*, Vol 14 Issue 4, 1 January 1982, Wolters Kluwer Health, Inc. Reprinted by permission.

Savage, R. and Armstrong, D: "Effect of a general practitioner's consulting style on patients' satisfaction: a controlled study". *BMJ: British Medical Journal*. Vol. 301, No. 6758. Reproduced with permission of the BMJ Publishing Group Ltd.

Sherman J. et al: "Telephoning the patient's pharmacy to assess adherence with asthma medications by measuring refill rate for prescriptions" from *Journal of Paediatrics*, Number 136 (2000) pp. 533. Reprinted by permission of James Sharman.

Shleifer, A: "Psychologists at the gate: a review of Daniel Kahneman's thinking, fast and slow". *Journal of Economic Literature* 50(4), 2012. Reprinted by permission.

Snyder, M. and DeBono, K. G: 1985. "Appeals to image and claims about quality: understanding the psychology of advertising. *Journal of Personality and Social Psychology*. Vol. 49 (3), 586-597 http://dx.doi.org/10.1037/0022-3514.49.3.586. Copyright © 1985 American Psychological Association. Reproduced with permission.

Tapper, K., Horne, P. J. and Lowe, C. F: "The Food Dudes to the rescue!" *The Psychologist*. Vol. 16, No. 1, 2003. Reprinted by permission of Kay Tapper, Pauline Horne, and Pat Lowe on behalf of the author, C. F. Lowe.

Tuckman, B. W: "Developmental sequence in small groups". *Psychological Bulletin*, 63 (6), 1965, pp. 386-387. http://dx.doi.org/10.1037/h0022100. American Psychological Association. Reprinted with permission.

Turley, L.W. and Milliman, R. E: Table from "Atmospheric Effects on Shopping" *Journal of Business Research*. Vol. 49, Copyright 2000 with permission from Elsevier.

James W. Varni: The PedsQL™ Pediatric Pain Questionnaire™, Copyright © 1998 J.W. Varni, Ph.D. Reprinted with permission.

Wang, J. et al: "Perfusion functional MRI reveals cerebral blood flow pattern under psychological stress". *PNAS*. Vol. 102, No. 49. Copyright (2005) National Academy of Sciences, U.S.A. Reprinted by permission.

Wansink, B., van Ittersum, K. and Painter, J. E: "How Descriptive Food Names Bias Sensory Perceptions in Restaurants" *Food Quality and Preference*, 16:5, 2005, 393-400. Reprinted by permission.

Weiss et al: "Vocational Psychology Research", University of Minnesota, copyright 1977. Reprinted with permission.

Wong, D. L. and Baker, C. M: "Pain in children: comparison of assessment scales". *Journal of Pediatric Nursing*, Vol.14, number 1, 1988, pp. 9–17.

Yamamoto, S., Humle, T. and Tanaka, M: "Chimpanzees' flexible targeted helping based on an understanding of conspecifics' goals". *PNAS*. Vol. 109, No. 9, 2012. Reprinted by permission.

BPS Guidelines for Psychologists Working with Animals (2012); 423 words from pp. 5, 8, 10. Reproduced with permission.

BPS Code of Human Research Ethics (2014); 1607 words from pp. 4, 7, 16–17, 18–19, 22, 24–25, 26 from http://www.bps.org.uk/what-we-do/ethics-standards/ethics-standards. Reproduced with permission.

BPS Code of Ethics and Conduct (2009); p.20. Reproduced with permission.

The ICD-10 classification of mental and behavioural disorders: clinical descriptions and diagnostic guidelines. Geneva: World Health Organization; 1992 (http://apps.who.int/iris/bitstream/10665/37958/8/9241544228_eng.pdf). Reprinted by permission.

Two tables from "An anchoring and adjustment model of purchase quantity decisions". *Journal of Marketing Research*, Vol. 35 published by The American Marketing Association. Reprinted with permission.

Generalised Anxiety Disorder Assessment (GAD 7) Version 1, March 2012, Wirral Community NHS Trust. Contains public sector information licensed under the Open Government Licence v3.0.

http://www.nhs.uk/Conditions/body-dysmorphia/Pages/Introduction.aspx. Contains public sector information licensed under the Open Government Licence v3.0.

Simulated Items similar to those in the Beck Depression Inventory-II. Copyright © 1996 Aaron T. Beck. Reproduced with permission of the Publisher, NCS Pearson, Inc. All rights reserved. "Beck Depression Inventory" and "BDI" are registered trademarks, in the US and/or other countries, of Pearson Education, Inc. or its affiliate(s).